FORMS OF MODERNITY: *DON QUIXOTE*
AND MODERN THEORIES OF THE NOVEL

RACHEL SCHMIDT

Forms of Modernity

Don Quixote and Modern
Theories of the Novel

UNIVERSITY OF TORONTO PRESS
Toronto Buffalo London

©University of Toronto Press Incorporated 2011
Toronto Buffalo London
www.utppublishing.com
Printed in Canada

ISBN 978-1-4426-4251-5 (cloth)

Library and Archives Canada Cataloguing in Publication

Schmidt, Rachel, 1963–
Forms of modernity : Don Quixote and modern theories of the novel /
Rachel Schmidt.

(University of Toronto romance series)
Includes bibliographical references and index.
ISBN 978-1-4426-4251-5

1. Fiction – History and criticism. 2. Cervantes Saavedra, Miguel de, 1547–
1616. Don Quixote. I. Title. II. Series: University of Toronto romance series.

PN3491.S35 2011   809.3   C2010-906446-1

This book has been published with the help of a grant from the Canadian
Federation for the Humanities and Social Sciences, through the Aid to
Scholarly Publications Program, using funds provided by the Social Sciences
and Humanities Research Council of Canada.

 Canada Council   Conseil des Arts
for the Arts   du Canada
 ONTARIO ARTS COUNCIL
CONSEIL DES ARTS DE L'ONTARIO

University of Toronto Press acknowledges the financial assistance to its
publishing program of the Canada Council for the Arts and the Ontario Arts
Council.

University of Toronto Press acknowledges the financial support of the
Government of Canada through the Canada Book Fund for its publishing
activities.

To Ken, Esther, Abigail, Mom, Dad, Luther, and Joanna –
Thanks for being there.

Contents

Preface

Form is an abstraction.

Rudolf Arnheim, *The Split and the Structure*

It has become a critical cliché that Cervantes' *Don Quixote* is the first modern novel.[1] Yet this epithet, 'the first modern novel,' begs several questions: (1) what is a novel? (2) what constitutes modernity in relationship to prose? and (3) why choose this novel, *Don Quixote*, as the progenitor of such a diverse and complicated genre? In order to answer these questions, I will undertake an analysis of several modern theorists of the novel, specifically Friedrich Schlegel, Hermann Cohen, Georg Lukács, Miguel de Unamuno, José Ortega y Gasset, and Mikhail Bakhtin. All of the thinkers covered in this book struggled overtly with the first question raised by taking Cervantes' novel to be the first modern novel: the definition of the novel. Indeed, with the exception of Hermann Cohen, their use of the term 'novel' is known in greater or lesser degrees by literary critics, and constitutes our basic approach to the novel. Michael McKeon has referred to Lukács, Ortega y Gasset, and Bakhtin as participating in the 'grand theory of the novel,' because 'each ... grounds an account of the distinctive qualities of the genre in an account of its historical emergence' (xv–xvi). Accordingly, these theorists problematize form, and see it reproduced in content (180). Moreover, they struggled with the other two questions, that is to say the definition of modernity and their choice of *Don Quixote* as an exemplary novel. Their hermeneutics of linking generic form to modernity will have a profound impact on the way *Don Quixote de la Mancha* is read. Indeed, the 'grand theory of the novel' itself has a telling history, emerging from specific philosophical traditions, namely, Romanticism and neo-Kantianism, and taking as its founding literary text *Don Quixote de la Mancha*. The definition of the novel will always involve for these thinkers a definition of modernity, whether explicit or implicit.

In spite of a tendency to decontextualize literary theory, we cannot help but read Schlegel, Lukács, Cohen, Unamuno, Ortega y Gassett, and Bakhtin after learning the lessons of a century in which nationalism and various political systems degenerated into barbarity, and intellectuals were consequently forced to examine the very foundations of ethical philosophy. Often their belief in the novel's power to critique and perhaps even correct the excesses of modernity might seem quaint, if not ill-conceived, to the contemporary reader. Even before the horrors of the two world wars, Nietzsche had unveiled the hypocritical grounding of conventional morality, just as Marx had revealed the compromising of literature by political and social conditions. Subsequently, Adorno and Horkheimer have undercut the moral pretensions of reason, and Derrida has put into play the location of truth in the word. The concept of individual freedom and autonomy, the human capacity to will and perform the morally right, seems naive and bereft of rigorous meaning.

Nonetheless, a continued belief in the novel's power to respond to, critique, and reform modernity underlies the work of many current theorists. Those who work within the Continental philosophical tradition, influenced by Descartes's and Kant's work on human freedom and Hegel's notion of modern subjectivity, see the novel as a formal and critical response to the problematics modernity creates for the individual. Anthony Cascardi, drawing heavily on the young Lukács, argues that the novel offers two means by which to counteract the formlessness of modernity: 'through the representation of a world that is objective, rational, and real; and through the creation of a free and autonomous individual, an independent self' (*The Subject of Modernity* 90). Some locate the novel's power in relation to social and ideological changes in which it participates. Ian Watt, although he eschews placing the novel's origins in sixteenth-century Spain in preference for eighteenth-century England, asserts that Descartes's emphasis on reconstituting 'the pursuit of truth ... as a wholly individual matter, logically independent of the tradition of past thought' constitutes modernity, and that '[t]he novel is the form of literature which most fully reflects this individualist and innovating reorientation' (13). Fredric Jameson figures that the novel's reshaping of the stuff of human life is in the service of capitalism: 'the novel plays a significant role in what can be called a properly bourgeois cultural revolution – that immense process of transformation whereby populations whose life habits were formed by other, now archaic, modes of production are effectively reprogrammed for life and work in the new world of market capitalism' (*The Political Unconscious* 152).[2]

Others locate its power in formal characteristics such as its ambiguity, irony, plurality, and heterogeneity. Take, for example, Julia Kristeva, who writes that '[t]he novel, and especially the modern, polyphonic novel, incorporating Menippean elements, embodies the effort of European thought to break out of the framework of causally determined identical substances and head toward another modality of thought that proceeds through dialogue (a logic of distance, relativity, analogy, non-exclusive and transfinite opposition)' (*Desire in Language* 85–6).[3] Northrop Frye, although he limits his own definition of the novel to realistic fiction typical of the nineteenth century, nonetheless grants that major works of prose fiction such as *Don Quixote de la Mancha* are a mixture of modes (novel, romance, anatomy or satire, confession) that include satire and cultural critique (303–12). Even when viewed from a Freudian point of view, the novel grants voice and liberty to the repressed. Marthe Robert writes that Cervantes displaces a part of himself that is unacceptable into the character of Don Quixote (*Roman des origines et origines des romans* 188). This displacement gives form to the liberty granted by the novel to the artist, who can write of whatever, and however, she pleases. This is not a comfortable state of affairs for the intellectual: 'For the critic, on the other hand, such freedom is highly suspect. He feels that some kind of boundaries should be established' ('From *Origins of the Novel*' 60). In short, the novel retains freedom and power even in an intellectual age when such human capacities have been questioned.

A curious transposition has occurred: agency and liberty have been transferred from the individual subject to a literary genre! Such a strange axiom of our own thought about literature deserves careful consideration. The lessons learned from studies of the reception of literary works need to be applied to works of literary theory. They are written in a specific time and place in response, either acknowledged or unacknowledged, to specific conditions. Given the location of our own perspective in time and space, it is essential to return to the period immediately prior to the First World War not only to reconstruct and thus appreciate the context in which these theorists of the novel wrote, but also to recover for ourselves whatever may be of value in the work of thinkers who were most certainly not simple or naive in their striving for an ethical foundation for literature. Indeed, precisely on account of this horrible and horrifying history, a return to the problem of ethics in general, and the ethics of literature in particular, is called for. As Emil L. Fackenheim states, 'After Eichmann [who stated at his 1961 trial 'Act so that, if the *Führer* knew of your action, he would approve'] a retrieval of Kant's categorical imperative is in any case necessary' (181).

Of central importance to this contextualization of the question of ethics and the novel is the examination of the thought of Hermann Cohen, a Jewish neo-Kantian philosopher at the University of Marburg who attempted to think through many of the problems that troubled not only Lukács, Ortega, and Bakhtin, but also continue to trouble us: the relation of the individual to society, the moral autonomy of the individual, the conflict between majority and minority interests and rights, and the location of truth vis-à-vis art. In short, these literary theorists struggled to reclaim one of the philosophical paradoxes central to Western thought from the time of the ancient Greeks: the equation of the beautiful with the good. Of the thinkers to be examined in this book, Cohen is the least well-known for historical – and even anti-Semitic – reasons that will be discussed.

In many important ways Friedrich Schlegel shapes the thought of the other theorists by defining the terms of the debate: the belief that the novel is an essentially modern form; the identification of irony as an essential element of the novelistic form; and the establishment of a canonical group of works and authors that exemplify the novel. Chief among these authors is Cervantes, and chief among his works is *Don Quixote*. Georg Lukács, I will argue, writes his *Theory of the Novel* in response to Schlegel; as a response, it is both an antithesis to, and a synthesis of, Schlegel's ideas. It is not an exaggeration to speak of Lukács's *Theory of the Novel* as a dissolution of Schlegel's theory of the novel. As such, its curious historical destiny is to entrench Schlegel's definition of the genre in twentieth-century literary theory.

Hermann Cohen and José Ortega y Gasset, although also responding to Schlegel, set out an alternative vision of the novel that is less tragic and ultimately more ludic in its representation both of the genre and of the modern individual's relation to society. Ortega, like many young intellectuals of his day, travelled to Marburg to study with the renowned neo-Kantian philosopher Hermann Cohen. It was there, in the summer of 1911, that the two read *Don Quixote* together. As an outgrowth of their respective philosophies as well as their personal friendship, another strand of the theory of the novel was born. In order to appreciate Ortega y Gasset's famous writings on the novel, I will first examine his mentor Cohen's writings on the novel within the entire framework of neo-Kantian philosophy; that is to say, in relation to aesthetics, ethics, and even logic. Then I will explore the young Ortega y Gasset's intimate involvement with Cervantes and *Don Quixote* in both its philosophical and political dimensions.

Mikhail Bakhtin is the theorist of most renown to contemporary scholars. He has been taken as a foundational thinker for cultural studies, and offers powerful ways to study literature in relation to social structures of power. But, as I will show, he writes about the novel in the tradition established by Friedrich Schlegel and drawing, to a certain extent, on Kant. Moreover, his work on the novel, particularly that of the 1930s, emerges as a critique of Lukács's Marxist notion of the novel by turning back, in part, to the Hungarian's *Theory of the Novel*, a work written fully in the Romantic, idealist tradition (Tihanov, *The Master and the Slave* 144–5). In Bakhtin's work, Cervantes' *Don Quixote* emerges once again as a novel that neatly and thoroughly problematizes modernity.

Miguel de Unamuno is an outlier in this tradition – not surprising given his self-definition as an intellectual provocateur. Indeed, his thought on the novel can be considered an anti-novelistics, opposed in fundamental ways to the other theories considered here. For example, he does not disassociate the novel from the epic, nor is he particularly concerned by the theoretical problem of irony. He considers Cervantes a rival, and boasts of his struggle with the original author for control over the figure of Don Quixote. Nonetheless, in his work he makes innovative points about the nature of literature, the relation between the author and his work, and the autonomy of the reader.

I write as a *cervantista*; my first loyalties are to Cervantes and his so difficult but so funny *Don Quixote* as well as his other multifaceted writings. I have approached this work with a certain amount of trepidation, for I recognize that all six thinkers are, first and foremost, philosophers. It is not my goal to explicate entire systems of thought, although some of that was necessary in the case of Cohen. My goal is to illuminate these philosophers' ideas on the novel through the eyes of a literary critic. I apologize to professional philosophers if I have oversimplified or decontextualized their ideas.

As a *cervantista*, I find it at times frustrating and always challenging to square the *Don Quixote* of modern literary theory with the text I know and teach. Why does Don Quixote, whose presumed sanity or insanity can never really be diagnosed in the actual novel, appear in theory in such two-dimensional terms? Why does the marvellous Sancho Panza, whose character and wit blossom as he wanders through Spain with Don Quixote, disappear from the theories of the novel? Why is it so difficult to put one's finger on the text's slippery but unquestionable humour and irony? Where is the author Cervantes, whose life as a soldier, prisoner of war, tax collector, jail inmate, and struggling author is worthy of a novel, in these learned disquisitions on modernity? Not to mention the following question: where is sixteenth-century Spain, imperial power, home to an explosion in new literary forms and figures as well as site of the Spanish Inquisition, in all this discoursing?

Serious misconceptions of Spain's place in European history and the sociopolitical context of Cervantes' times have given rise to a supposed paradox in the theory of the novel: the postulation of a non-modern work, *Don Quixote de la Mancha*, as the primogenitor of the modern novel. This apparent mistake has led to alternative histories of the novel, such as J.M. Bernstein's assertion that Descartes's *Meditations* constitutes the first modern novel (153–5) or Watt's assertion that the modern novel arises in eighteenth-century England. As the thinking goes, since Cervantes' Spain is assumed to be medieval or pre-modern, Cervantes' novel cannot be modern. Nonetheless, historians of Spain working in the last fifty years have consistently shown how and why sixteenth-century Spain can arguably be considered one of the first modern European nations. Moreover, since the landmark works on Cervantes by Américo Castro (*El pensamiento de Cervantes*, 1925) and José Antonio Maravall (*El humanismo de las armas en Don Quijote*, first published in 1948 and republished as *Utopia and Counterutopia in the* Quixote, 1991), Hispanists have continued elucidating the modern fictional techniques as well as sociohistorical context of *Don Quixote de la Mancha*. As I will show in chapter 1, *Don Quixote* is, in important ways, a modern work. I ask for my Hispanist colleagues' forbearance as I reiterate points already well known to them, for it is evident through my work on this project that what we take as a relatively standard approach to early modern Spain and its literature is shockingly new to non-Hispanists.

I take the point of one of the manuscript's readers (and I am quite indebted to both of them for their thoughtful, careful readings) that I am postulating 'material' conditions as constitutive of the production of Cervantes' text. However, I do not understand economic and social conditions to be, strictly speaking, material, for they are products of human mind and action. Ultimately, it is for this reason that I find Kant more compelling than Marx or Hegel. As I have reworked the manuscript, I have come to a greater appreciation of the emergent notion of the 'virtual' in these theorists. I suppose, if I were forced to define economic and social conditions, I might describe them as virtual, arising from human activity and thought, interacting with the realm of material objects, and creating an 'actual' and compelling reality for us.

I also write as a North American *cervantista* educated in the 1980s, at a time when literary theory was too often presented to graduate students as if it were a form of sacred scripture, above and beyond all historical context. It is now my turn to teach literary theory to my students, a task I honour but also question. In these days of post-structuralism and cultural studies, how can we not see literary theory as a product of a certain culture, fraught with the sociopolitical, economic, and ideological tensions of its time? Yet too often these texts are presented either as unquestionable dogma buttressed by all the authority and tradition embodied in the Ivy Tower, or as nifty decoding rings, the latest and greatest in hermeneutic technology. Both of these approaches to literary theory cheapen and degrade it. I also seek to preserve the epiphanic moments of illumination that literary theory can bring to a text – the eureka moments when one suddenly sees what was always there but invisible. One of my goals is to explain some of the charm, hypnotic or otherwise, that literary theory has held over North American academia for the last forty years to my colleagues outside this continent. By attempting to demystify literary theories, it is not my intention to discredit them. To the contrary, my methodology has been to accord them the same approach I would accord a literary text: a mixture of close reading, historical contextualization, and theoretical musing.

Acknowledgments

This book could not have been completed without the help of many persons and the aid of many institutions. For their guidance concerning Friedrich Schlegel, I would like to extend a special thanks to Paola Mayer and Hans Eichner, both of whom read and responded to my earlier writings on the German Romantic and provided me with essential tips and insights. I would not have been able to undertake this work without their support. I am grateful to Ciriaco Morón Arroyo and Svetlana Piskunova for encouraging me to delve further into Hermann Cohen's writings at a time when I doubted if I was on the right track. The support of my colleagues over the years at the University of Calgary has been most helpful, but I would like especially to remember the late Dean of the Faculty of Humanities Rowland Smith, who wisely understood that I needed a 'room of my own.' Thank you also to Dominique Perron, Elizabeth Montes, and Pauline Willis – and, of course, Kenneth Brown – for their intellectual companionship and friendship.

Librarians are the unspoken and invisible heroes of our work. I would like to acknowledge the librarians at the University of Calgary and the Netherlands Institute for Advanced Studies, as well as their counterparts in interlibrary loan departments across the world, for keeping me well supplied with reading materials. I would also like to thank the Netherlands Institute for Advanced Studies for supplying me with an office, computer facilities, and library service while my husband, Kenneth Brown, was a fellow there in 2001–2. I am also grateful for the access I was granted to the library and archives of the Fundación Ortega y Gasset, a lovely refuge of learning in the heart of Madrid.

This project has been generously funded through a standard research grant from the Social Sciences and Humanities Research Council of

Canada. Thank you to Anthony Wall for initiating the grant as principal investigator and helping me focus the topic. I would also like to acknowledge the support from the Aid to Scholarly Publications Program for the publication of this volume. Previous and much-amended versions of material contained herein have appeared in my following articles: 'Reassessing Friedrich Schlegel's Reading of *Don Quixote* in Light of His Early Writings,' published in *The Lion and the Eagle. Interdisciplinary Essays on German-Spanish Relations over the Centuries*, edited by Conrad Kent, Thomas K. Wolber, and Cameron M.K. Hewitt (New York and Oxford: Berghahn Books, 2000), 188–213; 'Bajtín y Foucault leen *Don Quijote de la Mancha*: el retorno del idealism,' published in *Don Quijote, cosmopolita. Nuevos estudios sobre la recepción internacional de la novela cervantina*, edited by Hans Christian Hagedorn (Cuenca: Ediciones de la Universidad de Castilla-La Mancha, 2009), 419–57; and 'Don Quijote y su lugar en la novelística y la estética de Hermann Cohen,' published in *Cervantes y su mundo*, vol. 2, edited by Kurt and Roswitha Reichenberger and Darío Fernández-Morera (Kassel: Editorial Reichenberger, 2005), 417–36. Thank you to the above-mentioned publishers for granting me permission to publish revised material from these articles. Thank you, also, to Richard Ratzlaff of the University of Toronto Press for guiding this manuscript through the review process, to Charles Anthony Stuart for his careful editing, and to Barbara Porter. My sincerest gratitude goes to the anonymous readers of this manuscript, whose careful attention and wise recommendations transformed this work. All mistakes herein are mine, not theirs.

Finally, I thank all of my friends and family who helped me survive the last ten years. This book would not have been finished without you. I name you in my heart.

Abbreviations for Cited Material

AA   Bakhtin, Mikhail. *Art and Answerability. Early Philosophical Essays*. Translated by Vadim Liapunov. Austin: U of Texas P, 1990.

ARG   Cohen, Hermann. *Ästhetik des reinen Gefühls* 1, 2. In *Werke*. Vols. 8 and 9. Hildesheim and New York: Georg Olms Verlag, 1982.

CHN   Unamuno, Miguel de. *Cómo se hace una novela*. Edited by Bénédicte Vauthier. Salamanca: Ediciones Universidad Salamanca, 2005.

DI   Mikhail Bakhtin. *The Dialogic Imagination. Four Essays*. Austin: U of Texas P, 1981.

DP   Schlegel, Friedrich. *Dialogue on Poetry and Literary Aphorisms*. Translated by Ernst Behler and Roman Struc. University Park: Pennsylvania State UP, 1968.

DQ   Cervantes, Miguel de. *Don Quixote*. Translated by Edith Grossman. New York: Harper Collins, 2003.

DQM   Cervantes, Miguel de. *Don Quijote de la Mancha*. 2 vols. Edited by John Jay Allen. Madrid: Cátedra, 2004.

ERW   Cohen, Hermann. *Ethik des reinen Willens*. In *Werke*. Vol. 7. Hildesheim and New York: Georg Olms Verlag, 1981.

IN   Ortega y Gasset, José. *Ideas sobre la novela*. In José Ortega y Gasset, *Meditaciones del Quijote/Ideas sobre la novela*. 9th ed. Madrid: Revista de Occidente, 1975.

KA   Schlegel, Friedrich. *Kritische Friedrich-Schlegel Ausgabe*. Ed. Ernst Behler, Hans Eichner, and Jean-Jacques Anstett. Paderborn: Ferdinand Schöningh, 1958–.

LN   Schlegel, Friedrich. *Literary Notebooks 1797–1801.* Edited by
       Hans Eichner. Toronto: U of Toronto P, 1957.
LRE Cohen, Hermann. *Logik der reinen Erkenntnis.* In *Werke*. Vol. 6.
       Hildesheim and New York: Georg Olms Verlag, 1977.
MQ   Ortega y Gasset, José. *Meditaciones del Quijote/Ideas sobre la
       novela.* Madrid: Revista de Occidente, 1975.
N   Unamuno, Miguel de. *Niebla.* Edited by Mario J. Valdés.
       Madrid: Cátedra, 1993.
OC   Ortega y Gasset, José. *Obras completas.* Madrid: Revista de
       Occidente, 1962–5.
PDP Bakhtin, Mikhail. *Problems of Dostoevsky's Poetics.* Translated by
       Caryl Emerson. Minneapolis: U of Minnesota P, 1984.
PF   Schlegel, Friedrich. *Philosophical Fragments.* Translated by Peter
       Firchow. Minneapolis: U of Minnesota P, 1991.
PP   Unamuno, Miguel de. *Pensamiento político.* Edited by Elías
       Díaz. Madrid: Tecnos, 1965.
RW   Bakhtin, Mikhail. *Rabelais and His World.* Translated by Helene
       Iswolsky. Cambridge, MA: MIT P, 1968.
SF   Lukács, Georg. *Soul and Form.* Translated by Anna Bostock.
       London: Merlin P, 1974.
TN   Lukács, Georg. *The Theory of the Novel: A Historico-philosophical
       Essay on the Forms of Great Epic Literature.* Translated by Anna
       Bostock. Cambridge, MA: MIT P, 1989.
UOC Unamuno, Miguel de. *Obras completas.* Madrid: Escelicer, 1966.
VDQ Unamuno, Miguel. *Vida de Don Quijote y Sancho.* 5th ed.
       Buenos Aires: Espasa-Calpe, 1943.

Note on Translations and Quotations

Unless otherwise indicated, all translations from Spanish are my own. In the case of German translations, I have used published translations where available. When I have cited the original German in the notes, it is because the English translation is my own. I regret not being able to work with the original Russian texts in the case of Bakhtin, and have relied on English translations.

In quotations, all indications of emphasis and use of italics are original, unless otherwise noted.

FORMS OF MODERNITY

1 *Don Quixote* and the Problem of Modernity

Don Quixote de la Mancha is a great novel about art, about the way it creates – and deforms – societies and persons. By taking Cervantes' *Don Quixote* as the basis for a novelistics, one posits that the novel as genre explores the power of art. The theories of the novel that I trace here represent a thoroughgoing questioning of the novel understood as 'realist,' in which mimesis is considered as faithful copying or reflection of what is 'real.' We take from Friedrich Schlegel, Georg Lukács, Hermann Cohen, Miguel de Unamuno, José Ortega y Gasset, and Mikhail Bakhtin, as well as Miguel de Cervantes, a deeper understanding of the complex and productive relation between human knowledge, society, language, and the arts that overcomes the limitations of realism defined as mimetic reflection or imitation. The more salient aspects of their novelistics, including the problematization of freedom and reason in modernity, hinge on the issue of art and its relation to the social and the scientific (rational or *wissenschaftlich*). In this tradition of the theory of the novel, art does not merely reflect, but rather critiques, produces, and creates. Inherent to this insight is the understanding that art exists as a mental category, arising from the functions of human mental life. It is here that the novel finds its modern definition and justification, for as a human product of reason and imagination it exists neither in the realm of the 'real' or the 'ideal' but rather the 'virtual.' I will call the virtual that plane of human activity and life made possible by the human mind. How clear it is now in the twenty-first century that this plane is as real for us as the physical world around us! We build economies, share information, carry on romances, and wage wars in the virtual sphere. This is the realm claimed for the novel by the thinkers covered in this book, and their insights about the novel illuminate certain unexamined corners of our virtual world.

The Novel and 'Realism'

Although this book deals with a Continental tradition of novelistics, it is necessary to begin with a few remarks about Anglo-Saxon theories of the novel. Ian Watt's influential book *The Rise of the Novel* links the genre to 'philosophical realism': 'the position that truth can be discovered by the individual through his senses' (12). Watt claims that this philosophical school arises from Descartes and Locke, and links it to the understanding of the individual in time and space. For Watt, the novel's realism is a function of its 'production of what purports to be an authentic account of the actual experiences of individuals' and its 'air of complete authenticity' (27). Verisimilitude is likewise seen as a function of authenticity, understood as the power to place the reader in the physical and temporal setting of the literary protagonist. Moreover, the novelistic plot turns on cause-and-effect relations, as a chain of causally linked events replaces the episodes and coincidences described by Aristotelian poetics. If we are to sum up Watt's definition of the novel's 'realism,' it would depend on the authentic re-creation of actual time and place for literary characters in the novelistic text and the unmediated accessibility of this re-creation to readers.

It is hard to accept such a 'common sense' definition of the novel after the epistemological insights of structuralism and post-structuralism into the nature of literary creation and reception. And yet, Watt continues to serve as the theoretical kingpin for the history of the novel within Anglo-Saxon academe. In general, this is due to his powerful, persuasive account of the historical conditions in eighteenth-century England that fuelled the interest in the novel, including Protestant individualism, the rise of the urban mercantile class, and the expanding number of female readers. In fact, one could argue that the latter two factors occurred in other times and places where narrative prose experienced a boom, including fourteenth-century Florence, sixteenth-century Spain, and the twentieth-century Americas. More pernicious is the possible chauvinism, sexism, and xenophobia reflected in the preference for 'realist' fiction. Margaret Anne Doody has argued that the injunction that authors write what they know through actual experience has resulted in exclusion based on gender, race, class, and culture in the 'realist' novel (292). The exclusion of the category 'romance' from the genre of the novel constitutes for Doody the greatest historical misdeed, for it obviates the existence of the ancient novel on the grounds that it is not 'realistic' enough (15–16). The marvellous, the exotic, and the culturally other all have no place in this form of realism, which would seem to be a way of denying them reality altogether.

Doody's thorough debunking of the 'realist' novel takes place, curiously enough, thanks to a conceptualization of the novel that has much in common with the tradition described in this book. The novel is a mixed genre, accepting and incorporating a variety of forms, languages, and experiences; it is open-ended and oriented toward the future; it expresses dissatisfaction with the systems of exploitation native to its sociohistorical moment, and expresses a deep yearning for individual freedom (471–85). Controversial as her claims for the novel as the genre of the ancient 'Goddess' might be (and it is not in the purview of this book to deal with the ancient novel), it is nonetheless clear that she writes within the parameters of the problem of the novel set forth by Schlegel, Lukács, and Bakhtin. Nonetheless, like Watt she makes a claim to the novel as a genre of the authentic: 'A novel *makes us feel the sense of being alive*' (479). What distinguishes Doody from Watt is that she situates this authenticity in the reader's experience of psychological and mental activity, yearning and thinking, dreaming and wondering. For Watt, novelistic authenticity arises from the recreation of the physical sensorial interaction with an outside world. Here is the crux of the difference: for Watt, writing as a 'philosophical realist,' sensorial experience is unproblematized and trustworthy, whereas for Doody, sensorial experience is a function of human mind.

The strong Kantian bent of the theories of the novel to be explored in this book rejects any notion of realism based on an unexamined faith in the senses. These theories of the novel are first and foremost about the human mind in all its creativity, activity, and limitations. As such, the theory of the novel must problematize freedom and reason within the context of modernity, for both are problematized in modernity. The modern novel becomes figured as the space of freedom, a freedom so complete that it is, according to Marthe Robert, 'total freedom' ('From *Origins of the Novel*' 60). But it is also conceived in relation – or opposition – to reason, and the other discourses where modern reason seems more naturally to reside. The very question of whether the novel can be 'true' or 'rational' is a modern question.

Modern Stories of Modernity

Watt's notion of 'philosophical realism' implies that modernity is in part a function of scientific progress based on sensorial observation.

Nonetheless, this account of the history of modern thought is now disputed. By re-examining the seventeenth century as a period of crisis in all spheres, from the economic and social to the intellectual and spiritual, Stephen Toulmin offers a vigorous revision of claims linking modernity to Cartesianism and the rise of modern science (71). Faced by uncertainty and instability, plus the increasingly censorious postures of the various institutions of the age, thinkers rejected the urbane, tolerant scepticism of sixteenth-century thinkers such as Montaigne and Bacon in favour of theoretical purity and certainty. Neither rhetoric nor case-based practical thought (casuistry) would allow for such an abstracted, de-contextualized endeavour, and were thus eschewed by scientists and philosophers; indeed, Toulmin dates the schism between philosophy (at least in its Anglo-American version) and the humanities to this seventeenth-century dream of a 'rational method, a unified science, and an exact language' (104). Four 'changes of mind' served to orient intellectual enquiry in a radically different direction: 'from oral to written, local to general, particular to universal, timely to timeless' (34). Only since the 1960s, according to Toulmin, have the social sciences and natural sciences turned back toward the consideration of the oral, local, particular, timely, rhetorical, and case-based.[1]

Toulmin's longing for a return to a 'kinder, gentler' modernity was not uncommon in the twentieth century, and reflected the widespread belief that modernity had entered a period of crisis. In the fields of academia and literature, this sense of crisis arose in inverse proportion to the declining influence of humanistic, hermeneutical, and narrative forms of knowledge. The schism between philosophy and the humanities interests us because it offers an explanation of the move to theorize the novel. On the one hand, literary critics and scholars claim to practise a form of rigorous, scientific enquiry if they can make a claim to theory. Theory provides 'system' and 'objectivity,' even in its most unsystematic forms. It provides the antidote to feeling and subjectivity. On the other hand, literature deals with the messy domain of human emotions and sentiment. As Toulmin notes, '[t]he apotheosis of logic and formal rationality struck deep roots, and for a long time had made the status of "feelings" or "emotions" problematic' (148). How could the exploration of the illogical and the irrational be taken seriously in an intellectual environment that favoured the logical and the rational? The compulsion to theorize literature needs to be seen within the context of modernity.

Taking reason as a problem constitutes a defining characteristic of modernity. J.M. Bernstein makes his somewhat paradoxical argument that Descartes's *Meditations* constitutes the first modern novel because in it the philosopher struggled with the problems of identity, knowledge, and belief that arise when it seems 'that there is something fundamentally wrong with our modes of justifying and accepting beliefs generally' (158). Modern scepticism about received, traditional wisdom throws into doubt authority, and requires that the individual reason and judge for himself or herself. Both Kant and Hegel wrestle with the problem of reason, Kant by exploring its limitations and aporia, and Hegel by associating it with history. In very broad terms, Kant differentiates reason from the external 'real' by locating it within the human mind, whereas Hegel links reason to the 'real' by arguing that being is thought (*Phenomenology of Spirit* 33). For Schlegel and our twentieth-century theorists of the novel, Kant will be an acknowledged predecessor insofar as he connects aesthetic activity to judgment, and thus to the mind. In other words, he provides an important link between reason and art. Hegel will be generally less acknowledged, even though his conception of the historical development of art in relation to society will underpin much of their thought.

Agnes Heller, writing at the very end of the twentieth century, offers an insightful vision of modernity's contribution to contemporary life that illuminates the continuing appeal of modern theories of the novel. Perhaps Lukács's most famous student, she postulates that the so-called postmodernity of our time is, in fact, modernity. Modernity, like postmodernity, eschews the ahistorical stability of premodern, traditional life by positing the lived experience of our time as 'a *transitory* state, stage, or world, compressed between the past and the future' (*A Theory of Modernity* 7). Heller denies that postmodernity is essentially different from modernity, but rather considers it the 'self-reflective consciousness of modernity itself' (4). Given that historical consciousness is one of the key aspects of modernity, postmodernity could be understood as a reflection on historical consciousness. In other words, postmodernity is aware of its awareness of historical transition and transitory nature. In this sense, all the thinkers to be approached in this book are involved in a postmodern undertaking: they are conscious and critical of their own historical condition.

Central to the modern mindset is faith in progress as determined by reason. For some, progress would occur through an upheaval or revolution that will permanently alter the order of history, whereas others imagine a gradual but undeniable movement of reform toward a perfected future. These mindsets (which Heller terms respectively 'Marxist' and 'liberal,' although we might now question whether the Marxist mindset has resurfaced in forms of religious fundamentalism) share four basic assertions.

> Firstly, the future is free – we (men) create it. Secondly, we can expect not just a betterment in the future, but a qualitatively better world and way of life. Thirdly, we can predict with certainty (scientifically) that we are going (freely) to create and achieve things in the future under certain conditions (evolution or revolution) which, however, can already be extrapolated. Fourthly, the constant development of technology is pivotal for progression. Although technology may develop nonteleologically, it opens up, wittingly or unwittingly, the *telos* for 'mankind' in (future) history. (8)

These assumptions create tensions that are evident in modern theories of the novel. Our theorists struggle with the first assumption that men freely create the future. For Lukács, the freedom is highly questionable and, if it does exist, can do so only if the individual is alienated from society. Thus, the first assumption morphs into the question of human agency in modernity, one of the central concerns of these theorists of the novel. Others, such as Unamuno, Bakhtin, and Schlegel, strive to configure a literary space in which freedom is possible. Their effort to construct such an alternative space for creativity, imagination, and the arts stands in opposition both to the scientific mode of knowledge and the development of technology. In effect, they work to gain a path alternative to the *telos* of technology. Cohen and Ortega y Gasset, ultimately more concerned with human knowledge than with literature, seek alternative notions of progress and knowledge. For Ortega, the task is to broaden knowledge from a narrow base in reason to include all of human experience. For Cohen, the task is to rescue the hope for progress by reconciling the possibility of reform with the impossibility of perfection.

The Emergence of Modernity in Spanish Institutions

An important element of the 'realist' philosophy of the novel has been to deny to Spain and to Cervantes participation in the modern. At times this prejudice was based on a lack of knowledge about the historical context in which Cervantes wrote, a prime case in point being Erich Auerbach's indefensible assertion that 'Don Quijote's adventures never reveal any of the basic problems of the society of the time' (345). At other times it seems to echo the Black Legend, anti-Spanish propaganda issuing from the early modern period when France and England vied with the more established Spanish Empire for world dominance. It is even a function of locating the origins of the modern in the eighteenth and nineteenth centuries, by which time Spain was in cultural and economic decline. Nonetheless, when we take into account recent theories of modernity such as Heller's and Toulmin's as well as the work of contemporary historians of Spain such as John Elliott and Henry Kamen, it is very difficult to deny that Spain in Cervantes' time was experiencing the crises and challenges posed by modernity. By extension, it becomes difficult to maintain that *Don Quixote de la Mancha* does not problematize modernity in a way typical of the modern novel.

Just as *Don Quixote de la Mancha* heralds the birth of the modern novel, so does the emergence of the nation Spain herald the birth of the modern nation state. Spain owes its modern boundaries, the predominance of Castilian as the unifying, 'national' language, and even its national identity to the monarchs, Ferdinand of Aragon and Isabel of Castile. They married in 1469, eventually joining their respective medieval kingdoms and expanding their jurisdiction over all of what we now know as Spain. The year 1492 was key in the history of this new state not only on account of Christopher Columbus's discovery of the New World, but also due to the final defeat of the Moorish Kingdom of Granada and the expulsion of the Jews from Spain. This historical moment serves to encapsulate an essential dialectic in the creation of a modern nation state: internal homogenization and definition of a national people coupled with external defence of and expansion of national interests. As the seat of the first modern international empire, Spain gave form to many of the institutions that have defined modern nation states. Indeed, there existed in Spain from the middle of the fifteenth century on at least three modern institutions: a professional army, a monetary economy, and bureaucracy, defined as administration by technical experts (Maravall 7). These institutions dedicated to the rationalization and centralization of social power dovetail neatly with Heller's logics of modernity. The modern army depends on technology and the monetarization and instrumentalization of human beings in order to promote political dominance. A monetary economy undermines and eventually destroys medieval notions of feudal allegiance and traditional class identity, and makes possible the establishment of modern states. Bureaucracy is perhaps the most telling manifestation of the technological imagination, for its enormous information-gathering machinery creates new forms of knowledge and control that allow political powers access into even the most personal realms of individual action.

To a large extent, the successful actualization of the new nation of Spain and its far-flung empire depended on a new notion of the monarchy. Until the 1590s, when the phrase 'Monarquía de España' began to circulate, there was not even a widely accepted term for this new political entity; it was referred to paraphrastically through phrases such as 'los reinos y estados de Vuestra Magestad' (I.A.A. Thompson 188). Unlike his French and English counterparts, the Spanish monarch was not considered to rule according to divine right nor to be God's deputy on earth; indeed, the sacralization of monarchy was considered by many Spanish intellectuals to be highly dangerous (Feros 69). The monarchy as an institution was subject to vigorous debate during Cervantes' lifetime, with a corresponding explosion in political treatises exploring the 'razón de estado,' often in anti-Machiavellian or pro-Tacitus terms by which the king's power would be limited by moral considerations (Tierno Galván, 'El tacitismo en las doctrinas políticas del siglo de oro español' 33). Matters of imperial policy were widely debated into the seventeenth century, to such an extent that much of the Black Legend was a mere repetition of harsh critiques of Spanish policy made by Spaniards themselves, including but not limited to Bartolomé de las Casas (Schaub 120). Nonetheless, the actual administration of this far-flung empire depended on a new, centralized bureaucratic organization, and on a modern conception of the king as administrator rather than warrior. It is no accident that the education of the prince exercised many leading minds of the sixteenth century, or that these intellectuals by mid-sixteenth century recommended humanistic training of king and advisors alike, as well as the creation of administrative councils, in order to produce leaders that were morally virtuous *and* good bureaucrats (Fernández-Santamaría 293). Hand in hand with the transformation of the warrior king into the bureaucrat king (seen in the transition from Charles V to Philip II) went the transformation of the warrior noble into the bureaucrat noble.

It is not surprising that scientific research in Hapsburg Spain depended highly on royal support and the interests of the state. One of the standard means by which to deny Spain participation in Western modernity (particularly pernicious, given that this approach was adopted by twentieth-century Spanish Fascism to reinforce its steely grip on the country) is to deny its scientific and intellectual heritage. Such a supposition rests on the notion that the modern sciences emerged in seventeenth-century Protestant lands, where individual thinkers threw off the received dogma to practise individual research unfettered by political oversight or financial exigency. Spain is viewed, from the years of the Black Legend on, as a culture in which intellectual enterprise is controlled, if not completely stifled, by dogmatic belief. According to this version of history, Hapsburg Spain was populated solely by a Catholic population composed of mystics, Inquisitors, and soldiers/adventurers. Having internalized this vision of their own culture, Ortega y Gasset and Unamuno turn to Cervantes at least in part as a means to fill the missing gaps in their national intellectual heritage.

Nonetheless, historians of science are now recuperating the story of Hapsburg Spain's contributions to the emerging sciences of astronomy, geography, botany, and even anatomy. This new interest in early modern Iberian science stems from an understanding that the 'emergence of empirical and mathematical scientific activities, in particular, resulted from the commercial and imperial activities of the sixteenth and seventeenth centuries' (Barrera-Osorio 59).Take, for example, the emergence in sixteenth-century Spain of a new model for natural history, in which classical cosmography gave way to accounts of peoples and places based on 'empirical epistemological criteria' (Portuondo 33). José de Acosta expresses the surprisingly modern attitude toward received wisdom typical of sixteenth-century explorers; based on personal experience in the Americas, he not only rejects classical beliefs that equatorial climes must be torrid and inhabitable, but even dares to laugh at Aristotle while he, Acosta, shivers in the cold, equatorial regions of the Andes (Book II, chap. 9). The astronomer Jerónimo Muñoz, too, dares to contradict Aristotle, when his observations of the 1572 supernova contradict the Aristotelian conceptualization of the celestial spheres (3r). Even the potentially heretical could be tolerated if it served imperial interests: Copernican ideas were regularly taught in the University of Salamanca astronomy and mathematics curriculum until the last decades of the seventeenth century because they provided the basis for better navigational tables (Navarro Brotons 90).

Not surprisingly, scientific and technological advances were largely linked to the interests of the Spanish crown in governing and benefiting from the new colonies in both the Americas and Asia. Philip II, in particular, recognized the need for improved scientific methods and information in order to manage his worldwide empire, and thus both funded and hoarded the innovations and knowledge accumulated under his auspices.[2] A master of bureaucratic design, he assigned the collection of scientific information and the promotion of technological innovation to entities such as the Casa de Contratación in Seville, which controlled all colonial commerce, and the Consejo de las Indias. The Hapsburg court, reflecting the international empire, became a magnet for inventors and thinkers across Europe, and attracted the likes of the anatomist Andreas Vesalius and the German metallurgist known as Juan Tetzel.[3] Spanish advances in navigation, metallurgy, astronomy, and geography, among other fields, were circulated among the other powers vying for colonial power. Botanical information from the Americas, some of it compiled by indigenous scientists such as Juan Badiano and Martín de la Cruz, filtered to Europe through Spanish authors such as Nicolás Bautista Monardes and Francisco Hernández, whose work was published in the anthologized version compiled by Nardo Antonio Recchi by the Roman Academy of the Lynx almost a century later (Cañizares-Esguerra 28– 30). It is no accident that sixteenth-century Spanish treatises of all types – not just literary – were quickly translated into French and English, and enjoyed numerous reprintings.[4] When translations were not available, other means to access this information were attempted. Richard Hakluyt, author of major works on navigation and the Americas and a particularly avid proponent of the Black Legend, gleaned his information not only from José de Acosta's printed work but also by interviewing disaffected Portuguese exiles who had worked for Philip II (Portuondo 264). When capturing Spanish ships, Thomas Cavendish and Francis Drake gained valuable maps and treatises and took Spanish ship pilots captive (264).

Even the Spanish Inquisition can be viewed as a modern institution, for its methodical and insistent enquiry into the most intimate actions and beliefs of Spanish citizens exercised an intrusion of institutional power into domestic and personal spheres in a way unimaginable to previous generations.[5] Historians and students of Spain have yet to determine the full effect of the forced expulsion of Jews and Moors, as well as the conversion to Christianity that many chose over exile, on the general tenor of Spanish society.[6] By the second half of the sixteenth century, the Inquisition had established a web of, according to one estimate, some twenty thousand informants, and thus constituted a pervasive form of social control previously unseen (Elliott 216). Concerning itself not only with religious practice but also with religious belief and sexual practice, it penetrated into the private lives and minds of citizens in a manner that approaches the control exercised by the modern totalitarian state. Joseph Pérez has observed the procedural similarities between the Spanish Inquisition and the Stalinist apparatus, noting the following points of contact: the anonymity of accusers; the social shaming of families of the accused; the distrust of those with foreign contact; and the stringent vigilance over those in positions of power and influence (383–6). One can even suggest that the Spanish Inquisition began to define individuals in modern terms as a function of its procedures: class status or occupation did not exempt anyone from prosecution, nor were local customs, laws, or institutions granted privilege over centralized law and organization (258). Personal identity was fixed in modern terms, being based on identifying a single individual with a single name, family tree, residence, and birthplace through documentary evidence and testimony. According to Irene Silverblatt, who works from Hannah Arendt's conceptualization of modernity according to nineteenth-century colonialism, the Inquisition served in the Americas to racialize individuals according to the modern categories of indigenous, Spanish (European), and black (102). The supposed exceptionalism of the Spanish Inquisition may, perhaps, be far from exceptional, anticipating as it did the apparatus of modern bureaucracy and modern concepts of identity.

Modernity in the Light of Spanish History

Too often histories of European modernity have been overly self-congratulatory and chauvinistic, so perhaps revisiting the history of Spain, France and England's colonial rival, will allow us to conceptualize modernity in more neutral terms. If Spain is one of Europe's first modern nation states, then certain aspects of its sixteenth- and seventeenth-century history shed light on overlooked aspects of our modernity. For starters, modernity does not move in only one direction: take the example of internal migration. Broad demographic changes occurred in this period in Spain, including the depopulation and repopulation of certain regions. In the sixteenth century, the total population of Spain expanded, eventually reaching a total of eight million around 1600, but this growth coincided with a depopulation of much of the countryside, as inhabitants left for the cities and the colonies. In the seventeenth century, repopulation of the countryside took place, in part due to the low birth and high death rates of cities, and renewed commercial activity on the coasts (Alvar Ezquerra 47). Social class structure (the *estamento*) fluctuated during this period. Rather than disappearing, it was reordered. New noble lines, such as the Manriques, were declared by the Crown (Ferdinand and Isabel were particularly active in this respect), whereas some older ones, such as the Mendozas, solidified their power by supporting the monarchs (Domínguez Ortiz and Alvar Ezquerra

94–5). Others, especially among the Andalusian and Castilian nobility, suffered from the monarchy's distrust and lost prestige (96–8). The nobility was 'domesticated' in various ways: through the confiscation of lands, the institution of new orders of nobility and royal-controlled military orders, and even personal humiliation and conviction for criminal activity.

The second class of medieval Spain, the clergy, also experienced radical change, as individuals and institutions operated in a flux between increased control exercised over Church institutions by the state and a capacity for individual freedom of action and thought. The Church had to give in to demands to contribute to the state coffers. Seen as dangerously rich and serving two masters (the Crown and Rome), religious orders were sometimes viewed by the monarchs in antagonistic terms. Gaspar de Guzmán wrote to Philip IV in 1624 that the clergy was on its way to owning everything (144). Some of the Crown's most notable critics were highly educated clerics, including the Dominican Bartolomé de las Casas, who wrote a scathing critique of the treatment of the indigenous peoples in the Americas, and the Jesuit Juan de Mariana, who critiqued Philip III's government and wrote a doctrine justifying tyrannicide. The number of parish clergy grew, and became intimately involved not only in the moral education of their parishioners, but also in improving literacy levels. As is clear, the reordering of the social class system was highly conflictual, and resulted from the clash between different institutions armed with different sorts of power. Moreover, modernity tended to rigidify the distinctions within a class and eliminate intermediate categories (106).

Spain's imperial ambitions and successes offer another example of modernity in its genesis. The first level of empire was Iberia itself, home before the marriage of Ferdinand and Isabel in 1469 to the Christian kingdoms of Portugal, Castille, Navarra, and Aragon, and the Moorish Kingdom of Granada. Even though the marriage of the so-called Catholic monarchs united their kingdoms in a couple, they remained separate in significant ways. The case of Aragon is telling, for the Kingdom of Aragon would retain its own laws and government institutions in their entirety until 1592. In 1591, Antonio Pérez, a former secretary to the Crown, fled from the jail cell in Madrid in which he was awaiting trial for murder, to Calatayud, where he claimed that as an Aragonese he was exempt from being taken prisoner by the king and should be transferred instead to Zaragoza. His plea occasioned two public riots in Aragon, for which about a hundred persons were processed by the Inquisition. Unable to tolerate continued jurisdictional diversity, the

Hapsburg crown intervened in Aragonese law, and revised its medieval statutes. Elliott is correct when he affirms that early modern Spain was 'a plural, not a unitary, state and consisted of a series of separated patrimonies governed in accordance with their own distinctive laws' (82). This same plurality extends to the languages of Spain, where, unlike the case of France, Galician-Portuguese, Catalan, and Basque exist alongside Castilian as living, spoken languages to this day. Perhaps it was the heterogeneity of government and language that impelled the forced unity of faith (106). Or perhaps it was the opposite – all other differences could be tolerated because they were of much less import for the nation. Regardless of the explanation, from this multiplicity one type of modern state was born. The traditional coexistence of castes defined by religious and ethnic identity, but joined by propinquity, is replaced by the modern nation, where adherence to a prevailing ideology is favoured above all else.

Spain's overseas empire comprised European principalities subsumed under the traditional Hapsburg crown and newly discovered colonies. The justification for Spain's colonization of the Americas was based on the old social form of the religious crusade, but it clearly served the strengthening of a modern state and a mercantile economy. Thus, we witness an example of the process of reoccupying traditional social and ideological forms that Blumenberg signalled as typical of modernity. The Spanish Empire was modern in several important functional aspects. It was an international empire not only in its expanse but also in its operations, and its functioning depended on what has been called a 'web of relationships […] in which non-Spaniards frequently played a decisive role' (Kamen, *Spain's Road to Empire* 11). Its economic value was to fund the imperial projects of Spain in other corners of the world, although its effect on the internal Spanish economy was in all likelihood injurious, as the influx of gold and silver fuelled inflation and immigration drained the peninsula of its more enterprising individuals. Foreign bankers, who continued to underwrite the Crown's continuous lack of funding, were the only clear economic winners, along with a handful of Spaniards who returned rich to the peninsula. The metallic capital of Latin America – its gold and silver – fuelled Spain's ideological capital, but served to impoverish the Latin American and Spanish people alike. The ascendency of ideology – over and against the conditions of actual existence – reared its ugly head early in modernity.

Even in terms of the arts and literature, the case of early modern Spain has lessons to teach us about modernity. It is here that the first explosion of prose fiction since the Byzantine era took place. Indeed, it is only outside the realm of Hispanism that Cervantes' *Don Quixote de la Mancha* can so easily be taken as the *first* modern novel. Other candidates for this title from within Spain include Fernando de Rojas's *La Celestina* (1498) and the anonymous *Lazarillo de Tormes* (1554).[7] *La Celestina*, deemed by its author to be a *tragicomedia*, is an intriguing and engaging mix of bawdy humour and an elevated love story. If one defines the modern novel as a mixed work incorporating many genres and discourses, then it would be difficult to dismiss this work summarily. Although it is written in the form of dialogue, its prose is fluid and colourful, and captures richly the varied idiolects of the characters, representing a gamut of social classes. Soldiers and prostitutes tease each other in overtly sexual terms; members of the lower classes comment on their masters; an aging father proffers a rhetorical discourse on fate at the end.

Lazarillo de Tormes, for its part, is generally considered the first picaresque novel. It shares the same mixed nature, as classical allusions and elite rhetoric mingle with the speech of the beggars, petty criminals, and juvenile delinquents who populate its pages. Moreover, the anonymous author's use of irony and narrative voice is ground-breaking. The first-person narration is very sophisticated, and depends on a doubling within the protagonist. Lázaro the adult narrates the tale of Lazarillo the child, and they are indeed quite different in their outlooks on the world. The mature Lázaro directs his account to some unnamed member of the upper class, and the text implies that this autobiography functions as a sort of self-justification. The novel itself ends on an enigmatic note, as it is never clear from which charge the *pícaro* defends himself. Anticlerical commentary abounds in the work, leading some readers to find an Erasmian context. Regardless, there is no doubt that *Lazarillo de Tormes*, like *La Celestina*, contains references to social issues of its day.

In these major works, Spain already experienced a revitalization of prose fiction in terms that accord with the characteristics generally attributed to the modern novel: a mixture of genres, use of irony, open-endedness, and ambiguity, incorporation of discourses and dialects pertaining to different social classes, and even social critique. Both *La Celestina* and *Lazarillo de Tormes* enjoyed notoriety and popularity such that they spawned unauthorized continuations, and deserve more recognition in the history of the modern novel. When one also takes into account the many texts of sentimental and pastoral fiction as well as chivalric romance produced in sixteenth-century Spain, it becomes apparent that Cervantes was writing in a time of much fertile experimentation with prose. This historical phenomenon of an explosion in prose fiction in early modern Spain has not escaped the attention of Hispanists. The works of E.C. Riley, Stephen Gilman, Cesáreo Bandera, Javier Blasco, and Robert ter Horst, among others, deserve a wider audience among non-Hispanist students of literature, for they illuminate the ways in which Cervantes' *Don Quixote* did not spring *ex nihilo*.

Don Quixote's Clash with Modernity

Cervantes' *Don Quixote*, originally conceived of as a humorous parody of chivalric literature, is by no means the obvious choice for the exemplary modern novel. Don Quixote, a middle-aged, landed gentleman of the lowest rank who has squandered his resources buying books of chivalric romances, sets out into sixteenth- or seventeenth-century La Mancha to resuscitate the defunct institution of knight errantry. Fully aware of the anachronism of his undertaking, he bemoans the lost practice of knight errantry, along with its attendant values of chivalry and nobility based on deeds. Don Quixote's performance as a knight errant at times enacts a sharp criticism of the new order of his time. Wealth is concentrated in the hands of the few, who force others to live a life of subservience; personal virtue is eroded by two constant threats, one being the evil deeds of those who would take advantage of the innocent and pure, and the other being a mercantilist economy that values acquisition of material goods over honour. Even the practice of warfare is cheapened, having been transformed from the confrontation of two valorous individuals into the anonymous melee of mercenary armies by the introduction of gunpowder. In short, Don Quixote is conscious of living in a new age, a time that is, in important ways, modern.

One of his more eloquent speeches refers to a lost golden age of utopic harmony and abundance, a time prior to the establishment of personal property and an economy based on the exchange of labour and goods. Addressing himself to a group of confused goatherds and a Sancho Panza more interested in physical repast than intellectual sustenance, Don Quixote waxes poetic: 'Fortunate the age and fortunate the times called golden by the ancients, and not because gold, which in this our age of iron is so highly esteemed, could be found then with no effort, but because those who lived in that time did not know the two words *thine* and *mine*' (*DQ* 76).[8] Not only did human beings share with each other, nature also gave freely of its bounty: the oaks invited humans to pluck their acorns, the streams offered their sweet waters, the bees shared their honey, and the cork trees readily and courteously gave of their bark. Just as the fertile earth remained pure and unviolated by the plow, so did the maidens wander untouched through hill and dale. Clothing was simple and unadorned, as were the affairs of the heart. There was no need of justice, for there were no crimes or criminals. But the growing wickedness necessitated the institution of knight errantry to defend maidens and aid widows, orphans, and the other deserving needy. This lost golden age is associated in Don Quixote's mind with the reign of King Arthur and the fellowship of the Knights of the Round Table (Endress 48–9). Thus, Don Quixote declares and defends his vocation, but it is a calling out of tune with his own times. Maravall, upon situating this speech within the context of other sixteenth-century Spanish works evincing a similar nostalgia for pastoral solitude and freedom, labels it pre-modern or medieval, insofar as it explicitly rejects the organization of human life by the state (225). Nonetheless, many authors of Cervantes' time opposed the communalist notions of utopia, and insisted that a utopia would include private property, and promoted strengthening the middle class of urban merchants and well-to-do farmers (Jehenson and Dunn 33–6, 97). The topic of communal vs private property was clearly a hot button in early modern Spain, and Don Quixote sides with communalism. In point of fact, the reference to the liberal generosity of the oak trees that gave freely of their fruit to any hand brings to mind the protest of the Spanish *Cortes* against the royal practice of selling off stands of oak that had once been communal property (Salomon 144). Communal lands held by medieval organizations, be they towns or religious orders, were in the sights of the cash-starved Crown, and led to many conflicts throughout the sixteenth century.

Contrast this golden age in which nature gives up its fruit without the intervention of human technology – or even human sweat – with modernity. Pastoral nostalgia for nature, combined with the classical *beatus ille* topic, flavours Don Quixote's speech with an anti-technological savouriness (Castro, *El pensamiento de Cervantes* 177–87). One of the axes of modernity is technological use and knowledge, and the notion of science as a form of progress that pervades the modern world view. For Heller, the logic of technology turns everything into an instrument for solving a problem; even the human being becomes an object to be used and manipulated (*A Theory of Modernity* 69). Since the La Mancha traversed by Don Quixote and Sancho Panza is still largely pre-modern in technological terms, one cannot overlook the fact that the episode that has most captured the imagination of readers throughout the centuries is Don Quixote's attack on the windmills. Although exactly when and how windmill technology arrived in Spain is not clear, milling technology was traditionally associated with the Moorish presence in Iberia, and windmills date from at least the fourteenth century. Not only did they render arable dry landscapes throughout Spain, they also served to grind grain and olives, make cloth and paper, and mint coins. Windmills, in particular, clearly represented a technological advance over other technologies insofar as they reduced human labour. A popular proverb of Cervantes' time stated that he who had a windmill enjoyed little work and much money – *molinero de viento, poco trabajo y mucho dinero* (González Landa and Tejero Robledo 151). Nonetheless, both Don Quixote and Sancho Panza abandon their traditional ties to the land, the former as a landowner and the latter as a peasant, in order to take up the practice of knight-errantry, that is to say soldiering.

The maddened Don Quixote seems disturbingly prescient as he situates himself in the cusp of an era twice removed from the golden age of virtue and abundance; not only is his Spain distant from a pre-economic and pre-agricultural utopia, but it is also distant from the era of knight errantry. When the barber insinuates through a story about a man who believes himself to be Neptune that Don Quixote is crazy, the latter responds with anger by referring to the decadent time in which they live: 'I only devote myself to making the world understand its error in not restoring that happiest of times when the order of knight errantry was in flower' (*DQ* 464).[9] Don Quixote further labels his age 'decadent,' for the knights of his time have given up chainmail, and are content to adorn themselves in damask and brocades. Don Quixote's rant leaves no doubt concerning what he views as the moral inferiority of his time: 'Now, however, sloth triumphs over diligence, idleness over work, vice over virtue, arrogance over valor, and theory over the practice of arms, which lived and shone only in the Golden Age and in the time of the knights errant' (*DQ* 465).[10] The medieval caste of the warrior noble finds itself rendered into effete courtesans in a new modern order, in which political order and justice emanates from the state and not the individual, and in which personal value accrues from economic power rather than virtue.

As Don Quixote laments, the military has already been greatly transformed by the technological innovation of gunpowder.[11] During a discourse on the relative value of arms and letters, a Renaissance *topos*, the self-proclaimed knight errant digresses to a denunciation of the changes that the use of artillery has introduced into modern warfare:

> Happy were those blessed times that lacked the horrifying fury of the dia-
> bolical instruments of artillery, whose inventor, in my opinion, is in hell,
> receiving the reward for his accursed invention, which allows an ignoble
> and cowardly hand to take the life of a valiant knight, so that not knowing
> how it comes, or from where, a stray shot is fired into the courage and
> spirit that inflame and animate a brave heart, sent by one who perhaps
> fled in fear at the bright flare when the damned machine discharged it,
> and it cuts off and ends in an instant the thoughts and life of one who de-
> served to enjoy many more long years. (*DQ* 332–3)[12]

The depravity of modern warfare, as expressed by this madman, is that technology renders the valour and courage of the individual meaning-less. The bravest soldier no longer necessarily defeats the coward, who, aided by the accursed machine, fells his moral superior. The end of the Middle Ages offers several historical instances of just such defeats: French knights were defeated at Crécy (1346), Poitiers (1356), and Agincourt by English archers (1415); the knights of Burgundy were de-feated by Swiss infantry at Morat (1476); even Francis I was taken pris-oner in Pavia because his horse was felled by a Spanish archer (1525; Lloréns 52).[13]

It is important to note that Don Quixote's denunciation of gun-powder does not rely on its greater power to kill and maim, but rather on the way it turns the valiant warrior into cannon fodder. In this way, the would-be knight errant's critique of the technology of modern war-fare dovetails with what Heller terms the essence of technology, that is to say the technological imagination. Modern individuals think in terms of the subject/object relation espoused by the sciences in which 'the subject treats the world ... as the arsenal of things for human use. Men themselves are objects for use. The whole universe is instrumen-talized or is in waiting as a "standing reserve" for subsequent instru-mentalization' (69). In the case of gunpowder, technology renders the soldier an object of war rather than a subject of war, an instrument of the mechanical arm he wields rather than an arm wielding an instru-ment. Don Quixote himself recognizes this loss of agency, stating that 'it still fills me with me misgivings to think that powder and tin may deprive me of the opportunity to become famous and renowned throughout the known world for the valor of my arm and the sharp edge of my sword' (*DQ* 333).[14]

Don Quixote's misgivings reveal the futility of his attempt to win fame and honour through the medieval office of knight-errantry in modern warfare. This transformation of the noble knight into the mercenary soldier is a telling example of Heller's second logic of modernity, that of the new social arrangement according to the monetarization of social roles, apparently chosen by the individual, as opposed to the pre-modern arrangement of caste identification and roles determined by one's birth. As Heller explains, 'For in the fiction (and imagination) of the modern social arrangement, function and being are not identical. The *function a person performs is not an organic aspect of the person's being'* (58). Don Quixote engages in a modern undertaking when, to all intents and purposes, he knights himself, albeit with the amused assistance of an innkeeper. The medieval order of knight-errantry is essentially coterminous with nobility, in which the knighting of a valorous progenitor by his sovereign is perpetuated among his descendants, and persists to such an extent in early modern Spain that the absurdity and hubris of Don Quixote's undertaking was censured by the readers of the first part of the novel. According to Sansón Carrasco's recounting of the various reactions of readers, the nobles accuse Don Quixote of not being content with his 'vine or two and a couple of fields,' whereas the knights resent competing with 'those squirish gentlefolk who polish their shoes with lampblack and mend their black stockings with green thread' (*DQ* 471–2).[15] Even in these derogatory comments, however, one notes how the role of the nobility, if not its inherited transmission, has changed: the nobles associate nobility with the accumulation of wealth, and the knights associate knighthood with the possession of status symbols. These gentlemen reveal themselves as participants in the modern order of the market, in which money replaces inherited status or personal virtue. According to Heller, 'The question to ask is no longer "what" or "who" (What do you own? Who were your ancestors? Who are you?) but "how much" (How much do you earn? How much have you inherited?)' (85). This shift can be seen in the linguistic usage of the term 'ricos,' which in its medieval form as 'ricos omnos' referred to nobility based on lineage and virtue but, as Diego Covarrubias noted, was taken by the seventeenth century to refer to those who were noble only as a function of wealth (Jehenson and Dunn 89–90).

The downgrading of social class that most bothers Don Quixote is the transference of the military office from the noble to the mercenary, and the transformation of the knight into the courtier. The function of soldier reverts to the underclass, and it is no accident that Don Quixote encounters a young man on his way to join the infantry who sings, 'To the wars I am driven by lack of pence,/If I had them, nothing would get me hence.'[16] In fact, the life of a sixteenth-century soldier was so difficult that often only the rural poor, already accustomed to penury and misery, were able to tolerate it (Salazar Rincón 196); moreover, by the 1590s Spanish civic governments complained of the impoverishing effect of taxation to support the myriad wars on the overall population, leading to broad public discontent with Spain's imperial commitments and the eventual suspension of debt payments by the Crown in 1599 (I.A.A. Thompson 168–71). In an insightful reading of this episode, Jaime Fernández observes that the young soldier does not recognize Don Quixote as a knight errant, nor does Don Quixote mention his chivalric occupation. In the figure of the young man, Don Quixote recognizes a sad reality, for all that awaits him is the dark uncertainty to which he is pushed by necessity – even though he believes himself to be freely choosing his fate (110–11).

The professionalization of the military by Ferdinand and Isabel of Spain tended to undermine the political power of the nobility; indeed, by 1493 the first permanent professional troops (Guardias Viejas) were established in Castille (Lloréns 58). Don Quixote's clash with the new monarchic law comes to a head when he runs across a group of criminals being led in chains to fulfil their sentence by serving as galley slaves in the Spanish military. His conversation with Sancho as to the identity of these men captures faithfully the transition from a medieval view of justice to a modern one, and thus merits careful analysis. Sancho identifies them as 'a chain of galley-slaves, people forced by the king to go to the galleys' (DQ 163).[17] Don Quixote responds in anger, 'Is it possible that the king forces anyone?'[18] At this, Don Quixote decides to put into action his chivalric code of righting wrongs and aiding the distressed and downtrodden, to which Sancho, ever the modern thinker, replies: '"Your grace shouldn't forget," said Sancho, "that justice, which is the king himself, does not force or do wrong to such people, but sentences them as punishment for their crimes"' (DQ 163–4).[19] In spite of his servant's protestations, Don Quixote proceeds to free the men, who, in turn, pelt him with rocks and flee.

The description of the galley slaves being led in chains is brief, but telling. Strung like beads on an iron chain, they are metonymically absorbed into a machine-like unit. Only their subversive and inventive use of language serves to grant them an individual identity (José F. Martín 27–34). Indeed, their destination to the galleys will completely assimilate them into the great mechanism of the Spanish warship, dependent upon their rhythmic and unified motion for its propulsion. In part II of *Don Quixote*, during their stay in Barcelona, Don Quixote and Sancho board a galley, in which the crew acts as an inanimate instrument: 'The crew hoisted the yard as quickly and noisily as they had lowered it, and they did it all without a word, as if they had neither voice nor breath' (*DQ* 877).[20] These galley slaves en route to the sea clearly go by force, the nature of this force causing the debate between Don Quixote and Sancho. Sancho, professing the modern perspective, explains that the force of justice, that is to say the king, sends them to this fate as fair recompense for their misdeeds. Indeed, the espousal of modern justice by this illiterate peasant serves as proof of the success of the Spanish monarchy's centralization and regularization of justice. Don Quixote's notion of justice, according to which this ragged group of petty criminals enjoys free will commensurate with that of the king, 'resonates with ideas then common' and summed up by Francisco Suárez's assertion that all men are born free, with no natural jurisdiction of one over the other (Jehenson and Dunn 128–9). Although sixteenth-century academics and jurists such as Martín de Azpilcueta and Suárez had insisted that power resided in the community and not the king (with Azpilcueta having done so in Charles V's presence), Don Quixote is once again on the losing side of the debate (118).

In Cervantes' Spain under Philip II and Philip III, justice resided ever more firmly in the king, whose arm of the law was the Santa Hermandad. Another example of Ferdinand and Isabel's genius for adapting and transforming medieval institutions into modern ones, the Santa Hermandad was established in 1476 based on the unified control of the popular brotherhoods (*hermandades*) that had served local leaders in earlier times. The Santa Hermandad 'combined in itself the function of a police force and a judicial tribunal,' and had jurisdiction over crimes that took place in the countryside, as well as acts of sedition against the monarchs (Elliott 85). Although its power, jurisdiction, and ferocity decreased with the gradual cessation of revolts against the monarchy, it still suffices to make poor Sancho tremble in fear, as he imagines the reprisal he and his master are to suffer for having freed the galley slaves. As González Echevarría remarks, 'The knight's act of freeing the men, as Sancho rightly observes with alarm, makes them, along with the former prisoners, fugitive outlaws. Theirs is a serious *caso de corte*,

for they have committed a crime against the crown, setting free men condemned by the king's courts, whose representatives they have fought
and injured in the process' (6). Curiously, the Santa Hermandad was
commissioned with the duties that had belonged to medieval knights:
helping the weak and poor and serving justice (Salazar Rincón 141).

When justice does catch up with the fugitive Don Quixote and Sancho
Panza toward the end of book I, its representatives resemble the
Keystone Cops in their incompetence and illiteracy. A barber, whose
basin and saddle Don Quixote has stolen and imaginatively transformed into the giant Mambrino's helmet and horse harness, appeals to
the judgment of four officers who happen by the inn, just as Don
Fernando and the priest refuse to acknowledge his claims that the objects in question are merely a basin and saddle. One angry trooper exclaims, 'If that's not a saddle, then my father's not my father, and
whosoever says otherwise must be bleary-eyed with drink' (*DQ* 394).[21]
Don Quixote's violent reaction is by now predictable; the narrator informs us that the blow he directs at the trooper would have felled him
if the officer of the Crown hadn't ducked in time. Calling for the help of
the Santa Hermandad, his companions, including the innkeeper, join
the assaulted trooper, and a general melee ensues. Don Quixote, imagining himself to be in the battle of the plains of Agramonte depicted
in *Orlando Furioso*, manages to restore order by announcing that such
high personages should not battle over insignificant things. As much
out of confusion as anything else, the troopers stop fighting with the
inn's guests – for a moment.

During the fight, two details reveal social and political implications
that go beyond the merely slapstick humour of a bar brawl. Upon heav-
ing his lance at the offending trooper, Don Quixote makes a class-based
slur: 'You lie like a peasant knave!'[22] Don Quixote, in both his real social
identity as an *hidalgo* and in his assumed social identity as a knight errant, cannot accept criticism coming from a lower-class rustic. A similar
note of class tension reoccurs in the narrator's description of the noble
Don Fernando's willing participation in the fighting: 'Don Fernando
had one of the officers under his feet and was trampling him with great
pleasure' (*DQ* 394).[23] Class memory lasts long, and neither Don Quixote
nor Don Fernando appears to have forgotten that the Santa Hermandad
was established to reduce and control the power of the local nobility.[24]
Nor was the difference in class lost on these four officers; as the narrator
notes, 'So it was that the officers stopped fighting when they heard the
rank and station of their opponents, and they withdrew from combat

because it seemed to them that regardless of the outcome, they would get the worst of the argument' (*DQ* 396).[25] Clearly, the power of the police, centralized though it might be in the king, was still called into question by the lowly class status of its members.

Cervantes' obvious interest in this conflict between class-based nobility and modern justice leads him to keep the fight going. Even as the officers decide to cool down, the one who had been beaten by Don Fernando conveniently remembers that 'among the warrants he was carrying for the detention of certain delinquents, he had one for Don Quixote, whom the Holy Brotherhood had ordered arrested, just as Sancho had feared, because he had freed the galley slaves' (*DQ* 396).[26] The beaten officer will have his final say, or so he thinks, with the arrest warrant, evidence of his power ordained by bureaucracy and ultimately the king. Cervantes' description of his search for and reading of the warrant is both humorous and telling, for it reveals the doubled identity of a modern police officer as a physical enforcer and a state bureaucrat. Like a good bureaucrat, 'he decided to make certain that the description in the warrants tallied with the knight.'[27] Nonetheless, the officer is only marginally literate, and so he reads the document slowly and painfully while comparing it with the man. Upon confirming Don Quixote's identity, the trooper appeals to the document as justification for action: 'In the name of the Holy Brotherhood! And so everybody can see that I'm serious, read this warrant ordering the arrest of this highway robber' (*DQ* 396).[28] Once again, Don Quixote physically attacks the officer whom he views, as evidenced by the narrative focalization, as a 'peasant highwayman' (*villano malandrín*). The noble Don Fernando stops the subsequent scuffle, even as the officers protest that they are serving the king and the Santa Hermandad by arresting Don Quixote.

Echoing the quarrel over the disputed identity of the barber's basin/Mambrino's helmet, the identity of Don Quixote as an alleged highway robber becomes the main bone of contention. Three different discourses are used to justify not arresting the would-be knight errant. Don Quixote, of course, appeals to the law of knight-errantry, a law unto itself and beyond the modern judiciary. In a lengthy harangue, Don Quixote for the third time labels the officers as 'crude and lowly born' (*gente soez y malnacida*): 'Who was the dolt who did not know that knights errant are exempt from all jurisdictional authority, or was unaware that their law is their sword, their edicts their courage, their statutes their will?' (*DQ* 397).[29] The knight errant's rejection of the Santa

Hermandad's jurisdiction over his actions reverts to the traditional noble attitude of those such as the Marquis of Villena, who claimed that people of low station had no right to use arms against knights (Maravall 43–4). Don Quixote's logic, of course, holds no sway in this occasion.

It remains to the lettered priest and the rich Don Fernando to resolve the conflicts. The priest, while Don Quixote thunders away, argues to the officers that the man is crazy, and thus his arrest would only be revoked once he was found to be insane. The priest's logic appeals to Spanish law dating from at least the thirteenth-century Siete Partidas, according to which the insane and minors under the age of ten were not held criminally responsible for their actions (González Echevarría 71–2). Thus, the law itself exonerates Don Quixote, at least as far as the Santa Hermandad is concerned. The barber and the innkeeper, both of whom have suffered financial losses in their dealings with the madman, require justice in kind. Don Fernando pays the innkeeper, and the priest pays the barber, from whom he receives a receipt and the promise not to engage in further legal action. At the end of the day, money suffices to smooth over the differences.

Don Quixote's relationship to money is problematic, to say the least.[30] Throughout book I, he refuses to pay the expenses incurred at inns, noting that knights errant are not required to do so. Don Quixote's tirade against the Santa Hermandad, in which he defends his position above their law, continues with an exclamation of exasperation against taxes: 'What knight errant ever paid a tax, a duty, queen's levy, a tribute, a tariff, or a toll?' (DQ 397).[31] Once again, we are privy to a class-based complaint; tax (pecho in the original Spanish) clearly refers to taxes charged against the lower classes. Hidalgos, who were exempted from paying taxes, were opposed in the social system of values to pecheros, who did pay taxes, or in the case of the countryside, to labourers (labradores; Salazar Rincón 88). Alonso Quijano, although an hidalgo, does not merit the title of caballero, nor should he use the honorific don due to a thoroughly modern problem: he does not have enough financial worth. Knighthood was not a legally defined estate in the nobility, and thus a knight was simply a noble who had enough money to lord over his peers (Salazar Rincón 90).

One could argue that the highest strata of the nobility, the so-called grandes de España established in 1520, received, in return for their loss of military might, monetary power. By 1530, they might have owned as much as one third of the nation's wealth; the Duke and Duchess who torment Don Quixote and Sancho in part II, as well as Don Fernando,

Dorotea's seducer in part I, could represent this level of nobility (Salazar Rincón 18–29). If this is the case, then Cervantes demonstrates a loss of civility and noblesse oblige among the richest nobles concomitant with their increased monetary power. They can – and do – buy whatever their heart desires. Hunting is for them devoid of its medieval class significance; once an exercise for war, it is now a merely frivolous pastime (Quint 149–50). Indeed, their hunt seems to extend to Don Quixote and Sancho Panza, who become the objects of many charades and jokes. The nobles' thirst for novel entertainment is such that they even waylay the protagonists on the road once the pair escapes their palace. Novelty in such a context is Janus-faced: on the one hand, it fuels the never-' satisfied desires of a financially enriched, but existentially impoverished, ruling class; on the other hand, it threatens the ruling class's power, as lower classes push for the new – reform and even revolution – to overcome their subjugation. Don Quixote himself recognizes the threat novelty poses for the status quo when he remarks that in newly conquered lands, the rulers fear that some *novelty* will destroy social order (1: chap. 15; Salazar Rincón 31–2). Ironically, the novelty that actually threatened the finances of the Spanish grandees in the sixteenth century was inflation, which ate into their purchasing potential, at the same time that they adopted an ever more lavish lifestyle (38–41).

The third logic of modernity, according to Heller, is that of political domination. Although she fails to give a precise definition of this logic, it becomes apparent from her writing that modern political domination depends ultimately upon the power of ideology embodied in the 'historical imagination.' In this sense both constitutional and totalitarian governments are modern, since historical imagination 'mobilizes past memories and places them in the holistic frame of an ideology' (*A Theory of Modernity* 107). Whereas Don Quixote's ideology appears to be medieval, based on the ethos of knight-errantry, his knowing reenactment of it as both antiquated and yet contemporary is typical of the double bind described by Heller as the modern predicament. 'Thus, the double-bind characterizes the world of the moderns: problem-solving and interpretation, planning and recollection, calculation and reflection. The double-bind needs to be "double"; it needs to bind modern men and women to different historical places and spaces, to different activities, different evaluations' (107). Don Quixote chooses to become a knight errant in part to address the problems of his existence; he must plan and calculate his performance, for he is acting outside the social roles of his own time. His entire endeavour depends upon both a critique, albeit a conservative one, of his time and place, and the historical imagination to envision a solution, albeit an ancient one.[32] One could even conceive of Don Quixote as the embodiment of modern historical imagination when taking into account Heller's description of it: 'The internal structures of institutions past are not preserved in the deep chambers of historical consciousness, but through the acts of men and women … The fragments of past worlds are presenced in imagination' (101).[33]

The obvious objection is that Don Quixote represents only himself, and perhaps Sancho Panza's limited material interests, but not the larger body politic of sixteenth- and seventeenth-century Spain. Don Quixote becomes the target of the Santa Hermandad, after all, because he has challenged the king's right to exercise justice over the galley slaves, thus setting forth the historical memory of knight-errantry as a power opposed to modern justice. Nonetheless, this conflict between the power of Don Quixote's enactment of medieval justice and the claims of the centralized state to power through the medieval institutions of monarchy and nobility is precisely the element that underlines the novel's modernity. The general impulse among Cervantes' contemporaries to reinvigorate old values responds, in fact, to the anxieties created by the changing times. Recent studies have shown that Spanish sixteenth-century readers of chivalric romances, the literature that inspires Don Quixote's madness, were largely noble, ranging from the Hapsburg monarchs themselves to highly placed courtesans to the lower classes of *hidalgos* (Salazar Rincón 144–53). It is even possible that the literature of knight-errantry, focused on the free adventures and exploits of the individual noble, represented an escape from the rigid protocol and royal control to which the sixteenth-century noble was subject (Chevalier 101). Certainly no noble of Philip II's court would operate as a freelance, so to speak, for the bureaucratic structure so deftly perfected during this monarch's reign made such individual action unthinkable.

Don Quixote, as a literary work representative of modernity, depicts a world in which social order is no longer 'natural,' but rather conventional. No final and unassailable principles underlie the world; rather, it is free to be worked and reworked, founded and re-founded. According to Heller, freedom *'is the foundation that grounds nothing'* (*A Theory of Modernity* 12). Don Quixote is free to remake himself, and free, at least in his mind, to live a critique of his time that serves to reveal the conventional and contingent order of his world. Cervantes' response to this moment of transition from a traditional society in which status depends on birth to modernity, in which one can rise or fall, is to value individual virtue over the prerogatives of social status (Salazar Rincón 83). Take, for example, Don Quixote's image of the two kinds of lineages as either an inverted or an upright pyramid: '[S]ome … trace and derive their ancestry from princes and monarchs, which time has gradually undone, and in the end they finish in a point, like a pyramid turned upside down; and others have their origin in lowborn people, and they rise by degrees until they become great lords' (*DQ* 161).[34] Don Quixote views his profession of knight-errantry as a way to elevate his own status, and soon convinces Sancho that he could become governor of an island, in spite of his lowly heritage. Sancho's wife responds at first with derision to such a notion, and comments on the peasant's ambition to marry their daughter to a noble with this insight: the husband 'might take a notion to insult her and call her lowborn, the daughter of peasants and spinners!' (*DQ* 487).[35] Moreover, Teresa is astute enough to know that the social pressure to maintain traditional divisions comes not only from above, but also from her own class. It is for this reason that she at first rejects the idea of giving herself the title *doña*, for her old friends would gossip about her behind her back. Nonetheless, Don Quixote's desire to raise his station is not simple insanity, but is common practice at the time. Sancho is soon won over to his ambition, and later even Teresa accedes. It is only after having served as governor of Barataria, a charade organized by the Duke and Duchess, that Sancho realizes the emptiness of his ambition. On his way home, he falls into a pit, where he reflects on his experiences as a leader and the slipperiness of fate.

Reason and *Don Quixote*

Don Quixote is one of the most gloriously irrational characters of world literature. He succumbs, after all, to the 'reason of unreason' (*la razón de la sinrazón*) of the fantastic, irrational literature of knight-errantry (1: chap. 1). It is due to this unreason, though, that the novel *Don Quixote* can be read as a discourse on the problems of reason. The conflict over the barber's basin analysed above also represents a conflict over the correct interpretation of reality. The fact that class distinctions come into play does not obviate this, but, in fact, casts doubt on the objectivity of reason. Leo Spitzer's famous analysis of the term *baciyelmo*, a combination of terms that encapsulates the two opposing interpretations of the object in question as either barber's basin or Mambrino's helmet, emphasizes the linguistic freedom that Cervantes takes for himself as evidence of the modern author's creative freedom (60). By returning to Américo Castro's early reading of Cervantes within the context of sixteenth-century humanist thought, we can understand why and how imaginative freedom emerges as a function of the modern problematization of reason. Our mad protagonist, Don Quixote, recognizes that the object in question appears differently to different people, and tells Sancho: 'what seems to you a barber's basin seems to me the helmet of Mambrino, and will seem another thing to someone else' (*DQ* 195).[36] For Castro, this capacity to accept and tolerate the different appearances of the same object links Cervantes' novel to Renaissance idealist and neo-Platonic thought, which Cervantes would have known through León Hebreo, and which foreshadowed Descartes's in the questioning of appearances and reality (*El pensamiento de Cervantes* 81).

The obvious rejoinder to such an assertion of modern doubt in Cervantes' text is to insist that he participated in a Baroque understanding of the world as illusion, best exemplified in the Spanish context by Pedro Calderón de la Barca. After all, the protagonist of *Life Is a Dream* (*La Vida es sueño*, 1635), Segismundo, comes to the conclusion that this world is a false appearance because reality exists in the afterlife (see chap. 5). Liberty understood in this intellectual context is, in Luis Rosales's words, 'liberty before God,' and thus linked to Christian notions of free will and individual responsibility (88–9). Unlike Rosales, I am not convinced that this post-Tridentine twist on neo-Platonism and liberty characterizes Cervantes' writings. In spite of the conversion narrative in the captive's tale, *Don Quixote* is surprisingly bereft of religious content. Sancho throws in a few phrases, often classical in origin, that he has heard from his village priest, and insists that he is an old Christian on several occasions. Don Quixote, on the other hand, is often silent about religion. Indeed, the explanation he provides for the multiple appearances objects assume in his world is decidedly pagan: enchanters and wizards cause the confusion.[37] Following the illogical logic of the literature of knight-errantry, Don Quixote brings into his early modern La Mancha a pre-modern form of belief in which the physical world is subject to magical manipulation. This combination of magical thinking and sceptical doubt is not, of course, uncommon to sixteenth-century European thought. As more historical work is done on the intellectual and scientific community in sixteenth-century Spain, it will become easier to situate Cervantes in that context (see above).

Insofar as Don Quixote's imaginary world brings him into direct conflict with those around him, it is possible to find in the text indices of the transition between medieval culture and modernity. Among the flashpoint issues we have identified are justice, social class structure, and money. Nonetheless, Don Quixote's awareness of the anachronistic nature of his undertaking to resuscitate knight-errantry at some point calls into question the supposition that mental illness is the chief cause of his deranged activity. To date, attempts to diagnose Don Quixote's madness according to either sixteenth- or twentieth-century understandings of mental illness are either inconclusive or contradictory.[38] The psychiatrist Carlos Castilla del Pino gives the most convincing explanation of this interpretive aporia: Cervantes narrates in this novel not a case of mental illness, but rather *'the transcendence of error in the construction of one's own life by any human being in general.'*[39] Error is a dislocation of judgment vis-à-vis reality; one misjudges. Furthermore, misjudgment leads to the dislocation of the individual vis-à-vis reality: 'the subject *dis-locates*, leaves his "place," his reality and his context. Whoever dislocates pays dearly, because his dislocation has consequences sometimes so serious that they interfere with his survival.'[40]

Castilla del Pino arrives at a conclusion shared by many leading Cervantes scholars; namely, that Cervantes understands life as a process of self-making, no matter how perilous or errant the journey might be. Américo Castro perhaps sums up the central place of this self-creation for *Don Quixote* and subsequently the modern novel: 'The modern novel was born of the conflict between one "I" and another "I", not from the conflict between situations, or between good and bad, or even arising from the anxiety of love, requited or unrequited.'[41] For Castro, this conflict arose out of the existential dilemma of leading a double life, or having a double self, epitomized by the situation of the *converso*. Other critics pose different explanations. For Juan Bautista Avalle-Arce, life is itself a work of art – a sort of self-creating. Don Quixote lives the dilemma of Calderón's *Life Is a Dream*: according to Baroque Catholicism, the life of this world is a mere appearance, but one must live as if it were real and train oneself accordingly toward virtue (212–13). Don Quixote's and Sancho Panza's notion that they can make themselves into something other than that determined by their birth and social station is obviously modern and challenges the traditional social order. It is no surprise, then, that they are frequently criticized, not so much for their delirious imaginings, as for their stepping

out of their stations. Nonetheless, their belief that they can and must remake themselves is a function both of modern freedom, in which identity
is dislodged from traditional forms, and the questioning of reason, by
which the self enjoys a distinct, unique perspective on the world.

Reason and Form

The unmooring of reason from the traditional anchors of tradition and
authority that accompanies modern freedom creates a crisis in form. By
the nineteenth century, form did not enjoy the same sempiternal solidity of earlier times, nor could it be seen as metaphysically related to
artistic power. The material content of form is now humanity – form
changes and shapes humankind. Nietzsche's deeply pessimistic concept of formal consciousness, expounded in *Beyond Good and Evil*, uses
the term 'form' to signify empty structures of thought and behaviour.
In the absence of reason, force informs: '[L]ife itself is *essentially* a process of appropriating, injuring, overpowering the alien and the weaker,
oppressing, being harsh, imposing your own form, incorporating, and,
at least, the very least, exploiting' (153). Even less pessimistic thinkers,
ranging from the sociologist Georg Simmel to the philosopher Hermann
Cohen, consider the disappearance of communal reason as involved in
the modern crisis of form.

The crisis of form is particularly acute for the arts and humanities, for
they do not lay claim to the formal modern reason exemplified by the
scientific method. Georg Lukács, in his essay 'On the Nature and Form
of the Essay,' identifies form as a modern problem that appears once
science separates from the arts. Because science claims to treat of facts,
it appropriates content and leaves form to art. Subsequently, 'science
offers us facts and the relationships between facts, but art offer us souls
and destinies' (*SF* 3). Given the young man's proclivities toward
Hegelianism, the attribution of soul and destiny to the realm of form
clearly elevates it above the mere content of science; in effect, form
treats of both life and living. Form mediates between the individual
and whatever transcends the individual; for this reason, it can even be
said to create the soul. Form still confers on the individual symbolic
meaning and destiny. Moreover, form as a power of abstraction is the
express subject of critics. The critic, identified by Lukács as the essayist,
deals with the general and the fundamental, as opposed to poets, who
treat of the 'unique and the incomparable' (*SF* 5). The analysis of form
undertaken by the critic identifies the principles that separate forms

from one another, including the type of material used and the creator's perspective on the world, but it also draws on the individual's feelings and experiences of form (*SF* 7–8). By grasping the formation of life, the critic also enjoys the power to reshape it. Reform, it is hoped, can spring from the critique of form. This is the work of the cultural critic: making a problem. According to Lukács, the essayist or critic works the salvation of an issue by accentuating its problems as much as possible and by radically digging to its roots (*SF* 15). This radical rooting about and uprooting constitutes modern critical reason.

Now we can begin to understand the context in which the great theories of the novel were written. The novel as form illustrated the way the individual's life and destiny coincided. In the case of modernity, the basic formal relationship between the individual and society was that of alienation and separation. Forms as social orders for living life appear as material manifestations of historical power structures. Forms have a history specific to their culture, time, and place. This is the contribution of nineteenth-century materialist thought to the theory of the novel. Forms as founding principles of experience, however, offer the critic a means by which to rise above and stake a view of material reality. Following the idealist trends of Plato, Kant, and Hegel, Lukács argues for form's power to simultaneously delimit and make visible the limits that define what would otherwise be chaotic and illusory (*SF* 7). In other words, form is intimately linked to mind. For the theories of the novel, the otherwise indefinable and ungraspable experiences captured in the novel are those that form the life of an individual in a society – the social forms narrated in the novel are, therefore, historical. Notwithstanding, they take on literary forms that are intimately linked to forms of perception, cognition, and interpretation in the human mind.

Forms and Society

In spite of the idealist tendencies of our theorists of the novel, they all agreed that the material forms of modern society limited individual autonomy. In general, they held what we would call socialist-democratic beliefs, according to which the conditions of society were seen as shaping the conditions of experience (see chapter 8). It is difficult to consider their belief in social forms thoroughly materialist, for they viewed social forms as the products of human activity, and human activity as the product of the mind. The materialist element to their thought could be said to be Aristotelian in its opposition of form and matter. As indicated in Aristotle's *Physics* by his frequent recourse to architecture and sculpture, this opposition of form and matter lends itself to (or perhaps originates from) the image of making and creating. Form does the work of definition, as the sculptor would define the stone or the architect the building. The subservience of matter to form is made quite clear in Aristotle's infamous personification of matter as woman: 'Yet the form cannot desire itself, for it is not defective; nor can the contrary desire it, for contraries are mutually destructive. The truth is that what desires the form is matter, as the female desires the male and the ugly the beautiful' (328). Not only does form define and complete defective matter, it also serves as its end and cause. Nature, being composed of matter and form, is twofold, and yet form is the essence because it puts matter into motion, causing and orienting motion (340). In *Physics* Book 3, Aristotle refers to form as what the mover transmits to matter, as in the case of human reproduction: 'The mover will always transmit a form, either a "this" or such or so much, which, when it moves, will be the principle and cause of the motion, e.g. the actual man begets man from what is potentially man' (344). In this sense, form is potential, and thus it is no accident that Aristotle equates it with essence and archetype. Form makes of matter what it is essential to be. Aristotle links form to change by considering it to be cause and motion. Indeed, even his frequent use of artistic metaphors (the bronze and the sculpture, the architect and marble) emphasizes the power of form to create change. Nonetheless, Aristotle sidesteps the issue of form's fluidity by identifying it with essences. Form might effect change, but essences do not change. Form enacts the motion necessary for creation and propagation, but the motion itself is stable and essential.

The writings of Karl Marx serve as well as any to demonstrate the anxieties surrounding the concept of form in the nineteenth century in response to the economic, political, and social realities of modernity. Although Marx clearly starts from the Hegelian notion of Idea infusing form, he removes the Idea segment from the spiritual realm to what he calls the material – that is to say, what infuses the form with meaning is no longer the Idea or the spirit but rather the value arising within economies of exchange. As Marx shows, however, economies of exchange are the product of human activity and signification. The notion of form anchors many crucial elements of his thought: forms of exchange and intercourse between individuals and groups (*Verkehrsform*); forms of property; forms of the state; forms of labour; forms of experience (bourgeois enjoyment of luxury). History, as viewed by Marx, is composed of the evolution of forms. Writing of the social forms of intercourse, he describes history as the alternation and replacement of forms: '[I]n the place of an earlier form of intercourse, which has become a fetter, a new one is put, corresponding to the more developed productive forces and, hence, to the advanced mode of the self-activity of individuals – a form which in its turn becomes a fetter and is then replaced by another' (*The German Ideology* 124). An analogical series of replaced forms underlies Marx's notion of the value-form that distinguishes commodities. Using the example of 20 yards of linen converted into a coat, Marx notes that it is through the creation of value-forms that human labour becomes a commodity. In the capitalist notion of the exchangeability of commodities (what Marx refers to as the language of commodities), the equation 20 yards of linen = coat expresses a relation in which 'the bodily form of commodity B becomes the value-form of commodity A, or the body of commodity B acts as a mirror to the value of commodity A' (*Capital* 1:77).

The relation of exchangeability between the coat and the linen, that is to say the notion that one is equal to the other, bestows on them the double identity that defines the commodity: it is both a physical object and a value-form. Thus, value is itself relative, and depends on the social relations that generate exchange value. Moreover, the chain of relations of exchange is open-ended since 20 yards of linen = 1 coat or = 10 lbs of tea or = 40 lbs of coffee, and so on (1:91). The parallels between Marx's notion of value-form and structuralist notions of language are striking: both systems depend on the equivalent value of objects that have both a physical form and a value-form, the latter being generated according to social conditions within a system of exchange that is essentially open-ended. Marx was not unaware of this similarity, for he refers to the system of commodity value and exchange as the 'language of commodities' (1:77). In an ironic aside, Marx even associates form-value with resemblance and sacrament: 'Thus the linen acquires a value-form different from its physical form. The fact that it is value, is made manifest by its equality with the coat, just as the sheep's nature of a Christian is shown in his resemblance to the Lamb of God.' Indeed, the commodity's value-form corresponds to the doubled nature of metaphor, which establishes through relations of equivalence and exchangeability a double identity and a double value. After all, speaking in the strictest rhetorical terms, the notion that 20 yards of linen is a coat is, indeed, a metaphor. The implications of Marx's thought for form are interesting, for once it is associated with value it enters a system of exchange, where it can, of course, change in its value.

Form and the Mind

Plato is never far removed from the thought of Schlegel, the young Lukács, Cohen, or Ortega – and probably not so far removed from Unamuno and Bakhtin. The German Romantics adopted a Platonic notion of intuition, corresponding to the '"vision of the forms" of the *Republic*, the "inner seeing" of the *Enneads*' (Beiser 60). Platonic dialectics as described in Book 7 of the *Republic* correspond adequately to Romantic notions of critique, for in both cases one seeks to uncover the principles, logical steps, and conclusions underlying thought. In the dialogue *Meno*, Socrates uses geometry as proof that knowledge already resides in the soul (Plato, *Five Dialogues* 70–6). It is the recourse to a notion that knowledge, or at least the forms of knowledge, are already present in and constitutive of the human mind that will influence the theorists of the novel. In the case of the young Schlegel, Plato served not only as a model philosopher, but also as a model stylist. Combining but not fusing the different generic styles (dithyrambic, fantastic, sentimental, rhetorical), Plato produces texts that are prose works of art (*LN* #102–3). Moreover, Socratic irony, the wisdom that masks itself as foolishness, serves as the model for Schlegel's notion of Romantic irony.

One of Hermann Cohen's important contributions to modern philosophy was his revalorization of the Platonic Idea as hypothesis, a move by which he linked Kantian thought to the Platonic tradition. Cohen conceived of form as intimately linked to thought. By positing Idea as hypothesis, the German philosopher grants it the power to found concepts (Poma, *The Critical Philosophy of Hermann Cohen* 14). Idea coincides, then, with the Kantian *a priori* insofar as it provides the structure and foundation for experience. Furthermore, Cohen differentiates between materialism as the belief that reality resides in matter with idealism as the search for 'the meaning of concrete reality' (27). Cohen's critical methodology, in which he sought to identify the *a priori* forms that make experience possible, depends on the examination of concrete phenomena and the mental processes by which it is experienced. Andrea Poma describes the function of *a priori* forms in this way: 'First of all, transcendental investigation does not deduce experience from a priori forms, but on them founds "possible experience," or rather "the possibility of experience." Thus we are dealing with a formal, not an ontological, foundation' (10). The examination of actual novels (concrete phenomena) combines with the critique of the forms that emerge from reading these novels to make possible the reader's experience of certain key elements. Thus, *Don Quixote* serves both as an example of the novel as a genre and as a foundation for the reader's experience of the social problems it explores.

The Appeal of Kant

Kant's conception of form resonates throughout modern theories of the novel. In the *Critique of Pure Reason*, Kant defines form in opposition to matter: 'That which in the phenomenon corresponds to the sensation, I term its *matter*; but that which effects that the content of the phenomenon can be arranged under certain relations, I call its *form*' (41). Subsequently, matter appears as an *a posteriori*, but form adheres *a priori* to the mind itself, independent of external sensation. The internalization of form to the human mind has its aesthetic analogue in Kant's formalistic notion of beauty, as seen in the *Critique of Judgement*. Sensation, because it is bound to the individual experience, cannot serve as the basis for beauty, which must be universal. Form, on the other hand, appeals to the mind, and gives pleasure through the dynamic play of cognitive faculties. In what Kant calls the formative arts, including painting and sculpture as well as architecture and horticulture, line is preferred over colour because delineation creates form, and thus mental pleasure. 'Every form of the objects of sense (both of external sense and also mediately of internal) is either *figure* or *play*. In the latter case it is either play of figures (in space, viz. pantomime and dancing) or the mere play of sensations (in time)' (*Critique of Judgement* 61). Figure occupies the spatial dimension of mental form, and play, as Kant himself clarifies, occupies the temporal. In this way, beautiful forms correspond to and excite *a priori* mental faculties. As Kant's excursus on ornamentation (*parerga*) indicates, form links what would otherwise be extraneous (frames, for example) to the whole, and thus complements the whole. In short, Kant's notion of formal beauty gives rise to the practice of aesthetic judgment as an interpretation of forms. Everyone will produce for him or herself an 'ideal of beauty,' a representation of the beautiful. As Kant explains, 'Although we are not in possession of this [ideal of beauty], we yet strive to produce it in ourselves' (69). In this way, Kant links the pursuit of beauty to the pursued perfection of the individual through free will and ethical action. Form serves to negotiate between the individual and the universal, for taste is refined to adapt to the *sensus communis*, but the individual (either person or art object) is appreciated as a whole.

The tradition of novelistics traced in this book begins with the young Friedrich Schlegel, playing and working to formulate – albeit in fragments and aphorisms – a concept of modern literature. Kant represented for Schlegel the most modern tendencies of philosophy as well as a political spirit of revolutionary enquiry. Kant's publication of the *Critique of Judgement* influenced, challenged, and stimulated the young Friedrich in diverse ways: to further explore the limitations of the human mind through the positing of irony; to question the relation between art and philosophy; and to view art itself as critique. Schlegel's debt to Kant rests on the following innovations in Kant's thought: 'first, the establishment of the autonomy of the aesthetic realm; second, the definition of aesthetic pleasure as "disinterested satisfaction," … and finally, the discernment of the uniqueness of aesthetic judgments in contrast to … scientific and moral ones' (Ernst Behler, 'Origins of Romantic Aesthetics in Friedrich Schlegel' 53). With these notions Schlegel will free the study of poetry from purely moralistic and didactic uses: imagination does not have to serve reason. He will strive, like the other theorists of this book, to associate literature with the ethical, not through the exposition of moralizing content, but rather through the training of moral judgment. In addition, from Fichte, who attempted to turn Kant's thought into a theory of the subject, Schlegel will adopt his notion of 'the dynamic thought process of philosophical reflection' (57). This notion of the unending aesthetic project not only grounds Schlegel's aesthetics of the arabesque, but also the other theories of the novel we will explore here.

Neo-Kantianism emerged as a major field of Continental philosophy toward the end of the nineteenth century in part as a response to an increasingly empirical psychologism in which material causes for all psychological phenomena were sought (a period not unlike our own in that sense). Hegelian notions of absolute spirit and reason could not withstand advances made in the sciences that threatened the very bedrock of philosophy and the humanities: interpretation, logic, and tradition. In the words of Michael Holquist, this is 'an age when relativity dominates physics and cosmology and thus when *non-coincidence* of one kind or another – of sign to its referent, of the subject to itself – raises troubling new questions about the very existence of mind' (*Dialogism* 17). Kant was particularly attractive to thinkers such as Cohen, Ortega y Gasset, and Bakhtin because he located the aesthetic function in the human mind. One must not forget that Cohen's chief academic antagonists were those who proposed a purely material explanation for all mental activities. The fictive nature of progress as expressed in neo-Kantianism spurred the individual toward ethical action at the same time that it prevented the representation of man as pure spirit (divine) or pure material (animal), and is not to be confused with the Hegelian movement of the spirit. Ernst Troeltsch describes the difference between Cohen and Hegel: 'Process is for Cohen only a thought image created with *a priori* necessity by human thought. Hegel assumed process to be a living movement of the divinity itself that can reconstruct the finite spirit, and every positional point within development, from its own depth and movement of life as absolute reality rooted in the Absolute' (Kluback, 'The Jewish Response to Hegel' 10). The notion of process as fictional rather than historical – albeit a useful and ethically necessary fiction – will also resonate in Ortega's and Bakhtin's novelistics. Kantian thought, as reimagined by Cohen, provides a way to conceptualize fiction in relation to both ethical action and epistemological process without resorting to a sort of literary mysticism. Fiction remains very much a human mental activity, and one of the interests of our theorists is to chart both its faculties and its limits.

To sum up the appeal of Kant for these literary theorists, he offered a theory of the beautiful that centred beauty in the activity of the human mind. Not only did this allow for the form to be studied as an integral element of meaning (an aspect also present in Hegel's aesthetics), it also allowed for the problematization of the reception of the artwork. With the possible exception of Lukács, all the thinkers we examine here are interested in reading as an exercise in judgment. They go far beyond the eighteenth-century interest in the development of taste to argue that reading develops both interpretive and analytical skills as well as ethical judgment and what we would call social consciousness. Even Unamuno, in his radical affirmation of the reader's power to re-create the text, assigns to this activity an ethical justification. Reading is the making of the ethical self, free to use reason and the other powers of the mind to judge for one's self. Our theorists were far from unique in their return to Kant, for many sociologists, philosophers, and politicians of the era turned to the eighteenth-century philosopher in their search for a cultural critique of modernity alternative to that offered by Marxism. Kant's categorical imperative that individuals not be treated as means but rather as a self-sufficient, autonomous individual is reworked in a myriad of disciplines. The novel offers an ethical critique of modernity insofar as it represents the cheapening and instrumentalization of human life and labour in modernity, and as it instructs the reader in ethical judgment.

Hegel as Inspiration and Foil

Hegel's notion of form starts with the Kantian assertion that form ad-heres not to the matter but to the organizing principle of art: '[The] content of art is the Idea, while its form is the configuration of sensuous material' (*Aesthetics* 1:70). For Hegel, beauty serves not so much to fur-ther the pursuit of the ethical by the individual, but rather to actualize beauty. Whereas Kant places the beautiful in the mind, Hegel places it in the spirit, which resides in mind but also beyond it. According to Hegel, '[t]he content of this world [of actualized beauty in art] is the beautiful, and the true beautiful ... is spirituality given shape, the Ideal, and more precisely, absolute spirit, the truth itself' (1:83). The arts, serv-ing as the realm of absolute spirit, are both the object and knowledge of spirit (1:93–4). As manifestation and consciousness, art makes truth present in a way similar to the incarnation of Christ in Jesus (1:103). Therefore, the study of art is linked to the study of religion and philoso-phy. Nonetheless, Hegel's most important contribution to aesthetics is to ground philosophically the study of the history of art. Since Hegel sees the working of the spirit in art, he associates individual works of art with their sociohistorical context, and proposes some of the main tenets of what will become art history and literary history. Of chief im-portance for formalism is his insistence that form and content coincide. Form is not accidental and has a dual function: it actualizes the spiritual in the sensuous, but then 'the external shape, whereby the content is made visible and imaginable, has the purpose of existing solely for our mind and spirit' (1:71).

Although Hegel's association of historical development with generic literary form was not unique (one has only to read Schlegel's earlier musings on historical genres to appreciate this), his tale of the develop-ment of forms in Western history serves as an inevitable backdrop to modern theories of the novel. Art begins as the 'urge of imagination ... in striving out of nature into spirit' (1:517). In this earliest period, it is associated with cultic activities in which the divine is brought to earth through the diviner. Epic belongs to classical society, in which reason has not yet freed 'the divine Being from its contingent shape' (*Phenomenology of Spirit* 451). He who sings the epic sings the unity of the divine and the human, and vanishes in his song as he simultaneously links the people through its heroes to the gods (441). Tragedy represents a higher form as the individual is inserted into the universal, for in it the hero speaks directly to the audience through the self-conscious activity of the actor

(444). Comedy takes self-consciousness one step further through irony (451). Beauty is attained in the classical period through the 'adequate embodiment of spirit's own substantial individuality' in form (*Aesthetics* 1:517). In the medieval (what Hegel calls 'Romantic') period, the 'simple solid totality of the Ideal is dissolved and it falls apart into the double totality of (a) subjective being in itself and (b) the external appearance, in order to enable the spirit to reach through this cleavage a deeper reconciliation of its own element of inwardness' (1:518). Honour, love, and chivalry are the stuff of medieval art because they represent values of the spirit internalized in individuals. The progress of art for Hegel, associated as it is with the historical development of the spirit, culminates in its death. Already in his time, Hegel remarks that art is 'a thing of the past' because one no longer just enjoys it, but also subjects it to judgment (1:11). Perhaps because of his announcement of the death of art, Hegel remains an often invisible interlocutor with the theorists of the novel. Nonetheless, there can be no doubt that his concept of the epic and the medieval vis-à-vis individuation and self-consciousness resonates in their thought, if only insofar as the association of literary form with social forms of being and ways of thinking is taken as axiomatic.

Galin Tihanov asserts that 'Hegel is the source of Lukács's understanding of the novel in one crucial aspect: the accommodation of the novel within a dialectical narrative that presents the history of mankind as the history of its (artistic) consciousness' (*The Master and the Slave* 114). Indeed, the same can and should be said for Unamuno, Ortega, and Bakhtin. Hegel would seem to be the natural starting point for this tradition. Like Hegel, our theorists of the novel accept that art is the expression of a time and a place – of a nation. They also tend toward formalism of the sort proposed by Hegel in which form cannot be considered accidental, but rather expresses and communicates meaning. Certainly all of the theorists working after Hegel read his work. Given that Hegel did mention Cervantes in his *Aesthetics*, there are points of contact that will be discussed in the appropriate chapters. The young Lukács most closely adheres to a Hegelian understanding of the participation of the ideal in art, whereas the others tend to appropriate Hegelian concepts only to redefine them, or employ Hegel as a useful foil. Unamuno draws on Hegelian notions of the spirit residing in the nation in his concept of *intrahistoria*, yet departs from Hegel's assertion that the individual will disappear by insisting on the personalization of history in the individual (Earle 327). Although Ortega uses Hegel's analysis of the limit to analyse the perceiving and conceiving human eye, the definition of the concept he proposes in his *Meditations on Don Quixote* could not be further removed from the Hegelian notion of the immanence of absolute truth in form. Similarly, Bakhtin's notion of the task – related as it is to Cohen's notion of *Aufgabe*, endless work – is similar to Hegelian teleology in its projected working out of meaning but differs from it in its final form because it proposes multiple meanings rather than one final end (Holquist, *Dialogism* 24).

The similarities and the differences between Hegelian poetics and the novelistics of the thinkers covered in this book become clearer if we examine Hegel's comments on Don Quixote. In fact, Hegel has much more to say about Don Quixote, the character, than *Don Quixote de la Mancha*, the novel:

> Don Quixote is a noble nature in whom chivalry becomes lunacy, because we find his adventurousness inserted into the midst of the stable specific situation of a real world precisely depicted with its external relationships. This provides the comic contradiction between an intelligible self-ordered world and an isolated mind which proposes to create this order and stability solely by himself and by chivalry, whereby it could only be overturned. (*Aesthetics* 1:591)

Hegel concurs with previous commentators on Cervantes' novel concerning the comic contradiction between the world and the isolated mind – except that he labels Don Quixote's nature noble. Early readers of the novel found Don Quixote's self-proclaimed nobility to be risible lunacy. Not only was the would-be knight errant mad, he was also presumptuous, claiming a noble identity that he did not truly possess. Nonetheless, Hegel asserts Don Quixote's nobility by comparing him to Shakespeare's characters: 'In his lunacy Don Quixote is a heart completely sure of itself and its business, or rather this only is his lunacy that he is and remains so sure of himself and his business' (1:591).

For previous readers, Don Quixote's self-satisfaction and impervious stubbornness was yet another symptom of his madness, but for Hegel it transforms the lunatic: 'Without this peaceful lack of reflection in regard to the object and outcome of his actions, he would not be genuinely romantic, and this self-assurance, if we look at the substance of his disposition, is throughout great and gifted, adorned with the finest traits of character' (1:591–2). Let us remember that Hegel defines 'romantic' art as medieval. In contrast to the classical period, it is 'absolute inwardness,' and its form is 'spiritual subjectivity with its grasp of its independence and freedom' (1: 519). As such, it is the character Don Quixote that manifests the spirit of the age: a self-assured inwardness independent and free of constraint. Moreover, the conflict between our self-assured hero and his world is not, for Hegel, a function of modernity. To the contrary, such independence arises in the medieval world of chivalry and feudalism. The justice system of the modern world has taken over the chivalric role of 'righter of wrong' and 'helper of the oppressed,' and thus whoever lives by the chivalric model 'falls into the ridiculousness of which Cervantes gave us such a spectacle in his *Don Quixote*' (1:196).

The problem is that Hegel defines the 'romantic' (medieval) form in the figure of the literary character and his relation to society, and not in the work as a whole. Hegel subsumes the comedic element of *Don Quixote de la Mancha* into romance tales of Don Quixote's adventures. Although the work makes a mockery of chivalry, 'the adventures of Don Quixote are only the thread on which a row of genuinely romantic tales is strung in the most charming way in order to exhibit as preserved in its true worth what the rest of the romance dissipates comically' (1:592). That is to say, Hegel proposes a theory of the 'romantic' (medieval) individual manifest in Don Quixote rather than the modern novel manifest in Cervantes' *Don Quixote de la Mancha*. In short, Hegel offers a theory of poetry, but not of the novel, as revealed in the fact that he includes works of narrative prose such as *Don Quixote* in the category of epic poetry. Thus, the distinction between epic and novel that characterizes and defines the tradition of novelistic theory started by Schlegel does not even exist in Hegel. Moreover, even though Hegel's use of the term 'poetry' extends to include prose, his basic definitions of the substance of poetry make it clear that he primarily understands poetry in opposition to prose. Poetry is older and more authentic than prose; poetry is distinguished from ordinary speech; poetry grasps the totality of the world, whereas the prosaic mind thinks only with the categories of understanding such as cause and effect, ends and means (2:973–6). As we shall see, this opposition between the poetic and the prosaic does not exist in the novelistics of thinkers such as Cohen and Bakhtin, for whom another defining characteristic of the novel is its capacity to straddle the boundaries of the prosaic and the poetic, absorbing and incorporating both discourses. In addition, most of the axiomatic beliefs that Hegel does share with the twentieth-century novelistics dealt with in this book (modernity, formalism, the link between nation, literature, and thought) already occurred in Friedrich Schlegel, and are not even necessarily original to Schlegel.

Hegel was a problematic figure at the turn of the twentieth century, and thus the rejection or appropriation of Hegel was not merely a philosophical turn, but also a political act. Unamuno went through a period of Hegelianism in his youth before rejecting Hegel's firm belief in the absolute spirit. In his case, it was probably a spiritual crisis after the brief life and death of his anencephalic son that hastened his disillusionment with Hegel. For Spaniards such as Unamuno and Ortega, a Hegelian interpretation of world events would propose that the spirit had abandoned Spain and moved on, a proposition unacceptable for these two men who so earnestly and energetically strove to reform their country. Moreover, unless one opted for orthodox Marxism, as Lukács eventually did, the historical circumstances of the twentieth century made it difficult to accept notions of the absolute. Cohen associated Hegelianism with pantheism, and its nationalistic teleology with the growing German identity movements. In fact, Cohen proposed in his notion of the infinitesimal a means to reject both the Hegelian notion of the actualization of the spirit in world history and the empirical denial of the existence of the Idea. Cohen's Kantianism was at least in part a function of his Jewish belief that God as Idea was completely separate from humanity (Kluback, 'The Jewish Response to Hegel' 9). Because Hegel insisted on the manifest nature of the absolute in this world, Cohen considered Hegelianism a form of paganism or pantheism.

On the other hand, our thinkers do at times participate in what Lukács termed 'romantic anti-capitalism.' This critique of modernity stems from an internal contradiction operative in modern capitalism that corresponds to the conflict between Don Quixote and his world described by Hegel: 'Capitalism gives rise to independent individuals who can carry out socioeconomic functions; but when these individuals evolve into subjective individualities, exploring and developing their inner worlds and personal feelings, they enter into contradiction with a universe based on standardization and reification' (Löwy and Sayre 25). Even before Hegel, when Friedrich Schlegel speaks of creating a new mythology rather than returning to an old one, he emphasizes a modern turn to the future at the same time that he critiques the materialism and solipsism of modern capitalism (Löwy and Sayre 29–43). Romantic anticapitalism appears with renewed vigour in German academia around the turn of the twentieth century. In its neo-Kantian and socialist manifestations, it bases its critique of modernity on the instrumentalization of human labour as contrary to the Kantian moral imperative, but it also envelops other strains of thought, including a nostalgia for supposedly lost times of communal unity typical of Hegelianism. Max Weber provides the most basic concepts for a critique of capitalism with his notions of the disenchanted world created by the rationalization and quantification necessary for capitalist production (Löwy and Sayre 29–43). Marxist 'romantic anticapitalism' comes out of this milieu, and is best represented by Lukács. His early Marxist critique of capitalism's 'non-culture' depends on contrasting it with a highly idealized notion of pre-capitalist cultures; moreover, his critique of reification in *History and Class Consciousness* relies heavily on Tönnies, Weber, and Simmel (104–7). This utopian longing for a lost pre-capitalist era largely stems from Hegel's pastoral characterization of ancient Greek culture as founded on agrarianism and crafts, and will persist in later writings about the novel influenced by Lukács, particularly those of Benjamin, Adorno, Goldmann, and Auerbach (Miles 29–33). Indeed, Lukács's eventual turn to Marxism has been interpreted as the only way he could 'save' the Hegelian narrative that he borrowed in the *Theory of the Novel*, by supplying a collective hero and a determined end (Bernstein 262).

Irony, the Limits of Reason, and the Novel

The theories of the novel covered in this book eschew an aesthetics of the absolute not only by turning to Kant, but also by re-engaging with literary modes such as irony, humour, tragicomedy, and dialogue.[42] If these theories deserver the moniker 'romantic,' this is true only insofar as they redeploy Romantic irony. Friedrich Schlegel's definition of Romantic irony was far removed from the debased image Hegel provides of it as nothing more than a superior sneer. To the contrary, Romantic irony turns the ironic eye not only on the content of art, but also on the process of creating art, and the limitations and foibles of the artist herself. Schlegel rejected the possibility of absolute knowledge at the same time that he argued that one must continue on its trail like a bloodhound. 'Irony is a tool that puts us on the trail of the [a]bsolute, helping us to approximate it' because it provides multiple frames for reflection on representation and knowledge (Millán-Zaibert 173). Humour is a cousin of irony, and, for a thinker such as Cohen, ensures a humble, self-deprecating view not only of others but also of the self. When our theorists write of tragedy, they will always couple it with comedy. Unamuno and Ortega y Gasset return to the sixteenth-century prose genre of the *tragicomedia* to ground the novel in both the serious and joking modes. Dialogue as a literary and philosophical form emerges often in these novelistics, not only in Bakhtin's dialogism but also in Unamuno's joking, ironic *nivola*, Cohen's definition of language as action, and Ortega's perception of multiple perspectives.

Although this critical tradition starts out in Friedrich Schlegel as a theory of the *Roman* (novel), it is not particularly 'romantic' if one understands Romanticism as the valorization of sentiment and the irrational over reason, the cult of the genius, and the exaltation of folk and national traditions. Rather than rejecting reason in favour of the irrational, or enshrining it as Reason, the thinkers analysed in this book tend to approach reason as a function of the human mind. Unamuno, Bakhtin, and Ortega go one step further and insist that the reasoning human mind functions according to social circumstances and constraints. In general, interest in Cervantes' authorial intention and creativity is minimized. Unamuno openly wrests Don Quixote away from Cervantes, and Lukács continues to sow the old chestnut that Cervantes was a literary idiot savant. Schlegel and Ortega, the most respectful of poor old Cervantes, view him as a peer, an intellectual made in their own likeness. Cervantes is never lionized as a superhuman genius, and only in the case of Unamuno is heroic stature shifted to Don Quixote. Finally, all of the twentieth-century figures – Cohen, Lukács, Unamuno, Ortega, and Bakhtin – understand the novel as a genre critical of modern society. Far from bolstering the myths of national identity, the novel serves to demythologize tradition and undo social convention through a form of ironic critique. Therefore, it can be considered a Romantic tradition only under the sway of Romantic irony. In addition, the very notion of Romantic irony, implying as it does an alternative to mimetic reflection, leads these thinkers to what is perhaps their most fruitful enterprise: the problematization of the relation between physical reality and the social, mental realm in which we spend so much of our lives. It is this re-evaluation that ultimately leads us to a greater understanding of the power of art and its relation to the plane of the virtual.

2 Arabesques and the Modern Novel: Friedrich Schlegel's Interpretation of *Don Quixote*

One of the most important early theorists of the novel is the German Romantic Friedrich Schlegel, who proposed a radically new understanding of the genre as part of the circle of young writers and literati in Jena at the turn of the nineteenth century. Although he, as well as his brother August Wilhelm, simplified and perhaps even bastardized the thought of his youth in their conservative, popularizing writings and seminars of the 1830s, Friedrich's early musings continue to interest literary theorists to this day. In addition, Hispanists have attributed to Friedrich Schlegel's reading of *Don Quixote* such importance that he would seem to have changed forever (and, usually according to these versions of history, for the worse) the overarching interpretation of Cervantes' novel. The foremost spokesperson for such a stance is Anthony Close, who argues that the Romantic reading typified by thinkers such as Friedrich Schlegel establishes a set of assumptions about *Don Quixote* that continue to influence critical interpretation of the text to this day. This approach is typified by: 'a) the idealisation of the hero and the denial of the novel's satiric purpose; b) the belief that the novel is symbolical and that through this symbolism it expresses ideas about the human spirit's relation to reality or about the nature of Spain's history; c) the interpretation of its symbolism, and more generally, of its whole spirit and style, in a way which reflects the ideology, aesthetics, and sensibility of the modern era' (*The Romantic Approach to Don Quixote* 1).

One must caution, however, that the history of the reception of Friedrich Schlegel's thought approaches that of Cervantes in its complexity and contradiction. Like Cervantes, Schlegel has proven to be one of those writers whose musings seem to adjust themselves to the tenor of the reader's times. The reception of Friedrich Schlegel's thought is as worthy of study as the reception of Cervantes' masterpiece, since the young thinker has proven to be as much a lightning rod for the enthusiasms and manias of his readers as has Don Quixote. In earlier interpretations one encounters a young Schlegel who is either a champion of individualism or a reactionary genius. Ernst Behler argues that both these apparently contradictory readings of early Romanticism stem from Hegel's failure to recognize the systematic nature of Schlegel's thought ('Die Auffassung der Revolution' 212). Others go even further to argue that Hegel's absolute idealism grows out of German Romanticism. Whereas the German Romantics held forth the notion of system as an unattainable but necessary goal, Hegel affirms the possibility of reaching a complete philosophical system (Beiser 66–7). Among the readers more sympathetic to our contemporary leanings we count Walter Benjamin, whose backward-facing angel of history seems a figure for Schlegel's epigram that the historian must be a prophet, and Werner Hamacher, who finds fuel for his deconstructive fire in the young Romantic's musings on the not-said of language. Philippe Lacoue-Labarthe and Jean-Luc Nancy epitomize the vision of Friedrich as our contemporary, remarking that he led the first avant-garde group in history (8) and that '[the] Athenaeum is our birthplace' insofar as we believe politics to be involved with the literary and the theoretical. It would perhaps be wise to approach the young Friedrich's current incarnation as a postmodern or deconstructive thinker with a grain of salt.

Nonetheless, despite the excesses of certain contemporary interpreters, the editing and publication of the young Friedrich's private notebooks in the second half of the twentieth century contributed to a new vision of a more difficult, nuanced, and relevant thinker than the previously imagined young fantasist. As Schlegel himself famously quipped, philosophy without philology is only half a philosophy. By further illuminating his public writing, the private writings of the young Romantic recovered by philology have indeed revealed a philosophical thinker of note who, troubled and stimulated by Kant and Fichte's enquiries into epistemology and idealism, recognized many of the problems that would dominate twentieth-century literary theory. Friedrich and his companions, far from rejecting Enlightenment questioning of all received truths and traditional institutions, linked critical thinking not only to philosophy but also to literature (Beiser 50–3). In his literary notebooks of 1797–8, Friedrich Schlegel contrasts various kinds of novels, ranging from the fantastical and the sentimental to the philosophical and the critical (*LN* #511, 69). Significantly, the absolute novel would include all of these characteristics. Such is the case of *Don Quixote*, insofar as it offers a negative representation of the sentimental and the fantastic, and positively develops philosophical and critical characteristics (*LN* #690, 85–6). Schlegel's influence on literary theory ultimately stems from his assertion that literature can perform the critical and philosophical enquiry normally ascribed to non-fictional forms of discourse. Andrew Bowie remarks that 'Schlegel's conception of "transcendental literature" … opens up the space for some of the most significant theories of literature in modernity, from Lukács' *Theory of the Novel*, to Bakhtin's theory of polyphony and Adorno's stringent demands on the truth-content of modern literature and art' (82). Friedrich Schlegel and the other young poets and thinkers of his circle demonstrate a telling ambivalence toward modernity that will be repeated in subsequent literary theories. Modernity is at once desirable, linked to individual freedom, progress, and cultural critique, and yet to be lamented as it breaks the bonds of community.

As indicated by the very word *Roman*, which literally means the novel and reverberates in the term Schlegel uses to define modernity, *das Romantische*, the novel is inextricably linked to modernity. It is, for reasons both obvious and subtle, the modern genre. In point of fact, the novel is *a* modern genre, given that there were very few long works of fictional prose in the ancient times, with the obvious exception being the Byzantine novel, a form generally considered inferior to the epic, lyric, and dramatic verse of the Greek and Roman periods. That it would be *the* modern genre is not so self-apparent, and yet this is the central definition of the novel that all readers of Schlegel have appropriated from his fragmentary writings. The fundamental questions of this analysis follow: what is modernity, and why does the novel embody it? Recent commentators on the young Friedrich have correctly insisted on the need to investigate the context of his thought, overcoming both the strong hermeneutical temptation to delight in the play of his thought to the exclusion of its historical and biographical setting, and the previously dominant tendency to read the early work through the distorting lens of his later conservative Catholicism and pro-Hapsburg politics. When the young man is viewed within his time and place, it becomes apparent that modernity is, for him, a crisis, both promising and troubling in its revolutionary tendency.

Jena Circa 1800

As is the case with Lukács and Ortega y Gasset, Schlegel writes his theory of the novel as a young man involved in the passions of youth: love affairs, intense intellectual friendships and enmities, ambitious plans to win fame or infamy, and politics. Friedrich arrived at Jena at a time when the university was attempting to recover from a series of disruptive and even violent student riots in the early 1790s. Goethe was the university's patron, and had contact with the Schlegel group in October 1799. Because the university paid poorly, it hired young academics that would use it as a stepping stone to move onto other more prestigious universities; nonetheless, this granted it a greater academic freedom than found at more staid institutions. Thus, Schiller, Fichte, and Hegel all passed through Jena, where they excited followings among the students; moreover, Fichte and Schiller discoursed in public lectures upon the necessity of reforming the university to make it an engine for producing philosophical scholarship that would reform society. Even Friedrich briefly lectured there from October 1800 to March 1801, although without much success among the students (Eichner, *Friedrich Schlegel* 92). Nonetheless, there emerged what Theodore Ziolkowski has called the 'Jena mode of discourse,' critical writing based on the academic forms of lectures, seminars, and Socratic dialogues in which various and at times conflicting ideas would be aired and evaluated. Friedrich was one of the practitioners of this form of discourse, as seen in his *Dialogue on Poetry* so central to the history of the theory of the novel (252–66). This work contains several discourses given by the literary characters that are members of this group of friends on topics such as the novel and mythology. Indeed, Schlegel described the university as 'something quite arabesque ... a symphony of professors' (261). As we shall see, the arabesque is also a metaphor for the modern novel.

In the heady days of Jena, Friedrich and the other members of his circle, including his brother August Wilhelm, Ludwig Tieck, and Novalis, were steeped in Cervantes' *Don Quixote* from 1797 to 1800, precisely when Friedrich was producing his most innovative musings upon the novel as a genre. As he wrote to his brother in 1797, he wished to translate the novel, noting its central importance to his life with great enthusiasm. 'I would not deviate from the orbit of my studies if I translated *Don Quixote*. At some point, the novel will certainly be a subject for me of as great importance as the ancients, among whom I now again live and breathe.'[1] The group as a whole proposed to stage parts of the novel. Friedrich took for himself the name Cardenio, a character from the novel that went mad from love and served as a counterpart to Don Quixote, who went mad from reading (Bertrand 83). Dorothea Veit, the daughter of Moses Mendelssohn, wife of Simon Veit, and lover and future spouse of Friedrich, even reported that Cervantes appeared to her in a dream.

Moreover, Schlegel and his fellow Romantics read *Don Quixote* in an age marked by major social and institutional changes that would effect their reading of the novel. Not least among these was a new approach to insanity. From approximately 1790 to 1820, debates raged throughout Germany and Europe as to the nature and treatment of mental illness. Theodore Ziolkowski lists the burning questions:

> Is madness caused by humors or by such social factors as the Revolution? Should its classification be etiological or symptomatic? Is it essentially psychic or somatic? Should it be treated 'morally' or medically? Who is the appropriate person to care for the insane: physician, layperson, theologian, professional governor, or mad-doctor? There was agreement on virtually nothing except the necessity for reform. (146)

Even Kant wrote on mental illness, distinguishing between *Wahnsinn* (dementia), in which the individual fills the normal mental faculties with delusions, and *Wahnwitz* (insanity), in which one fails to judge properly (151). Clearly, Don Quixote would conform to the former category of madness. It was perhaps then no accident that the Romantics were so interested in two great madmen of previous literature: Don Quixote and Hamlet (154). To sum up, insanity offered itself as a potential source of insight and poetic creativity alternative to the dry reason of the Enlightenment.

Revolutions and the Romantic

In terms of the nineteenth- and twentieth-century theories of the novel, Friedrich Schlegel's most important contribution is his identification of the novel as the genre typical of modernity. There is no doubt that his concept of the Romantic alludes to what was perceived as the historical uniqueness and promise of his time. Indeed, it was the notion of the historical difference, that is to say the distinction between contemporary and ancient times, which established the grounds for early Romantic aesthetics (Behrens 99). According to Hans Eichner, Schlegel's concept of the Romantic served for him 'both as a historical term and a normative term, referring simultaneously to a segment of the past and setting up a goal for the future' ('The Genesis of German Romanticism' 229). Schlegel's historical slice of modernity starts with the Italian Renaissance, and encompasses his own time and those epochs still to come. His use of the term 'Romantic' to describe this era harks to several associations: the genre of the early modern romance (including chivalric literature), the literature of the romance languages, and the genre of the novel, in German *der Roman*. The chivalric romances, like the literatures from which they sprang, largely Italian and Spanish, exemplify for Schlegel eroticism and the free play of fantasy. Subsequently, such freedom of form and thought should characterize the Romantic, that is to say post-classical and post-medieval literature.[2] As we shall see, the play of fantasy for Schlegel is not merely a belle-lettristic term; rather, it is the foundation for his form of idealism, his understanding of the relationship of art to the world, and his definition of the novel.

The power of fantasy underlies Schlegel's apparently absurd claim that Goethe's *Wilhelm Meister* is of equal historical importance to the French Revolution: 'The French Revolution, Fichte's *Theory of Knowledge*, and Goethe's *Wilhelm Meister* are the three greatest tendencies of the age' (Athenaeum Fragment 216, *DP* 143). It is difficult now to imagine the shockwaves sent by the French Revolution through Europe; moreover, there was the expectation, on the part of many Germans as well as even Madame de Stael, that revolution would next erupt in the Nordic countries (Behler, 'Die Auffassung der Revolution' 193). For Schlegel, this political event not only signified the possibility of a wilful and arbitrary break from the past, but also entailed the isolation of the individual from contemporary state and society. Moreover, it was precisely this alienation that distinguished the modern from the classical world. Schlegel and his contemporaries did not understand revolution so much as a political event, but rather as a wilful break with history that would initiate a new era (Behrens 19; Mennemeier 28). Schlegel identifies this will for revolution with modernity when he writes that '[t]he revolutionary desire to realize God's kingdom on earth is the elastic point of progressive development and the beginning of modern history. Whatever is without relationship to God's kingdom, is for it only accidental' (Athenaeum Fragment 222, *DP* 144). This aphorism discloses two profound comments on the nature of revolution, both of which are clearly linked to the nature of the modern world for Schlegel: (1) the kingdom of God, that is to say ordained order, is found to be lacking in the modern world, hence the necessity that humankind institute it; and (2) everything that is not conceived to be integral to this order is of lesser importance and status, hence its disposability.

Schlegel continues his thoughts on the French Revolution by stating that, in addition to being a great historical event and an archetype of revolution, it can also be considered within the contexts of the French nation and modernity itself. When viewed as a French phenomenon, it is the focal point and high point of French character, where all paradoxes are condensed together (Athenaeum Fragment 424, *DP* 148). Lest we attribute this comment to German chauvinism, we must then move to Schlegel's musings upon the French, who dominate in this time since they are a 'chemical' nation (Athenaeum Fragment 426). His time (modernity) is likewise a chemical time. Schlegel attributes this chemical nature not only to modern revolution, but also to business, society, and the arts: 'Revolutions are universally not organic but rather chemical movements. Commerce on a large scale is the chemistry of economy on the large scale; it is indeed an alchemy of sorts. The chemical nature of the novel, of criticism, of humour, of social life, of the newest rhetoric, and of the prevailing history is self-evident.'[3] The reference to alchemy in this quote illuminates Schlegel's understanding of chemistry, since he does not necessarily associate the term with our concept of scientific method (Allemann 61–3). Whereas chemistry as we understand it depends on the repeatability of results within the context of a controlled experiment, Schlegel's chemistry is rather the capacity for improvisation, leaps of imagination, and inventive associations typical of *Witz*, or humour. In fact, the reasoned method and predictability of chemistry as science would be merely mechanical in Schlegel's eyes, for as he wrote elsewhere, reason is mechanical, humour is chemical, and genius is organic (Athenaeum Fragment 365, *KA* 2:232).

Instead, Schlegel's concept of *Witz* owes much to the Baroque, for the young Romantic understands wit as the binding together of distinct images into one unity, a concept quite close to Gracián's notion of *ingenio*.[4] Revolution could not take place within the realm of natural law, for the laws of nature are immutable and do not allow for difference. Hence follows Schlegel's observation that genius was somehow more natural in ancient times: 'The individual great ones remain less isolated among the Greeks and the Romans. They have fewer geniuses, but more originality. All antiquity is original. The entire ancient era is one genius, the only one that can be called, without exaggerating, absolutely great, unique, and unattainable' (Athenaeum Fragment 248).[5] Accordingly, ancient culture forms a whole, expressing one genius or spirit. This unique integrity grants classical culture its status of unattainable grandeur. The young Friedrich Schlegel is, of course, not alone in this reverence for antique art as the organic expression of a unified culture, but rather follows in his analysis both J.J. Winckelmann and Friedrich Schiller.[6]

Schlegel most clearly enunciates the power of the unified classical culture with respect to its literary output in the *Dialogue on Poetry*, in which three literary characters, Andrea, Ludoviko, and Antonio, propound the author's concept of the relation between classical and Romantic literature. This work follows the format of a university seminar rather than a true dialogue, and presents us with four papers that mirror in their order Friedrich's own intellectual development (Theodore Ziolkowski 266).[7] Classical literature is the most original because it is the origin of European culture. Thus, Andrea, in his discourse on the 'Epochs of Literature' ('Epochen der Dichtkunst'), states unequivocally that Hellenic poetry, theatre, and epic are poetry itself. Everything that follows is mere residue (*Überbleibsel*), echo (*Nachhall*), and even resentment of these works of Olympic stature (*KA* 2:293). In the 'Talk on Mythology' ('Rede über die Mythologie'), the character Ludoviko laments the lack of mythology in the modern world. As Ludoviko explains it, mythology represents a shared middle ground, a cultural repertoire, and even a system of values common to all educated persons, such that the ancients were able to combine it with poetry, the latter understood as style or technique: 'For mythology and poetry are one and inseparable. All poems of antiquity join one to the other, till from ever-increasing masses and members the whole is formed. Everything interpenetrates everything else, and everywhere there is one and the same spirit, only expressed differently' (*DP* 82). The same spirit originates in all of antique writing, just as it originates in antique culture. Revolution, as abrupt, wilful change proceeding from difference, would have no place in classical art just as it would have no place in classical politics, for the same spirit, self-identical and thus incapable of internal fracture, emanated in all.

In both the discourses on the history of the genres and on mythology set forth in the *Dialogue on Poetry*, a profound sentiment of belatedness, if not loss, tinges the generally optimistic tone of the analyses. For Andrea, all literature subsequent to the Greeks is a mere leftover, and so it is not surprising that, in the discussion following his lecture, Lothario recommends that the ancients serve as a model (*Urbild*) for poets. Historical time for the Romantics comprises both presentiment and remembrance, and thus the Golden Age is made ever present in poetry

(Behrens 137–8). Antiquity serves Schlegel as a sort of negative model, related through difference rather than similarity to the modern period and to Romantic art; it follows that the absence of the classical is one of the defining characteristics of modernity, and that the artist would seek to make this absence present (82–3).[8] Indeed, the modern artist competes with the antique model, which in and of itself does *not* constitute a perfect origin (Ernst Behler, *Irony and the Discourse of Modernity* 63–6). Lothario, in his discourse on mythology, not only laments the lack of a mythology in his time, but also calls for a new mythology based on idealism. Returning to the connection between the French Revolution and Fichte's idealist philosophy, which insisted on the power of the individual to create reality, Schlegel uses Lothario to propose idealism as the revolutionary new mythology. Lothario states that idealism is not only the maxim of this revolution, but of all revolutions, since revolution itself is the outbreak of individual power and freedom. Curiously, and perhaps paradoxically, this revolution would not institute a new order, but rather revive the classical one and proclaim the future's debt to it: 'Remote antiquity will become alive again, and the remotest future of culture will announce itself in auguries' (*DP* 83). Revolution for Schlegel would be quite similar to revolution for Don Quixote: the present enactment through human endeavour of the lost past. The present, in this line of thought, becomes the point of contact in which the past and the future meet.

Having established Schlegel's understanding of the nature of revolution with respect to history as an active and wilful engagement with the past for the sake of the future, we can now move to his concept of the novel as the literary genre typical of his present, what he calls the Romantic era and what we understand as modernity. When the young thinker claims for Goethe's novel, *Wilhelm Meister*, the same importance as the French Revolution, he is clearly granting art the power to transform reality equal to that wielded by politics. Moreover, Schlegel grants to Cervantes' *Don Quixote* a status he never cedes to any of Goethe's works: that of a *romantische Roman* (Beiser 116). *Don Quixote*, therefore, achieves what *Wilhelm Meister* only promises. What, precisely, is the revolutionary power of the novel? According to Schanze, it is the genre's capacity to express a multitude of new and different experiences (64). Friedrich Schlegel repeatedly insists upon the novel's multivalent nature manifest in its melding of genres, tales, and themes. Typical of this view is Antonio's assertion in his 'Letter about the Novel' ('Brief über den Roman') from *Dialogue on Poetry*, that he cannot imagine a novel as other than a mixture of narration, song, and other forms. Precisely at this moment he refers to Cervantes, who combined genres as well as different stories in *Don Quixote*, noting that 'Cervantes never composed otherwise ...'[9] Schlegel's conception of the novel as a mixed genre by definition reveals the young Romantic's view of modernity, since the novel is, as indicated by its very German name, *der Roman*, the Romantic genre. Antonio states, excusing himself for having coined a tautology, that '[a] novel is a romantic [*romantisches*] book' (*DP* 101). In other words, the novel is the genre representative of the Romantic era.

Modernity and the Romantic

From Schlegel's concept of the novel (*Roman*), it is possible to glean the young man's concept of modernity. As noted above, antiquity is marked for Schlegel by a unity of spirit that gives rise to a unified literature. Modernity, in contrast, suffers from a lack of mythology, that is to say a lack of unified spirit. It follows that the novel as a modern genre would be similarly fragmented. Nonetheless, Schlegel wishes to propose a genre that will challenge the ancients, and thus the novel must somehow overcome this fragmentation. Significantly, Schlegel, in his 'Letter about the Novel,' distinguishes between a modern novel and a Romantic one, by disparaging as modern *Emilia Galotti* and praising as Romantic Shakespeare. The Romantic is as different from the modern as paintings by Raphael and Correggio are from eighteenth-century prints. The centre of the Romantic can be found, according to Schlegel, in the early modern period, the Renaissance:

> This is where I look for and find the Romantic – in the older moderns, in Shakespeare, Cervantes, in Italian poetry, in that age of knights, love, and fairytales in which the thing itself and the word for it originated. This, up to now, is the only thing which can be considered as a worthy contrast to the classical productions of antiquity; only these eternally fresh flowers of the imagination are worthy of adorning the images of the ancient gods. Certainly all that is best in modern poetry tends toward antiquity in spirit and even in kind, as if there were to be a return to it. Just as our literature began with the novel, so the Greek began with the epic and dissolved in it. (*DP* 101)

Schlegel espouses a particularly humanist aesthetics by stating that the modern must return to the ancient, and then somehow transform it into the contemporary. The genres to which he refers as truly Romantic ones are those of the early modern romance, the Renaissance literature of the romance languages, and the genre of the novel, or in German *der Roman*. Both the romances and the literature from which they sprang, largely Italian and Spanish, exemplify for Schlegel eroticism and the free play of fantasy. Subsequently, such freedom of form and mind should characterize Romantic, that is to say modern, literature.

As Antonio continues to develop his line of thought in 'Letter about the Novel,' the greatest distinction between the modern and ancient, at least in literary terms, is that the Romantic is not linked specifically to the genre of the novel; indeed, for Schlegel such a concept is odious. It follows that the modern novel must somehow embrace all genres, and perhaps overcome the modern condition of fragmentation. By comparing what Schlegel considers Romantic poetry to the Greek epic, he also establishes the relation of the novel to modernity. Just as the epic is the mirror of ancient time, so is the novel the mirror of modern time, as Schlegel states in the famous Athenaeum Fragment 116: 'Romantic poetry alone can, like the epic, become a mirror of the entire surrounding world, a picture of its age' (*DP* 140). Lest the reference to the freedom of fantasy lead us to doubt the mimetic relation of Romantic poetry to its time and place, this quote reminds us that Schlegel does not question, but rather insists upon, the mimetic relation of literature to the world from which it springs. The novel, understood in its larger conception as Romantic poetry, must reflect upon its surroundings. This reflection is the work of fantasy; more precisely, it is the work of the Romantic poet granted according to the author's unique position between both the text and the world it represents. As Athenaeum Fragment 116 continues: 'And yet, it too can soar, free from all real and ideal interests, on the wings of poetic reflection, midway between the work and the artist. It can even exponentiate this reflection and multiply it as in an endless series of mirrors. It is capable of the highest and the most universal education; not only by creating from within, but also from without, since it organizes in similar fashion all parts of what is destined to become a whole; thus, a view is opened to an endlessly developing classicism' (*DP* 140–1).[10]

Romantic poetry provides a unique viewpoint upon the world and the text, allowing the writer to hover unencumbered by interest, free to see an endless row of reflections.[11] By shattering the mirror image into countless mirror images, Schlegel adapts the notion of mimesis to his notion of modernity. If the reality of modernity is multiple and fractured, then only an infinite row of images would sufficiently reflect it. From this new metaphor for mimesis follows Schlegel's conception of both the hovering artist and the text unified in its multiplicity. The individual, when viewing one mirror directly, can see only one image of the reflected reality; when hovering over multiple images, she can see, albeit obliquely, many images. Hence Schlegel's following assertion that Romantic poetry is to art what wit (*Witz*) is to poetry: the capability to make synthetic, creative associations among seemingly disparate and disconnected objects. Likewise, Romantic poetry, as a form of wit, gathers these distinct units into a unity, and thus approaches the unity of the work of art in the classical world. Thus, the novel as a form of Romantic poetry must be multifaceted in its embrace of both generic and thematic difference.

Once Schlegel fractures the single mirror of mimesis into multiple ones, he also introduces time as a necessary component of the image. The hovering subject can only begin to view the infinite row of mirrors through time understood as open and infinite. Consequently, Schlegel characterizes the Romantic as the genre of becoming (*werden*), never finished or completed (*vollendet*): 'Other types of poetry are completed and can now be entirely analyzed. The Romantic type of poetry is still becoming; indeed, its peculiar essence is that it is always becoming and that it can never be completed' (*DP* 141). Hence we can also understand Schlegel's description of Romantic literature as progressive, not in the sense that it will reach a teleologically determined end, but rather that it will continue progressing and becoming. Ernst Behler, noting the frequency with which Friedrich used the adverbs 'not yet' and 'as long as,' explains the link between the notion of progressive literature and modernity: 'the words "as long as" and "not yet" do not designate a transitoriness to be overcome by accomplished knowledge or a temporary deficiency, but the actual state of our knowledge, its permanent form' (*Irony and the Discourse of Modernity* 61). Modernity itself takes the form of endless movement toward a never-reached perfection. Implicit in this notion of progression must be a certain optimistic hope, if not belief, that the endlessly increasing progression of mirrors will attain a more all-embracing reflection of the fragmented world.

The Copernican Revolution in Aesthetics: Schlegel and Kant

Yet to be problematized in this image of the modern form of mimesis is the condition of the subject who views reality reflected in the mirrors. In Athenaeum Fragment 116 Schlegel seems to personify this reflective subject as Romantic poetry, and thus it is that Walter Benjamin states that this image is free of self-consciousness since art not only provides the reflecting mirror, but also frees the reflecting self from self-consciousness (I-1, 139). Nonetheless, we can only appreciate Benjamin's insight into Schlegel's thought if we understand Schlegel's position vis-à-vis Fichte and Kant. The freeing of the self from self-consciousness should not be read as an erasure of the self in the act of reflection on art, especially given the primary importance Schlegel assigns to Fichte's thought, which he designates as one of the three great tendencies of the era alongside Goethe's novel *Wilhelm Meister* and the French Revolution. Schlegel clearly owes to Fichte his concept of reflection, namely, the concept of the second power of thought: the thought of thought (Benjamin I-1, 22). The young Romantic also owes a debt, however, to Kant's concept of transcendent thought as thought about thought itself, and thus we can explain Schlegel's frequent description of this sort of self-reflexive thought and literature as transcendental (Huge 103). Indeed, the intellectual revolution preceding Fichte is Kant's turn away from philosophical investigation of the material world toward investigation of the human mind, referred to as a Copernican revolution.

It would seem strange that the novel as a genre, and Cervantes' *Don Quixote* in general, when understood to be representative of societal schisms and personal incompletion and alienation, could be deemed aesthetically pleasing. It is salutary to remember that some neoclassical readers found Cervantes' masterpiece to be indecorous in subject and flawed in composition, not to mention unseemly in its prose. These readers, including the Frenchman René Lesage and some Spanish followers, based their criticism of the work on its perceived incompletion, lack of proportion, and lack of internal consistency or harmony. Nor do Schlegel and the other theorists of the modern novel examined in this book deny the validity of these aesthetic judgments; to the contrary, they turn these negative values into positive ones. The groundwork for revalorization of aesthetic imperfection – understood here most completely through reference to its Latin etymology as incompletion – lies in Kant's *Critique of Judgement*. Indeed, in aesthetics as in epistemology, one could argue that Kant signals another Copernican revolution, in which the experience of the subject, rather than the perfection of the object, takes pride of place in aesthetics. By considering the faculty of taste to be constitutive of the aesthetic experience, the philosopher centres aesthetic enquiry upon the spectator or reader rather than the art object itself. In order to prevent subjective taste from taking over completely his notion of beauty, Kant distinguishes between the beautiful, which is universally recognized and thus not a matter of subjective taste, and the pleasant and the good. To the contrary, a satisfactory experience of the good or the pleasant depends on the viewer's interests and desires, and thus becomes an end or a purpose to something else. More precisely, the pleasant gratifies; that is to say, drinking a fine glass of champagne either gives physical pleasure by producing a nice buzz or social pleasure by demonstrating the drinker's good taste. The good must conform to an idea, and therefore, is also linked to purpose; for example, I find the apple I have eaten to be good, not only because of the taste in my mouth, but also because I believe it to be healthy. The beautiful, by contrast, which is experienced by true taste, i.e., disinterested satisfaction, 'is the form of the *purposiveness* of an object, so far as this is perceived in it *without any representation of a purpose*' (*Critique of Judgement* 73). Despite the seeming obscurity and internal contradiction of this passage, Kant has previously made his meaning quite clear. The intentionality of the art object, art having been defined as that which has no utilitarian purpose or merely gratifies sensual desire or social interest, is to make visible or manifest moral ideals, such as 'goodness of heart, purity, strength, peace, etc.' (72).

So far Kant's representation of art as the manifestation of the ideals of the good seems a mere reiteration of old Platonic themes. Nonetheless, he has replaced the ancient or classical focus upon describing the object of beauty with the modern analysis of the subject's experience. In other words, Kant places the burden of correctly representing beauty not only on the artist, but also on the spectator, who must actively recognize and recreate the object in the mind's eye: 'The visible expression of moral ideas that rule men inwardly can indeed only be gotten from experience; but to make its connection with all which our reason unites with the morally good in the idea of the highest purposiveness – goodness of heart, purity, strength, peace, etc. – visible as it were in bodily manifestation (as the effect of that which is internal) requires a union of pure ideas of reason with great imaginative power even in him who wishes to judge of it, still more in him who wishes to present it' (72).

The decisiveness of this second Copernican revolution for the theory of the novel will become evident throughout this book, as Kant's thought upon judgment forms a constant backdrop for later thinkers. Rejecting the capacity of the human mind to know directly the outside world except through the very structures or faculties of the mind, Kant's opus establishes the philosophical necessity of thought about thought. The faculty of judgment takes on particular significance, therefore, because it must sift through the sense data to make sense of it. Commenting upon the centrality of Kant to the Romantic questioning of classical epistemology, Bowie notes in such a precise manner that it bears repeating: 'Importantly, Kant stresses the fact that reflective judgement need not arrive at any final determinations and can be allowed to function for its own sake, by making links and analogies between differing aspects of the empirical world. There is therefore the possibility of an interplay between the categorisation performed by the understanding and the image-producing capacity of the imagination, in which neither need become dominant. This interplay generates aesthetic pleasure' (59). Given that judgment is also the faculty of aesthetic experience, the German Romantics subsequently bestow upon poetry (understood as all creative production) a centrality of place in philosophical musing.

Indeed, one could argue, as does Bowie, that Schlegel was led to poetry as the site to reflect upon truth precisely because of the implications of Kant's thought concerning the impossibility of knowing the outside world (206–7). Benjamin's reading of Schlegel then follows: the 'I' perforce takes the place of the object of reflection, as thought about thought; this leads to an inner doubling of the 'I' as both subject and object; therefore, 'reflection is not mere observation, but rather an absolute, systematic form of thought, a conceiving.'[12] Thus, art and literature can assume a privileged position in thought as a space where the mind reflects upon itself in order to put an end to what Bowie terms the 'regress of reflections' (209), and that, for Schlegel, actually constitutes literature viewed as the product of the 'I' thinking on and about itself (83).

The positive approach that both Benjamin and Bowie take toward reflection as the basis of creativity and even thought for Schlegel glosses over a problem implicit within in the image of the 'I' thinking the 'I': that is to say, the identity – and even self-identity – of the self. In the 'Talk on Mythology,' Ludoviko calls idealism the spirit of revolution in this age, and claims that it must overtake all forms of learning and art. Here Schlegel defines idealism as a stepping out of oneself and a return to oneself in a sort of pre-Hegelian dialectic: 'Just as it is the nature of spirit to determine itself and in perennial alternation to expand and return to itself, and as every thought is nothing but the result of such an activity; so is the same process generally discernible in every form of idealism, which itself is but a recognition of this very law. The new life, intensified by this recognition, manifests its secret energy in the most splendid manner through the infinite abundance of new ideas, general comprehensibility, and lively efficacy' (*DP* 83). The self is involved in an endless leaving of itself to encounter the other and a returning to itself renewed, even doubled as indicated by the word *verdoppelte*. Just as the mimetic mirrors multiply and reduplicate endlessly, so the self renews itself in an expansive movement of leaving its own bounds and returning to them. Indeed, the concept of transcendence describes the superposition of this image of the doubled self to the row of mirrors; as Schlegel states in Athenaeum Fragment 116, the self hovers over the mirrors. If the mirrors are infinitely dividing and receding, then the self, too, must constantly change position by leaving and re-entering itself in order not to lose sight of reality.

Nor is there only one self, for Schlegel's description of this inward and outward movement in 'Talk on Mythology' is immediately followed by this qualification: 'Naturally this phenomenon assumes a different form in each individual; this is why success must often fall short of expectation' (*DP* 83). A dark note enters the optimistic description of reflective thought in this almost off-the-cuff statement; since there are many individuals, the phenomenon will take many forms, hence perfect success is unattainable. Nostalgia for unity, as seen earlier in the discussion of his concept of antiquity, shades Schlegel's notion of idealism. Peter Szondi's observation that modernity is for Schlegel a time of discontinuity and disintegration, isolating the individual from those around him and thus necessitating the ironic stance of Romanticism, calls attention to the anxiety underlying the young Romantic's at times almost cavalier assertions concerning the power of literature and reflective thought (67–8). The lack of a modern mythology represents both a freedom and a burden for Schlegel and his contemporaries. In 'Talk on Mythology,' two opposing pictures of the work of the ancient and the modern poet are offered: the ancient, living in a unified world, is as the inhabitant of Arcadia who merely plucks the acorns from the trees, whereas the modern must mine to new depths:

For it will come to us by an entirely opposite way from that of previous ages, which was everywhere the first flower of youthful imagination, directly joining and imitating what was most immediate and vital in the sensuous world. The new mythology, in contrast, must be forged from the deepest depths of the spirit; it must be the most artful of all works of art, for it must encompass all the others; a new bed and vessel for the ancient,

eternal fountainhead of poetry, and even the infinite poem concealing the
seeds of all other poems. (*DP* 81–2)

Not only must the Romantic, that is to say modern, poet dig deep for
poetry, she must also somehow embrace all the other arts in her poetry.
The image of transcendental unity offered in Athenaeum Fragment 116
in which the poet can somehow hover above difference and embrace it
in her all-encompassing vision now cedes to that of the digging, toiling
miner, whose creation must contain the seeds of other, different creations. The requirement to enfold the seeds of others in the poem attributes to the work of art a certain pregnant quality, as it carries
difference within itself. Subsequently, if one insists on the mimetic quality of art, as Schlegel does in *Dialogue on Poetry*, then the reality that art
seeks to embrace and embody is of itself multiple. The ancients had immediate, sensual access to reality because it was, in their time, one; the
Romantic must dig to deeper subsoil where the seeds of difference can
be found mixed together. Modernity, not only in its surface but even in
its very roots, is composed of difference and multiplicity.

The multiplicity of modernity, in which art in itself is multiple and in
which various individuals give form to various works of art, implies also
the lack of a rule. Even in his early writings on Greek and Roman art,
Schlegel rejects a neoclassical disdain for freedom and links it, rather, to
both reason and fantasy understood as spontaneity (Mennemeier 38–9).
In the image of the hovering self of Athenaeum Fragment 116, he describes
Romantic poetry as free from all real and ideal interests. This freedom
entails, then, flight that transcends the bounds of convention and allows
precisely for this new form of all-encompassing art. Freedom is not only
typical of Romantic poetry, but also of Socratic irony, a genre that Schlegel
associates with wit *(Witz)*: 'It [Socratic irony] is the freest of all liberties, for
it enables us to rise above our own self; and still the most legitimate, for it
is absolutely necessary' (Lyceum Fragment 108, *DP* 131). The image of the
transcending self of Romantic poetry doubles with that of the free self of
Socratic irony and wit in a way that reveals the same underlying thought:
freedom is, perhaps paradoxically, the transcendence of one's own self. In
Lyceum Fragment 16, Schlegel specifies that genius is 'not a matter of
arbitrariness, but rather of freedom, just as wit, love, and faith, which once
shall become arts and discipline' (*DP* 122). It is noteworthy that Schlegel
uncouples freedom from the concept of *Willkühr*, or mere arbitrary
wilfulness, only to couple it with art and discipline. Indeed, in this very

fragment he associates genius and freedom with Kant's idea of a categorical imperative, thus loading the terms with overtones of moral obligation. Subsequently, in Athenaeum Fragment 168 Schlegel states that the philosophy of the poet 'is the creative; it emanates from freedom and towards belief, and then shows how the human spirit stamps its precept on everything, and reveals how the world is its work of art.'[13] The freedom from which poetry springs empowers humanity to imprint its thought on the world, and even to make the world its work of art. The potential of freedom is tremendous, then, as the human being grasps the power to remake the world. The genius claims this freedom without fear, overcoming doubt and embracing the capacity to depict the world (Athenaeum Fragment 283). In fact, the freedom of genius offers Schlegel a means to overcome the sense of historical solitude that plagues so many modern thinkers, that is to say, their nostalgia for the lost classical era. As the young Romantic so poetically describes this freedom, one should not call upon antiquity as an authority, for spirits do not let themselves be grasped; rather, the shortest and briefest way to approach them is through the belief in the happiness of solitary production (*KA* 2:152).

Don Quixote as *the* Romantic Novel

Having established that Schlegel's vision of modernity is characterized by division and difference coupled with a notion of the modern individual enabled by freedom to recast the world, we can now explain why the young Romantic conceives of the novel as the Romantic art form *par excellence*. The novel in its multiplicity, its capacity to embrace and subsume all other genres, is the form that best captures the multiplicity of modernity. Likewise, it is the form that grants the Romantic poet the most freedom to remake this multiplicity. We are also now prepared to appreciate how Cervantes' novel *Don Quixote* fits into Friedrich's historical conception of the novel. According to Eichner, the novel as a genre represents for Schlegel the 'dominant form both of the earliest and the most recent postclassical poetry' ('Friedrich Schlegel's Theory of Romantic Poetry' 1021). From his personal notebooks we can glean the young man's musings upon literary history, remembering that Schlegel himself considered poetry in its highest power to be history (Note IX: 340; *KA* 16:282). His literary notebooks from 1799 to 1800 first present a model of Romantic literature based upon a triangular conception of the three classical genres of epic, lyric, and dramatic poetry. In note IX: 209 he links unity to the epic and infinite multiplicity to drama, noting that lyric lies somewhere in the middle, a suggestion that makes sense if one views the epic as the unified vision of a unified culture, drama as the multiple stories of multiple individuals, and lyric as the multiple story of one individual (*KA* 16:271). In note IX: 215 the young Schlegel clarifies further this manner of relating and distinguishing the three genres: 'The form of lyric is original, of drama individual, of epic universal.– In epic all that is pathetic must be joined with ethics. The *motivated* springs from the permeation of ethics and pathos and hangs together with individuality.– Epic = objective poetry.– Lyric = subjective/Drama = objective/subjective –.'[14] There is a transition implicit in this triangulation of the three genres from the objective nature of the epic through the subjective nature of lyric to the mixture of the objective and subjective in drama. The objective nature of epic poetry is related to its universality, that is to say, the wedding of the individual hero's experience of joy and suffering (pathos) to the communal values of his society (ethos). In Schlegel's literary history, this movement away from epic objectivity toward a mixture of objectivity and subjectivity is the movement from the classical to the Romantic (Lovejoy 219). It is also the movement toward the Romantic genre, *der Roman*, that is to say, the novel.

In a diamond-shaped diagram in his literary notebooks (Note IX: 683), the young Romantic mused on the cycle of the earliest Romantic poetry in such a way that it reveals not only the historical importance of each figure, but also the progression, or rather becoming, of the novel.

Petr[arch]

0/1

<Shak[e]sp[eare]   Dante>

–   +

Cerv[antes]

1/0   (*KA* 16:311)

This diamond, when compared to other notes of the same period, clearly represents the historical development of what Schlegel considers Romantic literature in the early modern era, beginning with Petrarch and Dante and culminating in Shakespeare and Cervantes. Keeping in mind Schlegel's assertion that Romantic poetry is that of becoming, we can glimpse several evolutionary processes captured in this diagram: the positivity of Dante represented by the plus sign refers to the transcendental and epic quality of the *Divine Comedy*, whereas the subjectivity of

Petrarch represented by the sign for zero refers to the lyrical and sentimental quality of his poetry. This observation coincides with Schlegel's
own comment that epic and lyric dominate the first epoch of Romanticism.
The mimetic and dramatic qualities of Shakespeare's theatre distinguish
the Englishman as a more progressive figure, typical of the second epoch
in which drama and the arabesque dominate.[15] In this way, this representation of Schlegel's Romantic forebears subsumes the earlier triangular
progression he traced between the genres of the epic, lyric, and drama, in
which the movement from epic to drama is also the movement from the
one epic to the many dramas through lyric. The reference to Petrarch
discloses how the lyric shatters the epic: by expressing the subjective experience of the individual unmediated by communal ethos, lyric poetry
negates the integral relationship of the epic hero's personal trials and
experiences to the social values and structure of his society. One protagonist's narrative no longer stands for an entire culture.[16] Consequently,
the many stories of theatre take centre stage, representing the variety of
human experiences (thus subjective) in a medium not focused by the
character's own viewpoint (thus objective).

   This multiplicity of experience, achieved to such great effect by
Shakespeare, will nonetheless reach its zenith in the novel, precisely
because the latter genre is defined by its multiplicity of form. Antonio
describes the novel in 'Letter about the Novel' as so similar to drama
that the latter is in fact the former's foundation. Nonetheless, Antonio
insists that the novel's generic identity depends on its capacity to include and embrace other generic forms: 'Indeed, I can scarcely visualize
a novel but as a mixture of storytelling, song, and other forms. Cervantes
always composed in this manner and even the otherwise so prosaic
Boccaccio adorns his collections of stories by framing them with songs'
(*DP* 102). Returning to the diamond represented above, it is now apparent that Cervantes' inclusion refers to the culmination of Romantic
poetry in the novel, more specifically in *Don Quixote*. As note V: 69 reveals, Schlegel assumes the genre of the novel to be the offspring and
culmination of the other three genres: 'The stuff of the Romantic: (1)
among the ancients: epic and drama. The beginning of mixed poetry in
prose and mystical, sentimental love (erotica); (2) the absolutely mystical
wonderful, the uniquely Romantic; (3) Don Quixote –.'[17] In these brief
jottings to himself, we glimpse Schlegel's genealogy of the novel, find-
ing its roots in ancient epic, drama, and prose, the latter of which the
young Friedrich does *not* designate with the term *Roman*, or novel. The
Romantic then passes through the mystical and wonderful expressions

of the romance, presumably understood here as medieval and Renaissance works of fantasy including the chivalric romances, but peaks in Cervantes' *Don Quixote*. The novel is, therefore, the genre of the post-classical age, connected in lineage to its predecessors, but surpassing and transforming its heritage. Cervantes' masterpiece even more specifically represents this transformation; if we read between the lines of this jotting, *Don Quixote*, as a parody of the chivalric romances, subsumes and renews the genre.

Likewise, the novel as a genre subsumes and transforms all other genres, thus establishing its definition as the mixed genre. A good example of this concept can be found in note V: 420, where Schlegel refers to the absolute novel as a mixture of psychological, philosophical, fantastic, and sentimental novels, combined with the absolutely mimetic, sentimental, fantastic, poetic, and rhetorical forms of the novel, plus prophecy (*KA* 16:120). Schlegel's understanding of the inclusivity of the novel has enjoyed much critical commentary; indeed, it is the one definitive quality upon which all scholars can agree. The space of the novel is for Schlegel essentially a mediating space, one so defined by polarities and dualities that it encompasses them all. Significantly, Schlegel often indicated the absolute with the mathematical notation $1/0$, the same one we see attributed to Cervantes in the Romantic diamond (*LN* 12). Arthur Lovejoy suggests that the young Romantic borrows this concept of the absolute, or infinity (*Unendlichkeit*), from Kant via Fichte, and uses the term to imply that 'art should be characterized by a constant enlargement of its boundaries and an endless progression towards an unattainably remote ideal' (216).[18] The novel, as a space circumscribing polarities, is the most suitable medium for an all-embracing art form. Thus, Schlegel's conceptualization of the novel as a genre blends into his understanding of the Romantic as the aesthetic of the modern: 'Romantic poetry is a progressive universal poetry' (Athenaeum Fragment 116, *DP* 140).

This mathematical notation associated with Cervantes – $1/0$ – proves to be fruitfully polysemic for Schlegel; not only does it associate the novel with the absolute, but it also associates it with chaos. Mathematically, $1/0$ represents the division of one, the perfect integral unit, by nothing; mathematically, then, $1/0$ represents an irrational, absurd concept. In another diagram found in his literary notes, Schlegel assigns the same place at the bottom of a diamond to the chaotic. Above the chaotic, at the apex of the diamond, he lists the sidereal, to the left the terrestrial, and to the right the ethereal. Given the manner in which

Schlegel reworks his ideas in the literary notebooks, it is significant that he defines the chaotic once again according to mathematical principles in note IX: 973: 'Mathematics is the principle of the chaotic/The mathematical form arises through the irrational, raised to a higher power/ Combinational progressive.'[19] The chaotic takes the irrational to a new power, thus linking it to the progressive and combinatory capacity of Romantic poetry. Echoing the statement in *Dialogue on Poetry* that Romantic poetry requires a new mythology, Schlegel states in note IX: 421 that the only essential, primary form of mythological poetry is absolute chaos (*KA* 2:421).[20] Chaos constitutes the very stuff of Romantic literature and mythology, an assertion that makes sense if we return to Friedrich's concept of a multiple and multiplying reality. Schlegel's concept of chaos approximates Schelling's, for whom it is the eternally alive ground of origin for the world, something that can never be completely acknowledged by thought (Huge 108). For Schlegel, the work of the Romantic writer is to take this chaotic stuff and systematize it, and even in this Cervantes serves as an example by manifesting a 'tendency' toward a system (Note IX: 728; *KA* 16:728). Thus, we find Schlegel placing the novelist in the position of the Romantic poet, hovering over a chaotic reality that is embraced and transformed in the systematizing impulse of the work of art. As the young thinker sums up: 'Chaos and the epic are certainly the best explanation of the Romantic.'[21] The objective order of the epic and the chaos of modern reality combine, then, as the content and the form of Romantic art. Cervantes, by enfolding the epic form in chaotic modernity, epitomizes Romantic literature in his *Don Quixote*.

Although many have accused Schlegel of being unsystematic in his thought, Benjamin rightly reminds us that the young Romantic's goal was to establish a systematic process of thought capable of progressive development through the contemplation of art. Ulrike Zeuch observes three manners by which the object might be apprehended by the Schlegelian subject: (1) abstraction, in which the observer through concentration perceives what the object shares in common with others of the same sort; (2) combination, by which the observer compares, conjoins, and summarizes different representations of the object in order to determine its specific qualities; and (3) reflection, through which the subject is aware of the very process of perception (64). This characterization of Schlegel's understanding of the reasoning process undertaken by the 'hovering' subject goes a long way toward illuminating how the Romantic poet can be understood to systematize chaos through the novel. The writer abstracts from his own perception of reality certain characteristic types; then he submits them to an almost experimental process whereby they interact with other types; and finally, he reflects upon his own perspective relative to this experiment. It is no accident that *Witz*, wit understood as the chemical combination of disparate elements, constitutes the basis of the novel in Schlegel's thought.

Irrationality, Irony, and *Don Quixote*

The questions follow as to what sort of chaos does Cervantes embrace, and how does he systematize it. Given the fact that 1/0 is an irrational number, one can link absolute chaos with the notion of absolute irrationality in Schlegel's literary notebooks. In fact, the irrational distinguishes the novel from the lyric and drama in yet another literary note, IX:132: 'Absolute irrationality is the essential distinguishing characteristic of the novel.'[22] Schlegel finds a complete catalogue of irrationality, and not without reason, in Cervantes' *Don Quixote*; folly (*Narrheit*), stupidity (*Dummheit*), and malice (*Bosheit*) make up the chaotic mythology of the work (Note IX:63; *KA* 16:260). Folly in all its forms can be considered the chaotic stuff of Cervantes' masterpiece, since Schlegel calls it the truly divine aspect of this novel (Note V:429; *KA* 16:121). The representation of foolishness in the characters of Don Quixote and Sancho Panza falls under the first step of reasoning, abstraction, since each person has within him both a Don Quixote and a Sancho Panza (Note VII:2; *KA* 16:205). This assertion of the universality of the characters of Don Quixote and Sancho Panza links Schlegel to earlier eighteenth-century readings of the novel, in which the story was understood as a universal satire. Schlegel further refines the abstracted notion of foolishness into several categories, specifically in the case of Cervantes' two protagonists, folly (*Narrheit*) and stupidity (*Dummheit*). In fact, the difference between foolishness and stupidity is one of degree rather than essence. Both are different from madness, because they are not arbitrary but rather wilful in their origin; that is to say, the fool and the stupid person choose to be so (Athenaeum Fragment 79, *KA* 2:79). The distinguishing characteristic between the two is their relative degree of education, for the fool is a scholastic (*Scholastiker*) and the stupid one a man of the world (*Weltmensch*; Note V:616; *KA* 16:137). The degree of education (perhaps the German concept of *Bildung* is more apt here) hinges upon the person's own capacity for self-reflexivity, as indicated by this passage from Schlegel's novel *Lucinde*: 'A stupid person is one who does not believe what he sees. A fool is one who is wilfully stupid, and does not believe that he is; he is stupid out of artfulness.'[23] The fool, unlike the stupid person, has the reflexive capacity to believe in his own stupidity, and yet out of artfulness or cunning does not. On the other hand, unlike the merely dumb person, the fool manifests an absolute perversity, in the sense of a refusal to participate in his own time and place, that Schlegel calls 'an absolute wrongness of tendency, a complete lack of historical spirit' (PF 56–7).

Given these definitions of stupidity and foolishness, it is tempting to ascribe the first attribute solely to Sancho Panza, the simple peasant who follows his master's imaginative lead, and the second to Don Quixote, the man of letters who wilfully chooses to adopt the anachronistic vocation of knight-errantry. To the contrary, the interplay between Don Quixote and Sancho Panza in the novel operates for Schlegel according to his second step of reason, combination. Schlegel once again compares the novel to the epic and drama in its compositional form, this time specifying that the form of the novel is combination: 'In construction is to be found the essence of drama. In epic it is deduced; in the novel it is combined.'[24] In the chemical experiment that is Cervantes' novel, foolishness and stupidity are mixed in the two protagonists. According to the above definition of stupidity, Don Quixote is not only foolish but also stupid, for no better description of his psychology can be offered than that he does not believe what he sees. Schlegel also hints at Sancho's movement toward foolishness through the influence of his master when he notes the following in his plans for a proposed arabesque: '"Through me one enters into eternal foolishness." Sancho sinks into ever deeper sorrow and desire behind his master.'[25] Sancho's sentimental education alongside Don Quixote draws him toward self-reflexivity, and thus foolishness. The interchange between the two characters, rendered active and reactive by the catalysts of foolishness and stupidity, is for Schlegel nothing less than a parody of Platonic dialogue (Note VI: 38; KA 16:197).

The genre of the novel is, for Schlegel, the Socratic dialogue of modernity, in which the wisdom of life is differentiated from mere book learning (Lyceum Fragment 26, KA 2:149). According to Schlegel, Socratic irony depends on dialogue for its flowing form of 'speech' and 'counterspeech.' Moreover, it is not linked to dialectical, Hegelian movement toward a *telos* but rather has 'a bottomless sliding as its main feature' (Ernst Behler, *Irony and the Discourse of Modernity* 83). In the well-known and oft-cited Lyceum Fragment 108, Schlegel offers an explanation for his assertion that the novel is a form of Socratic dialogue.

In this sort of irony, everything should be playful and serious, guilelessly open and deeply hidden. It originates in the union of *savoir vivre* and scientific spirit, in the conjunction of a perfectly instinctive and a perfectly conscious philosophy. It contains and arouses a feeling of indissoluble antagonism between the absolute and the relative, between the impossibility and the necessity of complete communication. It is the freest of all licenses, for by its means one transcends oneself; and yet it is also the most lawful, for it is absolutely necessary. (*PF* 13)

The same play of oppositional and contradictory terms that Schlegel uses to describe the novel are present in this description of Socratic irony: humour and seriousness, openness and depth, common sense and academic knowledge, nature and art, limits and limitlessness, impossibility and necessity. The freedom that one acquires in Socratic irony is the same that the Romantic artist achieves: the ability to transcend one's own limits. It is no accident, then, that the young philosopher reiterates in so many places that poetry, understood as literature in general, is philosophy. The interplay between Don Quixote and Sancho Panza is, then, a form of philosophical enquiry, although Schlegel, far more conscious of the parodic nature of this exchange, refuses to assign philosophical schools of thought to the two characters. That Don Quixote might represent the ideal and Sancho Panza the real, to mention later readings, is of little importance to Friedrich Schlegel. What is important is that their dialogue, based on wit and irony, represents Romantic thought at its best.

One of the most crucial elements for establishing the pre-eminence of *Don Quixote* is that it exemplifies how one can subsume the old into the modern through parody. In literary note V: 1122, Schlegel observes that it is possible to translate entire genres through parody, a form of witty translation (*KA* 16:177). Cervantes' *Don Quixote* is a parody of two ancient genres: the romances of knight-errantry and Socratic dialogue. As such, it epitomizes the Romantic artist's quest to transcend one's own time, free of the constraints of and yet bound by necessity to the past. *Don Quixote* approaches, in fact, a theory of the novel in itself when read in the light of Schlegel's thought. Further to Fichte's concept of the self-reflexivity of thought, it would only follow that the perfect theory of the novel would be a self-reflective novel. Just so opines Antonio in the 'Letter about the Novel':

Such a theory of the novel would have to be itself a novel which would reflect imaginatively every eternal tone of the imagination and would again confound the chaos of the world of the knights. The things of the past would live in it in new forms; Dante's sacred shadow would arise from the lower world, Laura would hover heavenly before us, Shakespeare would converse intimately with Cervantes, and there Sancho would jest with Don Quixote again. (*DP* 102–3)

Schlegel turns to his conceptual diamond of Romanticism to describe what this theory of the novel would contain: the epic objectivity of Dante, the lyric subjectivity of Petrarch, the subjective objectivity of Shakespeare's drama, and the ironic Socratic dialogue of Cervantes. In this novel – or theory of the novel – the old reappears in modern forms, fantasy enjoys free flight, and chaos is subsumed. In spite of the mention of other writers, however, it is the figure of Cervantes who by necessity dominates in this fantastic vision; he is, after all, the only one who wrote a novel, and it is irony that defines both the modern novel and the stance of the modern thinker. Ideas Fragment 69 clearly defines irony, and by so doing links it inextricably to the novel as understood by Schlegel: 'Irony is the clear consciousness of eternal agility, of an infinitely teeming chaos' (*PF* 101). The clear consciousness of both agility and chaos belongs to the Romantic author and is revealed in the world of the novel.

Schlegel's theory of the novel, despite the fact that it was never published in one coherent text but must be pieced together from all the different fragments of his writings, reveals itself to be the undisputed progenitor of all later theories of the novel. The very revolutionary quality of the young Romantic's thought can be appreciated when one compares his approach to *Don Quixote* to that of an earlier literary theorist, Johann Jakob Bodmer. In his treatise of 1741, *Kritische Betrachtungen über die poetischen Gemälde der Dichter* (Critical Observations on the Poetic Pictures of the Writer), the Enlightenment critic dedicates a chapter to Cervantes' *Don Quixote*. Like Schlegel, he notes the presence of both foolishness (*Narrheit*) and wisdom in the title character, and, like Schlegel, also notes how Sancho serves as a reasoned counterpoint to Don Quixote in the first part, only to be won over by Don Quixote's foolishness in the second part. The doubled character of the would-be knight errant, although duly noted, receives a cursory, unsatisfactory explanation in Bodmer's work: he is a symbol of the Spanish nation, led into error by the fantastic exploits of the fictional knights errant (518–19). Sancho Panza, whose gullibility serves merely to add pleasure to the text, is necessary only as an eyewitness to the main character's adventures (542). Fantasy itself is not a liberating, creative force, since it is what drives Don Quixote into his self-deception and feeds his wrong-headed interpretations of reality. Nowhere in Bodmer's reading is there any sense that the novel defines modernity in terms that go beyond the particular state of Spain, nor that modernity itself is an ambivalent state of both limitless possibility and limiting alienation from the past. The double-edged sword of freedom, which both severs the individual from tradition and society and yet enables him or her to transcend it, does not hang over Bodmer, who reads Cervantes' prose work as a simple, albeit entertaining satire on Spanish customs. Indeed, the responsibility of the writer, as seen by Bodmer, is limited to amusing and instructing the reader, and imitating some small slice of reality. Schlegel's call some sixty years later for a novel that must somehow encompass all the diversity, fractiousness, and irony of modernity is a very different theory of the novel indeed.

System, Fantasy, and the Arabesque

We have already seen how the Romantic writer is to create order from chaos, and how this capability depends on the author's hovering stance above his material. The autonomy of the fictional world stems to a certain extent from a new concept of authority in relation to structure. The novelist as an autonomous self creates from chaos, and from that creation emerges a new world that has its own internal logic, which Eberhard Huge has aptly described as an indwelling tendency toward motion and motive (113). Schlegel calls this *System*, although we might be more comfortable with the idea of an internal logic; notwithstanding the variety of terms, the central concept introduced here by the young Romantic is that the world created by the Romantic writer obeys its own rules, and does not subjugate itself to those of real life. In the positing of the arabesque as a system or a tendency, the German Romantic confronts the modern problematic of the dissolution of reason based on authority. In Schlegel's postulation of artistic independence, according to which the individual poet enjoys creative autonomy from authority, there still remains the issue of how to structure and write a text in such a manner that it is understandable. When the poet or novelist is freed from traditional or authoritative forms (say the precepts of neoclassicism and its overwhelming concern for mimesis understood in the most reductive sense), she must still face the dilemma of communicating with the reader. The reader, in turn, must adapt a new approach to appreciating and evaluating the work of art.

As Schlegel remarks in Athenaeum Fragment 173, 'In the style of a true writer nothing is ornamentation, but rather everything is a necessary hieroglyph.'[26] Interpretation depends not on comparing the work to an outside standard of taste and verisimilitude, but rather on observing its own inner language, a process that demands that the reader find meaning for even the apparently meaningless aspects of the work. The *necessity* of the signifying hieroglyph emerges from the system, or the arabesque, that structures the text. Insofar as it exists independently of tradition, the literary work is freed from being seen as a means to an end, but is rather viewed as a subject unto and sufficient to itself. In short, the literary work enjoys Kantian dignity (*Würde*) as an entity integral unto itself rather than an instrument for something or someone else. But in order for it to communicate, it must embody its own internal logic or system of reason in a manner accessible to the attentive reader. From the chaotic state of modernity – the lack of traditional authoritative reason – the poet wrests the arabesque system. Consequently, any lessons contained within the novel must be communicated through the whole of the work, rather than in single parts (Athenaeum Fragment 111, *KA* 2:181).

The notion of the arabesque, uniquely polyvalent among the arts, attracted the attention of the German Romantics for various reasons. In the visual arts it was associated both with the Islamic world and its organic, but often non-figural, decoration, and with the classical world; indeed, classical and classicizing grotesques were often subsumed into the category of the arabesque. Nor was it shunned by artistic geniuses; the great Renaissance painter Raphael designed arabesque ornamentation for the Vatican.[27] The discovery of vegetal ornament and grotesque decorations in Pompeii in the eighteenth century contributed to a renewed interest in the form and its presence in many aspects of the century's art and design. An academic controversy concerning the propriety of the arabesque, associated with the grotesques found in ancient art as well as Islamic architectural ornamentation, occurred in Germany in the 1780s and 1790s. Whereas some attacked the arabesque as tasteless, excessive examples of artistic licence, others (including Goethe) defended it as a minor art form (Polheim 17–21; Muzelle 649–63). It became an important form of Romantic music; Robert Schumann, for example, was influenced by Schlegel's notion of the arabesque as a treatment of nothing (*Nichts*), and subsequently a reflection on the nature of creative activity itself (Nonnenmann 243–54). The arabesque linked the visual arts to architecture, architecture to music, and music to literature. Schlegel himself sought to write arabesques, and left unfinished plans for arabesques, including one with Sancho Panza as its protagonist. Patricia Stanley suggests that the section 'Treue und Schmerz' ('Fidelity and Pain') from Schlegel's *Lucinde* represents a completed literary arabesque (402).

Within Schlegel's thought, the arabesque is linked to *Fantasie*; in addition, it offers means by which to reconcile chaos with system. As Patricia Stanley remarks, 'Arabesque is the term Schlegel used to indicate the ideal synthesis of chaos (in human nature and in the universe as a whole) and the underlying order of the universe' (404). Indeed, in one note the young Schlegel juxtaposes the system of chaotic philosophy (an oxymoron, if ever there were one) to a transcendental arabesque (Polheim 112). The image of the arabesque lends itself quite well as a support for understanding the systematic nature of the young Romantic's thought, for it depends on forms occurring in nature but embodies the problematics of modern aesthetics (Mennemeier 344). In the lines of its spiraling self-production, it embodies the continual movement between opposites that forms the revolving underpinning of Schlegel's understanding of philosophy, literature, and even the relation of the self to the world.[28] A visual design, ornamental in nature, the arabesque is based on spontaneous interweaving of line and fantastic elaboration of twists, spirals, and all sorts of interpolated forms. It seems free from the constraints of mimesis, and thus allows the artist to engage in whims and caprices, although, as Alois Riegl has shown, it depends conceptually and historically on natural patterns. The underlying principle of the Islamic arabesque is *infinite rapport*: 'As a rule, a simple element – even if it is a composite one – provides the basis of the entire decorative conception: either by duplication or division, so as to establish a continuous pattern of interrelation' (272). The similarity between this *infinite rapport* observed by Riegl in the arabesque and Schlegel's concept of *unendliche Fülle* (infinite abundance or fullness) is striking. Indeed, Schlegel repeatedly associated *unendliche Fülle* with *unendliche Einheit* (infinite unity) in such a way that Karl Polheim sees the relation between the two concepts as an arabesque (56–62). Moreover, the infinite pattern and play of the arabesque in Persian carpets is recreated in the border motifs, where the whole notion of border itself is complicated. As G.R. Thompson asks, 'Are borders limiting or limitless?' (179). Finally, the arabesque has the capacity to surprise and engage the viewer in its unending intricacy. Ornament, including the arabesque, is essentially ambiguous, requiring of the viewer that she interpret mixed signals and complete incomplete forms (Trilling 35–9). The ornamental forms of Pompeii and subsequent Islamic decoration leave the image unbounded, requiring the viewer to fill in the missing parts (Riegl 277). Nonetheless, it is a form based on a vertical division, in which one side must mirror the other. Thus, from the fantasy arises an order, self-contained as the one side repeats the other.

Scholars have noted that Schlegel associates the arabesque with Sterne's *Tristram Shandy*, in which case the category of the arabesque refers to his attribution of the concept to narratorial intervention and irony in the text (Polheim 217–22; Garber 33–40). Nonetheless, the connection between the arabesque and Cervantes' *Don Quixote* has gone unremarked. For example, Schlegel quips that the arabesque is to Cervantes what the study is to Goethe (Note IX: 182; *KA* 16:269). In the *Dialogue on Poetry*, Schlegel calls for a mythology that would have the form of an arabesque in its transformative and metamorphic powers. In fact, the structure of *Witz* seen in Cervantes and Shakespeare is the same as the arabesque, which Schlegel calls the 'oldest and most original form of human imagination' (*DP* 86). The description of Cervantes' wit is an apt description of an arabesque: 'Indeed, this artfully ordered confusion, this charming symmetry of contradictions, this wonderfully perennial alternation of enthusiasm and irony which lives even in the smallest parts of the whole, seem to me to be an indirect mythology themselves.' Through the figure of the arabesque, Schlegel attempts to bridge the gap between modernity and the antique, returning to the origins of human culture. The Romantic remains, however, to buttress this span with the figures of Shakespeare and Cervantes. In addition, the arabesque form, in its inclusion of contradiction, ordered contradictions, and irony, is none other than that of the modern novel. For what does the arabesque permit one to see but chaos and confusion? 'Neither this wit nor a mythology can exist without something original and inimitable which is absolutely irreducible, and in which after all the transformations its original character and creative energy are still dimly visible, where the naive profundity permits the semblance of the absurd and of madness, of simplicity and foolishness, to shimmer through' (*DP* 86). Once again, foolishness and idiocy serve to create wit.

The arabesque is an apt image for Cervantes' *Don Quixote* because it embodies what Schlegel calls the 'primordial and necessary' dualism of Don Quixote's and Sancho Panza's dialogue. According to Schlegel, 'Cervantes handles the characteristics of Don Quixote and Sancho musically and playfully throughout [the novel], without any psychology or development of base consequences. The free will and the sudden starts in Don Quixote's and Sancho's witty sayings are the finest aspects of their character. The dualism between them is original and necessary.'[29] This note is remarkable insofar as it establishes how completely Schlegel reads *Don Quixote* according to his own theory of the novel. The dialogue between the knight errant and his squire is described in such a way that it encompasses several traits of Romantic irony, particularly freedom, spontaneity, and transcendence. Musicality describes the way the Spanish author transforms this dialogue into something higher, more unified, and transcendent. Schlegel also emphasizes the musicality of Cervantes' prose in his review of Ludwig Tieck's translation of *Don Quixote* (1799), and observes that the Spaniard 'fantasizes the music of life' (*KA* 2:283). Cervantes, thus, provides a model for the representation of reality in a way that is not demeaning, hateful, or cruel. It is this quality that leads the young Schlegel to differentiate Cervantes from the 'raw, vulgar' Lope de Vega and the 'hard, acidic' Quevedo (Mennemeier 311–12).

The implications of the arabesque for both Schlegel's aesthetics and his ethics are profound. When applied to his concept of dialogue, it explains how two free parties engage in a playful, musical exchange, simultaneously stimulating and limiting each other. Don Quixote's and Sancho's dialogue is, then, a playing out of their dualism, in which the resulting form encloses both their difference and their coming together. In many ways, the arabesque corresponds to the parody in literature, in that it contains both one thing and its reverse. When Schlegel writes that the knight errant's and his servant's conversation is a parody of dialogue, he implies paradoxically that it *is* dialogue. This capacity of both dialogue and arabesque to encompass assertion and negation underlies literary note IX: 175: 'The most masterful aspects of *Don Quixote* part II are cultivation (*Bildung*) and intellect, and the parody of cultivation, of intellectual speech, of serious history, of aristocratic society.'[30] According to Schlegel, the second part of Cervantes' novel, like the arabesque, can present culture and reason, as well as their negation, through parody. The arabesque of this literary note is, however, somewhat lopsided, for only cultivation and understanding (*Verstand*) are presented in their positive forms. On the one hand, *Bildung*, understood as intellectual and moral development, takes place between Sancho and Don Quixote, as the pair grows together. *Verstand*, understanding as well as intellect, also takes place within their dialogue as the two teach each other. On the other hand, serious history and aristocratic society appear only in their negative forms, particularly in the episodes that take place in the palace of the Duke and the Duchess, where both the knight errant and his squire endure cruel teasing for the sport of the nobles. Against the novelistic model of Don Quixote's and Sancho's dialogue, Cervantes juxtaposes the parody of a society built on hierarchical difference in which the lesser serve only as means for the entertainment of the great.

Sancho's Arabesque

Present in Schlegel's notebooks dating from 1799 to 1801 are several outlines for extended literary works that the young Romantic labelled arabesques. The most detailed and comprehensive of these plans stars as its protagonist none other than Sancho Panza, who takes a trip to the underworld in search of his deceased master, Don Quixote.[31] In spite of the obvious lacunae in a plan that was private and, to our knowledge, never further developed, Schlegel's notes give enough of an indication of its proposed structure and content to reveal key ideas pertaining to his conception of a literary arabesque, as well as pertaining to his interpretation of Cervantes' *Don Quixote*. In a later notebook from 1807, Schlegel refers again to the proposed work, labelled 'Sancho's Descent into Hell' (*Sanchos Höllenfahrt*), as a comic tale of a hero (Polheim 318). Indeed, this proposed arabesque should suffice to dispel any lingering misconceptions among Cervantes scholars concerning Schlegel's supposed failure to observe the comic nature of *Don Quixote*. Parody and satire are the dominant modes of the proposal; moreover, the joking extends beyond parodying the literary *topos* of the heroic descent into hell (with obvious references to the Orpheus myth and Dante's *Divine Comedy*) to encompass references to contemporary politics, writers, and philosophers. Parodic references to other literary works include an allusion to *terza rima*, the poetic form used by Dante in the *Divine Comedy*, as well as allusions to various literary devils, including Mephistopheles, Klopstock's Abbadona, and Lesage's Asmodeus (Polheim 336). The arabesque, if it were ever completed, would have also functioned as a satirical *roman à clef* populated by risible characters based on philosophers such as Kant, Garve, and Nicolai, and literary figures such as Klopstock, Schiller, and Jean Paul. Curiously, Schlegel's proposed arabesque bears a striking resemblance to a mock-heroic poem described by Nicolai as a 'burlesque tale of a hero' that he and Lessing supposedly planned in fun in the winter of 1756–7 (Thayer 579–81). In Lessing's and Nicolai's proposed poem called *The Poets*, Gottsched and a follower ride out as knight and squire to battle the angels of Friedrich Gottlieb Klopstock. Perhaps this might explain Schlegel's enigmatic reference in the proposed Sancho arabesque to Nicolai as 'an ultramarine in burlesque' ('Nicola als Ultramarin in Bürlesken'), and the lengthy quote of an 'I' complaining of the virulent boredom and loathing for the Enlightenment he experienced sitting next to Nicolai.

These six enigmatic paragraphs describing Sancho's descent into hell obviously contain many allusions worthy of further consideration; in the interests of this study I will limit myself to the questions concerning Schlegel's notion of modernity, the novel, and *Don Quixote* that it raises. One must not lose sight of the fact that this underworld imagined by Schlegel is both intimately linked to his own epoch and undeniably comic. As Schlegel noted, 'Hell [is] taken as extremely pleasurable and funny, with parody of Klopstock.'[32] Klopstock published an epic poem called *The Messiah* (1748–73), inspired partially by Milton's *Paradise Lost* and seriously intended as a disquisition on the Christian account of the conflict between good and evil. Schlegel, however, opts for parody, and indicates in this plan that irony (*Witz*) is to Christendom what beauty was to Greek mythology (Polheim 315). This bold statement granting irony such a central role in Christian European culture indicates that the structuring principle of the arabesque is ironic reversal such as that seen in the comic underworld visited by Sancho. The ironically upsetting relation to Greek literature envisioned by Schlegel for this arabesque also appears in references to Aristophanes's *The Frogs* and the pseudo-Homeric *Batrachomyomachia*. The proposed descent of Sancho into hell in search of Don Quixote alludes to Bacchus's descent to Hades to bring back Euripides, a trip recounted in *The Frogs*. First, Schlegel refers to the fable of the frog and mouse war from the *Batrachomyomachia*, a battle that Zeus finally ends by creating crabs to intervene. Schlegel links this battle to revolution, and further suggests the superposition of animal fable on contemporary history by relating Renard the Fox to the history of nation states (Polheim 315). According to the plan, a similar reversal of the Greek by the popular would occur later on, when Till Eulenspiegel, the German trickster hero of folklore, would be ousted from the throne of idiocy (*Narrheit*) as Aeschylus was ousted from the underworld throne of tragedy in Aristophanes's *The Frogs* (Polheim 316). Common to these parodic reversals are references to European folk literature (Eulenspiegel, Renard the Fox) based on characters of lowly status that use their savvy to upset the social order. A remark calling for a German Lazarillo specifically invokes the picaresque, and serves to enhance further the socially transgressive nature of Schlegel's parody.

The young German Romantic goes further in his planned critique by linking identifiable figures of his time with his three categories of idiocy: vulgarity (*Plattheit*), worldly stupidity (*Dummheit*), and the more learned and arrogant foolishness (*Narrheit*). Of these, vulgarity occupies a lesser status and is linked to boredom (*Langeweile*), which one must imagine would be for the young Schlegel a far greater faux pas than the more entertaining stupidity and foolishness (Polheim 332). In the Sancho arabesque, it is only referred to when an unidentified Kantian is expelled from the circle of idiocy (*Narrheit*) to the circle of vulgarity (*Plattheit*). Schlegel exempts Kant from critique by imagining even a second-rate follower spared from the circle of idiots. As we have shown earlier, *Narrheit* and *Dummheit* form the basis of Don Quixote's and Sancho Panza's dialogue; Schlegel pursues this insight further in the proposed arabesque. In the first sections of the arabesque, worldly stupidity (*Dummheit*) predominates. Not only does Reynard the Fox preside over national history, but Sancho, the voice of popular refrains and common knowledge in *Don Quixote*, receives a warm welcome among the English, who all reside in the circle of *Dummheit*. Nonetheless, one moves toward the circle of *Narrheit* with the introduction of masks representing German characters. Following the removal of the Kantian from the circle of *Narrheit*, a voice, presumably Don Quixote's, echoes the words of Christ as it proclaims: 'Man enters eternal foolishness through me.'[33] Schlegel continues immediately to describe Sancho's emotional despair as he searches for his master: 'Sancho sinks into ever deeper grief and longing for his master.'[34] The implications for Schlegel's interpretation of the relationship between knight and squire are clear: Don Quixote leads Sancho down the path of foolishness (*Narrheit*), presumably away from stupidity (*Dummheit*). This movement away from the more common stupidity toward the erudite foolishness repeats itself in the image of Till Eulenspiegel's unseating from the throne of *Narrheit*. Popular wisdom, associated with *Dummheit*, cedes before the advance of *Narrheit*. In fact, toward the end of the planned arabesque there would appear a symphony of university professors, linked conceptually to 'reversed Socratic irony.'[35] Polheim notes that in the 'Letter about the Novel,' Schlegel observes that when stupidity (*Dummheit*) reaches a certain height, it becomes foolishness (*Narrheit*), the loveliest and final origin of the truly amusing (330). By reversing the movement toward the underworld, Schlegel takes the turn necessary for an arabesque, in which the motifs must interweave and mirror each other in all directions.

It is now possible to imagine the proposed work as an arabesque. Formally, the Sancho arabesque would consist of several repeated *topoi*: the descent into hell, the dethroning of popular wisdom, and the heroic quest. High and low genres would interweave like the warp and the woof; one would supersede the other, only to recede again in an endless cycle. Figures of animals would alternate with figures of men in such a manner that they would become entwined and confused. Literary figures would serve as masks for historical figures, rendering the entire arabesque an allegorical representation of Schlegel's modernity. Genres, figures, and *topoi* alike would repeatedly emerge through three distinct circles: that of *Plattheit*, *Narrheit*, and *Dummheit*. According to Polheim, this conceptual string of categories of idiocy links the arabesque to Schlegel's notion of *Kritik*, the critical analysis of text and society based on polemics, satire, parody, and caricature (335). As an example of the exercise of Romantic irony, the Sancho arabesque gives shape to a form of critique based as much on imaginative representation as on analytical insight. As such, it serves as a model for the modern novel conceived of as a form of social and philosophical critique. The other form of the modern novel, based for Polheim on the erotic string of love, fantasy, and imagination, is that of Schlegel's *Lucinde*, an exploration of the interior world of desire, sentiments, and the psyche (344–5).

In later theories of the novel, this alternation between a vision of the novel as an instrument of analysis and critique and its idealization as a vehicle of love and sentiment will recur. Schlegel's concepts of irony and modernity constitute his greatest contributions to our understanding of the novel. Cervantes' *Don Quixote* provides him with a model for dialogue capable of interweaving difference into a whole. It also provides him with a means to dignify parody and to privilege comic reversal and descent. Sancho's proposed journey into hell echoes several of the character's adventures in *Don Quixote II* as the lowly rustic ascends and descends the social ladder. His flight on Clavileño reveals the insignificance of the earth below; his fall into an empty well while returning home after being deposed as governor of Barataria reveals his own insignificance. Enlightenment comes only with the disillusionment caused by the distant, cool perspective of irony.

3 The Emptiness of the Arabesque: Georg Lukács's Theory of the Novel

Georg Lukács's *The Theory of the Novel* presents us with a challenge commonly associated with canonical works of literature: the hermeneutic task of attempting to read it within the moment it appeared. Few other works of literary theory are so obviously tinged by subsequent interpretive history; therefore, it is necessary at some moment to acknowledge its specificity, that is to say, to lift it from the author's lifework and appreciate it as a work unique to itself. The young Lukács began writing this essay on the eve of the First World War, and first published it in 1916 in the German journal *Zeitschrift für Aesthetik und allgemeine Kunstwissenschaft* (nos. 3–4), several years before his transformation into one of the foremost Marxist philosophers of the twentieth century. The interpretive thrust of most subsequent criticism of *The Theory of the Novel* has been simultaneously (and, of course, paradoxically) to divorce it from and connect it to his later writings. Indeed, Lukács himself could not resist such an attempt to appropriate his own past and make it adequate to his present when he wrote a prologue to a 1962 edition. After putting forth a number of observations concerning the intellectual indebtedness of this work to other thinkers that prove to be at the same time useful guideposts and red herrings, the Georg Lukács of 1962 sets out some limits for the 'correct' reading of this essay: it can be read as a 'pre-history of the important ideologies of the 1920s and 1930s,' but will only disorient the reader looking for guidance in the book (*TN* 23). In other words, Lukács argues in 1962 that not only should this book *not* be read in its own right as containing interesting or useful ideas about the genre of the novel, *neither* should it be read within the context of its actual historical moment, Lukács's pre-Marxist period, but rather in relation to the Marxist ideas of the following decades.[1] The older Lukács's reference to this essay's disorienting effect is not without validity; nonetheless, the difficulty and contradictions of the work do not warrant a merely disdainful attitude.

The interlocutor we seek for Lukács is Friedrich Schlegel, the previous writer to attempt a full-fledged theory of the novel, albeit in the form of fragments and his own novel, *Lucinde*. The relation between the German Romantic's theory of the novel and the young twentieth-century Hungarian's is complicated, revealing an extensive fertilization of the latter's thought with the former's as well as an attempt by the young Lukács to distinguish his theory from the young Schlegel's. In spite of Lukács's later rejection of Schlegel, as a young man the Hungarian thinker had a much more positive reception of the German Romantic's ideas, if not necessarily the conservative bent his politics and thought took after 1804. In fact, at one point Lukács proposed to write a book-length study on Friedrich Schlegel, but it has been suggested that the specific book never came to fruition because *Soul and Form* constitutes Lukács's response to Schlegel (Kruse-Fischer 11, 123). One of the main links between the two young men, separated by a century, was their sense of homelessness, that is to say, the alienation of the individual in modern society. For Ute Kruse-Fischer, the principal link between the young Schlegel and the young Lukács is their desire to overcome the essential duality of life (134). As shown in the previous chapter, Schlegel countered this split between individual and society with the forms of Romantic irony and the arabesque. It is not accidental, then, that Lukács introduces into his *Theory of the Novel* these two Schlegelian concepts: Romantic irony and the arabesque, both constitutive of the novel as a modern genre. From these notions the young Lukács elaborates his own understanding of the novel. Using a new concept of time, based on Henri Bergson's notion of *durée*, Lukács transforms Schlegel's concept of the arabesque into a figure evolving in time.[2] Nor is the moment and place in which *The Theory of the Novel* was written so easily disregarded. It was widely acknowledged among his friends that Lukács's literary essays were largely autobiographical in the problems they treated (Gluck 119). In his overweening interest in subjective experience, Lukács mirrored the young Schlegel, just as he and his friends mirrored the young German Romantics in their attempt to set up a circle of aesthetic revolutionaries.

The Young Lukács and Modernism

As a young man, Georg Lukács was fully engaged in the modernist enterprise, insofar as this is understood as the desire to reform modernity through avant-garde artistic and intellectual activity. Lukács belonged to the so-called Sunday Circle, a group of young Budapest intellectuals that met on Sunday afternoons from 1915 until the exile of many of its members following the fall of the Hungarian Socialist Republic in 1919. The Sunday Circle is described by Lukács's friend, the poet and librettist Béla Balázs, as a spiritual or ethical academy (Congdon 118). This group included important creative artists, such as Balázs and the composer Béla Bartok, and budding scholars such as Karl Mannheim and Arnold Hauser, as well as a number of talented women artists and intellectuals who never achieved such levels of international recognition or accomplishment due to sociohistorical limitations, such as the poet and artist Anna Leznai and the philosopher Edit Hajós. In spite of their heterogeneous ideological viewpoints, they did agree on one important point: modern culture was ethically and intellectually bankrupt and in need of renewal.

In their attempt to transcend the fractured culture of modernity and achieve a new, holistic one, the members of the Sunday Circle self-consciously followed in the footsteps of the German Romantics. Lukács suggested that their conversation be recorded so that persons of the next century could envy them just as they envied the Romantics (Gluck 20–1). They considered modern culture to be essentially one of alienation, and looked back to idealized models of supposedly unified cultures such as those of ancient Greece and the Middle Ages. Karl Mannheim, writing in 1918, traces a genealogy of the concept of alienation that clearly links the young Hungarians to the German Romantics: 'Perhaps the earliest spokesman of alienation … was Rousseau, and there is a direct line that leads from him … to Schiller, whose concept of sentiment, and to Schlegel, whose notion of irony, signal the identical fact from different sides' (Gluck 22). In addition, they felt affinities for the different branches of European modernism, which the young Lukács had first encountered, ironically enough, in Max Nordau's conservative denunciation of the new art in the book *Degeneration* (1893; Kadarkay 41). According to Lukács, 'the modernists stood for an "inner revolution" whose intention was to transform the internal life and the consciousness of individuals, not merely their external power relationships in the social and political world' (Gluck 65).

In spite of his close associations with fellow artists and intellectuals, the young Lukács from childhood on found social intercourse difficult, and sought solitude to carry out his work. Three social factors conditioned his alienation: his family, his identity as a Jew and a Hungarian, and modernity itself (Congdon 3–11). His relations with his banker father, who had bought the honorific 'von' for the family name, were always troubled, although the senior Lukács never failed to assist Georg or his friends when they found themselves in a financial or political bind. His relations with his mother were even worse for he seems to have considered her guilty of the empty formalities and hypocrisies typical of the haute bourgeoisie. Anti-Semitism dogged Georg's attempts at attaining an academic post, and might have been decisive in his rejection by both the Universities of Budapest and Heidelberg.[3] The year 1911 was particularly devastating, for it was the year of his friend Irma's suicide (brought about in part by Lukács's inability to love her) and his best friend Leo Popper's death from tuberculosis. Even Lukács's first marriage, to the Russian Ljena Adreyevna Grabenko, was a marriage of convenience occasioned by the First World War and intended to grant her Hungarian citizenship. Grabenko had served time in a Russian prison for terrorist activity; specifically, she had transported bombs beneath the blanket wrapping up a baby she had borrowed for the purpose (Congdon 89).

 The Theory of the Novel was written at a time when Lukács found himself even more alone than usual thanks to the First World War. Living in Germany when the war broke out, Lukács's active denunciation of the war and of the presumption of German cultural and military superiority alienated him to a certain degree from his colleagues and friends, including Max Weber and Georg Simmel. Decades later, Lukács recounted a conversation he had with Marianne Weber, the wife of his teacher in Heidelberg, Max Weber, in which he posed the rhetorical question: 'Who was to save us from Western civilisation?' (*TN* 11). Lukács viewed the outbreak of war in Europe as yet another example of the cultural and ethical bankruptcy of modernity. In a letter to the German writer Paul Ernst from July of 1917, Lukács comments that the two friends have parted ways politically: 'Just as I protest in my soul against the aggressive plans of England and France, so do I protest any action of that sort on the German side. I wish for a peace based on the *status quo*, not because nothing else is possible but because that *alone* would give some meaning to the senselessness of the war and would put an end to its madness' (*Selected Correspondence* 276). The madness of the war not only stemmed from Western civilization but threatened it, causing a doubled loss of meaning. Lukács's opposition to the war was so strong that in 1917 he and his friend Balázs proposed a Hungarian pacifist organization called, curiously, the 'Knights of Europe,' which would call for the creation of a United States of Europe (Congdon 133).

Lukács's theory of the novel is more than an exercise in the study of literary generic form; in fact, it is an exposition on the state of European modernity and an important cultural critique. Nonetheless, it should not be understood as a completely pessimistic writing on the death and impossibility of culture in the West, even though the older Lukács, perforce, describes it as a work of absolute despair, written prior to his complete adoption of Marxism shortly thereafter. Georg Simmel, who espoused the belief in the tragic death of Western culture, was Lukács's teacher in Heidelberg, and clearly exercised a great influence on the young man. Of particular import to Lukács's thought was Simmel's theory of money; indeed, Lukács's supplemented Marx's analysis of capitalism with Simmel's concept of alienation and objectification as results of capitalist production (Grauer 46–7; Löwy, *Georg Lukács* 98; Arato and Breines 15–18). Max Weber, who welcomed Lukács into his circle and fought over several years to get him an academic position at Heidelberg, also exercised significant influence over the young man and his conception of reification and rationalization (Congdon 82–9; Löwy, 'Figures of Weberian Marxism' 432–5; Tarr 131). Michael Löwy sums up the three main components of what he calls the 'tragic vision' common to Weber, Simmel, and various German neo-Kantians thus: '1) A metaphysical variant of the problem of alienation, reification, and commodity fetish … 2) A neo-Kantian dualism whereby the sphere of values was divorced from reality, and the realm of the spirit from the realm of social and political life … 3) The feeling of "spiritual impotence" when faced with an uncultured, barbarian-civilized, and vulgarly materialist "mass society."' (*Georg Lukács* 66–7).

To the contrary, Lukács strove in *The Theory of the Novel* to examine the type of artistic work, and the form it took, that could overcome the supposed inadequacy and impotency of the human being before the seemingly immoveable and impenetrable forms of the exterior world (Márkus 8–11). As Corredor maintains, *The Theory of the Novel* had been 'conceived in a revolutionary spirit' (73). The fact that a cursory reading of *The Theory of the Novel* makes it appear to be so completely despairing is perhaps a result of its incompletion. In another letter to Ernst, from the spring of 1915, Lukács announces that he has begun writing his 'new book on Dostoevsky … The book will go beyond Dostoevsky though; it will contain my metaphysical ethics and a significant part of my philosophy of history' (*Selected Correspondence* 244). Lukács's war service in the Office of Military Censorship in Budapest cut short his planned *opus magnum*; in a letter to Max Weber from December 1915, the young man laments that he will not be able to finish the book and will publish only a fragment that does not include his new metaphysics based largely on Dostoevsky. Moreover, he attributes to the portion to be published as *The Theory of the Novel* a 'dissonance that cannot be dissolved' (254).

We find clues to what this Dostoevskyan new world and its corresponding literary form would be in Lukács's extant writings. Toward the end of *The Theory of the Novel*, Lukács hints at the emergence of a new literary form in Dostoevsky's work, this new form representing a new age in which the individual would enjoy certain creative and formative power in the world.[4] Like Weber, Lukács was fascinated by Dostoevsky, particularly by the puzzle posed by the Russian author's Grand Inquisitor: Do the masses really want freedom? (Löwy, *Georg Lukács* 39, 113–24; Tihanov, 'Ethics and Revolution: Lukács's Responses to Dostoevsky' 610–11). Russia, in its major writers Tolstoy and Dostoevsky, represented to both German and Hungarian thinkers in the 1910s and 1920s an alternative to the West, based, paradoxically enough, on its supposedly more soulful, mystical nature as well as its proletarian revolution (Löwy, *Georg Lukács* 77). In an exchange that reveals much about Lukács's interpretation of Dostoevsky, his first wife, the Russian revolutionary Ljena Grabenko, asked him in a letter why he was so interested in God if God was dead. Lukács replied he would study Dostoevsky's atheist protagonists who were nonetheless 'profoundly suffering, profoundly seeking brothers of the new Christians' (Congdon 101). These new Christians would herald the coming of a new world in which the individual would live in unfettered society with his or her community. Concerning the nature of the individual, there would exist the sort of goodness seen in Dostoevsky's anti-heroic protagonists that, mindless of societal norms, originated from within the individual in adequate response to the needs of the surrounding persons. Concerning the nature of society, there would exist a community based on cultural, not social, forms. Given the merely suggestive nature of this vision of a post-modernity based on individual norms for good action and a society founded on something other than convention, *The Theory of the Novel* in its entirety propounds the broken nature of modernity that gives form to the individual's plight in this epoch.

Soul and Form

Lukács's first major publication, *Soul and Form* (1911), is composed of essays on aesthetic matters, ranging from lyric poetry to tragedy. In both their content and form, these essays serve to situate the themes and problems that characterize *The Theory of the Novel*. Foremost among them is an analysis of the essay as a scientific, critical, and artistic genre. As Lukács maintained throughout his life, the essay's paradoxical and fragmented nature reflects truthfully modern reality. It is a worthwhile exercise, then, to engage the essay in a careful, serious analysis of its own form and content without excessive reference to either the ideas of the young theorist's predecessors or his own later musings. Lukács, describing his proposed work *Soul and Form* in a letter to Leo Popper, noted his intention to subtitle the work with the Hungarian *kísérletek*, meaning experiments (*Selected Correspondence* 81). Nonetheless, the essay-experiment remained a fragmentary genre that would lose its value if viewed within a larger system: 'But this longing for value and form, for measure and order and purpose, does not simply lead to an end that must be reached so that it may be cancelled out and become a presumptuous tautology' (*SF* 17).[5] Given the essay's status as a form of infinite reflection, it is not surprising that Kruse-Fischer sees Lukács's essay as variations on Schlegel's fragments (13). Perhaps the young Lukács's most startlingly original assertion is that the essay arises from the same impetus for giving form to consciousness and experience that characterizes the novel.

Lukács's book of essays *Soul and Form* gives evidence in its very title of the centrality of form to his thought. Indeed, Lukács's debt to neo-Kantianism appears most clearly in his concept of form.[6] Following in the footsteps of Simmel, Lukács imagines form according to both the Hegelian historicity of social forms and the Kantian belief that form shapes realms of experience (Bernstein 77–8). Like Hermann Cohen, Lukács assumes that art in its form serves as a vehicle for self-consciousness, not only of an individual but also of a culture. For the young theorist, form has a doubled nature: not only does it create reality, it also symbolizes clarity and perfection, allowing us to name reality. It is, therefore, critical, providing one with analytical capability (Grauer 20). In addition, it is ethical, serving as a standard for the empirical task of living (25). Finally, the way in which Lukács conceptualizes the essay as an open-ended form, unbounded by delimiting finality, parallels Cohen's notion of the unending movement of the novel form toward, but never reaching, an endpoint that gives the genre direction rather than limitation. There is, however, also a Hegelian level to Lukács's notion of form insofar as he views form as manifesting truth. As a critical genre, not only is the essay to be valued as a work unto itself, it is also

beholden to express something truthful about reality. Lukács problematizes the essayist's duty to speak to reality thus: 'Here too there is a
struggle for truth, for the incarnation of a life which someone has seen
in a man, an epoch or a form; but it depends only on the intensity of the
work and its vision whether the written text conveys to us this suggestion of that particular life' (*SF* 11).

The essay approaches reality through struggle and must embody life
through the granting of form; nonetheless, it must also appear to be
truthful to the reader. Mimesis, understood as the capacity to produce
the convincing appearance of reality, becomes the essayist's goal.
Subsequently, reality itself escapes the essayist's grasp, just as it escapes
the portraitist's paintbrush, for, to borrow two examples proffered by
Lukács, who is to say that Velázquez's Philip III or Schlegel's Goethe is
the real one, even though they seem real. The neo-Kantian insistence on
the inaccessibility of the *Ding an sich* founds, curiously enough, Lukács's
notion of verisimilitude. In the absence of direct knowledge of the object, the struggle for truth takes place in the production of mimetic representations, the truth-value of which depends on their capacity to
convince the reader. The writing of the essay is inextricably linked to
the audience, since they are the ones to be convinced. Appropriately,
Plato's Socrates embodies the essay's form, as he lived in immediate
dialogue with his interlocutors. Indeed, he embodies the form of the
problematic individual, who seeks oneself and one's own meaning:
'The essayist must now become conscious of his own self, must find
himself and build something of his own out of himself' (*SF* 15).
Therefore, Lukács, in his role as essayist, understood himself to be involved in the same search for meaning as the novelistic heroes of whom
he wrote (Derwin 13).

Lukács wrote a dialogue about the novel, published in *Soul and Form*
under the title 'Richness, Chaos and Form. A Dialogue concerning
Lawrence Sterne' (dated 1909). The intertextual links of Lukács's essay
on Sterne to Friedrich Schlegel's *Dialogue on Poetry* are indubitable,
since both the situation and the content hark back to this important essay on the novel. Indeed, one is tempted to read Lukács's essay as a
caricature of Schlegel's dialogue.[7] Moreover, in a letter to Popper,
Lukács discusses precisely this essay in relation to two of Schlegel's
most well-known quotes. Quoting from the famous Athenaeum
Fragment 116 in which Schlegel defines Romantic poetry as continually
evolving, Lukács diagnoses German Romanticism's 'frivolity' as a result of its seeking after the infinite (*Selected Correspondence* 103). He does

concede, however, that Romanticism also involves irony, and thus cites Schlegel's image of irony as an endless row of reflections in mirrors. Seeing himself in Schlegel's mirror, Lukács states in this same letter: 'Well, my life to a large extent is a critique of the Romantics' (104). As he exclaims, one cannot critique Romanticism without critiquing the form of the novel: 'Oh no, it is not by accident that the word *Roman* (novel) and "romantic" are etymologically related!'

In Lukács' dialogue on Sterne, many of Schlegel's central concepts come in for a lively and at times acerbic examination as two young university students vie for intellectual victory before the eyes of their mutual, unnamed beloved. Vincent, described as a handsome young blond man, is the enthused but hapless mouthpiece for popularized versions of Schlegel's ideas, including Romantic irony and the arabesque, while Joachim, darker and more poorly dressed, ends up denouncing the same concepts as chaotic and unethical. Consider the way in which Joachim shatters the mirror image central to Schlegel's Romantic irony. Linking irony to *Weltanschauung*, Vicent argues that '[n]o writer and no work can do more than give us a reflexion of the world in a mirror which is worthy of reflecting all the world's rays' (*SF* 139). The individual then absorbs the world's variety through a mystical feeling of unity between the self and totality. Joachim deflates the image by asking which piece of the self is worthy of reflecting all the brilliance of this world.

The arabesque suffers a similar deflation. Vincent links the infinite form of the arabesque with sight, which has horizons rather than limits. This form is modelled by both medieval chivalric literature and Sterne's novel, as adventure follows adventure. According to Vincent, who refers specifically to Schlegel, the arabesque unwinding represents a sentimental affirmation of life (*SF* 145). For Joachim, who claims that Friedrich Schlegel did not hold the arabesque form in particularly high esteem, the arabesque ultimately represents chaos of sentiment and thought. Lukács describes this essay as a 'critique of all of my writing and of my entire way of life, that is, the critique of the fact that a life has only one use – it exists only for the purpose of intellectuality and thus has become superfluous here' (*Selected Correspondence* 102).[8] The superfluity of the intellectual exchange manifests itself in the young men's failed attempt to gain the beloved woman's affections.

Although this essay treats primarily of Sterne, Lukács does refer several times to Cervantes; indeed, *Don Quixote* as read here is an excursus on inadequacy. Curiously, Lukács focuses in this dialogue on the relation between Sancho and Don Quixote, an integral part of the novel and its reception that he fails to mention in his later *Theory of the Novel*. Lukács, through the voice of Vincent, employs a theatrical metaphor to describe the pair's interdependency: 'The Spanish knight and his fat squire stand side by side, like actor and scenery, and each is no more than a piece of scenery for the other. They complement each other, certainly, but, only for us' (*SF* 129). This reciprocal relationship is ultimately empty of actual human interaction. In fact, they reflect each other in a distorting mirror (*Zerrspiegel*) that serves as a symbol for the impossibility of human reciprocity in life. It is not surprising that Vincent reduces the pair to the doubled image of Daumier's caricatures, stating that Cervantes' writing is only illustrative text of these images, which are in themselves the manifestation of an idea (*SF* 130). Moreover, their figures, one large and thin, the other small and fat, have a mask-like quality that reduces their relation to the to-and-fro of adventures. Joachim objects to this characterization of Don Quixote and Sancho Panza not in its analysis, but rather in its heavy-handed tone, by reminding Vincent of the humour at the heart of Cervantes' and Sterne's novels. In accordance with the ancient, allegorical origins of theatre as described by Hegel, one must wear a mask through the whole performance and become a sort of epigram (*Phenomenology of Spirit* 444). But, as Joachim reminds Vincent, 'any mask ... is still an obstacle to interaction between men' (*SF* 135). Cervantes' *Don Quixote*, then, serves the young Lukács as a symbol for the emptiness of human relations.

The Theory of the Novel

It is not a stretch to read Lukács's *The Theory of the Novel* as a dialogue – perhaps even a satirical dialogue – with Friedrich Schlegel. As such, Cervantes' *Don Quixote* assumes a central position within the work, because it served as one of the exemplary manifestations of the genre for the young Schlegel. One cannot help wondering, however, whether Lukács felt much affinity for *Don Quixote*; certainly, Dostoevsky's work engaged him at a much deeper level, both psychologically and intellectually. It is perhaps Daumier's Don Quixote rather than Cervantes' that inspires Lukács's analysis of the novel. Like Daumier's caricatured figure of the would-be knight errant reduced to a stick figure, Lukács's reading of Cervantes' novel presents us with a doubled reduction: the novel *Don Quixote* serves as a form of the novel as a genre, and the character Don Quixote serves as a form of the novelistic – read modern – hero. Ultimately, the vision of Don Quixote as an abstract idealist is

Lukács's lasting contribution to the historical reception of Cervantes' novel. In order to arrive at this point, the theorist performs a dissolution of the complex novelistic character into a type reminiscent of Daumier's caricatures in its insistence upon a few defining traits. Form, the generic type, serves, according to Lukács, to make visible the life of the individual (Renner 14). It follows that the form of the novel reveals the lived experience of the modern individual.

'The composition of the novel is the paradoxical fusion of heterogeneous and discrete components into an organic whole which is then abolished over and over again' – thus Georg Lukács summarizes his image of the novel in *The Theory of the Novel* (*TN* 84). Lukács requires of us a stretching, if not an outright breaking, of deeply ingrained categories of ontological being; that is to say, we must picture the melding of discrete, heterogeneous pieces into a whole, while at the same time imagining the whole continually dissolving. To call this paradoxical is an ironic understatement on the theorist's part. Whereas paradox merely requires us to think one self-contradiction, this definition of the novel invites us to think the self-contradiction inherent in the statement, 'heterogeneous and discrete pieces are combined into an organic whole,' while at the same time thinking a second self-contradiction: 'melding and dissolving take place at the same time.' Paradox is, to borrow a term from the early Romantics, potentialized or taken to a higher power. The novel exists in a precarious relation to both time and space; just as spatial unity is undermined by disunity, so temporal unity is undermined by the competing processes of integration and disintegration. It is here that we see most clearly Lukács's debt to Hegel, as being and nothingness, self and other, intertwine.[9] What remains to be seen, however, is whether Lukács's notion of the novel will allow itself to be resolved or remain unfinished and open.

This, then, is the stuff of the novel for Lukács: paradoxical dissolution and resolution of the parts into the whole and back out again. The writer continues to explain this paradox in ethical terms, through recourse to ideas now quite widely recognized from Romantic theories of the novel. The juxtaposition of opposing figures in a unified form that Lukács uses as the figural basis for his definition of the novel clearly calls to mind Friedrich Schlegel's concept of the arabesque. Lukács practically paraphrases Schlegel's thought when he remarks that, in the novel, the creative ethic of lyrical subjectivity must be combined with the normative ethic of objectivity typical of the epic. Moreover, like Schlegel, he maintains that such a doubled perspective is achieved through irony. Indeed, the Lukács of the 1962 prologue recognizes his indebtedness by mentioning that 'the young Friedrich Schlegel's and Solger's aesthetic theories (irony as a modern method of form-giving) fill out and concretise the general Hegelian outline' (*TN* 15). Nonetheless, the wording by which he asserts irony's dominance in the form of the novel warrants analysis, as it points out for us unique aspects of Lukács's theoretical stance toward the novel: 'This interaction of two ethical complexes, their duality as to form and their unity in being given form, is the content of irony, which is the normative mentality of the novel. The novel is condemned to great complexity by the structure of its given nature' (*TN* 84). *The Theory of the Novel* itself represents Lukács's attempt to overcome the Kantian split between critical thought and art, since both will be subsumed into theory (Kruse-Fischer 44). In a parallel manner, the individual will overcome the dissonance between reality and utopian ideals through the attempt to live ethically. This requires the capacity for irony seen in the essayist, who balances and mediates dissonance between differing opinions and viewpoints (68–9).

Perhaps Lukács's most salient departure from previous literary thought is his assertion that irony has content. As a rhetorical device, traditional poetics can only envisage irony as a form available for the writer's application to whatever content she prefers. It is a vessel for meaning, but it does not contain any meaning inherently its own. Friedrich Schlegel, by linking irony to other forms, such as the Socratic dialogue and the arabesque, and by linking it to modernity, opens the door on irony's transformation from form into idea. Moreover, when we ask about its content, that is to say its idea, we are confronted with a form: the formal duality of the ethics of the lyric and the epic unified in the formation that is the novel. Hence, Lukács serves up another paradox: the content of irony is the form of the novel. In other words, content is form – and so we arrive at one of the central paradoxes of high modernism, if not modernity itself. Márkus fittingly sums up the primacy of form: 'For Lukács, form designates all the functions connected with the creation of meaning. It enables the multiplicity of facts, events and all the other elements to life to be arranged into *meaningful* structures, *organized patterns of meaning*' (10–11).

Form becomes a meaning-giving construct precisely because there is no generally accepted, ordained meaning in modernity (Bernstein 70; Corredor 77). In fact, it is the young Lukács's contention that modernity is bereft of meaning, content, and, in his words, God. It is in this sense that Lukács borrows from Fichte the concept of modernity as the age of complete sinfulness. Lukács holds forth pantheistic classical Greece as the model of a God-filled golden age, which he understands to be a unified culture reflected by Homer's epic verse. For Lukács, God is not a providential deity arranging human events from another realm, but rather consists of immanent meaning that pervades all of human society and activity. In this he follows Hegel, who calls 'Spirit … an *artificer* … [that] produces itself as object' (*Phenomenology of Spirit* 421). Nonetheless, immanent meaning has abandoned modernity, with the result that the metaphysical drive is itself an attempt to transcend the separation between individual and society and find immanent meaning (Gluck 152). J.M. Bernstein aptly sums up the role of antiquity: '*In Lukács's theory it is the dissonance of the ancient epic which allows the novel to be brought to historical consciousness; the comprehension of that dissonance in the novel is the goal of his history*' (75). Modernity is sinful, therefore, insofar as meaning no longer resides in the social forms.

Lukács begins this essay on the novel with an elegy to a lost time and place, noting a harmony between the individual soul and its surroundings: 'Happy are those ages when the starry sky is the map of all possible paths – ages whose paths are illuminated by the light of the stars' (*TN* 29). Martin Jay sees in this opening sentence an allusion to Kant's image of the starry heaven as representing a higher reality linked to the intellect seen by the individual who holds, within his corporal being, a sense of morality (46).[10] Even though Lukács sharply distinguishes between the world and the 'I,' he imagines their mutual indwelling through the metaphor of light and fire. The fire of the soul reflects and draws upon the light of the world, and so one can speak of a completed, full relationship between the two in spite of their duality. The fullness of meaningful activity is figured as round: 'rounded, because the soul rests within itself even while it acts; rounded because its action separates itself from it and, having become itself, finds a centre of its own and draws a closed circumference round itself' (*TN* 29). The form of epic society is the circle. Meaning pervades the whole circle, and the individual, secure of meaning, completes the circle through action. Through its inherent balance, symmetry, and unity, the circle certainly lends itself to the utopic vision of antiquity. A more perfect image, perfect in the sense of completion and fullness (*vollendet*), does not offer itself. Indeed, the circle is the image Hegel uses for both the philosophical whole, each part complete and rounded upon itself, and the 'good infinity' of circular history perceived as a totality (Jay 56–9). Significantly, in the very first paragraph of this essay on modernity, Lukács refers to the ideals of the two giants of modern philosophy, Kant and Hegel, only to reject them as representing pre-modern culture.

Immediately upon figuring this perfection through the starry sky and the circle, Lukács turns to the stark contrast of modernity by quoting the Romantic writer and friend of Schlegel, Novalis, who defined philosophy as the homesick urge to be everywhere at home. Due to this homesickness, philosophy is symptomatic 'of the rift between "inside" and "outside", a sign of the essential difference between the self and the world, the incongruence of soul and deed' (*TN* 29). The quote from Novalis, juxtaposed against Lukács's own poetic description of Greek antiquity, immediately contrasts the lost fullness to modern emptiness. Indeed, the young Hungarian's formulations of the epic as a genre representing the wholeness and connectedness of the ancient world, and its generic correspondence to the novel as the work best reflecting modernity, stem from Friedrich Schlegel's writings (Szondi 63). Lukács takes the Romantic image of homelessness as a metaphor for the modern individual's feeling of isolation and alienation in a world bereft of immanent meaning. Nonetheless, Schlegel's Athenaeum Fragment 277 clarifies the difference between the attitudes of the German Romantics and Lukács vis-à-vis the ancients: 'To believe in the Greeks is only another fashion of the age. People are rather fond of listening to declamations about the Greeks. But if someone were to come and say, here are some, then nobody is at home' (*PF* 56). For the German Romantics, who wavered between deep respect for the Greeks and Romans and equally deep dedication to a renewal of modern literature and culture, it was important to search for a way that modernity would subsume the ancients. To simply believe in the possibility of restoring ancient values was ridiculous, since there were no longer any ancient Greeks at home. Lukács has expanded on this aphorism to argue that, in modernity, there is no one at home at all. Modernity cannot subsume antiquity, for it cannot provide a resting place for anything at all.

As Lukács expounds in *The Theory of the Novel*, not only is modernity severed through temporal and historical difference from antiquity, it is also profoundly and irrevocably fractured from within. Philosophy originates from the modern necessity to grant meaning to the person lost in a world forsaken of meaning. This assertion might surprise the reader, for where is the birthplace of modern Western philosophy to be found other than in ancient Greece? Nonetheless, Lukács hastens to explain that there were no philosophers then and there because everyone was a philosopher, and meaning was immanent in the world. Upon asserting the necessity of philosophy in the modern world, Lukács specifically links it to literature as it bestows both form and content upon modern art. This inherent relationship between philosophy and literature operates on at least two levels: first, in its mimetic function literature reflects through both form and content the symptom of modernity, the split between the self and the world; second, it uses as its instrument of reflection the philosophical stance or tool of irony. Taken one step further, if there are no longer authoritative given forms, then literature in the genre of the novel becomes the space in which the individual can create meaning through form (Bernstein 96).

Irony and Modern Consciousness

Lukács doubtlessly owes much to the early Romantics in his conception of irony. He does not deny the possibility that an author might write without irony, a position he significantly describes as one of leaving no empty room between idea and reality to be filled by the writer's wisdom (*TN* 75). It is ironic writing that distinguishes the epic from the novel, for the epic writer merely makes recognizable the given meaning of the world, but the novelistic writer must reflect upon the world to find meaning (Krückeberg 72). Ironic writing is defined precisely as reflection, indeed reflection upon reflection, and this reflection becomes its content: 'His reflexion consists of giving form to what happens to the idea in real life, of describing the actual nature of this process and of evaluating and considering its reality' (*TN* 85). The allusion to Schlegel's image of the mirrors reflecting upon mirrors, multiplying reality through reflection, is an obvious subtext here (Derwin 26). For Lukács, the ironic content of literature consists of ironic reflection upon the sad fate of the idea in reality, which continues multiplying into ever more fractured images. Lukács also specifies what is implicit in Schlegel's writing on irony: the function of the narrator as a space of ironic reflection. That is to say, the author's reflection upon his own reflection upon the world expressed through his writing will become the stuff of another level of reflection as irony is taken to another level (*TN* 85). The narrative stuff, the story of the idea in the real world, must also be reflected upon, this time presumably through the form of the narrator (*Erzähler*). The narrator, conceived of as the reflection upon the story itself, occupies, then, the place between the idea and the world. She also occupies a dramatic moment in the narration, where reality will be viewed from many perspectives through the multiplying mirror effect of reflection (Krückeberg 73).

This understanding of irony clearly moves beyond a purely rhetorical conception of irony as saying what one does not mean toward the Romantic concept of irony as the reflection of a transcendent self upon the chaos of the world. Nonetheless, whereas Schlegel imagines a Romantic ironist who can create beauty and order from disorder, Lukács imagines an individual condemned to watch the tragic destiny of the idea when placed in action in the world. The twentieth-century theorist makes specific an aspect of the ironic self already implicit in Schlegel's imagery: the interior fragmentation of the self. It only follows that any self, subject to the mirroring effect of irony as it rises above one's self as well as the world, will appear in multiple personae. The modern writer's ironic stance, as seen by Lukács, involves two contradictory personages: that of a passive witness as well as an active creator. An important passage illuminates exactly how Lukács abstracts the concept of an internally divided subject from the notion of Romantic irony: 'The self-recognition and, with it, self-abolition of subjectivity was called irony by the first theoreticians of the novel, the aesthetic philosophers of early Romanticism' (*TN* 74).

The urgent need for irony in the novel responds to the danger that it may be written from a purely subjective viewpoint; subsequently, Lukács, like Schlegel, sees irony as a means of complementing subjectivity with objectivity. Judith Norman has demonstrated in Schlegel's thought how rising and reflexive irony is a critical act, allowing one to see the 'illusory status' of the object presented in art (141). When the self becomes the object of irony, the process of recognizing, destroying, and sublating the self that Lukács recognizes in Romantic irony serves as a means of seeking novelistic objectivity. Objectivity itself is the longed-for and never completely reached goal of the novelist, for it cannot be approached without the questioning of subjectivity that takes place in irony (Mészáros 52). Don Quixote, as the epitome of the abstract idealist type, suffers from nothing other than the lack of objectivity, the incapacity to experience distances as realities.

In Lukács's *The Theory of the Novel*, irony, from which Don Quixote does not suffer, is 'an act of form-making' (Cascardi, *The Subject of Modernity* 77). Lukács also recognizes that this dissolution of the self in irony, in spite of all the epistemological and creative advantages it offers, entails a negative aspect: the fragmentation of the self: 'As a formal constituent of the novel form this signifies an interior diversion of the normatively creative subject into a subjectivity as interiority, which opposes power complexes that are alien to it and which strives to imprint the contents of its longing upon the alien world, and a subjectivity which sees through the abstract and,therefore, limited nature of the mutually alien worlds of subject and object, understand these worlds by seeing their limitations as necessary conditions of their existence and, by thus seeing through them, allows the duality of the world to subsist' (*TN* 74–5). The writer, in order to create a novel, must be divided into two: protagonist and narrator. One subject understood as interiority confronts and interacts with the world; the other transcends the first in order to grasp the necessity and, indeed, the meaning of the world. The novel as a form may be understood, perhaps too simplistically, as a genre constituted of a central protagonist in conflict with reality and a narrator transcending this point of view to offer a more nuanced and complete vision of the interaction between the main character and the world.

Yet Lukács hastens to add that even the unity of vision offered by the second self, the narrator, is provisional. He explicitly states that the conflict between the subject and the object *cannot* be transcended through a Hegelian *Aufhebung*; to the contrary, the subject/object opposition must merely be recognized as necessary. Thus, the second self submits to another round of ironic reflection (*TN* 75). Lukács immediately follows his assertion of the necessity of ironizing the ironist by stating that 'this irony is the self-correction of fragility.'[11] As Lukács's use of a colon immediately following *Brüchigkeit* indicates, the word 'fragility' refers to an arabesque construction of abstractions in which inadequately construed relations could lead to misunderstandings and oversight, and in which everything can be seen from many sides, indeed as polar opposites. To paraphrase Lukács's description of the subsequent disordered order, the same things could be isolated or interconnected, important or unimportant, abstract or concrete, in bloom or in decay, causing pain or suffering injury. The point of view determines the object's meaning. The fragility that irony corrects pertains to interpretation, when one understands interpretation as the process of giving form and meaning. Irony corrects the vision of things in relation to each other by locating them in the novelistic world, and thus brings the writer closer to objectivity.

Whereas this situation is advantageous from the Romantic point of view because it allows the writer freedom to create, for Lukács such irony confines both the story and the storyteller to their respective fate (*Schicksal*). According to Lukács in 'On the Romantic Philosophy of Life. Novalis,' the German Romantics made poetry the centre of their existence because in literature everything takes on symbolic value, including the very individuals who lead their lives according to literature

(*SF* 49). An individual's fate is her place in a symbolic narrative. By extension, the narrator of a literary work must likewise look upon herself, just as she has looked upon the protagonist, and see her own inescapable destiny, her own bond to reality as well as her symbolic function. This liminal space of irony, defined according to fate rather than freedom, is more a crack or crevice trapping the writer and storyteller than an open point of floating or hovering. A deep paradox underlies Lukács's linking of irony and fate, since irony would normally seem to, at the very least, mock the power of destiny. What is the taking of an ironic persona other than an attempt to somehow undermine one's given identity? And yet the ironic splitting of the self corresponds by necessity (*als notwendig*) to the state of modern consciousness.

Consequently, imagery of cracking and splitting appears frequently in *The Theory of the Novel*, and is always associated with the modern situation. For example, Lukács refers to the seductive power of the ancient Greeks, whose example led modern individuals to 'forget again and again the irreparable cracks in the edifice of their world and tempted them to dream of new unities – unities which contradicted the world's new essence and were therefore always doomed to come to naught' (*TN* 37). Cracks are essential to modernity, and are recreated in the novel through irony, as Lukács indicates when he notes that the non-ironic writer leaves no 'empty space or distance' between reality and fiction that would be filled by the writer's reflection (*TN* 84). The split between the world and the idea, between the narrative and the narrator, is also repeated within the very self as the 'unfathomable chasm which lies within the subject himself' (*TN* 37).[12] Nonetheless, Lukács insists upon the paradoxical identification of this confined space of irony, which both restrains the subject from without and severs him from within, with the highest of freedoms possible in modernity: 'Irony, the self-surmounting of a subjectivity that has gone as far as it was possible to go, is the highest freedom that can be achieved in a world without God' (*TN* 93). One can imagine the writer climbing ever higher (or deeper, for in this image they are the same) into the crack between idea and reality, and thus nearing the point where they might converge. Indeed, Lukács holds forth the possibility of such a point understood, aptly enough, as form. Given that modernity is a godless world, immanent meaning or content cannot serve as the unifying factor between idea and reality. Hence, it must be created through literature.[13]

For the theorist irony serves as the negative mysticism of modernity, and the author is a mystic who, by taking the path of negation, will arrive at a meaningful state, that is to say, freedom via the paradoxical loss of freedom. The mystic represented for the young Lukács a figure of revolution, of the possibility of changing the world. In fact, mysticism would be another means of achieving what the young Lukács sought in his aesthetics, 'the triumph over subjectivity' (Gluck 160). Even what appears to the ironist to be knowledge must be understood as an expression of his own subjectivity, and thus eschewed as not-knowledge. Lukács states unequivocally that authorial irony is a form of negative mysticism for godless times: 'It is an attitude of *docta ignorantia* towards meaning ... and in it there is the deep certainty, expressible only by form-giving, that through not-desiring-to-know and not-being-able-to-know he has truly encountered, glimpsed and grasped the ultimate, true substance, the present, non-existent God' (*TN* 90). Following the *via negativa* of irony, the novelist refuses to delve for meaning by creating an internal system of ethics that destroys the interior self (Radnóti 64). Through this refusal of the self and of knowledge, the ironist arrives at the point where meaning exists – in the case of modernity, the place precisely where the absence of meaning presents itself. This absence of meaning, this purposeful refusal to know, establishes the modern novel's objectivity. If one follows Lukács's imagery through to its logical conclusion, this meaningful non-meaning occupies the ironic cleft between reality and idea in the novel.

The novel's objectivity, understood as its lack of meaning, could seem to represent a telling moment of aporia, in which Lukács runs up against a wall in his own pursuit of meaning. Nonetheless, if one accepts the theorist's first premise, that modernity is bereft of meaning, then the second premise follows logically. If there is no meaning in the modern world, then the only truth of the novel, understood as the genre of modernity, is that meaning is absent in the world. This is the novelist's certainty, the point where the idea and reality converge. The only certainty is the lack of certainty. Note the way Lukács characterized the existential situation of the German Romantics in his Novalis essay: the eighteenth century is 'dying' (*SF* 42); rationalism has 'dethroned all existing values' (*SF* 43); the French Revolution has devolved into terror with 'cruel and bloodthirsty logic' (*SF* 42); Germans are confined to 'revolution of the spirit' rather than real revolution (*SF* 43). Finally, 'when Kant appeared on the scene to destroy the proud armouries of both warring parties [rationalism and sentimentalism], there seemed to be nothing any longer capable of creating order in the ever-increasing mass of new knowledge or in the opaque depths below' (*SF* 43). Things have simply gone downhill in the century between Schlegel and Lukács as the alienation caused by modernity has been heightened by increased industrialization, the reification of human labour, and the alienation of the individual from cultural and social institutions. Lukács returns to the German Romantic era to encapsulate the relation between the novel and modernity: 'The novel is the form of the epoch of absolute sinfulness, as Fichte said, and it must remain the dominant form so long as the world is ruled by the same stars' (*TN* 152).

Lukács asserts that this truth can only be expressed through form. The Hegelian truth-bearing quality Lukács grants to form rests on its relation to the historical, or in Lukács's terms the historico-philosophical, milieu from which it arises.[14] Ancient epic verse differs from the modern novel not because they are particularly distinct genres, but because they spring from different worlds: 'The epic and the novel, these two major forms of great epic literature, differ from one another not by their authors' fundamental intentions but by the given historico-philosophical realities with which the authors were confronted' (*TN* 56). The epic and the novel express the form of extensive totality, that is to say, the external world in all its variety and multiplicity, as opposed to the tragedy that deals with the intensive totality of the individual (Parkinson 25). Lukács shares with Schlegel what Szondi has called the latter's 'anticlassicism,' that is to say, the preference to elevate the novel above tragedy as epic's counterpart since both epic and novel are the genres truly reflective of the society from which they spring.[15] For Lukács, authorial intention cedes before historicism, for the cultural moment in which the work is produced determines the genre's form. Thus he states: 'The novel is the epic of an age in which the extensive totality of life is no longer directly given, in which the immanence of meaning in life has become a problem, yet which still thinks in terms of totality' (*TN* 56). On one hand, the ancient epic arises from a culture in which total meaning exists, that is to say, in which societal values and individual action form a cohesive whole. On the other hand, modern culture yearns for such an integral relation precisely because it has been lost. The intellectual debt Lukács owes German Romanticism in his configuration of classical totality and modern fragmentation could not be more clearly expressed.

Don Quixote as a Critique of Modernity

The lack of concordance between social and individual values gives form to two types of novelistic heroes, the abstract idealist and the disillusioned romantic, both of whom are typically problematic, marginalized persons. Because the marginalized, whether a child, a woman, a criminal, or a crazy person, does not have a socially fixed place of meaning, their search for meaning opens up the space for novelistic representation of their relation to society (Bernstein 149). The prototype of the abstract idealist is Don Quixote, whose psyche suffers a maniacal narrowing as his insistence on ideals leads him into conflict with the world. The prototype of the disillusioned romantic is Frédéric, the protagonist of Flaubert's *A Sentimental Education*, whose interior life is so full that the world cannot possibly satisfy it. Only Goethe's Wilhelm Meister offers an alternative to these two empty prototypes, as the individual comes to terms with his or her surroundings (Arato and Breines 67–8). In the case of the abstract idealist such as Don Quixote, his incapacity to problematize his own interior life, and his subsequent inability to experience the outside world as a reality, give shape to the novel as the 'structure-determining problematic' (*TN* 97). The protagonist refuses to recognize the corrective of the outside world, and becomes ever more obsessed by his own interior world, which leads to a further round of increased conflict with the outer world (*TN* 89). It is his refusal to recognize the reality of the external world that marks Don Quixote as a representative 'narrow' soul (Parkinson 27). In fact, the inner world of the abstract idealist is static, closed, and completed or perfected in itself (*TN* 100). According to Lukács's language of forms, the soul of the abstract idealist is a circle in itself, echoing the circular totality of the ancient world. That is to say, the protagonist believes that his ideals are in complete accordance with reality, both ideal and real, and thus fails to distinguish an outside world independent of his own vision. This circle, unlike that of antiquity, does not correspond, however, in any way to society, and thus the relationship between the hero and his world, seen from outside, is that of a deep cleft rather than a circle.

The inner dynamic of the novel's action, given the hero's inability to see beyond the circle of his own soul, is one of intensifying difference and violence. The outside world carries sufficient resemblance to the abstract idealist's own interior world that he can continue to be confused even as he hits up against 'the real nature of the existing world, the self-maintaining, organic life that is alien to all ideas' (*TN* 100). The hero's determination turns grotesque as his fight continues and his personality hardens into rigidity, at the same time that the world, closed off from the hero's ideal, destroys it. In aesthetic terms, the structure based on the abstract-idealist protagonist fluctuates between the sublime and the grotesque; just as the hero becomes more rigid in the pursuit of the ideal, he may appear more sublime and the world more grotesque in its stubborn resistance (*TN* 104). Ultimately, the mixture of the sublime and the grotesque is mimetic in the case of the abstract idealist. As Lukács summarizes the existential dilemma, attaining meaning inwardly causes the loss of meaning, and thus the sublime becomes mad and monomaniacal (*TN* 100).[16] Such is the case of Don Quixote, whose inner moral code of knight-errantry condemns him to come into conflict with modernity, the consequence of which is falling into madness.

Cervantes' masterpiece *Don Quixote* enjoys pride of place in Lukács's theory of the novel precisely because it appears at the beginning of modernity, the moment of the great split between the totality of the medieval world and the fragmentation of our own. The theorist's description of this historical moment neatly expresses the bifurcating arabesque of his thought (indeed, his very sentence structure is that of a bifurcating arabesque). The Christian God of the Middle Ages abandons the world; humanity becomes lonely and homeless; the world is left to its own meaninglessness. At this point in time a crack opens that causes a whole array of ill effects. In just this moment does Cervantes write *Don Quixote*, a novel giving form to this collapse into anarchy. The parody of chivalric romances on which Cervantes bases his novel is historically and philosophically pertinent because the genre had lost its connection to meaning. Once the medieval value system based on a Christian God of providence that intervened in the exploits of heroes to ensure the doing of right disappeared, chivalric romance ceased to be a mimetic form.[17] The Middle Ages, unlike modernity, offered the individual an external scale of values by which to refine the self. Given the absence of God, Don Quixote turns himself into a sort of God (a demon in Lukács's parlance) who struggles to maintain the existence of medieval ideals in a thoroughly modern world.[18] Don Quixote (although probably in Lukács's rather simplified reading unaware of the problematics of his undertaking) is an ironic figure, as he takes it upon himself to fill in the gap between the ideal and the real. In this endeavour to fill in meaning, he becomes a representative of the fate of the novelist in general, who struggles to give form (and hence meaning) to modernity. Indeed (although Lukács does not seem to acknowledge the psychological development of the character), the Don Quixote of the second part of the novel is intensely aware of the futility and emptiness of his own position, to such an extent that it arguably leads to his death.

The novel *Don Quixote* also exemplifies the arabesque structure of the novel in which the discrete parts must have 'a strict compositional and architectural significance' in order to prop up the precarious whole constituted of heterogeneous elements woven together through opposition and juxtaposition (*TN* 76). Like Schlegel, Lukács sees the lightness of touch necessary for the balancing of such parts in Cervantes' successful inclusion of the short stories interpolated throughout *Don Quixote*. Moreover, *Don Quixote* as a novel treats of the opposition and juxtaposition of forms of life and thought. If we focus on the forms – internal, external, and interactive – that Lukács describes in *The Theory of the Novel*, we notice a pattern of opposition and bifurcation. Whereas the hero's soul may be self-contained, it inhabits a reality characterized by division, echoed in the verbs Lukács repeats in their many forms: divide, separate, split, etc. Division into polar opposites takes place on multiple levels: on the phenomenological level, perceived reality vs actual reality; on the psychological level, mania vs heroism; on the spiritual level, the demonic vs the divine; on the aesthetic level, the sublime vs the grotesque; on the ontological level, subject vs object. This constant bifurcation creates a layering of splits upon splits, a form that branches or shatters, depending on one's point of view. Juxtaposed to this multilayered splitting is the dynamic element of intensification through time. Temporal elaboration of the form creates a spiralling dynamic as the polar opposites exist in dialectical relation, feeding and fuelling each other in a potentially open-ended escalation. Lukács figures here none other than a form of arabesque; starting with a simple bifurcation, he multiplies and intensifies it through continued bifurcation into a progressively more complicated image. The novel form itself figures an arabesque.

Cervantes does not fare so well in Lukács's theory of the novel. Certainly, the cleft between idea and reality that Lukács considers the site of irony appears in *Don Quixote*; one has only to mention the series of narrators, including the unreliable Cide Hamete Benengeli, to invoke the notion of ironic reflection. Cervantes, who wrote the first novel of this novel time, would seem to be blessed with extraordinary ironic insight, and yet Lukács reduces this image of the literary artist to that of a befuddled scribbler. The theorist clearly recognizes the paradox of this portrait, but does nothing to undo or explain it. In one passage, he contrasts the naive writer Cervantes, unaware of the dangers of the novel form he invents, with another Cervantes, the intuitive visionary of the moment (*TN* 130). In fact, this dualistic characterization of Cervantes as the author of *Don Quixote* reveals how Lukács's contradictory image of the ironist as a negative mystic breaks down. Lukács writes that the author who wishes to sacrifice subjectivity and 'simply accepts, transform[ing] [one's self] into a purely receptive organ of the world, can partake of the grace of having the whole revealed to it' (*TN* 53). For Lukács, Cervantes embodies this *via negativa* in 'the leap Cervantes made when, becoming silent himself, he let the cosmic humor of *Don Quixote* become heard' (*TN* 54). He silences himself in order to let something else speak. In another passage, Lukács develops the idea that the author somehow refrains from expressing his own opinion by remarking that Cervantes, a believing Christian and naive patriot, gave form to the great problem of modernity, the transformation of heroism into grotesquerie and madness. Given this characterization of the author of *Don Quixote*, one must assume that he somehow did so intuitively, without the benefit of ironic reflection.

Clearly, Lukács has fallen into a logical trap here, for how could the first novel, instituting the genre of irony, be written by a naive author incapable of irony? Not only does the form of the novelistic hero's misadventures take the form of the arabesque, but also the form of the author's writing as activity. Upon asserting that irony, as the constituent form of the novel, involves a splitting of the writer's self into two, one that experiences the world as alien and the other that recognizes the necessity of the world's otherness, Lukács describes the text this second self creates in the novel as a complex of interdependent, mutually binding and bonding alterities: 'At the same time the creative subjectivity glimpses a unified world in the mutual relativity of elements essentially alien to one another, and gives form to this world' (*TN* 75). The novelist recognizes and preserves the duality of reality in which objects and subjects define each other through their bordering opposition, and yet creates a unified world. This unified image of opposing and alternating entities can only be an arabesque. Indeed, such a delicate and precarious union of oppositions characterizes *The Theory of the Novel* itself (Mészáros 58).

Lukács names the melancholy of historical time as the speaker of the truth about modernity contained in *Don Quixote*: 'The profound melancholy of the historical process, of the passing of time, speaks through this work, telling us that even a content and an attitude which are eternal must lose their meaning when their time is past: that time brushes aside even the eternal' (*TN* 104). This sentence is remarkable both for its paradoxical logic and its rhetorical complexity. Upon attributing to it melancholy, Lukács personifies historical time, distinguished from time in general (*Zeit*) by the term *Ablauf*, meaning quite literally the running away of history. Then, Lukács personifies history's attribute, melancholy, by writing that it speaks. One understands through synecdoche that it is history that speaks, an assertion that returns us to the allegorical figure of the classical muse of history, Clio. Curiously enough, personification of historical time leads to depersonalization of the novelistic author. Although Lukács does not invoke the muse, his use of personified abstractions to describe Cervantes' achievement functions as if the author of *Don Quixote* were a mere instrument of another force, in this case history. In other words, upon refusing to grant Cervantes the intellectual and moral insight necessary to write the first critique of modernity, he must grant it to someone or something else presumably working through the author. This is the contradiction contained in positing an ironic novelist who is also a mystic; in the case of *Don Quixote*, Lukács downplays Cervantes' capacity for active reflection on his era in favour of his supposed passivity as a voice for history.

That the novel is a critique of modernity Lukács does ascribe to Cervantes through recourse to the metaphor of the spring or well. According to the theorist, chivalric romances had lost their transcendent value and thus became trivial precisely because they were grounded in the Christian values of the other world. Once God abandoned this world, the form of the chivalric romance lost its relevance to this world. Cervantes' critique of this genre reveals how an old 'idea' becomes subjective and fanatical because it lacks 'any objective relationship' to reality (*TN* 103). The objective certainty of transcendent meaning fades away, and can only be grasped at through stubborn madness, as in the case of Don Quixote. Cervantes' novel, by giving form to its historical moment, leads us to a critique of modernity. And yet the speaking voice of this greatly critical novel is history itself. The author becomes the mouthpiece of his time, intellectually unaware of the ramifications of his masterpiece and himself subject to the blind religiosity and patriotism of his surroundings. In fact, Cervantes is not the only human to lose a capacity for agency before the sheer force of time or history. As Lukács explains toward the end of *The Theory of the Novel*, it is only time that unworks the seemingly epic and eternal repetition of the events in *Don Quixote* (*TN* 130). Even the protagonist Don Quixote cedes before the power of time.

Bergsonian Time and the Novel

If form is the stuff of the novel, then it is time that emerges in Lukács's *The Theory of the Novel* as its true author and main character. Lukács's stylistics in this work depends upon such a constant personification of abstract concepts that it is at times quite awkward to translate. The novel seeks form, the historical moment determines its form, form gives meaning – these are the active forces in his thoughts. Writers or poets rarely do anything but bear witness to the metamorphosis of form. The passivity of the literary author does not only come to the fore in his portrait of Cervantes. Writing of Flaubert's *A Sentimental Education*, Lukács notes that time alone can bring together into a whole all the fragments of the central character's experience. Indeed, only time can piece together any identity in the modern world, for its unhindered and uninterrupted flow serves as the one force capable of creating something homogeneous out of the pieces of modern existence (Corredor 86–8). Forms themselves depend on time for their being in a meaningless world in which they are no longer simply embedded. As Lukács describes time, it 'brings order into the chaos of men's lives and gives it the semblance of a spontaneously flowering, organic entity; characters having no apparent meaning appear, establish relations with one another, break them off, disappear again without any meaning having been revealed' (*TN* 125). The relationship between figures (understood by the term *Gestalten* as both abstract forms and literary characters) depends entirely on the passage of time; only time weaves their appearances and their disappearances, as well as their meetings and their leave-takings. History envisioned as the flow of time takes on the attribute of other classical figures (again unmentioned by Lukács), that of the Fates. Even the lives of men and women take on abstract meaning and form for Lukács. It is no accident that he used as the epigram for his essay 'On the Romantic Philosophy of Life' the following quote from Novalis: 'The life of a truly canonical person must be symbolic throughout' (*SF* 42).

It would be erroneous to understand the fateful workings of time in modernity according to an ancient or Christian notion of a link between worldly time and another realm. Modernity's godlessness creates a different form of time, understood by Lukács in *The Theory of the Novel* according to Bergson's concept of *durée*. This is the time of human experience, a present unlinked to external objective measures or to a providential ending, but shaped by past experience and directed toward future action (Bergson 4–10). Upon placing time within the locus of human perception, Bergson makes it constitutive of the subject's identity, her interaction with the world, and, indeed, her origins in the world. The French philosopher applies the scientific concept of evolution to the essence of human experience in order to compose a new vision of the human being, no longer differentiated from the rest of organic being as special, unique, and, indeed, godlike. When Bergson hypothesizes about human freedom and consciousness by remarking on the liberty of movement that enables protozoa and amoebae to move about their environment in search of the stuff of nourishment, he has radically decentred humanity from its traditional location between God and nature (118–27). In this sense, Bergson's thought is typical of what the Hungarian philosopher considers the godless nature of modernity. Humanity represents merely the culmination of one of nature's tendencies toward mobility and consciousness. Bergson's approach also radically destabilizes form, since it no longer resides in a realm somehow beyond nature but is, in fact, nature's doing. Accordingly, life itself is flux, and so what appears to be stable is actually constantly changing. Referring to the new insight made possible by photography, Bergson remarks: 'But in reality the body is changing form at every moment; or rather, there is no form, since form is immobile and the reality is movement. What is real is the continual *change* of form: *form is only a snapshot view of a transition*' (328). Time understood as change, endurance, and transition is the true stuff of reality.

Lukács takes from Bergson's notion of *durée* the concept of its constitutive relation to reality itself, while at the same time rejecting the French philosopher's fundamentally optimistic notion of an ever-evolving and progressing natural world. Indeed, the Hungarian's understanding of *durée* does not correspond to the benevolent flux imagined by Bergson (giving rise to such perfect adaptations as vision and consciousness culminating in humanity); to the contrary, it is a constant flux sweeping the individual up in its tidal force.[19] Lukács carefully distinguishes this modern time of *Dauern* from time in the classical epic, in which the passage of time has no effect on the substance of the characters, or from time in the mystical experience, in which the individual leaves the personal time of *durée* in order to achieve the timeless dimension of the cosmos (*TN* 122). To the contrary, modern time is stripped of any relation to another realm, and thus itself constitutes meaning, both in modern experience and in the genre that adheres to it, the novel. The debt to Bergson is clear, up to a point: time, once meaning is no longer immanent in this world, takes its place; essence, which previously had granted form to the world, recedes; and so time takes over its form-giving function. Nonetheless, Lukács's concept of time menaces rather than produces the individual human being.

Thus, time becomes the antagonist of every novelistic hero as it forms the external world's cold and rigid indifference to subjective experience. Obviously Don Quixote provides the perfect example since he struggles in and with modern times to re-enact the values and social systems of the medieval era. It is precisely this personification of time as the enemy of the individual that allows Lukács to write: 'In the novel, meaning is separated from life, and hence the essential from the temporal; we might almost say that the entire inner action of the novel is nothing but a struggle against the power of time' (*TN* 122). Once Lukács grants time such force, not only in the life of the individual but also as the form-giving dynamic of modernity, it follows that the individual becomes dehumanized. That is to say, when time is understood as an all-powerful antagonist, the human being becomes a mere piece of flotsam in the overwhelming force of its tidal wave. This seems to be Cervantes' fate, as Lukács figures him giving voice to history in a nonintellectual, if not unconscious, manner.

Irony, Humour, and Fragmentation

The diminishing of the author that we have seen in the case of Cervantes follows logically from Lukács's adaptation of the Romantic concept of irony. This twentieth-century theorist clearly takes Schlegel's notion of a hovering ironist to its logical conclusion, and there finds only fragmentation and impotence. The references to this hovering point of view are multiple, and are usually associated with the limitations of this perspective. For example, Lukács devotes a substantial passage to a meditation upon the humoristic author, of whom Cervantes would, of course, be exemplary. He begins by describing precisely the Schlegelian paradigm of the hovering viewpoint of the ironist in which the self attempts to transcend the objective world in a search for totality: 'However high the subject may rise above its objects and take them into its sovereign possession, they are still and always only isolated objects, whose sum never equals a real totality' (*TN* 53).

Lukács rejects Schlegel's optimistic hope that a new totality can be achieved in art through the sovereign gaze of the ironist. The human being can never rise to such a point that the perspective would encompass all of reality; indeed, this is the viewpoint of God, who has abandoned the world. Clearly, the artist who aspires to such a vision also aspires to take a divine form, in this case that of the completed circle

that would contain the entire cosmos. Lukács, again, rejects such a possibility out of hand: 'Even such a subject, for all its sublime humour,
remains an empirical one ... and the circle it draws round the world-
segment thus selected and set apart defines only the limits of the subject, not of a cosmos complete in itself' (*TN* 53). The border between
subject and object remains, and the subjective circle can only enclose
itself, because the human being cannot escape empirical existence. For
Bernstein, it is because Lukács does not recognize fundamental differences between his notion of historically caused social fragmentation
and Schlegel's notion of a transcendent conflict between the infinite
and the finite that the Hungarian's analysis of novelistic irony fails
(191). Although Schlegel already understood modernity to be implicit
in Romantic irony and fragmentation, he did tend to emphasis the
poetic capacity of both – poetic in the sense of *poeisis*, self- and world-
making.

Lukács, on the other hand, conceives of *poesis* in a much more div-
isive, even violent manner, and thus he turns from irony to humour. At
this point in *The Theory of the Novel*, Lukács discards the Romantic notion of irony's creative, productive capacity to insist upon the destructive drive of the humorist: 'The humorist's soul yearns for a more
genuine substantiality than life can offer; and so he smashes all the
forms and limits of life's fragile totality in order to reach the sole source
of life, the pure, world-dominating "I"' (*TN* 53). By invoking the destructive power of humour, Lukács moves away from Schlegel toward
Kierkegaard, who wrote that '[h]umor has a far more profound skepti-
cism than irony, because here the focus is on sinfulness, not on finitude'
(Kierkegaard 329). Fragmentation for Lukács embodies the absence of
meaning rather than a dialogue or aphorism. Unlike the Romantic iron-
ists, Lukács argues in *The Theory of the Novel* that humorists, through
their desire to achieve the substance and totality of life, paradoxically
break down its substance and totality. This darker perspective on humour fixates on the subsequent destruction wrought on the subject itself: 'But as the objective world breaks down, so the subject, too,
becomes a fragment; only the "I" continues to exist, but its existence is
then lost in the insubstantiality of its self-created world of ruins. Such
subjectivity wants to give form to everything, and precisely for this reason succeeds only in mirroring a segment of the world' (*TN* 53).

The humorist, by breaking the world to which he belongs, also fragments the self. Schlegel himself hinted at this fragmentation, and yet
always insisted on the subject's power to transcend and create from this

fragmentation. Indeed, the fragment as a form was for Schlegel both a way to mirror modernity's fragmentation and transcend it. As he remarked in Athenaeum Fragment 206: 'A fragment, like a miniature work of art, has to be entirely isolated from the surrounding world and be complete in itself like a porcupine' (*PF* 45). For Schlegel, the work of art could spread its spines like the porcupine and establish its autonomy from the world's fragmentation, being itself a whole. In this sense, the arabesque serves as an alternative form of system, one capable of embracing contradiction and incongruity. Lukács, although he seeks such totality in form, can allow the ironic or humorous writer no such out, for the author is as much a part of the fragmented world of modernity as the literary object. The Hungarian theorist, unlike the German Romantic, insists on the destructive power of humour, and limits the productivity of irony to a moment of enlightenment experienced only by the novelistic hero (Bernstein 162, 205).

By insisting on the impossibility of authorial transcendence, Lukács needs to assume an essentially passive writer, subject to the waves of time. Indeed, the only writer to whom he grants any active transcendence is Dostoevsky, who, according to Lukács, writes a new genre belonging to a new time. The aporia of his theory of the novel is to be found precisely in the concept of agency. Having denied it to the authors of novels as mere flotsam in time, he nonetheless seems to assert the noble agency of novelistic protagonists through their appropriation of lived time, *durée*. Here Lukács turns once again to Bergson, who highlights the role of memory in the subjective experience of time: 'The cerebral mechanism is arranged just so as to drive back into the unconscious almost the whole of this past [experienced by the individual], and to admit beyond the threshold only that which can cast light on the present situation or further the action now being prepared – in short, only that which can give *useful* work' (Bergson 7). Thus, memory accommodates the past to the present, allowing the individual to use the past experience in the interest of the present. Memory, as a means to mediate *durée* and make it a tool, also inheres to the possibility of action, and thus links to the future. As Bergson notes, 'The more duration marks the living being with its imprint, the more obviously the organism differs from a mere mechanism, over which duration glides without penetrating' (42). That is to say, the more the individual enjoys consciousness, understood by Bergson as the capacity for movement, the more he or she bears time as meaning, both through memory of the past and intention or plans for the future.

The Novelistic Hero's Struggle for Meaning

Lukács models novelistic heroes according to this possibility for consciousness and action mediated through memory and hope implicit in Bergson's thought. These heroes, too, are subject to the flow of time, figured again as the bearer of the novel's elevated, epic poetry (*TN* 123–4). Unlike the novelistic author, as exemplified in the naive Cervantes, the novelistic protagonists, particularly those who are disillusioned Romantics, wage a virile struggle against this inexorable flow of time by creating meaning from the direction of its flow through memory and hope.[20] Unlike Bergson, however, Lukács sees no meaning in *durée*, at least in its modern variety, except that created by the individual. Novelistic heroes are 'problematic' because they are forced to seek themselves in a world that has no place or meaning for them (Parkinson 26). Through their mixture of resignation and courage, these heroes have access to 'experiences of time which are authentically epic because they give rise to action and stem from action: the experiences of hope and memory; experiences of time which are victories over time: a synoptic vision of time as solidified unity *ante rem* and its synoptic comprehension *post rem*' (*TN* 124). Although epic time cannot be simply recuperated, reflection grants the individual 'the form-giving sense of *comprehending a meaning*,' and thus provides the closest approximation possible to essence in a God-forsaken world. Naiveté exists within the moment (*in re*), that is to say, when the individual is subject to time, whereas reflexivity exists somehow outside the moment, either before or after it (*ante rem, post rem*). In this manner Lukács imagines irony not as transcending its spatial relation to the world, as a sort of hovering above it, but rather as escaping time. This moment in which time is transcended is denied to Cervantes, the author, precisely because he must somehow speak for history, or let history speak through him. To whom, then, do these experiences belong? Apparently, they belong to the novelistic heroes, who *give form* to experience through memory and hope and thus *seize meaning* from a meaningless world. This meaning-giving activity is epic in that it attempts to re-establish a meaningful relation between the self and the world.

Lukács posits as the best example of this experience of time Flaubert's *A Sentimental Education*, in which the lack of composition and integration most aptly reflects the broken nature of modernity. The main character remains incomplete in the sense that the author does not try to focus on his interior world or make him the absolute centre of the action. Mimesis resides, then, in the lack of authorial intervention to form meaning from the shards of experience, for reality is shattered into separate shards, hard, broken, and isolated (*TN* 124). Epic objectivity depends on the disappearance of the author, who merely copies modernity's fragmentation. Anna Bostock, in her translation of these crucial paragraphs, has included references to 'us,' a first-person plural, that approaches meaning and before whom form appears. Nonetheless, Lukács's German is devoid of any such pronouns. Experiences 'near,' and forms 'stand' – the personification of modernity is so complete that humanity, as both author and reader, cedes into passivity. The only human figures that act are the literary characters, mere simulacra of human beings. Moreover, positivity, the capacity to actually build or create something, belongs only to time: 'This victory is rendered possible by time' (*TN* 125).

Time in modernity seems to reoccupy the position abandoned by God; indeed, Lukács describes it as something alive and dramatic, existing for itself and creating an organic continuum. The only force that could somehow weigh in against this great antagonist would be one that could take it on its own terms, memory personified in the temporal figure of the moment (*Augenblick*). Whereas hope and memory attempt to grasp the future and the past, the moment overcomes the great unidirectional flood of time understood as *durée*: 'Duration advances upon that instant and passes on, but the wealth of duration which the instant momentarily dams and holds still in a flash of conscious contemplation is such that it enriches even what is over and done with' (*TN* 126). The moment takes on the attributes of Romantic irony; that is to say, from the chaos that is the ever-surging wave of time, it snatches meaning, envelops and encompasses the richness of experience, and achieves a contemplative stance. The very word *Augenblick*, literally meaning the blink of an eye, returns us through metonomy to the notion of a hovering, contemplating subject. Accordingly, Lukács's notion of *Augenblick* links to Schlegel's notion of *Witz*, the Romantic hovering of the ironist (Kruse-Fischer 27). But, unlike Schlegel, Lukács renders the individual passive. Just as in the case of the author who becomes a mouthpiece for history, the reflective individual, presumably the novelistic hero, cedes agency to the moment, for which he is the flicker of an eye.

Paradoxically, there is value in passivity. That is to say, in the moment when the individual recognizes defeat, then appears the source of life's fullness: 'What is depicted is the total absence of any fulfilment of meaning, yet the work attains the rich and rounded fullness of a true totality of life' (*TN* 126). Full absence (in the German text *völlige Abwesenheit*) – this is the paradoxical essence of modernity for Lukács, the meaningless plethora of being swept along by time. The disillusioned Romantic hero forms from this full absence of life experience a meaning instilled in the autobiographical impulse to order and explain one's existence. The heroic contemplative deed, complete with the recognition of failed action in the outside world, depends on memory. Memory itself serves to mediate the discrepancy between the object that resists the subject and the subject's ideal image of the object. That is to say, the individual reflects upon past experience, and by so doing is able to incorporate both the resistant object of desire and his or her own desires toward it into the life story. Memory does so not through a transcendence or sublation of the objective reality into subjective desire, but rather by maintaining what Lukács calls the 'resolving of its form-conditional dissonances,' in other words, by letting be the dissonances that reside in the form itself (*TN* 128). Schlegel's concept of the novel's multiplicity changes, in Lukács's analysis, into the notion that the novel is capable of encompassing both subjective and objective reality.

For Lukács, heterogeneity abandons subjectivity to reside only on the side of objectivity. That is to say, the protagonist must struggle to remain one, whereas the modern world is condemned to fragmented multiplicity. Ironically (in the fullest sense of the term), memory offers a means of homecoming for the homeless modern individual by granting meaning to the modern experience of the outside world's resistance to interior desires, ideals, and goals: 'That is why the unity of the personality and the world – a unity which is dimly sensed through memory, yet which once was part of our lived experience – that is why this unity in its subjectively constitutive, objectively reflexive essence is the most profound and authentic means of accomplishing the totality required by the novel form' (*TN* 128). Memory joins the past to the future while the present is granted a paradoxical permanence in the form of the novel, and thus offers a modern sort of home to the individual. But memory, as understood by Lukács in *The Theory of the Novel*, is only individual and never communal. The novel, as the genre asserting a life story through memory and hope, 'overcomes its "bad" infinity [that is to say, the discrete, heterogeneous infinity of modernity it reflects] by recourse to the biographical form' (*TN* 81). The reference to 'bad infinity' is Lukács's clearest debt to Hegel, who associated it with the Romantic notion of a limitless and never-ending time as opposed to his own notion of a closed, circular time (Jay 56). The novelistic hero, at the end of his story, finds out that 'a mere glimpse of meaning is the highest that life has to offer, and that this glimpse is the only thing worth the commitment of an entire life, the only thing by which the struggle will have been justified' (*TN* 80). The German word for glimpse, *Erblick*, reminds us of the transformation of the Romantic hovering gaze into this fleeting moment of recognition (*Augenblick*).[21] The structure of the novel, as conceived by Lukács, depends, paradoxically enough, on the fleeting moment of ironic recognition of limited meaning.

The Emptying of the Arabesque

This chronotope, or time/form, of the novel stretches the imagination. When viewed in terms of the irremediable separation of the modern individual from society, or the absence of transcendent values in the modern world, Lukács's theory of the novel is easily comprehensible. Yet after thorough analysis of his figuring of the form and time constitutive of the novel, we return to his own concise, but admittedly paradoxical, description of the genre's structure: 'The composition of the novel is the paradoxical fusion of heterogeneous and discrete components into an organic whole which is then abolished over and over again' (*TN* 84). Nonetheless, the figure can be pictured if we imagine a form transforming through time; this is, after all, the concept of an arabesque emerging in time. The discrete, heterogeneous parts adhere to one another through the dynamism of opposition and juxtaposition: the individual against the world, the subjective against the objective, time understood as impersonal duration against time understood as the experienced moment. The formal difference between Schlegel's arabesque notion of the novel and Lukács's is precisely the latter's introduction of time into the form as a constituent element. The whorls and tensions of the arabesque appear and disappear in time, constituting and reconstituting the ever-changing arabesque just as the pieces of a kaleidoscope arrange and re-arrange themselves into ever new totalities. Schlegel's novel transcends time, somehow subsuming the past model of the Greek and the coming perfection of poetry in its almost divine present; Lukács's novel is of time, flowing with historical *durée* as its literary formal expression while at the same time resisting it through the remembered life story of the protagonist.

The temporal arabesque of Lukács's theory of the novel eliminates the possibility of transcendence present in Schlegel's more optimistic thought. According to Schlegel, the novelistic author hovers above the work and the world in a semi-divine state of irony; according to Lukács, the novelistic author disappears into time as its mere mouthpiece, only to cede her ironic position to the protagonist. This fundamental difference is easily explained when one takes into account the two theorists' respective perspectives on the nature of reality in modernity: for Schlegel, abundance in the world, albeit chaotic, is still present, whereas for Lukács, the world is now empty. For Schlegel, the thinking follows thus: God is still in the modern world, even though it appears chaotic; the author can achieve a god-like view of this chaos through irony, thus managing to reconcile differences and order the chaos; the novel is the expression of the author's ordering of the world. For Lukács, the thinking follows thus: God has abandoned the world; the author cannot take the position of God and is thus subjugated to time; given the abandonment of the world by God and the subsequent impotence of the author, the novel is the expression of the protagonist's attempt at ordering the world. According to Schlegel, then, the model of the ironic author offers an example to the individual attempting to overcome the fragmentation of the modern world; subsequently, since the author can order chaos through art, there is hope for productive transformation, understood as aesthetic and moral revolution, in the modern world. According to Lukács, the author cannot offer a model of agency, since she is a mere mouthpiece for history; the only model left is that of the novelistic hero bravely fighting against modernity, whose triumph is reduced to a brief glimpse of meaning in all the meaningless battles of a lifetime.

The two theories of the novel form an arabesque of their own, as the ideas of irony, modernity, and generic complexity dovetail and diverge between them. Even the novelistic hero of Lukács's thought, the problematic individual, crosses between the two. But the oppositions in the arabesque of their interrelation can be seen most clearly according to their different interpretations of *Don Quixote*. For Schlegel, the author Cervantes, who achieves a hovering, ironic perspective on his own work and his society, is the hero; for Lukács, Cervantes is a mere scribbler who naively envisions the problem of modernity. To the contrary, for the latter theorist, Don Quixote is the hero, embodying one way of fighting against the intransigent lack of transcendent meaning in the modern world. Schlegel never loses sight of the would-be knight errant's madness, and always sees it in juxtaposition to Sancho Panza's stupidity. Together, the two characters form an arabesque dialogue of modernity. In *The Theory of the Novel* Lukács never mentions Sancho, an interpretive omission forced by his own theory that can be understood in the light of Lukács's subsequent turn to Marxism.

System and Misreading

Bernstein argues that the paradoxes of *The Theory of the Novel* can only be made to make sense by taking into account Lukács's later Marxist thought. In 1914 Lukács sees that Romantic irony 'becomes the trope of the alienated man whose consciousness of his predicament deprives him of the ability to act' (Bernstein 213). As has been shown, the young Lukács substitutes in the place of human agency time understood as *durée*, but the personification of time is ultimately yet another absence. For Bernstein, Lukács finds in Marxism the collective subject, the proletariat, who will fill this gap (262). Following this logic, he argues that Lukács's *History and Class Consciousness* (1922) supplies a new narrative context for the story of the novel: capitalist reification. Drawing on Marx's characterization of the commodity as a means by which to objectify human labour, Lukács builds his notion of the reified mind of the capitalist era. This phenomenon starts in the mystification of human labour into capital: 'man in capitalist society confronts a reality "made" by himself (as a class) which appears to him to be a natural phenomenon alien to himself; he is wholly at the mercy of its "laws', his activity is confined to the exploitation of the inexorable fulfilment of certain individual laws for his own (egoistic) interests' (*History and Class Consciousness* 135). The subjective experience of the 'natural law' that capitalism appears to be results in the internalization of the system of exchange and the loss of agency: 'But even while "acting" he remains, in the nature of the case, the object and not the subject of events.'

Thus the Kantian antinomies that structure theories of the novel such as Schlegel's (the finite and the infinite, the noumenal and the phenomenal) are bourgeois, arising from the historical material circumstances of capitalism. Transcendental thought seeks to overcome the shattered self and society of the reified mind in its demand for rational, universal system. But for the Marxist Lukács, this system is perforce empty: 'For a system in the sense given to it by rationalism – and any other system would be self-contradictory – can bear no meaning other than that of a co-ordination, or rather a supra- and subordination of the various partial systems of forms (and within these, of the individual forms)' (117). The drive for form serves a mystifying end, to give the appearance of necessary relations within a totalizing system that will overcome the stultifying split between individual and society. The individual, however, is trapped in the system and the forms, and thus unable to operate any sort of 'real' synthesis of the fragments of modernity: 'The freedom (of the subject) is neither able to overcome the sensuous necessity of the system of knowledge and the soullessness of the fatalistically conceived laws of nature, nor is it able to give them any meaning' (134). In 1922 Lukács reprises, critiques, and undoes the forms he has used to construct his novelistics. The split between individual and society that shapes modernity is now understood as the result of commodity reification. The arabesque devolves into the empty, formalist system of transcendental thought. Irony is the mere illusion of freedom as the individual remains trapped in the system. Time, the protagonist of *The Theory of the Novel*, is bifurcated into the rationalized, quantifiable time of labour (a time that becomes space; 90) and the historic tendency of the emerging proletariat. In this sense, the proletariat replaces time as the true agent of Lukács's revised narrative of modernity.

If there is in this work a revision to Lukács's novelistics, it depends on replacing *Don Quixote* as the first modern novel with *Robinson Crusoe*. The first movement toward the modern away from the medieval is the emergence of the bourgeois belief that all social problems are caused by human activity. The second step is the emergence of 'the individual isolated consciousness à la Robinson Crusoe' (135). The third step is that, by isolating the individual, the possibility of social action is obviated. Bernstein extrapolates from this new narrative of reified mind to postulate that 'in the same way as modern philosophy discovers the self as the ground of knowledge and right action, so the novel discovers the self as the primordial bearer of intelligibility in our understanding of experience' (246). Robinson Crusoe as the problematic individual of the modern novel enacts the charade of self-invention, of societal founding, and of the master/slave dialectic, for 'all the models have disappeared' (155). For this reason, Bernstein rejects *Don Quixote* as a modern novel, in which he makes the highly questionable claim that there exists a 'superabundance of models,' although no longer any usable ones. Bernstein's misreading of Cervantes' novel emerges in his incorrect assertion that Don Quixote's 'hapless comedy derives from his innocent assumption that all the old models are in working order.' To the contrary, as is shown in chapter 1, there is nothing innocent about Don Quixote's wilful representation of a way of life he fully knew to be anachronous and out of step with his own times.

Perhaps there is a cautionary lesson in Bernstein's misreading of *Don Quixote*, just as there is in Lukács's misreading. For both thinkers, the theoretical apparatus with which they are working – in other words, their system – forces the literary text to be altered to such an extent that indisputable elements of the novel are misunderstood or erased. In Bernstein, this results in the blindness to Don Quixote's lack of innocence, the dilemma of living a consciously anachronistic life that shapes not only his physical confrontations with his surroundings, but also his growing doubts and misgivings. In part II of *Don Quixote*, these doubts are played out in the relationship of the knight errant and his squire. Don Quixote needs Sancho to believe in and confirm his version of reality, so he pleads with the peasant to believe in his vision of damsels and knights errant in the Cave of Montesinos just as he promises, somewhat maliciously, to believe in Sancho's fantastic visions on the wooden horse Clavileño. Moreover, Sancho needs for Don Quixote to believe in knight-errantry, and it is he who pleads with his dying master not to give up his way of life – or to replace it with that of becoming a poetic shepherd.

In Lukács, the misreading is even more egregious, for he erases from the novel none other than Sancho Panza. To focus on the interaction of Don Quixote and Sancho would be to posit the possibility of companionship between individuals in modernity, in spite of their marginalization from society. This Lukács cannot seem to imagine, for it would undermine his insistence on the absolute loneliness of the individual and the impossibility of any meaning in sociable companionship. Subsequently, Lukács's interpretation of *Don Quixote*, because of the centrality of the novel's place in his theory, remains sterile.[22] The gentle humour that arises from the knight errant's and squire's conversation, the *Scherz* to which Schlegel so often refers, disappears in the face of Lukács's insistence on the cruel humour of the lone madman's confrontation with reality. The arabesque of their conversation, so full of delight for Schlegel, disappears before the cold, empty arabesquing of the self through time or history in Lukács's reading of both *Don Quixote* and the genre of the novel.

4 Ideas and Forms: Hermann Cohen's Novelistics

Hermann Cohen, a neo-Kantian professor of philosophy from the University of Marburg, serves as the pivotal figure of this history of the theories of *Don Quixote* and the modern novel. He is the mentor with whom Ortega wrestles, the standard-bearer of the philosophical idealism that Lukács eventually and definitively rejects, and the figure of neo-Kantianism that beckons to Bakhtin. Although his name has been forgotten, Cohen's work left a legacy to the field of literary theory, specifically the theory of the novel. Unlike the field of philosophy, where his ideas have been erased, Cohen's notion of the modern novel – although unacknowledged – continues to fashion much conventional wisdom about the genre. Even setting aside the influence upon his student Ernst Cassirer, Cohen's impact can be found among the young men and women who flocked to Marburg from across Europe at the turn of the century to study with him, and who in turn returned to their homelands with his books and ideas. Ortega's and Bakhtin's intellectual indebtedness to Cohen is now widely accepted among scholars. The young Spaniard attended his lectures at Marburg and enjoyed his tutelage. The young Russian knew of Cohen's thought through the influence of his friend Matvei Isaevich Kagan.[1] Bakhtin's and Ortega's theories of the novel can be legitimately viewed as responses to Cohen's aesthetic ideas. Indeed, one cannot understand either's concept of the modernity of the novel without taking into account their common teacher's ethical as well as historical placement of the literary genre. To the contrary, Cohen seems to have presented a negative influence on Lukács. Although he did not personally study with Cohen, Lukács presents in *The Theory of the Novel* a conception of modernity, irony, human will, and the novel that constitutes if not an outright rejection of the older scholar's more hopeful conception of the novelistic genre, at the very least a darker, pessimistic version of the neo-Kantian's belief in free will and virtue.

An Introduction to Cohen's Life and Work

At the beginning of the twentieth century, Hermann Cohen and his school represented for many the most progressive and the most modern tendencies in philosophy. In his obituary of Cohen, Bakhtin's friend Matvei Isaevich Kagan sums up the philosopher's appeal to young European intellectuals: he counteracted the pessimism of Schopenhauer and the individualism of Nietzsche as well as philosophy's isolation from the sciences (195). Since Cohen was a systematist, it is necessary to deal with salient points from his logics and his ethics in order to understand his aesthetics as well as his reading of *Don Quixote*. In general histories of philosophy, he is named as a neo-Kantian who explicated Kant's major works and devoted himself to the philosophical examination of the natural sciences, although this description only covers the first part of his philosophical career. In histories of Judaism, he is known for his final period, when he tried to reconcile philosophy and religious faith. Cohen's publishing history divides into three stages: (1) revision of Kant's critical system (1871–89); (2) founding of his own system (1902–12); and (3) renewed engagement with Judaism and subsequent revision of his own system (1915–19) (Orringer, *Hermann Cohen* 15). Although Cohen is often considered an idealist, it is equally appropriate to consider him a critical idealist, or just a critical philosopher. His goal was to critique knowledge through an analysis of the knowing or transcendent subject (not to be confused with the concrete, individual subject) and his relation to the material world. Cohen developed his critical philosophy or idealism in conscious response to two powerful, threatening tendencies of his time: materialistic explanations for social phenomena based on reductionist economic or biological analyses, and burgeoning religious and ethnic fundamentalisms (Holzhey, 'Hermann Cohen' 25–6). Cohen associated representation with materialistic accounts of the sensing subject (what he called the psychological subject), and tended to reject accounts of sensorial perception as uncritical (Poma, *The Critical Philosophy of Hermann Cohen* 63). Instead, he focused on the judging subject, in whom the mind brings internal concepts and categories to sensorial perception. It is judgment that creates categories of knowledge, and unifies the dialectical movement of separation and unification in thought (Holzhey, *Cohen und Natorp* 1:100–1).

Cohen's work of the second period has had the most influence on the sphere of culture and the arts. This is the time when Cohen presided as a teacher of almost mythical proportions over his circle of students at Marburg. Take, for example, Boris Pasternak's assessment of Cohen and the Marburg School as completely original: 'Whereas current philosophy speaks of what this or that writer thinks and formal logic teaches us how to reason at the baker's so as to be sure of getting the correct change, what interested the Marburg School was what was at the white-hot springs, the very sources of world discoveries' (192). As a teacher, Cohen exercised an almost priestly influence on his students, who flocked to Marburg from all corners of the world and created their own environment of cosmopolitan, intellectual headiness (Woland xii).

Given his crowd of disciples and professional prestige, it is surprising that Cohen was forgotten. Several factors combined to obscure his name in the history of philosophy. The course of German history condemned the Jewish philosopher to official oblivion during the Nazi period. Cohen became the lightening rod for the disdain aimed at the entire school of neo-Kantianism as the new generation of the 1920s fought to define itself against their predecessors (Gordon 31–4). Martin Heidegger was only the most vocal of the academic critics who unfairly glossed over and simplified Cohen's thought.[2] In this case, one suspects several motives: latent anti-Semitism as evidenced by Heidegger's eventual collaboration with Nazism; and his need to assert the primacy of his metaphysics over the unrelenting critical idealism of Cohen. Nonetheless, even the briefest perusal of the Marburg scholar's writings reveals his centrality to twentieth-century phenomenology as well as ethics. Peter Eli Gordon sums up the ironic fate of neo-Kantianism: 'to a striking degree, the memory of neo-Kantianism is a memory constructed by a *knowledgeable* opposition, students who were themselves schooled in the philosophy they then set about dismantling' (31–2). Jacques Derrida, too, reminds us that later philosophers defined themselves against the straw figure of Cohen. Heidegger and Husserl had to work in the context of Cohen's thought 'against neo-Kantianism and in another relation to Kant' (140).

Cohen became a controversial figure for Jewish intellectuals following the Second World War and the Holocaust. Cohen was born in 1842 in Cospig, Germany, and died in 1918; subsequently, 'he remained in spirit and outlook a child of the nineteenth century' (Jospe 464). The son of a cantor, he left his orthodox home to pursue philosophy in the German university system. Cohen never denied his religious heritage, and has been remembered largely for his purposeful, although often highly generalized, incorporation of Jewish concepts into his systems of ethics and jurisprudence (Schwarzschild, 'Introduction' viii–ix). He consistently defended the absolute monotheism of Judaism as spiritually, ethically, and logically superior to the panentheistic tendencies of Christianity. Nonetheless, he believed that the Jewish people should fully participate in a modern Germany. In 1880, when the historian Heinrich von Treitschke attacked the Jewish people as a foreign tribe, Cohen publicly defended his faith as akin to German Protestantism insofar as it shared with the German tradition the ideals of rationality, ethical behaviour, and humanistic values (Jospe 462–3). Moreover, he saw the Jewish messianic mission as the atonement of all humanity (Mittleman 41). It was this belief that the Jewish people should work for the universal good that conditioned his stance against Zionism. Undoubtedly, the oblivion into which Cohen's thought fell arose from the antipathy both his claimed heritages felt toward his attempt to reconcile the Jewish and neoclassical German intellectual traditions.

Scholars in a number of academic fields have begun to reassert Cohen's important relationship, often dialectical, to subsequent leading thinkers. In the realm of philosophy, Cohen's drive to examine thoroughly how the faculties of the mind (reason and will among them) condition scientific investigation has gained renewed importance (Patton 109–18). In an age when science appears in the popular imagination as 'common sensical' and self-explanatory, Cohen's critique of empiricism and psychologism touches upon problems as important for our time as for his (Ringer 306–15). His concept of freedom offers a possible Kantian response to naturalistic notions of morality that justify behaviour as 'natural' or 'native' to the human species (Coble 181–97). In the realm of theology, Cohen's influence on Karl Barth has been studied (Fisher, Lyden). Martin Buber's ethics of the I-Thou relationship seems to be even more heavily shaped by Cohen, in spite of the former's rejection of any such influence. Franz Rosenzweig did acknowledge Cohen's influence, taking from his logics the principle of origin or beginning (Funkenstein 285). Contemporary Jewish theologians have focused on issues in Cohen's work such as the relation between joy, suffering, and duty (Kaplan). In the field of law, his notion of the juridical person and his positing of jurisprudence as the *factum* of ethics have invited attention as of late.[3]

Kant and the Ethical Implications of Aesthetics

Cohen's attempt to systematize philosophy according to the disciplines of epistemology, ethics, and aesthetics posits a rethinking of Kant.

Cohen's intellectual (and in Ortega's case, personal) influence was such that it was impossible to read Kant in the second decade of the twentieth century except through or against Cohen. Aesthetics falls for Kant under the aegis of judgment, 'the faculty of thinking the particular as contained under the universal' (*Critique of Judgement* 15). Therefore, the study of aesthetics in its consideration of pleasure and pain offers the bridge between the particular faculties of the subject's desire, those linked to freedom, and the universal faculties of cognition, linked to nature. Without this link, there is a 'great gulf that separates the supersensible from phenomena' (32). The faculty of understanding, that which allows us to know nature as phenomena, implies but does not determine that phenomena are also supersensible, that is to say, beings in and of themselves. The morally necessary vision of others as beings in themselves (rather than ends to be used) depends then not on reason, but on the faculty of judgment. The development of individual taste through aesthetic experience lays the foundation for moral judgment by mediating between the particular and the universal, or in ethical terms between the subject in his/her situation and the norm of the good.

In other words, the aesthetic experience provides a template for morality; as Kant states, the beautiful is the symbol of the good. Perhaps most importantly, it offers a means by which to train the individual in the recognition of universal principles. That is to say, individual taste, ranging the gamut of human diversity, should be educated. The essence of the aesthetic experience, in other words, its basis in unique individual experience and sentiment, serves, albeit paradoxically, the purpose of educating moral judgment, through which the individual should be able to discern the common good. Kant provides the following reasons to explain the link between the assessment of the beautiful and the judgment of the good, all based on the supposition that judgment matures through aesthetic experience. First, the pleasure aroused in the subject by the beautiful is disinterested, and thus related to the disinterested pleasure aroused by the morally good. Secondly, the freedom of the imagination stirred in contemplating the beautiful corresponds to the law of understanding harmony; thus, it exercises in moral judgment the 'freedom of the will thought as the harmony of the latter with itself, according to universal laws of reason' (199). Finally, the subjective and the universal appear to merge as individual taste represents itself as 'valid for every man, though not recognizable through any universal concept,' just as morality must appear valid for both the individual and all humankind, and thus universal. Aesthetic experience provides the ground for the inculcation of morality in the individual by training her to conform freely to a sense of the universal. Ethical training dovetails with aesthetic training because the aesthetic object provides a site where the individual learns to value something, not according to any monetary or instrumental value, but rather according to its intrinsic worth. The valorization of art corresponds to the ethical valorization of other human beings, according to basic worth or dignity (*Würde*). Finally and most importantly, judgment enables the individual to fulfil the Kantian moral imperative to treat others as ends and not as means (Bowie 87–8).

Kant did not pursue any further explanation for his rather outrageous claim for the centrality of the aesthetic experience to the development of morality, nor did Friedrich Schlegel feel any need to elucidate such a connection. The young Friedrich's alternately appreciative and rebellious reception of Kant's philosophy indicates beyond a doubt that he could only conceive of artistic freedom in response to the latter's ethical formulation of the concept. Indeed, Schlegel locates humankind itself in the mediating space of the aesthetic, between the phenomenal and the noumenal, when he quips in *Idea* 28 that '[t]he human being is nature's creative backwards glance upon itself.'[4] Whereas Schlegel's poetics of the novel hints at moral concerns in the formulation of the concepts of freedom, creativity, and the ordering of modern chaos, the young man failed to develop explicitly the relation between literature and ethics. Despite Cohen's rather sharp rejection of Romanticism (likely grounded in the nationalistic and ethnocentric perversions to which it was eventually subjected), it is he who will most clearly explore the relation between the Kantian categorical imperative and the Romantic aesthetic imperative, through an ethics that emphasizes the moral necessity of an eternal, and necessarily incomplete, striving to understand the other.

The Innovations of Cohen's Epistemology

Cohen undertook not only a critique of Kant's theory of reason, understanding, and judgment, but also an exposition of his own systematic conceptualization of the three faculties in three major works: *The Logic of Pure Knowledge* (*Logik der reinen Erkenntnis* 1902, 1914), *Ethics of Pure Will* (*Ethik des reinen Willens* 1904, 1907), and *Aesthetics of Pure Feeling* (Ästhetik des reinen Gefühls 1912).[5] Cassirer explains that, for Cohen, '[t]he organization of the "mind that" idealism seeks can be deciphered nowhere else but in the structural relationships of natural science, ethics and aesthetics' ('Hermann Cohen and the Renewal of Kantian Philosophy' 98). A century later, one sees that Cohen's 'improvements' upon Kant arise from his adoption of several unique heuristic models, including the infinitesimal and the case. The strength of these models, according to Cassirer, is to highlight experience and mental activity as forms of cognition in relation to each other. Cohen's new understanding of the mind accomplishes the reintegration of art into the activities of the mind: '[L]ike the world of art, the world of empirical, spatiotemporal existence and, likewise the world of ethical values, is not "encountered" immediately, but rests on principles of formation that critical reflection discovers, and whose validity critical reflection demonstrates' (105). Moreover, 'art is that which represents the "principle" of these kinds and their relationship in a new sense.' That is to say, science and art both flow from cognition. The naturalist assumption that science deals directly with the real can be cast aside. By the same token, facile disregard for art as 'not true' is also overcome. Art and science rest on the same foundation: mental activity.

As a Kantian systematist, it was necessary for Cohen to establish the origins and limits of human thought and knowledge. His first innovation was his dialectical vision of the origin, in which he wrestled with the question of how something emerges from nothing. Unlike Hegel, Cohen does not link nothingness to being, and cautions that it is only through verbal accident that *Nichts* (nothingness) seems associated with *Nicht* (dialectical negation and alterity; *LRE* 104). To the contrary, nothingness is a station rather than an absolute (Holzhey, *Cohen und Natorp* 1:192). As Lukács explains, Cohen attributes to nothingness a fundamental ambiguity. Nothingness is the opposite of something, but it also serves as the means or path to something (*Heidelberger Ästhetik* 18–20).[6] In other words, Cohen posits nothingness as producing something, for it provides the 'indication of the direction of the problem, the origin of the determinability of content' (Poma, *The Critical Philosophy of Hermann Cohen* 96). According to Cohen, most approaches to the question of origin fail because they consider the 'given' to be external to thought. To the contrary, Cohen posits the given in a semiotic manner by posing the following question: if *A* serves as the sign of the simplest content, where does it come from? (*LRE* 82–3). This turns *A* (or in mathematics *x*) into the sign for determinability rather than the undetermined. Within the act of determining identity, then, being and nothingness are mutually dependent. Whereas the concept asks the question: what is it? judgement asks the question: what is it not? (*LRE* 92). Nothingness, conceived of as relative to being, serves as a springboard for thought and identity. Using the Platonic example of the immortal soul, Cohen shows how the determination of the soul's identity depends on the insertion of a negation ('the soul is not mortal') into the definition (Gordon 42). The essential duality of the origin also extends to Cohen's notion of founding or establishing a ground (*Grund*) for thought, since founding implies creating a base (Orringer, *Hermann Cohen* 16). By insisting that this foundational work is quite specifically a laying of foundations, Cohen avoids the absolute foundations associated with metaphysics (Holzhey, 'Cohen and the Marburg School in Context' 17).

Cohen's postulation of the origin in relation to nothingness also lays the foundation for his ideation of the infinitesimal. Following the model of calculus, the infinitesimal is an infinitely small unit used to approach a limit. According to differential calculus, one can approach an unreachable limit through the accumulation of infinitely small units, without, however, arriving at the endpoint. As such, the infinitesimal is a powerful mathematical heuristic device, allowing one an ever-closer approximation to a never reachable answer. The fact that one cannot reach it is overcome by the movement toward the end. This is the logical or mathematical basis of the infinitesimal; it is represented linearly as an aggregation of points toward a limit. The metaphysical basis for the infinitesimal arises from its use to measure change, as the quantity or extent, in relation to the quality of change, understood as intensiveness or power. We can imagine the logical notion of the infinitesimal in the relation plotted between movement and force in a tangent or curve; the metaphysical understanding of the infinitesimal depends on the notion of continuity.[7] Although the infinitesimal curve, figuring movement toward an ideal goal, resembles Hegelian tautology, Cohen understands it as a product of the human mind rather than an absolute. Indeed, the notion of the infinitesimal (as well as the case of *Aufgabe* to be considered shortly) represents Cohen's attempt to overcome what he calls the pantheism of Hegel's notion of the absolute, in which the difference between divine substance and natural substance is erased (*LRE* 329). In other words, the infinitesimal belongs to the human mind; as a human construct and method, it can only approach truth. Nor can it ever attain the status of Being, for that pertains only to God. In this sense, 'Becoming belongs to thinking ... [i]t is never Being' (Kluback, 'The Jewish Response to Hegel' 12). Importantly for our purposes, all mental activity is for

Cohen fictional insofar as it cannot partake in the realm of Being. It approaches the truth, but it is not the truth.

For Cohen, the infinitesimal serves as a device by which to explain the problematic relation between the enquiring mind and the object of study, or in Kantian terms, between the phenomenological (that experienced by the enquiring individual) and the noumenon (the object to be studied). For Kant, the noumenon remains inaccessible in itself, given that the human always 'knows' it only through her own mental structures and dispositions. Cohen recuperates this critical insight into the limits of human knowledge in order to counter what he sees as a dangerous trend among his contemporaries to materialize human experience in psychology and the social sciences. Not unlike scientists of today, many researchers of Cohen's time were attempting to locate qualities of human experience in matter (in certain areas of the brain). In Cohen's return to Plato, he finds mathematics as an antidote for the materialist/ idealist schism that was threatening scientific research in nineteenth-century Germany.[8] Cohen takes as an example experimental psychology that describes consciousness according to its constituent factors, such as the cognition of sensual data, emotions, etc. These factors, nonetheless, are hypothetical, for they pertain to the mind. To approach them as objective givens is epistemologically mistaken – in Cohen's terms, uncritical. Mathematics, for Cohen, 'allows us to demonstrate the proper balance of thinking [*denken*] and sensible intuitability [*Anschauung*] in philosophy, a balance that will then affect nearly every other feature of Cohen's work' (Moynahan 44). To the realm of sensible intuitability (*Anschauung*) belong similarity (or resemblance; *Gleichheit*) and size (*Größe*; Cohen, *Das Prinzip der Infinitesimal-Methode* 2–3). Although sensible intuitability is foreign to the realm of logic, it still plays an important role in cognition.

The infinitesimal contains an inherent paradox as it signifies both discontinuity (the points that never arrive) and continuity (the curve that extends and relates). Cohen illustrates the elusive, future-oriented nature of infinitesimals, a concept borrowed from Newtonian physics that describes 'building blocks of the universe, for in nature everything is continuous, nothing is discrete, and continuity is constructed from fluxions of fluents' (Samuelson 173). Moreover, Cohen uses the infinitesimal to figure epistemological problems in a manner that leads Samuelson to posit the infinitesimal as a figure for the idea: '[t]he infinitesimal is a kind of nothing in that it is less than anything positive and definite, but it points to something definite, viz., the object that is its limit or ideal end. It is not itself anything real, but at the same time it is that from which all reality is generated' (174). In order to understand the infinitesimal in relation to reality, we must remember that size belongs to the realm of sense-based intuition. The infinitesimal, although infinitesimally small, is a unit of size. Thus, the infinitesimal method of differentiation proposed by Cohen as the form of cognitive criticism (*Erkenntniskritik*) has the advantage of linking intuition to logic. In its metaphysical sense, the curve created by the relation of the infinitesimals to force creates a tendency, in other words a *Realisirung*. The infinitesimal method creates reality, but this follows only if one allows reality to be defined as the unified consciousness of science or scholarship. As Cohen concludes, 'But reality is – consciousness; and certainly not the material content of consciousness, but rather the legitimate foundational form of scientific consciousness, a type of integrated consciousness, a principle of cognition.'[9]

Philosophy and the Problems of Modernity

This extension of the Kantian categories into a new *triidium* of academic fields of study represents Cohen's overriding concern for safeguarding German society against the perils of nationalistic mythologies, racism, anti-Semitism, and decadent Romanticism in art and literature. These cultural phenomena threatened the individual by threatening his autonomy, thus separating him from the realm of critique.[10] As he clarifies, true idealism is methodical rationalism, or rather the reflection of reason upon itself (*ARG* 1, xii). By so doing, Cohen harks to the Aristotilean definition of philosophy as reasoning about reason, and Plato's dialogical idealism. Rejecting as nationalistic arrogance a self-seeking, false, and chauvinistic patriotism that has perverted German idealism, he calls for a return to the idealism of German classicism, in which 'the German spirit combined with the original power of ancient Greece' in order to seek out the rational (*wissenschaftlichen*) spirit of humanity (*ARG* 1, xiii). Indeed, it is impossible to appreciate Cohen's thought without viewing it as a reaction against both the intellectual movement of *Kulturpessimismus* and the popular writings on the German *Volkskultur* that appeared during his lifetime (Kluback, *The Legacy of Hermann Cohen* 61–70).

Humanity signifies quite emphatically for Cohen all human beings, as he distinguishes in his ethics between narrowly understood community (*Gemeinschaft*) and universality (*Allheit*), the all-inclusive grouping of humankind.[11] Cohen's critique of community based on particular identities, be they ethnic, religious, or political, rather than universal and all-encompassing citizenship, forms the substance of his critique of modern Western society, but he also draws heavily on the notions of pain and pleasure in his analysis of the absorption of the individual into the collective.[12] Unlike many others, he does not distinguish between antiquity, medieval times, and modernity as completely different epochs insofar as they configure ethical concerns. To the contrary, he finds the seeds of modern problems in ancient society and thought, and thus usually employs the term *neuere Zeit* (more recent times) instead of *Neuzeit* (modernity). However, he often – and almost always pejoratively – uses the adjective 'modern' to describe characteristics of his time. In general, Cohen diagnoses the ills of modernity as a result of the economic and ethical devaluation of human worth. Market-based capitalism serves to reify the worker, while the modern social sciences offer a false ethics based on the atomization of the individual. Ethics represents for Cohen the point where practical and theoretical philosophy should meet, through the action of the moral individual for and in the interests of all. Such action unifies the self, this being the final goal and inherent concern of ethics (*ERW* 80). The forces that tear the individual asunder and confound him or her in moral action are those emanating from the false unity of community: 'As long as he floats in a majority, which deposits in him its influences and reactions, his self is still not present. Unity [in *Allheit*] can give it to him for the first time, and can make him into a moral being.'[13] The purpose of ethics is none other than to locate the individual, torn apart by the many claims of specific communities, within the realm of the universal.

The concept of man as a creature driven by passions and pleasures is ancient, but it takes on particularly dangerous tones in modernity. The first danger is the way in which modern culture entwines pleasure and displeasure with worth, founding a certain type of modern bourgeois capitalism. Capitalism, in its emphasis on the human being as worker and consumer, links human value with exchange value based on utility (*ERW* 606–7). Capitalism personifies capital: 'Capital in itself becomes the worker; like the worker, it works; it produces worth, therefore objects.'[14] By casting capital as the correlate of work, it dehumanizes the individual into *Kapitalwert* (*ERW* 610). Cohen leaves no doubt concerning the false ideological power of modern capitalism: 'The mythology of capital itself brings about the delivery of the working person.'[15] Nonetheless, the modern worker exists as a thing, since exchange creates things. Cohen's critique of modern exchange value (*Wert*) leads him to propose an alternative: *Würde*, a term he borrows from Kant that means dignity or propriety, but can also refer to an earned rank, honour, title, or degree. This sense of worth understood as dignity rather than market value depends upon the concept of the person as having *Selbstzweck*, or being an end unto herself, which extracts her from the web of exchange value (*ERW* 322). Cohen's critique of the modern conceptualization of human worth in economic terms broadens as he links consumerism to pleasure-based consumption. When one accepts that pleasure and the lack thereof constitute self-consciousness, then the individual's only worth is found in momentary and individualistic pleasures. Even self-consciousness degrades into mere sensation of pleasure and displeasure: 'The driving thought always remains: there is nothing more powerful, more evident for life and consciousness than *hoia* (it's good for me) and its opposite. Hence pleasure and displeasure must be the sign and witness of life's worth.'[16]

As a Jewish intellectual writing in early twentieth-century Germany, Cohen perceives the dangers inherent in the conception of a people as *Volk*. He distinguishes between the anthropological perspective, in which the tribe is understood scientifically as part of universal humankind, and the political perspective, in which *Volk* most commonly represents an 'aggregate of particularities, and itself remains a particularity.'[17] All conflicts between peoples of different races and tongues are immoral, as they arise from a sense of the particular rather than the universal and impede the state's work for the well-being of all. The state, understood in its proper role, should offset the particularities of the tribe, and counteract the notion that the nation is determined through blood (*ERW* 34). This it performs by replacing the *Volk*, joined together in community (*Gemeinschaft*) on the basis of common tongue, ethnicity, and/or religion, with cooperative society (*Genossenschaft*). In his historical notion of the development of society from community, Cohen approximates Hegel's notion of the state based on 'universally binding law' (Novak 267–8). Cooperative society itself depends on the juridical notion of the person as an entity enjoying both rights and responsibilities in relation to the universal body. The ideal state, one based on rights and law (*Rechtstaat*), is most emphatically not the empirical state based on power (*Machtstaat*), which represents the status quo and subsequently defends the interests of the ruling classes and tribes. To the contrary, '[t]he idea of such a community is an indispensable and unwavering *regulative* of our action' (Cassirer, 'Hermann Cohen and the Renewal of Kantian Philosophy' 104).

Cohen's insistence on the ethical imperative for understanding the individual as intricately and integrally involved in a universal association arises not only from his critique of the exclusive tribes and religions of human history, but also from his critique of the Western cult of the individual. Emphasis on the heroic individual grows ever more dangerous in history, as the cult of the hero arises from stoicism and becomes transformed through the image of the man-God in Christianity. Cohen rejects the Hegelian notion of dialectical movement of the spirit through the individual as a form of pantheism that centres all being (*Sein*) and obligation (*Sollen*) in nature because this notion, present in Schelling's and Hegel's thought, dissolves ethics into logic, and thus deprives the individual of the freedom to act and evolve (*ERW* 44–5). History is wrongly viewed as the working of the spirit through these heroic individuals (*ERW* 30). Heroic political individuals seem to be forces of nature, and yet act only on their individual feelings of pleasure and displeasure (*ERW* 148). It follows that politics is perceived of as the sphere of great men, and that the political choice consists of electing individuals, who in turn represent a party, that is to say, a particularity rather than the whole. Cohen is clear about another consequence of the politics of individuals: when and where there is found lacking a clear sense of responsibility toward and representation of the all, the identity of the state becomes fatally entwined with the mythologies of nationalism, tribal identity, and group politics.

Contractual Ethics and the Work of *Aufgabe*

Does one speak of individuality or universality in relation to ethics? The very question, as Cohen understands it, can only originate within modernity, since modern philosophy transforms the ancient concept of consciousness into self-consciousness. Kant takes from Descartes the concept of *cogito* and from Leibniz the concept of a unified self of apperception, and subsequently adds a second level to metaphysics: the concern not only with the object but also with the subject (*ERW* 94). Modern philosophy deepens the concept of consciousness – literally understood by Cohen according to its etymological meaning of 'knowing with' (*Mitwissen*) – by problematizing the self that knows. Based on the concept of a transcendentally defined self, he finds hope in the possibility of an ethics based on more universal grounds than those offered by adherence to a particular creed or identity with a certain group. One may even speak of optimism in the philosopher's thought, a concept he openly embraces as the eudemonia of the eighteenth century and a force for freedom in modern politics (*ERW* 296).

One finds traces of a history of modernity in the milestones Cohen identifies in the development of key philosophical and moral concepts: the Reformation, the contract theory of the state and the law, and idealist philosophy. The Jewish philosopher's favourable evaluation of Martin Luther may seem surprising, and yet he finds in the reformer's attack on medieval Catholicism the seeds of both ethical freedom and of the modern state based on a notion of universality rather than religious or ethnic affiliation. Upon removing the Church's mediating function between God and the individual, Luther furthers the morally necessary work of developing self-consciousness: 'It is the interiority of moral self-consciousness, in all its awe and reverence, but also in all its faith and all its cheerfulness of moral certainty, which spreads here its wings.'[18] In spite of its negative manifestations, this self-consciousness announces the moral and aesthetic freedom of the new epoch (*der neuen Zeit*). The process of bringing the individual into direct contact with God is, for Cohen, a renewal, for it calls upon the ancient tragic problem of man, who struggles like Prometheus to bring divine fire to the earth. As the individual fights to approach the divine in the here and now, the difference between the worldly and the spiritual disappears. From this process emerges another positive characteristic of modernity: the Protestant concept of the state (*ERW* 308).

Cohen's notion of the state as an entity distinct from and even opposed to any groups based on religious or ethnic identity finds conceptual support in the notion of contract law and legal rights. In his revalorization of the social contract, he stands in opposition to Hegel, who rejected the notion of the contract because he believed that the citizen was born into the state and actualized his freedom through the state (Berry 691). Cohen rejects notions of citizenship as birthright on the grounds that such a notion leads to the equation of the state and the tribe. For the Jewish philosopher, all individuals have a contract with the state, and are equal before it in their civil rights (Coskun 317). Just as modern philosophy abstracts the individual into the subject, modern law abstracts the individual from his existence within a given situation into the legal subject of a state: 'The juridical person distances himself from the moral prejudices of individuality and its character within the grouping of the many; he constitutes himself on the ground of universality as a unity of the civil subject.'[19] Not only could the state stand for universal law against individual or group interest, it could also provide, under certain ideal conditions, for what Cohen terms *Aufgabe*, the working of the will toward ethical service.

The concept of *Aufgabe* is probably the most powerful innovation that Cohen brings to neo-Kantianism.[20] The philosopher's use of this term, which can mean, in German, 'problem,' 'exercise,' and 'duty' as well as 'resignation' and 'surrender,' is quite suggestive. In logical terms, *Aufgabe* means the general characteristic of judgment, as well as the 'combined action of methods that complement each other in pure thought, so that no single method can completely run its own course, but must always be almost halfway separated from the others.'[21] Cohen represents *Aufgabe* as occupying spaces between methods that are not diametrically opposed, but rather knitted into a web of convergences and divergences. Cohen's colleague and friend Paul Natorp defines *Aufgabe* in terms of struggle between unity and division: 'Thought (theory) depends on separation, tendency fights against separation; it is a restless advance, campaign, anticipation, but always in strict continuity: *Aufgabe*.'[22] The time of *Aufgabe* is eternity understood as the never-ending movement of the will (Natorp, 'Hermann Cohens philosophische Leistung' 98). Judgment itself must be understood as the mental capacity to juxtapose and distinguish, and thus the logical concept of *Aufgabe* takes its place in ethical and aesthetical thought as well.[23] In ethical terms, *Aufgabe* mediates between the inner world of the self and the outer world, and thus serves to clarify the problem of intention. Intentionality, as normally understood, posits an external world as a given; to the contrary, *Aufgabe* 'contradicts first of all the given; it abstains from the given; it makes up the given.'[24] It has the capacity to move either toward the outside or toward the inside, although movement from the inside out will always be limited by the external thing (*Ding*). In addition, the faculty of *Aufgabe* tends toward the inner world of striving, since only there can it complete itself (*ERW* 143). In moral matters, this capacity to judge and juxtapose provides the means by which to form the interior world in relation to the exterior and to reflect upon the internal emotional state. Subsequently, if the process of *Aufgabe* were ever completed, it would bring about its own annihilation and would presumably signify the annihilation of self-consciousness. In other words, Cohen understands the self as an entity in constant process, continuously striving toward, although never reaching completely, an ethical constitution of the self both in internal harmony and in harmony with others.

It would be easy to confuse Cohen's notion of the creation of the ethical self through *Aufgabe* with the Fichtean notion that the 'I' creates itself vis-à-vis the 'not-I.' Cohen himself insisted that such was not the case, primarily because he conceived of the ethical self in relation to other ethical selves, considered as *Nebenmenschen*. Cohen contends that Fichte lost sight of Kant's notion of the transcendent self, and thus stumbled into metaphysics whereby self is understood as the historical, perceiving person rather than the transcendent person of *Aufgabe*. The *Ding an sich* is no longer problematized, and the exterior world is reduced to phenomena experienced by the self (Poma, *The Critical Philosophy of Hermann Cohen* 74–5). This results in a dehumanizing ethics. When Fichte calls the external the 'not-I,' he falls into the error of defining the other as the not-human, since the 'I' is a human (Schwarzschild, 'The Tenability of Hermann Cohen's Construction of the Self' 362). In other words, Fichte understands the 'not-I' as object rather than another subject (Poma, *Yearning for the Form* 264). To the contrary, the ethical self can only act by recognizing the humanity of the other. In this recognition of the essential humanity of the other as *Nebenmensch*, Cohen not only rejects Fichte but also lays the groundwork for the ethical thinking of Buber (who will deny his influence) and Levinas (Wogenstein 168).

The faculty of *Aufgabe* is, if not coterminous, at least intricately related with action, both in terms of logic and ethics. Action itself is none other than the most basic problem of ethics, since through action the person reveals himself and enters into open relation with the outside world (*ERW* 72). In other words, 'pure will is morally worthless … [I]t is only the *action* that makes man into a man' (Holzhey, 'Cohen and the Marburg School in Context' 23). In logical terms, *Aufgabe* is the concept (*Begriff*), that is to say, not already given in thought, but rather carried out by judgment. Like the *Aufgabe*, the concept exists only in process and would suffer annihilation if ever ended. Moreover, its very existence takes place in its process of creation: 'Its existence endures only in its production, and its production accepts no ending, insofar as it is a true concept. That means: the concept is *Aufgabe*.'[25] This equation of the concept with the active faculty of *Aufgabe* allows Cohen to posit thought itself as an action. If *Aufgabe*, this continual process of judgment and juxtaposition, gives shape to thought, then thought is action. The notion of *Aufgabe* has serious methodological implications for critical thought, and gives rise to a three-part method: the presentation of a factual problem to be considered theoretically; the move toward a universal or transcendent principle with which to resolve the problem; and the return to the phenomenon in all its uniqueness and peculiarity (Orringer, *Hermann Cohen* 62).

Moreover, Cohen carefully distinguishes here between the German *Handlung* and *Tun*. Thought is not *Tun*, since this word signifies the production and completion of something else; rather it is *Handlung*, which has no completion and which produces nothing but itself (*ERW* 171). Cohen proposes that the difference lies in the relative function of action: *Tun* produces an object, aim (*Zweck*), and content, whereas in *Handlung*, action is itself the product, the content, and the purpose (*Ziel*; *ERW* 175). In this sense *Aufgabe*, as idea and action carried out through the will without end, corresponds to the Kantian categorical imperative against treating the other as an end. In fact, willing needs the other person in order that action not 'fly and scatter away in fanciful whims and impetuosity.'[26] Not only does the exterior world tame and calm the self's willfulness, it also serves as a necessary counterforce to action as the latter 'builds the internal, which face to face with the whole outside world turns into a sheer exterior.'[27] The logical consequence of Cohen's insistence on the constitutive power of *Aufgabe* leads to the notion of a subject in a constant state of self-creation. As Willliam Kluback succinctly states: 'This I is not given, it is set forth as a task' (*The Legacy of Hermann Cohen* 132).

Nonetheless, the self created by the action of *Aufgabe* does not exclude the other person or banish her to the exterior. One of the more influential innovations in Cohen's thought is precisely the way in which he expands the idealist conception of the self to include the other. Indeed, it is no accident that he introduces this issue in order to propose a model for political power and rights, for it forms the very foundation for his concept of the state. In a move that both foreshadows Buber's ethics and echoes Talmudic thought, Cohen bases self-consciousness on the relation between the I (*Ich*) and the Thou (*Du*). Self-determination, understood as self-consciousness through moral development, is most emphatically *not* based on conflict with the other, the third-person he (*Er*) whose approach we view as dangerous, and thus transform into an it (*Es*; *ERW* 248). Instead, self-determination understood as self-consciousness depends on the binding of the I with the Thou, just as the first person singular calls into dialogue the second person singular: 'I cannot say Thou without drawing you to myself, without joining Thee to the I in this relationship.'[28] Politically and ethically, this unification of the self with the other takes place through a double action similar to that seen in contracts. First, it takes away the mistrust and worry with which we see others as alien and threatening; secondly, it constitutes 'a claim of the right with which I lift the other up.'[29] Cohen is punning here upon the phrase in German to lay claim to something, idiomatically expressed as lifting up a claim, and thus displaces the purpose of one's action from the expression of a claimed right to the proclamation of respect for the other. In a second pun, he asserts that the claim to a right (*Rechtsanspruch*) is now a right action (*Rechtshandlung*). The contract has thus performed a remarkable transformation in the relationship between the self and the other, making a 'claim into speech.'[30] The model of the contract serves as an alternative means by which to understand the relation of the individual to the state, in which she participates not on the basis of birth but on the basis of mutual rights and obligations.

Truth and Freedom

Unlike Kant, Cohen posits the foundation of truth in both logic and will. Whereas the Kantian notion of the unknowable *Ding an sich* works for the natural sciences, it throws into doubt the validity of the idea, and thus threatens the validity of ethical judgment as well as other sorts of scientific enquiry (*Wissenschaften*) into the human state: 'It gives rise, then, to the suspicion that the idea was really only an idea that presented itself against and beyond that of the *Ding an sich* ... or rather hid and obstructed it.'[31] In other words, the possibility that the idea is divorced from the *Ding an sich* causes a grave doubt concerning ethical judgment. Indeed, moral obligation could appear to be even less than a list of commandments, but merely a fantastic realm of pious hopes (*ERW* 26–7). Instead, Cohen prefers to recuperate the legal notion of action as *Handlung* in order to provide a conceptual basis for ethical methodology, since the term carries a double meaning of both action and negotiation (*ERW* 65). Through this concept one can imagine a mutually productive relation between the individual and the idea, one in which the moral idea is acted out and created by the individual, at the same time that the moral idea acts and creates the individual.

Cohen appropriates Plato's notion of the idea as hypothesis – as something to be tested and brought into existence (*ERW* 97). Drawing on both Platonic and Jewish traditions, Cohen understands the idea as hypothesis as a 'giving account of,' the act of deriving an explanation of a phenomenon by returning to its origin and tracing its steps (Orringer, *Hermann Cohen* 44–5). The implications for ethics are obvious. The implications for ethics are obvious, as truth is understood not only in an empirical sense, but also in relation to action. Cohen could be no more insistent in this definition: 'Truth means the correlation and the accord of theoretical and ethical problems.'[32] But Cohen goes further, and equates truth with the search for truth, which could be understood logically as methodology, and ethically as correctly oriented action: 'The search for the truth, that alone is truth. The method alone, by means of logic and ethics joined as one and produced by this union – this unifying single method completes and authenticates truth.'[33] The implications of equating the search for truth with truth itself are far-reaching, and perhaps unintended by Cohen. If truth is no longer seen as a mere datum or fact of nature or history, but rather as method or process itself, then ethics, and by extension the study of the humanities, is revalorized alongside the natural sciences, mathematics, and logic. In addition, this reformulation of truth relocates it in the domain of the will. One must want to find the truth in order to find it, and this wanting constitutes the condition for truth. Upon locating truth with relation to the will, reason can no longer appear disinterested. Method must then harmonize the diversity of reason's fundamental interests (*ERW* 91). Cohen thus implies that method is not only judgment, that is to say, the capacity to discern and mediate between differences, but also *Aufgabe*, the capability to problematize and harmonize difference.

The concepts of the contract and the movement of *Aufgabe* in the constitution of the self ground Cohen's understanding of freedom. Freedom is central to Kant's and Cohen's ethics because it presupposes the human faculty to live and act in a moral manner. Cohen, unlike Kant, does not consider the ethical self a pre-given entity, but rather a continuous and ever-changing entity. As Cohen clarifies, 'the self is in no way nor in such an ideal form given beforehand, before it presents itself, and in no way is it only to present itself; to the contrary, it must first produce itself.'[34] Cassirer sums up Cohen's stance on freedom even more succinctly: 'as ethical subjects, we act not from freedom, but towards freedom' ('Hermann Cohen and the Renewal of Kantian Philosophy' 104). Cohen further defines the production of the self through pure will as *Aufgabe* (*ERW* 325). Indeed, if the subject were a given emerging from his milieu, then ethics would be anthropology or sociology (*ERW* 96). In short, Cohen identifies the first level of the pure self-consciousness as striving (*Bestreben*), in other words, the inner activity by which consciousness expands itself (*ERW* 133). This striving is not the Fichtean creation of the self and the other, for it occurs within the eternal time of *Aufgabe*, understood 'not as the succession of one moment after another, but rather as the projection as it were of the moments before one another. The future goes before us, and the past follows afterwards.'[35] The future itself becomes for the philosopher an ethical concept, and eternity is the endless work of *Aufgabe* toward *Allheit*.

Autonomy signifies the regulation of the self in regards to the interests of the other and the all (*ERW* 324), but freedom is oriented toward the historical, political, and social work of humanity. As such, freedom takes on different historical forms. In antiquity, freedom stands in opposition to pleasure, and represents the capacity of the self to overcome and transcend physical desires. In Socratic thought, freedom is linked to virtue as a form of knowing (*Wissen*), and thus signifies the possibility of thought and the knowledge of virtue (*ERW* 286). In medieval times, human freedom is merely the individual's freedom from sin, and does not refer to man's spiritual dignity or uniqueness, as it did in antiquity (*ERW* 288). In modernity, the problem of freedom is still that of the individual, but now in relation to the masses. Indeed, Cohen leaves no doubt that the individual of the masses is the problem that defines modernity (*ERW* 289).

Cohen argues that modernity reduces the individual to a 'being of nature' (*Naturwesen*) by categorizing and quantifying him or her through statistics within a mass. Moreover, statistics replace morality and theology in modernity (*ERW* 290). Birth, illness, death, as well as criminality, addiction, and other matters of the spirit – all find their explanation in statistics. Causality serves as a central logic of modernity insofar as the individual is viewed as powerless before the conditions of his or her time and place. Physiology, pathology, and even economics reduce the individual further still to a being hopelessly driven or confined by the milieu. In short, this is the logic of modernity, one that clearly structures the modern concept of society and of the social sciences. According to the modern social sciences, only causality allows insight. Moreover, causality is the law of the milieu or environment. Humankind is only an object of investigation within this milieu (*ERW* 291). The causal laws set forth by the milieu deny the individual his freedom, and he thus appears merely as the 'average man' or the 'profile' (*ERW* 292).

Finally, we can situate Cohen's work in relation to his concept of modernity. The modern individual lives shackled by his or her surroundings, having lost social, political, economic, and ethical freedom.

Society understood as a particular group binds the individual's identity to concepts of origin: family, nation, language, or religion. Politicians and political systems exploit this identity by pandering to and furthering the interests of particular groups against the interests of all. Capitalism continues to enslave the individual through treating work as capital, that is to say, as an object of exchange. The work of ethics in modernity is to restore freedom to the individual by redefining human autonomy through a reformulation of the relation of the self to the other and to all humanity. Cohen's own personal dedication to socialism as a political system constitutes a means by which to further the reintegration of the individual into a community based on universal rather than particular values. Indeed, the philosopher insists that political reform and revolution are periods of experimental ethics, in which the theoretical is tested (*ERW* 328). In this way he seeks to alleviate the physical (what he refers to as the problem of the stomach) as well as the spiritual problems of the modern individual. Both his ethics and his politics are quite explicitly, and by necessity, aimed toward the future as modern individuals strive to break the bonds that limit their freedom. Once Cohen has defined truth as the agreement of logic and the will, the very existence of truth depends upon the loosening of these limitations upon individual autonomy. If the person cannot freely will, he or she does not possess the ethical grounds upon which to seek the truth.

Irony as Virtue

Any ethics based on personal autonomy would be incomplete without a discussion of virtue. In our times this concept has been appropriated by the right, although there is a renewed interest in ethics within philosophy.[36] It is interesting that an avowed socialist such as Cohen would insist upon, and even attempt to lay the groundwork for, a renewed concept of autonomy and subsequently agency. The Nietzchean superman (*Übermensch*) is immoral, according to Cohen, because it implies by logical necessity its polar opposite, the 'underman' (*Untermensch*; *ERW* 562). To this effect, Cohen returns to Kant's revised version of the golden rule in which the individual should treat others not as means, but as ends unto themselves. '"Act in such a way that you always employ the humanity in your person, just as that of the other person, as an aim, and never merely as a means." In these words the deepest and most powerful meaning of the categorical imperative is expressed: they contain the moral program of modernity and the entire future of world history.'[37] Cohen believes that defining the individual as an end in his or herself evolves into the idea of socialism (*ERW* 321). Thus, the development of the person, in Cohen's vision of socialism, is the highest goal. Just treatment of the other, as well as of the individual in relation to the state, depends upon the will to strive for the development of each individual as a completely autonomous being.

The concept of virtue raises certain problems for Cohen because he writes within the modern context. Earlier standards for virtue, such as ancient manliness, depended on fear of the gods or, more immediately, fear of the masters. This fear created an ethical mentality, necessary so that the individual might internalize morality. Nonetheless, the notion of duty or obligation that it engendered was based on difference, whereas virtue should be the same standard for all (*ERW* 474). Even though these differentiating forces should disappear from modernity, yet there is still a need for fixity in moral issues. The virtues are to become signs (*Wegweiser*) delineating the path toward ethical behaviour. Like Kant, Cohen rejects a notion of society as based on the metaphor of conflict, opting instead for the idealist metaphor of a road toward a new order of virtue. This road, however, does not simply bifurcate into a wrong and a right path; it bifurcates into two paths, one toward the self-consciousness of the individual and the other of the whole. Cohen recognizes the central paradox of his prescription for social good: the individual's developing modern self-consciousness may place her on a collision path with the interests of the group, even when the group is understood as the whole. Cohen is fully aware that the two paths, the individual and the universal, must at times lead to serious conflict. Quoting Aristotle, he refers to the possibility of a middle path between the two, only to reject it.

Instead, Cohen states unequivocally that virtue is based on internal strife, and thus moral thought is tragic. Significantly, it is here that Cohen first refers to Don Quixote in a series of rhetorical questions: 'And does wisdom not turn into arrogance when it fails to recognize its own limits? And is Don Quixote perhaps only a fool? Or is Aristophanes a foolish poet, because he fastens a comical mask to tragedy? Plato has also pointed out the right way here. In the deepest night, when all carousing was finished and the rest slumbered, he let Socrates say it: that the tragedian alone can also be the writer of comedy.'[38] Cohen notes that these two literary modes, tragedy and comedy, parallel the cleft between two types of virtue, one that is oriented toward the universal interests of the whole (*Allheit*) and another oriented toward the relative interests of the particular community (*Gemeinschaft*). Internal strife is inevitable unless the two paths come together directed toward the universal body of humanity.

The reference to literary figures such as Don Quixote and literary categories such as tragedy and comedy precisely at this point in Cohen's ethics alerts us to his postulation of irony as a virtue. The virtues for Cohen include honour, modesty and moderation, bravery, loyalty, justice, and humanity. Cohen unlinks honour from any community-based identity or class orientation to insist that true honour is oriented toward the ideal state based on equality and inclusivity. Honour, based on the notion of equality, becomes the affect of virtue, and thus anchors action in the direction of the other seen as the Thou (*Du*), which then tends toward the We (*Wir*). Bravery constitutes the willingness to enact virtue in history. Loyalty springs from the natural impulse of human beings to join together, and can be harnessed for promoting the universal interests of humanity. Justice, in turn, orients this loyalty toward the state and establishes the basis for a methodology and a science (*Wissenschaft*) of rights.[39]

Modesty and moderation, both signified by the German *Bescheidenheit*, take their place as the second level of virtue in which one becomes aware of the fallibility of human nature and the limitations of human existence (Kluback, *The Legacy of Hermann Cohen* 10). The example of Socrates provides a model for modesty, a virtue linked to irony. Socratic irony serves Cohen as the model for what he calls Greek irony figured in the satyr, and embraces the contrast between the ugliness of Silenus and the divinity of Eros as the representation of wisdom (*ERW* 530). In other words, Socratic irony stands for wisdom because it insists upon the limits of knowledge, which in turn provide the necessary correction by which to approach truthfulness (*ERW* 531). Irony's insistence on scepticism is negative, but it becomes positive as it leads to the activity of criticism. Criticism possesses the virtue that it 'awakens the sense of the gaps and the limits of knowledge. And even if the gaps are filled in, the limits nonetheless remain.'[40] Irony informs the virtue of modesty and moderation as it counteracts dogmatism and the mistaken belief in the sovereignty of the self. Indeed, irony and its subsequent virtues, moderation and modesty, are important to the development of democracy because they warn against a concept of personal aristocracy that itself leads to the elevation of certain individuals over others and certain races over others (*ERW* 543). Finally, the virtue of modesty and moderation provides the individual a distanced point of view (*Distanzgefühl*) over his or her own circumstances that results from the process of *Aufgabe* within the self. In short, irony is linked to the process of internal moral *Aufgabe*, figured by Cohen as a continual strife within the self toward self-knowledge and self-consciousness (*ERW* 544). Moreover, it allows for knowledge of one's circumstances. Even though Cohen denies that the formative powers of the environment obviate autonomy, he affirms that the knowledge of one's circumstances builds the foundation for freedom (*ERW* 546).

The final virtue, humanity (*Humanität* or *Menschlichheit*), understood as moral action, has an aesthetic basis. The concept of humanity asserts the individual's worth in terms of morality rather than economic or class status, for it values the individual on her ethical action and treatment of others. This concept of humanity also means that one's character is not fixed, but is rather itself a process (*ERW* 631). Cohen figures this work of humanity both visually and through sound. In visual terms, it is the *Rücksicht*, respect and regard: 'The sharp, benevolent eyes for the particularities of cases, for the uniqueness of the person that thereby come into question, grant the gaze circumspection and a panoramic view ... Humanity turns its gaze toward all sides.'[41] Cohen further describes the all-encompassing aspects of the gaze as the form of just composure (*rechte Sammlung*), which collects unto itself all points of view and thus establishes tranquillity, security, harmony, and peace. Harmony is to be thought of not as simplicity but rather unanimity, thus joining the visual concept of composure with the musical concept of the melody based on the internal relations of harmony. Cohen further plays with the relation between visual and musical composition by describing the power of harmony as form-giving (*gestaltende*; *ERW* 632). Thus, internal coherence and integrity form the basis of all art for Cohen, as he will further explain in his aesthetics. This integration of the many and the particular into a harmonious whole carries great ethical significance for the philosopher. Art provides an example of the *Aufgabe* of humanity, understood as the production of a relation between the singular and the universal. Indeed, the relation between art and ethics is so close that at one point he defines humanity as the virtue of art (*ERW* 634). Love of humanity, as expressed in art, 'is oriented towards the political realisation of universal brotherhood among men and of peace' (Poma, *Yearning for the Form* 106). But it is also love of the individual, in all his or her peculiarities, made possible through humour.

Language as Ethical Action

Cohen's emphasis on the internal unity of art has obvious significance for twentieth-century aesthetics. In his *Aesthetics of Pure Feeling*, Cohen anticipates much phenomenological study of the arts, and so his work deserves study in the fields of musicology, architecture, and art theory. Nonetheless, I limit myself to a discussion of his understanding of literature and language. By transforming the contract into an ontological metaphor, Cohen sets forth a new basis for conceptualizing communication. In *Religion of Reason*, Cohen maintains that language establishes the relation of the self to the Thou rather than the He, and thus gives the model for the ethical stance of the individual vis-à-vis the other (Kluback, *The Legacy of Hermann Cohen* 110, 135).[42] Speech becomes the medium for ethical action, and is clearly another manifestation of *Handlung* (ERW 521). The metaphor of dialogue even grounds Cohen's understanding of the concept, which cannot be a complete and finished unit in itself. Instead, it is a question that invites an answer that is another question, and so on indefinitely. 'What is realized in the system of concept is a new kind of reciprocal conditioning or action: reciprocal action between question and answer' (Poma, *The Critical Philosophy of Hermann Cohen* 90).

The spoken word manifests the work of *Aufgabe* in its mediating operations between the interior and the exterior, and becomes an example of the relation of the individual to the whole. Cohen presents a taxonomy of speech based on both its internal and external functions. Tone (*Laut*) is the most basic of its instruments used to reveal the self in the world; through tone, internal speech refines and renders thought precise. As action (*Handlung*), speech directs itself not only toward internal self-knowledge, but also toward the outside world. Tone is the manifestation of the internal that pushes itself out and surrenders itself to the external: 'The tone is the most powerful and intense expression of the internal; the sign that the internal cannot manage to restrain itself inside its own borders, that it oversteps itself into the external, into expression.'[43] Speech, even in its most basic manifestation as mere sound, constitutes the impulse of the self to break out of its own boundaries. The tone is a sign; words, the next level of complexity, represent concepts, the building blocks of thought; and speech itself is thought.[44] In a provocative aside that echoes Romantic philosophizing on language, Cohen insists that words themselves could not exist without the sentences that bind them into meaning, for then they would be only tones and not words.[45] Sentence structure stabilizes sound through concept as thought, and then through concept into words (*ERW* 191). Speech as utterance, however, cannot be pure thought, for it binds the internal and the external (*ERW* 191). Speech is internal, a vehicle of thought, and external, exiting the self as sound.

Cohen moves beyond this definition of the word's dual nature to situate it within a second level of duality, in which, as an expression of the will, it morphs into action: 'The most precise medium through which the will bestirs itself into action and declares itself is the verbal expression.'[46] Thus, speech pertains to the realm of *Aufgabe*, the constant work of the self in relation to both the internal and the external. Moreover, in legal terms, speech makes possible the contract. Not only does speech enact will in the world (*ERW* 194), it also bridles and releases the feeling of the will (*Willensgefühl*). Language serves to calm and harness the power of feelings: 'First speech freely brings moderation and calm into the confusion of feeling; the volcanic turbulence is subdued and mastered. At the same time, however, the feeling for speech also operates, simultaneously unloosing and redeeming. It provides the foundation for the will's action, as it prepares a bed for the stream of emotion and channels them.'[47] As language serves a dual function relative to the feeling of the will by both taming and employing its power, it also springs itself from a feeling, *Sprachgefühl*. This German term translates literally as a feeling for speech, and describes a person's capacity for effectively and correctly using a given language. Feeling is thus associated with competency, and the feeling for language with the capacity to use speech in the exterior world as a form of action. Indeed, speech is no mere adjunct to will, but rather intrinsic to will itself: 'Whereas the will, in order to become will does not so much clothe itself in words, but rather grows within them, so it springs out of the feeling for words with which the conceptual words of speech continue to grow together.'[48]

Art as Power

In Cohen's *Ethics of Pure Will* (1904), poetry remains exiled from thought in accordance with Kant. Nonetheless, the organic metaphor of entwined growth that Cohen uses to describe the intertwined relation between the will and language leads toward his notion of the symbiotic relation between poetry and self-consciousness. Poetry cannot exist but as an entangling of the will and sentiment in the self: 'There would be no poetry, and no poetry that would begin to bloom toward thought, although not in thought, if this growing together did not endure and did not renew itself endlessly in the cultured consciousness. It is as much the morally as the aesthetically cultivated consciousness that strolls among these plantings.'[49] Thus poetry, through the mediating position of language between the will and the emotions, enjoys pride of place in consciousness as the refined garden in which the moral and the artistic meet and coalesce. Cohen quickly qualifies the primacy of poetry as presented within this image by first noting that, true to orthodox Kantianism, poetry cannot itself partake of thought. He backpedals even more by asserting that sentiment and the feeling of the will are but the motors for the motive of *Aufgabe*.[50] Given the philosopher's definition of truthfulness as the concordance of logic and ethics, he cannot so easily dismiss the possibility that art could contain truth, and so steers away from a dogmatic rejection of the image and imagination as purveyors of truth: 'Poetry never replaces scientific enquiry [*Wissenschaft*] and philosophy; rather it climaxes and penetrates them, but above all by absorbing their deepest contents (not just skimming off their catchwords).'[51] Nonetheless, his reservations signal that he might have let the genie of imagination and art out of the Kantian bag. In Cohen's thought, art exemplifies *Aufgabe*. Drawing from the German etymology of the word, Cohen writes: 'Art [*Kunst*] is power [*Können*], the capacity to create and to build, to form and to draft images that compete with nature for the appearance of actuality.'[52] Cohen reformulates Bacon's old chestnut that knowledge is power into art is power. He thus performs a careful realignment of art in relation to knowledge at the same time that he establishes art as an example of the subject's 'drive toward the outside' (*Trieb nach Aussen*) visible in other social constructions such as politics (*ERW* 59). Art takes central place in the development of aesthetic and ethical feeling, and is a function of the human impulse to build an actuality against that of nature.

Seven years later, in his *Aesthetics of Pure Feeling* (1912), Cohen rejects a clean split between aesthetic experience and knowledge. Although Cohen does not abandon the notion of genius, he deems that the Kantian division between thought and imagination has led to the individualization of aesthetic value in genius, thus isolating the aesthetic from ethical or social relevance. In addition, the exile of art from the realm of thought gives rise to the dangerous Romantic notion of the absolute, in which truth is to be found either in the ideal (in heaven) or in the real (on earth; *ARG* 1, 30–4). Cohen sees feeling as intricately bound to consciousness. His goal is to define feeling as a form of

Aufgabe. As Poma explains, 'The foundation of aesthetic experience as productive activity … is possible, if it can be demonstrated that feeling does not merely accompany the productive process of consciousness … but can also play its own independent productive role, through which, incorporating the meaning of the relative feelings, it overcomes them … in the independence of pure feeling' (*The Critical Philosophy of Hermann Cohen* 137). In ethical and aesthetic terms, pure feeling is, for Cohen, love. In short, by 1912 Cohen places poetry precisely in the centre of the individual's ethical as well as intellectual development.

Cohen links morality to literary form through a notion of perfection, fulfilment, or completeness (*Vollkommenheit*) that not only springs from historical difference and development, but even from imperfection and incompletion.[53] Fulfilment as an aesthetic category depends, ironically enough, on the awareness of the limitations of one's own viewpoint: 'Fulfilment is a visual image of a point of view; it does not lend the character sketch fixity nor security in the face of changes nor does it tumble into contraries.'[54] That is to say, fulfilment is not stable and unchanging, but rather subject to temporal transformation or even internal contradiction. Artistic fulfilment (*Vollkommenheit*) represents yet another manifestation of *Aufgabe,* and bears within itself complexity, difference, and contradiction reflecting the different moments and aspects of the eternal working of art. Since aesthetic consciousness is itself composed of movement, it creates a productive engagement with the artistic object that Cohen coins *Kunstgefühl,* a feeling for art that engages the viewer in reflection upon and exchanges with the art itself (Philonenko, *L'école de Marbourg* 101–2). Art depends for its completion on the receptor or viewer; thus Cohen asserts that 'form is the unity of soul and body.'[55] The viewing mind works with the art object, in a way parallel to the artist's mental work with the object. Moreover, the aesthetic sense of movement felt by the viewer upon forming a unity from the plurality of sensations is, in Cohen's terms, a form of thought, for it is the making of unity from plurality that defines thought in his logics (Dufour 101–2). The aesthetic movement experienced by the viewer offers Cohen a means by which to valorize abstract art (102–5). Aesthetic movement is also present in rhythm, where it plays not on the corporeal ebb and flow of breath and heartbeat, but rather on the movement of the mind.

Irony serves as an aesthetic virtue precisely because it highlights the multiplicity and incompletion of the process. As such, irony also historically assumes various and successive avatars: in antiquity, it appears as Socratic irony, and in medieval times, as humour. Moreover, humour fuels the transition toward modernity. Writing of Dante, Cohen quips that the Italian writer's modernity resides in the fact that his work's ethical problem is not religious, but rather political (*ARG* 1, 317). Cohen applies his history of modern times to that of literature, arguing that the shift from the medieval notion of religious tribe to the modern notion of state first occurs in the *Divine Comedy*. This ethical secularization has its counterpart in the aesthetic secularization that takes place in Dante's masterpiece, as the rigours of hell appear enjoyable (at least to the reader who imagines but does not experience them). Cohen terms this new feeling aroused in the reader 'humour,' and considers it the very basis of burgeoning freedom, as it rejects aesthetic dependence upon religion (*ARG* 1, 311). Here we see at work Cohen's concept of irony as the necessary acknowledgment of limitations in art: in the case of Socratic irony, it represents the limitations of knowledge, whereas in the case of medieval humour, it represents the limitations of religious belief.

Cohen expands his analysis of humour in his *Aesthetics* by correlating it to the sublime (Poma, *The Critical Philosophy of Hermann Cohen* 139–47). Whereas the sublime corresponds to knowledge in Cohen's systematic thought, humour corresponds to morality. In other words, the sublime depends on logical judgment, but humour depends on moral judgment in its ideal form: love. Humour recognizes humanity's frailty and limitations, but encompasses them in love. Ugliness as an aesthetic attribute signals humanity's beastliness or animal nature. Cohen figures humour as a loving force that transforms the beast into a man: 'Humour says: this scarecrow of humanity should be a human, God's image!'[56] Laughter is merely a symptom of humour, which in itself is a moment in the continuum of beauty. Beauty is now for Cohen a function of *Aufgabe* as well as material embodiment. As Poma explains: 'A work is beautiful because it is a realisation of the straining towards the infinite' (*Yearning for the Form* 153).

Although Cohen does not use these terms, we can find in his description of ugliness a new take on mimesis. If the ugly represents or signals part of mankind's animal nature, then it does reflect reality. Ugliness performs the ethically necessary function of showing us our limits, making visible what is determined in human nature. In that sense, it can be said to perform the ethical work of mimesis, mirroring humanity warts and all. Nonetheless, it also submits this ugliness to the power of love, and thus grants humanity to the bestial aspect. This is the moral work of humour for Cohen, a concept that distinguishes his interpretation of Shakespeare from Hegel's. For Cohen, Shakespeare's comedies offer a critique of society at the same time that they offer a glimpse of the utopic in the union of the sublime, the tragic, and the humorous (Uhlig 40). Cohen's elevation of humour also, as we shall see, distinguishes his notion of the novel as a genre.

Aesthetic modes, such as the humorous and the ugly, do more than merely reflect reality, for they participate in the ethical work of *Aufgabe*. Present in Cohen's writings on aesthetics is the concept of actuality (*Wirklichkeit*). Art makes present or actual something new. Art as oriented toward ethical action participates in the creation of an improved society – this Cohen makes clear. But I would like to draw attention to the new that is being actualized through art. Because Cohen is more interested in this actualization as a function of ethical future-oriented action or the modelling of mathematics, he does not seem to glimpse that he is, in fact, implying a distinct realm of actuality made through and by aesthetic activity. It is this other plane – what is created by the aesthetic – that will interest Ortega and Bakhtin as they attempt to understand the ontology of art. Moreover, it is this other plane that so interests us as the virtual, a plane that is not false, unreal, or derivative, but somehow true, actual, and productive. Cohen points us toward a third way, leaving aside both the Platonic notion of art as copy and the Aristotelian notion of art as matter.

Cohen's Theory of the Novel

The most obvious element common to Lukács's, Ortega's, and Bakhtin's theories of the novel is the differentiation between the epic and the novel, a distinction already drawn by Friedrich Schlegel. Nonetheless, it is Cohen's cultural and ethical characterization of the two genres that mediates between the Romantic and twentieth-century novelistics. Cohen's relation to Friedrich Schlegel can only be characterized as problematic. Quite clearly, he repeats many of the young Romantic's dicta concerning the novel, reworking such key concepts as incompletion and the mixed genre to fit into his own aesthetics. He fails, however, to mention Schlegel by name either in the *Ethics* or the *Aesthetics* – an omission rendered even more ironic when one takes into account how later generations of thinkers failed to mention Cohen's name, eventually erasing him from the philosophical record. Curiously enough, only pages before he repeats Schlegel's most basic sayings concerning the novel in his *Ethics*, he attacks the form of the aphorism as incomplete and morally dangerous.[57] One can attribute his strident attack on Romanticism to the degeneration of late Romantic art and thought that gave way to the dangerous valorization of the German *Volk*, making it possible that this general distaste for Romanticism causes him to omit naming Schlegel.[58]

Given the systematic connection between ethics and aesthetics in Cohen's thought, it is not surprising that the epic and the novel are first defined in his work on ethics. Cohen founds his entire novelistics on the assertion that modern art should be based on moderation and modesty, and thus opposes the novel to the epic: 'The aesthetic difference in the world epochs may reside in the difference of the epic from the genre that modernity has amplified as the novel.'[59] As the art form of modernity, the novel originates in an ironization of the heroic deeds of the novel begun in Boiardo and brought to fruition in Cervantes. Indeed, such a characterization of the way Cervantes creates a comic spectacle of medieval heroism in a modern world where justice is the work of the state echoes Hegel's reading of *Don Quixote* (*Aesthetics* 1, 196). Once again, the difference (and it is fundamental) between Hegel and Cohen is that the latter considers the modern form of the state with its contractual relation to the citizen to be preferable to what Hegel called the 'Heroic Age.' Given that irony is the mode of moderation and modesty, Cohen attributes ethical significance to the ironization of the epic. The novel operates as an ironic correction of the epic, for the epic naively represents the deeds of heroes who, in turn, represent their tribes. (*ERW* 537–8).[60] The great ethical danger of the epic, particularly in the modern world, is the manner in which it prolongs strife and conflict through the false appearance of peoples as good and bad. The good hero exemplifies the fundamental goodness of his tribe; the enemy exemplifies the fundamental weakness of his. The novel, therefore, has first and foremost ethical significance in its attack on the mythology of the hero and the nation understood as tribe or *Volk*. This it achieves through humour, the artistic force that links the highest aspirations of humanity toward divinity with its animalistic underbelly. In this way, humour corrects the epic by showing up its vanity, and creates a more complete picture of humankind.

In a similar vein, Cohen differentiates between good and bad novels, the bad ones being those that sugarcoat the pettiness and underhandedness of bourgeois life. Good novels, to the contrary, use humour to distinguish between good and evil, and reveal immoral motivations in even the most insignificant characters. In a long quote from *Ethics of*

Pure Will that bears citation because it so succinctly describes how Cohen understands the inner workings of the novel, he explains the poetic relation between good and evil in novelistic humour:

> But humour makes weakness the cause of wickedness; it also then points out flaws and frailties in comfortable morality. Thus, good and evil enter into an interwoven relationship, repeated in an entanglement of their smallest motifs, so that good character appears through it in all his oppositions and contradictions, and so humour brings forth harmony and reconciliation, where, moreover, the opposition builds a unique firmness and trust. Humour's grace is that, contrary to the solemnity and elevated rhetoric of high art, it lowers its gaze toward the baseness and conceit of human life, and for it claims indulgence.[61]

Humour (or irony, as the terms are indistinguishable at this point in Cohen's analysis) works to reveal the source of evil in small things, circumstances, and persons, thus undermining the grand scope of the epic. This smallness can even be taken as an aspect of modernity, given that bourgeois culture conditions the hidden corners of workplace, private home, and public house where the petty intrigues take place. No novelistic character is exempt from evil, unlike the epic hero whose character is a pure representation of social values for taken to be good. And yet humour has a beneficent quality as it creates a work of art in which the opposition of good and evil is reconciled through form and the aesthetic experience. Moreover, humour calls for humble indulgence from the reader. After all, the same mix of good and bad describes the reader's character as the protagonist's. In this sense, humour links up to irony and its corresponding virtue of humility. None are exempt from its penetrating gaze, and yet none are condemned by it. Notably, this concept of the overlapping of ironic gazes, reconciled through harmonic love, will carry over into both Ortega's and Bakhtin's novelistics.

In his *Aesthetics of Pure Feeling*, Cohen links the novel to poetry, the latter understood as a form of internal speech. Therein he develops a history of literary forms that mirrors in significant ways Schlegel's history of the literary genres. Epic is the original form of poetry because it internalizes discourse; that is to say, it speaks of people and not nature (*ARG* 1, 391). Lyric represents the second form of poetry, insofar as it internalizes thought about individuals rather than peoples and heroes. Moreover, through its reflexive consciousness of the image as likeness, it advances beyond the simple relations of identity put forth in the epic

(Wiedebach, *Die Bedeutung der Nationalität für Hermann Cohen* 166). Lyric's limitation is that it knows mainly the interior self, and approaches the exterior only in relation to itself (*ARG* 1, 394). A third form is drama, the genre of action and interchange between individuals (*Handlung*) and, therefore, the genre of ethical development (*ARG* 1, 395). Like Schlegel, Cohen understands the novel in this historical development as a mixed form, encompassing within itself aspects of all the past forms of poetry. As the aesthetic production of a complicated cultural period, it deals with the problem of communal identity found in the epic, the individual problem of love in the lyric, and the moral problem of action in the drama (*ARG* 1, 400).

Apparently referring yet again to one of Schlegel's aphoristic descriptions of the novel, Cohen notes that, in Cervantes' *Don Quixote*, 'poetry becomes the prose of the novel.'[62] The novel, as a form of poetry, should parallel music (*ARG* 1, 400–1). Poetry normally conveys feeling through metre, a form of tempo that links it phenomenologically to music. In its *Begriffsprache*, or expression of concepts, poetry parallels the tone values of music. Likewise, poetry and music contain parallel genres; epic is associated with oratorios, lyric with love ballads, and drama with opera. Cohen can imagine no musical parallel for the novel, mainly because its ethical content is too complicated. Nonetheless, the philosopher has already laid the foundations for a musical understanding of the novel when he describes its humorous workings as creating harmony out of discord and disagreement. The interweaving of conflict and opposition that worked out into a spatial and visual figure of harmony in Schlegel's novelistics of the arabesque takes on auditory tones in Cohen's thought. In Cohen's conception, the novel harmonizes the discords of good and evil present in all modern society.

It is but a short conceptual step to Bakhtin's figuring of this discord as discourses forming a novelistic whole reflective of the social strains of modernity. Craig Brandist argues that Bakhtin's notion of the polyphonic novel is indebted to Cohen's conceptualization of jurisprudence in the socialist democratic state in which '[a]ll consciousnesses have "equal rights" and are correlated with that of the author whose presence is in the perspective on the whole from without. The polyphonic novel is a cosmopolitan idea (Dostoevsky's "form-shaping ideology") that bears the universal principles of humanity' ('The Hero at the Bar of Eternity' 218). Indeed, Cohen invites such a politicization of his thought when he writes of the troubled relation between art and power (*ARG* 2, 389). The more the mighty increase and the weak decline in power, the more art will be pressured to reflect power. Nonetheless, there is a counter-tendency that must take place in art in order to analyse and offset this tendency: art offers those who are differentiated within society a means to imagine a condition in which they are not governed by arbitrary power.

Cohen's Reading of *Don Quixote*

We are finally prepared to approach Cohen's interpretation of Cervantes' masterpiece as the exemplary modern novel, having established both the philosopher's concept of modernity and his concept of the novel as a genre. Modernity represents for the philosopher certain perils, such as racism, nationalism, and the capitalistic cheapening of human dignity, as well as certain advances, particularly with regard to legal human rights and individual freedoms. The novel is the genre that perforce makes light of and critiques modern society. Cohen asserts that *Don Quixote* constructs for the epoch of modernity a foundational form (*Grundform*) toward which the forms of all modern novels tend (*ARG* 2, 119). Lest we consider Cohen's assertion that Cervantes' masterpiece is the foundational form of the modern genre to be prescriptive, it is essential to remember that this philosopher always understands the ideal form as something humankind strives for but never attains. Gregory Moynahan clarifies how the infinitesimal, in spite of its mathematical provenance, can serve to figure all of human thought: 'Reality is never directly given, but is rather the ideal category under which imagination unifies thought and intuition so as to achieve the greatest probable level of "determination" of the particular' (48). Cervantes' *Don Quixote* serves, then, as a curve composed of infinitesimals, limiting and orienting the image of the modern novel toward which all other novels will tend and strive. Indeed, Cohen describes the way the Spanish novel grounds all others in terms that link it visually to the curve created by a differential equation: 'From its breadth [or expanse] can one perhaps derive all the forms of the novel produced by modernity.'[63]

Don Quixote grounds the genre, then, not as a fertile field from which later works grow, but rather as an ideal curve defining (that is to say, limiting) the field of coordinates or sites for later works. The agricultural metaphor of grounding cedes to the mathematical metaphor of bounding. Modern novels, as Cohen continues to describe them, provide the coordinates for a new culture with a new spirit: 'Then they are all didactic poems of great style, spiritual cosmogonies, in which the creation, metamorphosis, and new formation of a culture of spirit is sought.'[64] Novels are didactic, not in a prescriptive manner, but in a productive manner, as they set forth the ideal points, lines, and curves of a new culture. Moreover, as Cohen explains in his *Logic of Pure Knowledge*, the concept of the point correspondent to a theory of infinitesimals is preferable to the traditional idea of the point as the limit of the line, for the point forming a curve serves not as an end, but rather a beginning. In other words, it sets forth the tangent, both the rule and the direction, of future movement (*LRE* 129). In this sense, *Don Quixote* serves as the beginning point for the modern novel, setting forth the genre's rule and direction in a way that is neither purely prescriptive nor descriptive, but rather productive.

Cohen affirms *Don Quixote*'s modernity by contrasting it with Dante's *Divine Comedy*, a move in which he was anticipated by Schlegel. Indeed, Cervantes' novel replaces Dante's masterpiece insofar as 'the sense of this new divine comedy is to engulf all the cultural relics and shrines in vanity.'[65] According to Cohen, although Cervantes took care not to offend the Catholic Church, neither did he favour its claim to the monopoly of salvation in another world over and against that of this world. His novel is modern because it ironizes the sacred commonplaces of his culture, going even beyond its critique of Catholicism to extend to matters of state. For Cohen, the representation of the modern statesman in the person of Sancho Panza is a much weightier issue than the representation of the knight errant in Don Quixote. As Cohen remarks, 'Sancho Panza becomes the ideal governor. That is an even more significant peak in this poetic mountain range than the fact that Don Quixote is an ideal knight errant.'[66] Cervantes would seem to echo Cohen's account of modernity, as he secularizes the medieval Catholic world and replaces religious social authority with that of the state. Indeed, Cohen seems a bit troubled that the creator of Sancho Panza might be making fun of government, just as he makes fun of knight-errantry, and resorts to a rhetorical question concerning Cervantes' possible opinion that each of the governor's presiding remarks might be evil. Because he has read Sancho as the figure of a just governor presiding over a just society, Cohen refrains from exploring the possibility of political parody in *Don Quixote*. Indeed, Cohen remarks that *Don Quixote*, and with it the entire genre of the novel, would not be so essential to modernity if Cervantes had limited his humour to the topics of chivalry and statesmanship. What is it about Sancho that makes him such an attractive figure of a governor for Cohen? Since Cohen does not explain, we must extrapolate from his politics. As a socialist, he worked for a democratic society in which all are involved in the process of governing. This inclusivity creates the whole (*Allheit*), and includes within it the working classes and the poor, among whom Sancho clearly numbers. Moreover, as a neo-Kantian socialist, Cohen advocated not only for political and economic emancipation of the lower cases, but also for their cultural, intellectual, and spiritual education – what the Germans understood as *Bildung*. Sancho's wisdom shows that he has experienced this complete education through his conversations with his master, a fact that Don Quixote himself acknowledges several times in part 2 when commenting on how his servant's language, manner, and rhetorical skills have improved.

For Cohen, love also assumes a central position in Cervantes' establishment of the modern novel's tendencies. Love is the universal feeling toward which art should train the individual, according to Cohen's understanding of art's ethical mission. Cervantes juxtaposes Dulcinea of Toboso, who represents love and lyric poetry, to the figures of Don Quixote and Sancho Panza. Indeed, Don Quixote's love for Dulcinea epitomizes the way the idea effects change in the surrounding world. The figure of Dulcinea functions in the novel as a form of infinitesimal, for she is both an entity and a shadow, existing in the knight errant's mind but effecting his actions in the world. Through the image of the beloved, Cervantes introduces the lyrical into the very centre of the novel, and thus Cohen, like Schlegel, defends the necessity of the love stories interpolated in *Don Quixote*. Moreover, Cohen, in a move that could be deemed stereotypically Romantic and idealist, maintains that all is appearance in this work except the heart. Nonetheless, the generic tendency away from the epic and toward the lyric that Cohen postulates in the novel is absolutely necessary within the philosopher's system. Love in the epic is merely 'a prize won in battle, certainly not an experience that … raises to a higher power the new characteristic value of the individual human life. The novel is therefore only externally the continuation of the epic, because it is internally much more the elaboration of the lyric.'[67] The moral superiority of the lyric – and subsequently of the novel – over the epic stems from Cohen's ethical understanding of love as an essential step in ethical development. On the one hand, the epic, as the genre of warring tribes and nations, represents an ethical construction of the other as enemy and the collective as composed of only neighbours and family. Love, on the other hand, constructs the self as essentially linked to the other. Referring to the Hebrew dictum, 'Love thy neighbour as thyself,' Cohen maintains that 'neighbour' is a mis-translation of the Hebrew *Rea*, which means, in fact, 'the other.' Subsequently, any understanding that the loved are only those close to us, be it on account of blood, language, religion, or tribe, is based on a fundamental misunderstanding of the commandment. The philosopher further claims that the only pure love of the other 'is the broadening of the very subject through compassion for another subject.'[68] With the fig-ure of widening or broadening the self, we arrive at a notion of love con-nected once again to *Aufgabe*, to the work of the self toward the exterior world, expanding its limitations and interaction with the other.

According to Cohen, Cervantes maintains love as the centre of the novel, even though he widens its stretch to embrace the entire culture (*ARG* 2, 123). Don Quixote's love for Dulcinea remains essential, for it represents one way by which the novelistic conflict between the ideal love of eternity and the earthly, relative love of wedlock can be medi-ated. How can eternal love be brought to earth? In the case of Don Quixote we have a clear example of the ideal leading to action in *Aufgabe*; even the existence of a possible physical manifestation of the other in the peasant Aldonza Lorenzo is transumed by Don Quixote's powerful vision of Dulcinea. It is helpful to turn to Cohen's reading of Goethe's *Elective Affinities*, for in this novel the philosopher finds the fullest working out of the tragic dimension of love. Charlotte and Eduard, a seemingly happily married couple, fall out of love with each other. Charlotte gradually moves toward Hauptmann, and Eduard en-ters in a passionate romance with the young Ottilie. Their true loves are, of course, doomed, for moral society cannot accept the propriety of such love. Charlotte's baby, sired by Eduard but with the face of Ottilie, becomes the victim of this tragedy, and dies by drowning. Indeed, the introduction of idealized love into earthly relations can only be tragic for Cohen, for the eternal and ideal cannot reside peacefully on this earth: 'Eternity is also here the restlessness of striving and struggling.'[69] Depicting this tragic restlessness is the work of the novel as it enters the space between eternal love and the real world, so to speak: 'There is no complete union in moral culture between the ideal and the actual. In this cleft of the spirit enters art.'[70] The contrast in imagery with Lukács's notion of a cleft or division is telling. For Lukács, the chasm that typifies modernity exists between the individual and society, as the latter pre-vents the former from realizing his goals. For Cohen, the chasm exists between the ideal and the actual (understood as product of human ac-tion), into which art moves. Within this cleft art occupies a mediating space – it brings the ideal near to the humanly produced actual. The novel, for Cohen, has the task of imaging or imagining ideal love in actual conditions: 'And so arises the work of the novel: to represent the eternity of love in the love story of mortal human beings, to which the human heart soars, and before which humanity's poor cultural condition must subside into misery.'[71]

Cohen's characterization of art as a liminal production situated in the tragic gap between the ideal and the actual holds true for all the major literary genres. *Aufgabe,* understood as the work of the self, or the working out of the self, toward the other, also underlies Cohen's understanding of both the lyric and the epic. Along with Schlegel and Lukács, Cohen characterizes the lyric as the genre of the individual, opposing it to the epic as the genre of a community. Likewise, he recognizes that the lyric problematizes the desire of the self toward another person. Cohen's breakthrough is to conceive of the loved or desired other as a *Du,* or Thou, rather than a he or she. Upon transforming the beloved from a third-person pronoun into a second-person pronoun, the lover moves into a relation with the loved one that is both more problematic and more promising. Lyric represents the confrontation of the lover with the beloved Thou. Love also promotes longing or desire, feelings that expand the self and extend it beyond its own boundaries (*ARG* 2, 26). Love, as represented in the lyric, furthers the ethical work of the self in engaging the beloved Thou (*ARG* 2, 23). Furthermore, lyric becomes a dominant form in early modernity, when humanism, the Renaissance, and the Reformation all free the self from the confines of the medieval communal ethos toward the new ethical freedom of the individual (*ARG* 2, 39). The novel, however, goes one step further than the lyric; that is to say, not only does it expand the self through loving engagement with another, but it also reveals or shows up the spiritual poverty of the society and culture in which individuals find themselves.

The difference between the lyric and the novel may be thought in terms of degrees or powers. The lyric expresses what Cohen terms the dual unity of the self as it interacts with the beloved Thou, but it is sufficient for the genre to stay within the confines of individual experience and the union of individual hearts. Cohen hastens to add that love itself is a more complicated phenomenon: 'Even its vicissitudes, its own ups and downs, deserve development, and its complications and entanglements with the surrounding world promote not only description, like the miscellany and news they offer, but also enquiry, as in legal proceedings and even in the observation undertaken in the diplomatic official documents of world history. They belong in the house archive of the human heart, which is not exhausted and dispatched through the epigrammatic heartfelt sighs of the lyric.'[72] Therefore, when Cohen describes the novel as a *Liebesgeschichte*, he does not define it merely as a love story, but rather as a *history* of love. As such, the novel represents not only the sentimental experiences of individuals, but also the way in which these experiences emerge and play themselves out in relation to society. We must take quite seriously the extended metaphor of this passage that equates the novel to legal and historical documents, for through the writing and reading of the novel a form of social enquiry takes place.[73] Here Cohen seems to share a common opinion with Hegel, who likewise finds in Goethe's idyllic novels a happy literary development. And yet for Hegel, Goethe succeeds because he 'has been able to find and present out of our modern world today characteristics, descriptions, situations, and complications which in their own sphere bring alive again what is undyingly attractive in the primitive human circumstances of the Odyssey and the pictures of patriarchal life in the Old Testament' – in other words, the lost heroic, pre-capitalist past (*Aesthetics* 2, 1110).

The comparison with Hegel serves to highlight Cohen's unique notion of the novel not as nostalgic recreation of a lost golden age, but rather as critique of modern society. The very image of the novel as the house archive of love involves a merging of the public and the private in the genre, what Cohen terms the collisions and conflicts of love with cultural institutions regulating morality (*ARG* 2, 122). As a form of research, the novel focuses on the conflicts between the sentimental and the social, a position not so different from Lukács's insistence on the novel as the genre problematizing the individual in relation to society. As Kluback reminds us, Cohen argues for the study of the individual in his historical milieu because '[t]he historical situation, the apparent consequence of a multiplicity of causes, is the true genesis of the problem of causation' (*Hermann Cohen* 28). As a form of enquiry, the novel takes on a theoretical bent, a position not so different from Schlegel's merging of philosophical and literary enquiry in the novel. Cohen furthers both these lines of thought by insisting that it is precisely this scientific, theoretical bent of the novel that necessitates the abandonment of metre (*ARG* 2, 122). Furthermore, by comparing the novel to legal proceedings and diplomatic treaties, Cohen pushes the envelope of the notion of the novel as a mixed genre. No longer does it arise from the intermingling only of literary forms, but rather of all forms of human discourse. It is now clear how Cohen lays the theoretical groundwork for Bakhtin's conceptualization of the novel as formed from various and opposing discourses. In addition, when Bakhtin proposes in 'The Author and the Hero' that the author enjoys a transcendent point of view allowing her to see the hero within the horizon of determining factor, the Russian grants the author the power of the judge (Brandist, 'The Hero at the Bar of Eternity' 216). Thus, Cohen's notion of jurisprudence is embedded within twentieth-century novelistics.

The neo-Kantian philosopher has grounded logically, ethically, and aesthetically many of the ideas glimpsed by Schlegel and accepted by the majority of twentieth-century literary critics concerning the nature of the novel as a genre. Cohen has defined the ethical problematic of the modern individual as being at odds with society. He has also maintained that the novel intensifies the confrontation of the self with other selves by placing it within the larger cultural framework. Even the very concept of *Aufgabe*, with its notion of a to and fro, or a give and take, between the self and the outside world, prefigures many of the epistemological problems concerning the nature of the aesthetic experience to be explored by later thinkers. The relativity of truth clearly implied and explored by Cohen will continue to trouble, both positively and negatively, coming thinkers. What is missing from these later formulations is Cohen's attempt to ground the novel epistemologically and aesthetically, and by so doing, to find a new ground for the notion of human liberty once modernity has completed its work of separating ethical standards from social and religious norms. It seems paradoxical to speak of an idealist system that seeks to ground, and yet that is clearly the philosopher's goal. It underlies his very idiolect, as he writes of grounding forms and ideas. Yet it is through the innovative and imaginative reworking of the idea as future goal, of the limit as infinitesimal, of the future as a tangent or direction, and of the work of the self in logical thought, moral activity, and artistic creation as *Aufgabe* that he strives to present his idealist system. His mature work may be viewed as transferring idealism onto an alternate set of values that will shape the work of later thinkers. Process replaces fixity, negotiation replaces certainty, and goals for the future replace eternal truths. Art in general, and the novel in particular, will perforce enjoy renewed prestige in this system, for they are fictions in the productive sense in which the Marburg School understood the term: cases that offer examples for study and models for future action.[74]

Cervantes' novel *Don Quixote* continues to serve Cohen as the modern novel par excellence because of the ways it fictionalizes the problems the philosopher sees as fundamental to modernity: not only the conflict between individual and community, or between imagination and reason, embodied in Don Quixote, but also the problems of social justice and good government manifest in the life and actions of Sancho Panza and the powerful ethical expansion of the self made possible through love exemplified in the knight errant's devotion to Dulcinea. Both the love of Don Quixote for Dulcinea and the relation of the knight to his squire figure powerful ways to break down the politics of modernity and envision a better social order in the future. The fact that Dulcinea is an ideal that Don Quixote strives to reach mirrors in a provocative way Cohen's notion of *Aufgabe* as an ethical striving toward an unreachable but guiding ideal. Attaining the ideal is impossible, but the struggle toward it should transform the self and society. Such an understanding of his quest for Dulcinea was, indeed, on Don Quixote's mind. Aware that Aldonza Lorenzo, the peasant girl who inspired his vision of Dulcinea, did not measure up to his ideal, Don Quixote defends his love for her even in the face of her possible non-existence and inaccessibility. As Don Quixote admits to the Duke and the Duchess toward the end of his journeys (2: chap. 32), 'God knows if Dulcinea exists in the world or not, or if she is imaginary or not imaginary; these are not the kinds of things whose verification can be carried through to the end. I neither engendered nor gave birth to my lady, although I contemplate her in the manner proper to a lady who possesses the qualities that can make her famous throughout the world' (*DQ* 672).[75]

Nonetheless, Cervantes presents a roadblock to Cohen's reading of the novel in none other than Don Quixote's death. The dying man reclaims his former identity as Alonso Quijano, and renounces his chivalric mission as foolish and dangerous. For Cohen to ground his ethical imperative – the work for a better society – he must turn to Sancho Panza. Even at his master's deathbed, Sancho does not abjure their adventures. To the contrary, he begs to return to the road, this time taking the guise of pastoral characters. Sancho's transformation, when read through the lens of neo-Kantian socialism, represents incremental motion toward an ideal society. Sancho has been improved through his exchanges with Don Quixote; he has experienced the German neo-classical ideal of *Bildung*: moral, social, and academic education. If Sancho, an illiterate peasant devoted to the flesh, can be educated, then so can the working class. If Sancho can be a good governor, then democracy based on the full incorporation of all into civil society can succeed. Cohen, however, cannot hold on for long to this vision of culture as redemptive of the relation between the self and the other, and in the final years of his life will return to his Jewish religion to ground loving, ethical action. The fate of both his nations – German and Jewish – in the near future will contradict all the values of socialism, education, tolerance, and civil society that he has so thoroughly attempted to ground, and throw into doubt the nature of human reason, will, and feeling.

5 The Poetics of Resuscitation: Unamuno's Anti-Novelistics

Miguel de Unamuno, novelist, poet, philosopher, professor of Greek, and rector of the University of Salamanca, lived a life-long struggle with Cervantes. Born in 1864, some three centuries after Cervantes' birth, Unamuno found his greatest intellectual and artistic antagonist to be the author of *Don Quixote*. When read against the backdrop of the various theories of the novel explored in this book, Unamuno's writings on *Don Quixote* present an anti-novelistics in which the major tendencies that unite Schlegel, Lukács, Cohen, and Ortega are denied, if not overtly ignored. Nowhere, for instance, does Unamuno consider the novel as opposed to – or even different from – the epic. Indeed, he equates great novels with epic poems and includes among them not only *The Iliad*, *The Odyssey*, *The Divine Comedy*, and *Don Quixote*, but also the major writings of Spinoza, Kant, Hegel, Thucydides, and the gospel writers (Navajas 73–4). If anything, the novel for Unamuno subsumes and includes all other genres and modes in an agonistic co-existence (Álvarez Castro 222). His musings on Don Quixote's heroism clearly position Cervantes' protagonist as a sort of epic hero. Although Unamuno problematizes modernity, he does not do so by advocating for scientific progress, artistic innovation, or socialist democracy. His critique of Spain's supposedly delayed modernity does not call for the adoption of European values and models, but rather a return to what he deemed Spanish values. Nor does he view the novel as a particularly modern genre. In short, Unamuno reads *Don Quixote* through the lens of his own thought, in which the novel participates in the tragic, epic, and comic modes and in which the answers to modernity's dilemmas are to be found in neither the political right nor the left. To sum up, he puts forth a poetics based on the problems of literary creation rather than a novelistics based on epistemological, ontological, or sociological problems.

It could be argued that Unamuno more fully integrates the Romantic notion of imagination (as opposed to reason) into his poetics. He certainly founds his notion of the ethical function of literature upon the imagination's capacity to create sympathy and understanding (Álvarez Castro 117). He also disassociates the literary from the mimetic function, grounding it instead in the free movement of imagination (128). His notion of the organic – as opposed to formal – genesis of poetry contrasts with the neo-Kantian dependence on mathematics, and recalls the Romantic appreciation of the lived, the irrational, and the imaginative as sources of art (La Rubia Prado, *Unamuno y la vida como ficción* 27). His main mode of discourse has been described as an open dialectic alternating between opposing sides or points of view (Valdés 'Salamanca 1898' 269). This understanding of dialectic links it to *poeisis*, the creative making of meaning. Don Quixote serves as the exemplar of the poetic self, struggling to actualize his interior world. Unamuno proposes a poetics rather than a novelistics precisely because of his focus on the character Don Quixote rather than the work *Don Quixote*. The Spanish philosopher María Zambrano describes Unamuno's approach as one of extraction and abstraction (111). Unamuno extracts Don Quixote from the novelistic whole and eliminates the complex world in which Cervantes places his protagonist. This process renders Don Quixote a tragic figure rather than a novelistic one, as Don Quixote is seen to enact the tragedy of will and faith (112).

Unamuno is often listed in literary histories as a member of the Generation of 1898, a group of young Spanish writers and intellectuals led to question their national heritage upon the defeat of Spain by the United States in the Spanish-American War and the subsequent loss of Spain's remaining colonies, including Cuba, Puerto Rico, and the Philippines.[1] He certainly wrestled with the place of post-imperial Spain in Europe (Zambrano 36–44). His long and active life as Spain's leading intellectual saw him involved (as supporter or foe) in all the country's major political moments: the dictatorship of Primo de Rivera (1923–30), during which he was exiled from Spain; the Spanish Republic of 1931, in which he began as an elected *diputado* but ended up as a vocal critic of its corruption and failure to prevent anticlerical violence; and Franco's uprising in 1936 initiating the Spanish Civil War. It is on account of this last political upheaval that Unamuno is most well-known as a political activist both inside and outside Spain. At first optimistic that the military revolt would lead to an ethical reform of the Spanish government during the summer of 1936, Unamuno quickly realized that what was actually taking place was the extermination of the movement's foes of all stripes and persuasions. The confrontation with Fascism came to a head on 12 October 1936, the so-called Day of the People (*Día de la Raza*), in a public ceremony at the University of Salamanca. Due to his initial support of the uprising, Franco and his followers had expected that Unamuno, rector of the University of Salamanca, would speak in their favour. Contrary to their expectations, Unamuno challenged their intolerance of Spain's multiple cultures, including his own beloved Basque people and mother tongue, and their bloodthirsty cult of death. In what Unamuno recognized as a final irony, he ended up denouncing central paradoxes of his own philosophy in his denunciation of Franco. The elderly philosopher was led from the auditorium by Franco's wife, Carmen Polo, to prevent an eruption of violence, and died a broken man on 31 December 1936.

The Spanish Struggle over *Don Quixote*

For both Unamuno and Ortega y Gasset, Cervantes was first and foremost a Spaniard. In nineteenth-century Spain, the interpretation of Cervantes' masterpiece was subject to the interests and machinations of the two broadly defined groups whose constant to and fro defined the political face of nineteenth-century Spain: the liberals and the conservatives.[2] The liberals, composed of the entire gamut of 'freethinkers,' running from mercantile liberals to anarchists, considered themselves the inheritors of Spain's all too brief attempt at broad-based constitutional, democratic reform under the Cortes de Cádiz (1810–13), the initiatives of which included the abolition of the Inquisition (1813) and the acceptance of the 1812 Constitution allowing for freedom of the press and limitations on royal power. The conservative group was composed of Catholic clerics and conservative laypeople, wealthy aristocrats objecting to the loss of seigniorial rights, some urban bourgeoisie, Carlists, and Castilian centrists. They deemed themselves to be the protectors of Spain's national identity epitomized by the defence of Catholicism and empire. During the second half of the nineteenth century, an uneasy arrangement of alternating conservative and liberal governments conserved order within the nation, although the liberal/conservative split was complicated by growing Catalan and Basque nationalist movements, the upsurge of labour unionism, and the appearance of several successive generations of disillusioned intellectuals.

Spanish interpretations of Cervantes' *Don Quixote* from this period reflect an almost crude caricature of the political situation. From the left appear books proclaiming the novel to be a critique of the Spanish monarchy, the Catholic Church, and the Inquisition, written by an author who championed religious heterodoxy – if not Protestantism or atheism – political democracy, and free-thinking in general. Typical of this reading is Nicolás Díaz de Benjumea's *Estafeta de Urganda* (1861). In response to Benjumea's vision of a liberal Cervantes whose masterpiece contained esoteric statements on the hypocrisy and corruption of the Church and state of his time, the Spanish novelist Juan Valera countered with the image of a conservative Cervantes. This Miguel de Cervantes was a true believer, an orthodox Catholic who defended the Church in all its doctrines and sacraments, as well as a loyal subject and soldier of Philip II. Unamuno's frequent eruptions at the so-called *cervantistas* expressed his impatience with a form of philology in which unproblematized authorial intention provided the only basis for correct reading of the text. Thus, the declaration in the first prologue – from the mouth of an anonymous friend – that this work was a satirical attack on the literature of knight-errantry, was held by many scholars of the time to be the only acceptable reading of *Don Quixote*. This stated intention then barred as unacceptable any reading of the text in which a deeper or hidden meaning was to be found. Valera affirmed this position by providing the dominant metaphor for such a reading of Cervantes' novel: a realistic painting produced with photographic fidelity ('Sobre la *Estafeta de Urganda*'). Cast aside all the rhetoric about sublime poetry, and we are left with the image of Cervantes as a faithful photographer, recording real life. The author provides a mechanistic but supposedly verisimilar snapshot of reality that the reader then accepts at face value. In brief, Spanish interpretations of *Don Quixote* remained integrally and visibly bound to the politics of the interpreter until the introduction of the philological method at the turn of the century.

In response to the crisis of 1898 arose the so-called Generation of 1898, among them the cultural critic Ángel Ganivet, and Cervantes' biographer, Francisco Navarro Ledesma. In an attempt to understand the causes of Spain's decline from a world power to a marginalized backwater, these intellectuals returned to the nation's literary myths and traditions, searching for the traces of Spain's 'essential' national character. Cervantes was not to be seen as liberal or conservative, but as Spanish first and foremost; likewise, Don Quixote's failure was not that of leftist or rightist ideology, but that of Spain as a people and a nation. Don Quixote was not only the extravagant idealist in this period, but also could stand for the indefatigable fighter, imperial soldier, enlightened scholar, or even proud nationalist and chauvinist, and thus his adventures could serve as the mirror for the political adventures and misadventures of various governments (Varela Olea 47). All of these visions of Don Quixote, despite their differences, grew from the assumption that Spain as a nation was not modern. Modernity, understood as European, was believed to have bypassed Spain.

Exemplary of the political appropriation of Cervantes' novel at the time was the centenary of the publication of *Don Quixote*, part I, celebrated throughout Spain in May of 1905.[3] First suggested by the liberal journalist Mariano de Cavia, this commemoration of Cervantes and his masterpiece was intended as a showpiece to celebrate the best of Spain. Cervantes was a figure in whom all Spaniards could take pride, and whose example could serve as a model for the future of Spain. The activities themselves reveal the ever-deepening rifts in Spain – even the briefest perusal of the many speeches, journalistic essays, and accounts of the various parades and spectacles read in retrospect as foreshadowing the Spanish Civil War to come three decades later. From the pulpit parish priests proclaimed that Cervantes was theirs, whereas socialist journalists proclaimed that he belonged to the proletariat. A country noblewoman lavished festivities on her minions, including a free bullfight for all, in order to offset the activities of labour union organizers. Catholic schoolgirls were instructed to write essays on the exemplary figures of feminine service and devotion to be found in Cervantes' work, whereas atheists and anarchists pointed to examples of anti-clericalism and critique of the Inquisition and monarchy to be found in the same texts. In short, the nineteenth-century debate between Benjumea and Valera was transferred to the pulpit, plaza, and classroom in the 1905 centenary. Unamuno published *The Life of Don Quixote and Sancho* in 1905 against the backdrop of these activities as a challenge to the official image of a patriotic, domesticated Cervantes proposed therein. For him, this act constituted the resuscitation of Don Quixote and the rejection of Cervantes' authorial intentions (*UOC* 7: 290). Making the text speak to the modern reader and reveal truths about the modern Spanish character is a political act born of necessity.

Cervantes in Unamuno's Writings

Although Don Quixote, Sancho Panza, and Cervantes were Unamuno's constant companions, I will focus on several key texts that epitomize the twentieth-century Spaniard's appropriation of *Don Quixote*.[4] The figure of Don Quixote looms in major philosophical writings by Unamuno, including his early *On Casticism* (*En torno al casticismo*, 1895) and his *On the Tragic Sentiment of Life* (*Del sentimiento trágico de la vida*, 1913). Don Quixote stands for the problem of modern Spain, although Unamuno's perspective on both the Spanish problem and the literary character takes a 180-degree turn by 1905. Nonetheless, *On Casticism* sets forth concepts that will shape the entire course of Unamuno's thought, such as *intrahistoria* and *casticismo*. *Intrahistoria* refers to Unamuno's belief that true history arises from the daily lives and customs of the people, whereas *casticismo* refers to Unamuno's notion of the Spanish people as a warrior nation valuing decisive, individual action and a form of mysticism that bypasses intellectual subtlety to seek the submersion of the individual in the whole. The contrasting events of 13 July 1898 epitomize *intrahistoria*: on the day when the Americans defeated the Spanish fleet in Cuba, Unamuno observed the Spanish *intrahistoria* at work, as he watched peasants working the fields in Salamanca, oblivious to the defeat (Rabaté 139). *Casticismo* is a centuries-old accrual of customs and thought patterns that arose from Spain's past, first in the centuries-long *Reconquista* of the Iberian peninsula from the Moors, and then in the Hapsburg era of imperial conquest and expansion. Don Quixote represents for Unamuno this national character; Sancho, speaking the common sense of the *pueblo*, completes the dyad; and Spain stands represented in the pair. In 1895 Unamuno calls for the death of Don Quixote so that Alonso Quijano, the voice of reason, can be reborn (*UOC* 1:854), and so that Sancho's voice of common sense can be heard (*UOC* 1:859).[5] In June of 1898, frustrated by the defeat of the Spanish military, he repeats the call for Don Quixote's death (Rabaté 135).

By 1905, Unamuno has not changed his reading of *Don Quixote*, but rather the terms by which he values it. Thus, he will no longer call for the death of Don Quixote, but rather his resurrection. Sancho's common sense is not to be heeded, but rather Don Quixote's example of immutable individual heroism serves as a counterpoint to the stifling conformity of the people. *The Life of Don Quixote and Sancho* (1905) is usually described as a commentary on Cervantes' novel, although Unamuno made it clear that it was in no way an erudite commentary, but rather a passionate statement of his own thought (Álvarez Castro 35). As such, it is a unique sort of commentary that combines often insightful perception into Cervantes' texts with wilfully idiosyncratic and paradoxical musings on larger issues such as life and death, truth and madness, Spain and modernity. Unamuno frequently interrupts the commentary to insert his own ideas and reactions (La Rubia Prado, *Unamuno y la vida como ficción* 127). He also resorts to an intimate dialogue with the reader, whom he addresses informally by using a collective 'tú' in his exhortations, remonstrations, and harangues (Roberts 104). The text is loosely structured according to the chapters in Cervantes' *Don Quixote*, but the author feels no need to follow them, often skipping one or combining several. By skipping the interpolated tales and discourses on such sixteenth-century topics as the arms vs letters debate, he highlights both Don Quixote's eloquent speeches and his frequent physical battering. Although his reading of Cervantes' novel is generally considered idiosyncratic by Cervantes scholars, it has influenced scholarly readings. Prefiguring Salvador de Madariaga's *Guia de lector del Quijote* (1926), Unamuno identifies the effect Don Quixote has on Sancho as the squire's 'quixotification' (Ouimette *Reason Aflame* 73). His notion that Cervantes' novel reveals Spain's vital *intra-historia* and polemic gives rise to much of Américo Castro's thought (Marías, *Miguel de Unamuno* 75–6). At times Unamuno considers the issues of literary genre, but only to ponder the tragic, epic, or comic elements of *Don Quixote*. At no time does he label Cervantes' text a modern novel. To the contrary, he only mentions the word *novela* twice, and then according to its early modern usage as the Italianate *novella* in reference to the interpolated story 'The Man Who Was Recklessly Curious' (*Curioso impertinente*), upon which he deigns not to comment except to assert that it is completely irrelevant to Don Quixote's story.

In *On the Tragic Sentiment of Life in Men and in Peoples* (1913), Unamuno addresses both the existential problem of the individual, faced by but unwilling to accept his mortality, and the development of national systems of belief and behaviour. The term 'sentiment' is crucial here, for Unamuno understands the human consciousness as persisting through the body (Luby 47). By calling attention to the self, pain rather than pleasure provides the greater consciousness of self (Ilie 36). The human mind is a 'a troubled space ... that merit[s] the dignity of being explored and civilized, respected and known' (Sinclair 31). In opposition to Descartes, Kant, Hegel, and nineteenth-century idealism, Unamuno puts forth the challenge that reason is, in fact, a product of society: 'Reason owes its origin by chance to language. We think through articulation, that is to say reflexively, thanks to articulated language, and this language sprang from the need to transmit our thoughts to our neighbours.'[6] He approaches this assertion from several vantage points, including the religious, the literary, and the biological. His argument for the genesis of reason and language as products of a species that manages to preserve itself and reproduce through social relations is based upon a Darwinist evolutionary stance (*UOC* 7: 120–31). Unamuno abolishes the distinction between reason and fantasy, stating on evolutionary grounds that reason springs from imagination. Given that the senses arose through chance as faculties that favoured the preservation of the species, our perceptible reality is itself based on what we have needed to survive as a species – and, for Unamuno, as individuals. Modern philosophy has discounted the physical and social basis of humanity, and thus turned the living being into a mere abstraction. Descartes's principal error, according to Unamuno, is beginning from the mind and setting aside the flesh-and-blood thinker who wishes not to die.[7] The tragic sentiment of life arises from the possibility that reason and life are opposed, and that the irrational and even the anti-rational are the actual bases of life (*UOC* 7: 129). Don Quixote figures as the hero of this work precisely because he refuses to live the distinction between what is vital and what is rational.

How to Make a Novel, or in Spanish *Cómo se hace una novela* (French version, 1926, and Spanish version, 1927), stands in stark contrast, both in content and form, to the modern theories of the novel examined in this book.[8] The title is best translated quite literally from the Spanish into the English, for the gist of Unamuno's text is that one makes a novel by making one's life.[9] In a letter from the period to Warner Fite, his American translator, Unamuno quipped that *How to Make a Novel* can be reduced to how to make a novelist, a reader, and an individual (Batchelor 78). To that effect, this work is the story of the protagonist, Jugo de la Raza, who, like Unamuno, leads a pointless life in exile in Paris. As Unamuno notes, this character is himself, and the name proceeds from his own: U being the first letter of Unamuno, Jugo being the last name of his maternal grandmother and the ancient family seat in Vizcaya, and Larraza being the Basque name of his paternal grandmother (*CHN* 187). Jugo de la Raza, meaning in Spanish 'the juice of the people,' links this figure not only to the author Unamuno, but also to Spain. Not much happens to this protagonist who debates whether he should finish reading an unnamed novel, for he fears that his life, like the skin in the novel, will shrink to nothing as he finishes the text. Unamuno read Balzac's *Le peau de chagrin* around this time, and was clearly inspired by the work to explore how history and legend consume the individual (Turner 117). The text's epigraph, the Augustinian quote *Mihi quaestio factus sum*, establishes the philosophical nature of the work as an inquest into the self (Franz 41–2). As a problematization of his own person, Unamuno described the work to his friend Jean Cassou as his tragic consciousness of his emptiness and Spain's abjection (Zubizarreta 66). In its political dimension, the text personalizes the problem of Spain into a conflict between Unamuno, figured as Don Quixote, and the dictator Primo de Rivera, a sort of Don Juan figure dedicated to self-gratification and self-preservation (Roberts 198).

The work itself poses a number of textual difficulties occasioned in part by its production. First published in French in Cassou's translation of Unamuno's text, it was then retranslated from the French back to Spanish by Unamuno.[10] Frequent biting references to Unamuno's exile and the politicians and generals responsible for it were expunged in the editions published in Spain during Franco's time. It is a fragmentary text, and calls to mind Schlegel's use of fragments (La Rubia Prado, *Unamuno y la vida como ficción* 30–4). Moreover, it contains almost all the literary forms in which Unamuno wrote: narrative, essay, diary, philosophy, and poetry (S. Roberts 206). These forms can themselves be subsumed under two categories within the text: the literary or fictional level, and the documentary level, based on autobiography and self-display (Zubizarreta 115).The text thus typifies Unamuno's notion of the unfinished and unfinishable autobiographical text, subject to continual reworking and even mutilation or recreation by active readers (be they censors, translators, or friends).

Unamuno vs Cervantes: The Struggle for Don Quixote's Body

Fundamental to Unamuno's reading of *Don Quixote* is his belief that the novel springs from a genius superior to that seen in Cervantes' other works. Such an observation was a commonplace of the time – indeed, arguably the greatest achievement of twentieth-century Cervantes scholars has been to rescue works such as *La Galatea, The Exemplary Novels,* and *Persiles and Segismunda* from oblivion. Unamuno makes no bones about it: the literary character Don Quixote is superior to his author, Cervantes. The supposed disparity between *Don Quixote* and the other works allows him to propose the following conundrum: that Don Quixote, in the guise of Cide Hamete Benengeli, dictated the narrative to Cervantes (*VDQ* 274). If Don Quixote dictated his story to Cervantes, then it is not beyond the pale for Unamuno to suggest that Don Quixote and Sancho whispered in his own ears as he wrote his story of their lives – which, indeed, he does suggest. The encounter between writer and protagonist is more than a mere whim for Unamuno, and will continue to haunt his writings throughout his life.

At times Unamuno figures his rivalry with Cervantes as a fight for Cervantes' or Cide's manuscripts, whereas at other times he figures it as a competition for Don Quixote's parentage. In chapter 9 of part I, there appears a torn-up old manuscript written in Arabic characters about the deeds of Don Quixote, which a narrator (the suggestion is Cervantes himself) finds by accident one day in the market of Toledo, located just outside the old Jewish quarter. By happy chance (yet not so accidental, Toledo being known for its medieval Jewish and Moorish communities as well as the School of Translation), he also finds there a young *morisco* who renders a translation of the manuscript in about six weeks in exchange for raisins and wheat. Cide's manuscript comes to us only through this presumably poor translation couched in Cervantes' text. To assert Cide's historicity, as well as that of Don Quixote, is a flagrant violation of all the narrative frames within which Cervantes has placed this fictional manuscript. Such a violation is typical of Unamuno's literary thought and creation, for from this transgression of boundaries he seeks to problematize authorship and readership as well as the status of fiction.

The missing manuscripts of *Don Quixote* serve to figure through metonymy and irony the struggle for authority over the story and its protagonists. In a 1905 article, 'On the Reading and Interpretation of *Don Quixote*,' Unamuno expresses his profound relief that Cervantes' original manuscript has never been found. If it were to show up, it would elicit a flood of literary analyses of Cervantes' handwriting, since the fetishizing impulse of the *cervantistas* would lead them to focus on the physical traces of the author rather than the text (*UOC* 1:1236). In an elaborate joke in the prologue to the 1928 edition of *The Life of Don Quixote and Sancho*, Unamuno claims to possess Cide's manuscript. This text purportedly affirms that he, Unamuno, was correct in attributing a certain passage in Cervantes' *Don Quixote* to Sansón Carrasco rather than Sancho in his *The Life of Don Quixote and Sancho*. Moreover, upon perusing this non-existent manuscript, Unamuno has come to believe that Cide was actually not an Arab but rather a Moroccan Jew. He repeats the same device of an embedded manuscript written by a named narrator, in this case a Spanish woman Ángela Carballino, who became the friend and confidante of a village priest being proposed for beatification, in the short novel *San Manuel Bueno, mártir* (1931). In this case, Unamuno emerges at the end of the novel in possession of her manuscript and declares his faith in her reality. His taking possession of Cide's manuscript is more convoluted due to the intervening and troublesome presence of Cervantes.

Unamuno attacks the obstacle that is Cervantes by claiming that the latter was born to write the novel, and that he, Unamuno, was born to comment upon it (*VDQ* 276). Such revelations serve to demonstrate what Unamuno calls the 'objectivity, the existence – *ex-sistere* means to be outside of – of Don Quixote and Sancho and their entire chorus outside of and above novelistic fiction.'[11] Not only does Unamuno flout all normal conventions for reading fiction, he also fashions a false etymology, since the Latin source for the word existence is *ex(s)istere*, which does not mean 'to be outside of' but rather 'to appear.' The joke goes one step further, for it is precisely the appearance of the fictional manuscript, as well as the fictional characters Don Quixote and Sancho Panza, that Unamuno claims as his own experience. In his writings, Unamuno uses the Latin root *sistere* to name his agonistic notion of life, one based on persistence, resistance, and insistence (Cerezo Galán, *Máscaras de lo trágico* 291). Through the appearance/existence of Don Quixote and Sancho, Unamuno affirms his right to them and to resisting Cervantes' authorial claim.

The metaphor of parentage is even more resistant to Unamuno's claims to Don Quixote. Cervantes avoided taking full paternity for his novel, and in his prologue to the first book of *Don Quixote* claimed that the work is his stepson. Moreover, the phrase that one is the 'son of his own works' (*hijo de sus obras*) recurs frequently throughout the novel. Unamuno, aware of Cervantes' hesitancy, insists upon exploring the possible permutations of Don Quixote's parentage.[12] In his 'On the Reading and Interpretation of *Don Quixote*,' Unamuno maintains that if one must say that Cervantes was Don Quixote's father, then his mother was the Spanish people – and what follows is that Don Quixote displayed more of his mother's heritage than his father's (*UOC* 1:1233). The genius of *Don Quixote* arises from the Spanish people; indeed, Unamuno defines genius as the individualized people (*UOC* 1:1234). The issue of paternity grows ever more complicated as Unamuno tends to figure Don Quixote as a Christ figure. In notes that probably date from the period when Unamuno was writing the original version of *How to Make a Novel*, he alludes to the virgin mother of Don Quixote as the Spanish people's fantasy expressed through Cervantes. This, of course, leads to the concept of the 'virgin father, another contradiction' (*CHN* 124). Even Don Quixote seems to work virgin births, as his works engender others. In *How to Make a Novel* Unamuno sets forth the follow-ing: if we are the sons and daughters of our works, are we not also the parents of our works? Then we, like Cervantes and Don Quixote, be-come our own trinity as fathers and sons of ourselves, with our work being the Holy Spirit (*CHN* 216).

For Unamuno, the roles of author and reader likewise blur. Because he defines human reality as largely textual, the human being performs life in the theatre of the world and participates in a chain of representa-tions (Navajas 60–1). Unamuno consistently uses the term 'poetry' to refer to all creative activity, for in this sense he recuperates the ancient Greek meaning of *poeisis* as creation (Álvarez Castro 76–7). The cult of Don Quixote the character, as opposed to *Don Quixote* the novel, par-ticipates in the poetic chain, for it foments continued creative activity among the readers (78). By the same token, it is the reality of the literary character that impedes its author from killing it off, let alone controlling its future readings. Don Quixote and Sancho live outside of Cervantes' novel through an active form of reading that is described as a consump-tion or eating of the text and that resonates with the biblical injunction to consume the scriptures (Revelations 10:8–11).[13] According to *How to Make a Novel*, reading and writing a novel are inextricably combined in the activity of becoming a novel. Indeed, the reader of a novel becomes a novelist, and the reader of history becomes a historian (*CHN* 217). Unamuno's radical affirmation of the reader's authority depends on his belief that the reader makes the literary text present through reading. The living text of Cervantes' *Don Quixote* is, then, what Unamuno reads it to be. As he asserts in *On the Tragic Sentiment of Life*, 'Its life is what I discover there, whether Cervantes put it there or not, what I put in it and under it and over it, and what we all put there.'[14] The use of the verb 'to put' here is telling, for it avoids the issue of signification and intention. The reader's interaction with the text involves a direct, un-mediated insertion of his or her self into the text.

An unread text is lifeless, and awaits the reader who will resuscitate it. Unamuno's recognition of the essential link between life and death through texts extends to his notion of the novel as autobiography. At several points in *How to Make a Novel*, he acknowledges that he is mak-ing a legend of himself through the text. Not only does he participate in this legend-making, but also his readers, whether friends or enemies. His agony upon writing springs from his knowledge that the process is collaborative, and from his fear that the legend-making might actually escape his control: 'Will I be as I believe myself to be or as I am believed to be? And here I have how these lines transform into a confession that is both unknown and unknowable for and before my unknown and unknowable self, unknown and unknowable to myself. Here I proffer the legend that I make in which I must bury myself.'[15] The choice is tragic: if Unamuno chooses to make his own legend, then he dies in the text; if he chooses not to do so, he dies completely by entering oblivion (*CHN* 197).

Although he toyed with the images of possessing Cide's manuscript and hearing Don Quixote's voice, Unamuno's strongest claim to *his* Don Quixote comes from his conceptualization of reading as a form of creation and re-creation. Indeed, Unamuno expresses surprise that anyone could have read *The Life of Don Quixote and Sancho* as other than a creative commentary, or in his words, 'recreative commentary' (*comentario recreativo*; *CHN* 133). As Unamuno explains, 'What this means is that the reputedly fictional beings have their own independent life and continue living. All of us who by knowing them recreate them – we give them life.'[16] A recreative commentary is not only recreational but also revivifying. Cervantes insisted on killing Don Quixote at the end of part II – be it in response to the pirating of his character by the pseudonymous Avellaneda, or to emphasize the satirical nature of his take on the literature of knight-errantry, or to enter into more levels of narrative and metafictional play. The death is narrated in several moments through diverse means: the narrator's account of Alonso Quijano's death, undertaken according to all the legal and religious rituals of the moment; the epitaph for Don Quixote's grave written by the Bachelor Sansón Carrasco; and Cide Hamete's speech upon hanging up his pen, according to which Don Quixote and his pen were born for each other. Unamuno cannot but insert himself into this final speech, insisting on the necessity of his own place in this triangular relation of author, characters, and reader/commentator: '"For me only was Don Quixote born, and I for him; he knew how to work and I how to write," the historian says to his pen. And I say that in order for Cervantes to recount his life and for me to explicate and comment upon it were Don Quixote and Sancho born; Cervantes was born to explain their life and I was born to comment upon it.'[17]

Heroism, History, and the Novel

It is at this point that we can begin to grasp the link between the individual, the novel, and history. To conceptualize reading as a means of resurrecting the text is to challenge death, the shadow that haunts Unamuno's thought throughout his life. For Unamuno, the ultimate spectre of the Spanish people as well as all humanity is death.[18] It is no accident that he begins his *The Life of Don Quixote and Sancho* by calling the reader to join him on a march to Don Quixote's tomb (*VDQ* 13). Several sources for Unamuno's vision of a heroic Don Quixote have been proffered: Hegel's knight of faith, Carlyle's and Schopenhauer's poetic heroism, Kierkegaard's leap of faith, Nietzsche's exaltation of the will, and Darwin's survival of the fittest.[19] A neologism Unamuno applies to Don Quixote is *erostratismo*, the drive to achieve glory and fame in order to triumph over death. Erostratus was an Ephesian citizen who sought glory through the infamous act of burning down the temple of Artemis; he stands as a figure of the individual who seeks fame through crime or misdeed. In Erostratus Unamuno was called to the wilful model of seeking fame and notoriety (Álvarez Castro 59). In this vein, Don Quixote as a figure of erostratism stands for the impulse to immortalize the self through fame, an impulse that underlies for Unamuno much of the world's cultural production. Unamuno contrasted *erostratismo*, the vain striving for individual glory that manifests itself in Don Quixote's person, with *egotismo*, the ethical working out of the self that transcends mere self-interest, and that is vital for the regeneration of society. This *egotismo* is also seen in Don Quixote, specifically in his noble aspirations to better society and succour others. *Egotismo* as such is linked to Kantian and Fichtean notions of the ethical work of the self, and depends on the agonistic relation in society with others engaged in the same *egotismo* (Cerezo Galán, *El mal del siglo* 534–9). Liberty becomes the unending struggle with the world, a struggle doomed to incompletion because, in Kantian terms, the world is a phenomenon resistant to what Schopenhauer and Unamuno term the *homo noumenon* (709).

There can be little doubt that Unamuno understood Don Quixote as an ethical hero (Ferrater Mora 80). His Don Quixote is clearly differentiated from Nietzsche's Superman, for the former wrestles with himself whereas the latter struggles to impose his will on others (Ouimette, *Reason Aflame* 14). By raising the issue of destiny and identifying the novelistic protagonist as a hero, Unamuno moves decisively away from modern notions of the novel that contrast it to the epic. Although Lukács expresses most profoundly the anti-heroism of the novelistic protagonist, almost all other modern theorists of the novel take it as a given. The novel's anti-hero, unlike the epic hero, cannot stand as the embodiment of his people's essence and destiny; to the contrary, he dwells in the inhospitable cleft between society and individual imagined by Lukács. At one level, Don Quixote's heroism, for Unamuno, consists precisely in the character's refusal to abide within the rational and social structures of his time and people. Don Quixote's lunacy becomes a heroic refusal to live according to common sense: 'Madness, true madness, is what we really need. Let us see if it will cure us of this plague of common sense that has strangled what is unique in all of us.'[20] Moreover, in *The Life of Don Quixote and Sancho*, Unamuno attributes Spain's perceived backwardness to its people's unwillingness to run the risk of being seen as crazy. Social pressure combines with common sense to stifle creativity and ingenuity, and thus limits the possible: 'Only he who tries out the absurd is capable of conquering the impossible. There is only one way to hit the nail on the head, and that is by hitting the horseshoe a hundred times.'[21]

Don Quixote's heroism is also a function of the different form of justice he enacts, a divine justice that is immediate and swift but that seeks to pardon (*VDQ* 90–1). His justice is based on the tenet of giving to each his due: *suum cuique tribuere*. It stands in contrast to what Unamuno defines as Sancho's justice: moderate, prudent, and based on human law (*VDQ* 88). Influenced by German and French Protestant theologians of his time, Unamuno attributes to Luther the secularization of vocation, by which all human beings are freed to pursue their conscience and passion, and of which Don Quixote is a prime example (Orringer, *Unamuno y los protestantes liberales* 195–221). Therefore, he compares the tragic appearance of Jesus Christ before Pontius Pilate (*ecce homo*) to Don Quixote's appearance before his ridiculers (¡*He aquí el loco!*).

In *How to Make a Novel*, the avatar 'U.' Jugo de la Raza's heroism coincides with that of the author, Miguel de Unamuno. Only by retracing the author's trajectory in exile can Jugo de la Raza embody heroism. This trajectory enacts not only Unamuno's personal story of heroic resistance to Primo de Rivera, but also key moments in the history of Spain. As such, it is *intrahistoria*, the history of the people living in and through the individual. It is for this reason that Unamuno's protagonist returns to the Arnegui bridge on the border of France and Spain, where the Carlist pretender to the throne, Carlos of Bourbon, withdrew in 1875. The prince's exile is linked to Unamuno's, who was arrested on 21 February 1924, exactly fifty years after Carlist bombs fell on his village (*CHN* 196). In this way, Spanish history conjoins with Unamuno's personal history, and casts a heroic light over Jugo de la Raza. The epic hero, who is defined by his identity with the historic destiny of his people, becomes a sort of Everyman in Unamuno's thought.

The consubstantiation of the historic in the individual is rendered intelligible by Unamuno's understanding of time. He states that '[i]n the innards of things, and not outside them, exist the eternal and the infinite. Eternity is the substance of the moment that happens, and not the enveloping substance of the past, present, and future of all temporal duration; infinity is the substance of the point at which I look, and not the enveloping of the breadth, length, and height of all its extensions.'[22] Traditional ontology views eternity as the container of time as experienced by human beings, and infinity as the container of experienced substance. By erasing the inside/outside dichotomy that separates eternity and infinity from lived experience, Unamuno can undo the paradoxical nature of his assertion that history abides in the individual. Those who deride and make fun of others who assume a heroic quest no longer lay claim to common sense. The individual is free, like Don Quixote, to render his life epic: 'Let us then hunt and swallow the poisonous flies that, buzzing and wielding their stingers, zoom about us, and may Dulcinea give us the power to transform this chase into an epic combat that will be sung throughout time in the whole earth.'[23]

The comic nature of this heroism is already manifested in *The Life of Don Quixote and Sancho* (1905), whereas its tragic nature emerges in later writings. When viewed in a comic vein, Don Quixote is associated with actors, known in Spanish as *comediantes* and *farsantes*. Unamuno takes advantage of the Spanish usage of the term *comedia* to describe all theatre, and insists that comedy is the profound knowledge of life's spectacular nature: 'The crazy person is usually a profound comedic actor, who takes comedy seriously, but does not fool himself, and who, while he seriously plays the role of God or the king or the beast, knows full well that he is neither God, nor the king, nor the beast.'[24] The knowledge accessible to the crazy person, then, is the awareness of social conventions. Unamuno differentiates between reason and truth: 'Reason is that on which we are all in agreement, more or less the majority of us. The truth is something else, but reason is social; the truth usually is completely individual, personal, and incommunicable. Reason unites us and truths separate us.'[25] Madness, as the unreason of reason, is determined socially rather than clinically; the madman is unique but not ill for he does not participate in socially accepted reason (Ouimette, *Reason Aflame* 91). By extension, Unamuno's notion of heroism involves the speaking of truth, even under circumstances when so doing contradicts common sense, and casts the individual as crazy. Moreover, truths are accessible through the individual, as they present themselves in the innards of infinity, eternity, and history. The crazy person becomes the modern prophet. What distinguishes the prophet or the crazy man from the reasonable one? According to Unamuno, it is nothing other than the will to endure ridicule in the name of truth.

Life Is a Dream: Unamuno's Critique of Modernity

Unamuno develops his critique of modern society through referencing one of Spain's greatest *comedias*: Pedro Calderón de la Barca's *Life Is a Dream* (1635). This play recounts the gradual civilization of the Polish Prince Segismundo, condemned to live in a tower by his own father, the King Basilio, in order to counteract a prophecy that he would be dethroned and killed by his son. The prophecy seems self-fulfilling, however, as the young prince is raised without social contact and the civilizing effects of human affection and education. Upon his release, Segismundo acts as a barbarian, killing a hapless servant by throwing him from a window, and attempting to rape Rosaura, an abandoned woman seeking revenge on the Duke of Muscovy, Astolfo. Basilio attempts to return him to the tower by convincing him that his experience of the outside world was nothing more than a dream. Nonetheless, at the play's end Segismundo has tamed his bestial impulses and educated himself through becoming aware that life is a dream. He leads an army against his father, whom he unseats, but it is understood that his own reign will be based on moderation and clemency. In the Catholic context of Calderón's play, this insight is based on the notion that this world is but a prelude to the true reality of heaven. Therefore, in order to attain entrance to the true reality, Segismundo must learn to act well (*obrar bien*), fully acknowledging that he now abides in a world of appearances and deceit. To that effect, Segismundo states in his famous soliloquy at the end of act 2:

What is life? A frenzy.
What is life? An illusion,
A shadow, a fiction,
And the greatest good is puny,
For all of life is a dream,
And dreams are dreams.[26]

As Calderón makes clear in his *auto sacramental*, *The Great Theatre of the World*, God's authority over and authorship of the world is absolute and not merely apparent (Regalado García, *El siervo y el señor* 136). Unamuno's concept of life as a dream, then, more closely approaches Shakespeare's meaning by which humans are the stuff of dreams (Marías, *Miguel de Unamuno* 22).

Unamuno conflates Cervantes' protagonist with Calderón's at the end of *The Life of Don Quixote and Sancho* by stating that Don Quixote's final insight is the same as Segismundo's: life is a dream. Unamuno sidesteps the troublesome renunciation of his deeds as Don Quixote that the newly sane Alonso Quijano performs on his deathbed: 'Poor Don Quixote! On the threshold of dying and by the light of death, he confesses and declares that his life was nothing but the dream of madness. Life is a dream!'[27] Asking whether we are but God's dream, Unamuno returns to the image of the windmills. These posit generous, heroic action as the means to transcend the dream: 'Rather than investigating whether what threatens us are windmills or giants, we should follow the voice of the heart and attack them, for all generous attacks transcend the dream of life. From our actions, and not from our contemplation, will we gain wisdom.'[28] At this significant moment, when Unamuno calls for heroic, ethical action, he simultaneously casts aside reason in favour of faith.

Unamuno returns to the equation of life as a dream in his *How to Make a Novel*. Having presented himself in the figure of Jugo de la Raza as a comically mad hero, he imagines an unfriendly reader who will accuse him of merely playing a role in his critique of the dictator Primo de Rivera. This indignation results from projection, for what truly insults the reader is the mirror Unamuno holds up to him. The reader is likewise a comic protagonist of his own life. In this later text Unamuno makes explicit what is only implicit in 1905: that the novel is a form of comedy. Insofar as Unamuno repeats his earlier critique of the insubstantial, farcical nature of modern society and reason, the equation makes sense. Indeed, this is the closest Unamuno comes to labelling the novel a modern genre. Yet the author also breaks down the barrier between fiction and life once again to assert that life itself is a comedy and a novel. Thus, Unamuno calls out to the reader: 'Let him make life of the dream, of his dream, and then he will have saved himself.'[29]

How does Unamuno manage to undo the ontological barrier between fiction and reality, historical individual and fictional character? One way is by positing that human beings and literary characters exist in a similar mode: they exist in time and within narratives (Marías, *Miguel de Unamuno* 25–33; Ferrater Mora 111). In a fascinating note from the 1920s, Unamuno suggests that the histrionic personality of Don Quixote – his wilful choice to play a role – defines consciousness itself. History, by placing the self within society, makes actors of everyone, even those who seem to occupy minor roles, whether playing a part in a village or pretending to read Chinese alone in a room. Consciousness creates the stage setting, for it implies an observer (*CHN* 122). Unamuno continues to define consciousness as 'he who, playing alone, looks over his shoulder,' and then concludes that the subconscious is not exactly the base of consciousness.[30] Consciousness exists in the observation of the self, and thus all selves are doubled. A double personality is normally diagnosed as insanity, and yet this doubled perspective is the very basis of human consciousness.

Unamuno is most overtly modern in the confluence of his thought on consciousness and death. Like Freud, Husserl, and Bergson, he approaches the individual as a problem and consciousness as an enigma (Zambrano 59–69). As Unamuno asserts in *On the Tragic Sentiment of Life*, consciousness is of death and pain, for the psychological and intellectual content of consciousness is knowledge of one's own limitations (*UOC* 7: 192). Death represents the greatest limitation and the possibility of nothingness, but it also represents the possibility for the individual to become self-conscious, knowing his existence and his agonistic struggle to exist in the face of death (Valdés, *Death in the Literature of Unamuno* 14). In order to confront mortality, Unamuno needs the notion of God as the dreamer of man who will hold or annihilate him in consciousness. The possibility of God provides for Unamuno a comic resolution to humanity's dilemma in the face of death, for God will continue to imagine man (*UOC* 7: 198).

Don Quixote as a Tragicomic Figure

One could say that consciousness is the image of God in man, but this consciousness participates in both comic and tragic modes. In its comic mode, consciousness is humorous and sceptical, for it is aware of its stage settings. Cartesian doubt is 'comic doubt, a purely theoretical and provisional doubt; in other words, the doubt of one who acts like he doubts without doubting.'[31] It does not achieve for Unamuno the status of true doubt because it deals only with reason and the mind, ignoring life, emotions, and biology. Unamuno also associates the comic mode with social existence, for the social world implies play-acting (Ilie 65). Tragedy forms the human experience in general, and the Spanish experience in particular. The tragic feeling arises from the individual's confrontation with death and nothingness, while she, committed to life and incapable of imagining nothingness, must live with the contradiction of her future annihilation in death. The culmination of the tragedy is eternal lack and pain as 'the soul, my soul at least, yearns for something else – not absorption, not calm, not peace, not extinction, but an eternal drawing near without ever arriving, an unending yearning, an eternal hope that will eternally renew itself without ever completely ending.'[32] The longing is tragic, because if one were to arrive at the desired end, being itself would end.

The better alternative, for Unamuno, is to live in the state of incompletion. Reason has no chance of arriving, for it would only limit the end through definition, and thus kill it (*UOC* 7: 208). One must choose to engage in the irrational and the emotional – in so many words, the literary – but neither do these offer access to the promised goal. The best Unamuno can proffer is to live with doubt and uncertainty in a faith built on doubt and uncertainty. It is no accident that Kierkegaard and Luther haunt Unamuno's thought, for it is in their acceptance of the incredulity necessary to faith that the Spanish thinker finds his only consolation – a consolation that cannot console. Moreover, it is this call to a doubting faith that explains Unamuno's own vision of his vocation – to upset, to unsettle, to overturn, in short, to make his fellow Spaniards uncomfortable with common sense.

Don Quixote must be tragic, or at best tragicomic for Unamuno. The tragic face of Unamuno's Don Quixote is perhaps more salient than his comic aspect, but also more difficult to define. In his *The Tragic Sentiment of Life* he presents most clearly this vision of Don Quixote – and Sancho. It is Sancho Panza who reflects Unamuno in his struggle between doubt and belief, and it is for this reason that Unamuno repeatedly expresses his desire to believe in Don Quixote, just as Sancho did. Standing in counterpoint to doubting thinkers such as Unamuno, the would-be knight errant is the very figure of headstrong leaps of faith. He withstands the derision and the laughter of the doubters yet remains firm in his vision of Dulcinea. The confrontation between the heroic believer and the abusive masses figures for Unamuno tragicomedy. Indeed, Unamuno draws the parallel between Don Quixote and Jesus by referencing the *ecce homo* scene in Pontius Pilate's palace.[33] This scene is repeated in *Don Quixote* in the palace of the Duke and the Duchess, as their servants lather up Don Quixote's face in order to mock him:

'"Behold the crazy man!" they would say. And the irrational, comic tragedy is the passion for ridicule and disdain. The greatest heroism for the individual as for the people is to know how to confront ridicule, and even better to know how to make fun of oneself and not lose courage in it.'[34] The tragicomedy of modernity is the ridiculing of the individual who speaks out against common sense, for the integrity of life. In other words, tragedy is accessible to the individual who chooses to undergo ridicule, whereas those who do not choose to suffer so but remain in the jeering throng live comically. The final determination as to whether a story is comic or tragic is its ending, and thus one's manner of death ultimately determines the mode of life. Those who laugh and jibe because they value thought and reason over feeling and faith die comically, whereas those who live in the opposite manner die tragically (*UOC* 7:294). Ultimately, God figures as the judge of comedy or tragedy. It is God's final joke on the ridiculers that renders their own lives comic.

Don Quixote's tragic aspect is his re-enactment of the medieval in modernity; it is 'nothing else but the most desperate fight of the Middle Ages against the Renaissance which emerged from it.'[35] Moreover, Unamuno asserts that Don Quixote was conscious of his anachronism. It is this self-consciousness that renders the would-be knight errant a modern individual as well as a model for modern individuals (*UOC* 7:298).[36] In a telling passage, Unamuno proclaims the painful self-consciousness seen in the tragicomic figure of Don Quixote to be a response to the human conditions described by both Freud and Marx: one should not bury oneself in the unconscious or dose oneself with opium, but seek ever more consciousness (*UOC* 7:275). The call for consciousness sounds anachronistic after Freud and Marx, whose great innovations were to uncover the unconscious depths of the soul and society. It is through this calling, which Unamuno refers to as the calling in the desert, that he sees himself as a Don Quixote, and his nation as Quixotic. And it is through this calling to self-consciousness that Unamuno seeks to reform his country ethically and politically.

The *Tragicomedia*, the *Novela/Nivola*, and Modernity

Unamuno's stance before modernity is more complex and contradictory than that of the other thinkers we are considering here. Wilfully adopting a paradoxical and often combative style, Unamuno certainly earned the epithet given him by Ernst Cassirer: *Excitator Hispaniae* (Marichal 102). In many ways, this complexity reflects Unamuno's will to theorize modernity from the specific vantage point of Spain (unlike Ortega, who adopts a pointedly 'European' perspective), while still adopting the Kantian moral imperative as the basis of his critique of modernity. Unamuno reworks the Kantian adage as 'work as if the world had an end and thus you will contribute to the existence of the end' (Cerezo Galán, *Máscaras de lo trágico* 287). Moreover, this return to Kant occurs in part through Hegel, and thus Unamuno from 1904 on writes of this work as 'heroic deeds' (*hazañas heroicas*; 288). Unlike Hegel, however, Unamuno insists that the real is irrational, and so the modern individual is trapped in a tragic dilemma (*Sentimiento trágico de la vida* 111). Don Quixote, by epitomizing the modern individual, must live tragically, for the world of values and the phenomenological world do not coincide (343).

Within the Spanish early modern literary tradition, it was not uncommon to use the term *tragicomedia* to describe works that combined serious philosophical and religious speculation and often tragic story lines represented in counterpoint to comedic secondary characters and subplots. Fernando de Rojas's ground-breaking *La Celestina* (1499) not only challenged the generic boundaries between prose and theatre, but was also originally titled *La tragicomedia de Calisto y Melibea* (see chap. 1). By opting to write of Don Quixote as a tragicomic hero and Cervantes' novel as a tragicomedy, Unamuno avoids the equation of the novel with modernity understood in the European terms of scientific positivism, radical doubt, and the belief in technological progress. The mode of the tragicomedy, with its deep roots in Spanish literature, offers Unamuno a means to theorize a specifically Spanish modern genre that will both reflect upon the European condition and offer Spanish insights into 'the anaesthetizing process of habit, mass-production and mass-government' (Batchelor 188). In the concluding chapter to *On the Tragic Sentiment of Life*, Unamuno refers to the tragicomedy that is the contemporary European condition. According to Unamuno, modern Europe is trapped in the cults of science and progress (*progresismo*), based on a notion of reason as transcendent rather than social. The symbol for this trap is the literary character of Doctor Faust found in both Marlowe's and Goethe's texts, although Marlowe's version rings more true, for in it there is no Margarita to return to Faust his stolen soul (*UOC* 7:285). Unamuno further maintains that Margarita stands for modern Europe's faith in culture, an ideal that will somehow return to it its soul.

Nonetheless, only Don Quixote provides a true model for the modern individual. The values wilfully championed by Don Quixote correspond to the traditional Spanish values Unamuno claims as the nation's *casticismo*. The Quixotic way of life and philosophy to be reclaimed is not only that of Don Quixote, but also of Ignatius of Loyola, the conquistadors, the Counter-Reformationists, and the mystics (*UOC* 7:293). Moreover, these Spaniards did not fight for ideas, but rather 'spirit.'[37] Taking into account Unamuno's own heretical stance toward orthodox Catholicism, let us remember that 'spirit' here refers not to theological dogma but rather to a recuperation of the emotional, the imaginary, and the lived components of human life. The tragicomedy of modern Europe is nationalized, with reason and progress situated in England, France, and Germany, and individual valour, faith, and mysticism situated in Unamuno's Spain. For this reason, Unamuno can argue for Don Quixote as Spain's philosopher, and argue that the Spanish people, unlike other Europeans, reject comedy for tragedy (*UOC* 7:282).

In many respects, Unamuno's most effective expression of his concept of the literary genre commonly known as the novel is a novel itself, *Niebla*, published in 1914. In short, *Niebla* enacts the problem of the author's authority over literary creations. The title *Niebla* means mist or fog, and is labelled on its title page a *nivola* rather than a *novela*. Critics have generally interpreted the title as a reference to Unamuno's proto-existentialistic view of life as a fog (Gullón *Autobiografías de Unamuno* 94). The term *nivola* is a neologism coined by Unamuno, and represents the fusing of the genre (*novela*) with the title (*Niebla*). As Unamuno was fond of puns, etymologies, and neologisms, it is worthwhile to unpack the term *nivola*. According to the *Real Academia de la Lengua*, the second usage of *niebla* is to refer to a spot or blurring in the cornea. The root of the neologism – *niv* – links it to adjectives meaning snowy (*nivoso, níveo*) as well as to the verb meaning 'to level' (*nivelar*). The *nivola* springs from confused, cloudy vision; its usefulness is to operate an obscuring of levels and hierarchies. That the author should consider the genre itself muddled, misty, and difficult to comprehend evidences yet again his ambivalence and sense of irony with respect to modern theories of the novel. As the character from *Niebla* who claims to have invented the term *nivola*, Víctor Goti, asserts, 'this way no one will have the right to say that it repeals the laws of the genre. I invent the genre, and inventing a genre is no more than giving it a new name, and I give it the laws that please me.'[38] The word *nivola* arises in a dialogue between Víctor and Augusto in which the former announces that his novel will have no set plot, but rather emerge on its own. Dialogue will be its principal form, from which the characters will 'go on making themselves according to what they do and say, but especially what they say; their character will go on forming itself little by little.'[39] Monologues will become dialogues, for Goti will add a dog to listen to them (Augusto's dog has the final word in *Niebla*). The entire genre of the *nivola* grows out of human taste for dialogue, what Víctor calls the 'enchantment of conversation, of talking for the sake of talking, of broken and interrupted speech.'[40] It is thus hybrid and spontaneous, eschewing psychology and description (Ribbans 128).

The novel's plot is uneventful, not to say unmoving, if it were not for its irony. The text is so metaliterary in its content and form that one critic has compared it to René Magritte's famous painting *This Is Not a Pipe* (Øveraas 93). The intertextual references to *Don Quixote* are plentiful, affording many similarities between the plot of *Niebla* and Cervantes' work, particularly in the protagonist's love for Eugenia (Ribbans 116; Øveraas 34–9).[41] Its protagonist, Augusto Pérez, is a bored young man who hails from a wealthy family in Madrid – in other words, the exemplary dandy or *flâneur*. Wandering the streets, he falls in love with an unknown girl of his same class, the piano teacher Eugenia. He devotes himself as much out of ennui as infatuation to winning her hand in marriage. In the meantime, he falls in love with the girl who brings him his ironing, Rosario, with whom he shares a kiss, and occasionally lusts after his cook, Liduvina. When Eugenia elopes with Rosario's fiancé, Mauricio, Augusto finds himself rejected and disgraced. Seriously considering suicide, Augusto reads an essay on the subject by his author, professor of Greek at the University of Salamanca, Miguel de Unamuno. Deciding to consult the expert, Augusto Pérez boards a train from Madrid to Salamanca in order to plead for his life with his maker.

The confrontation between author and character hinges upon how much authority an author has over her fiction. Informed of Augusto's determination to kill himself, Unamuno replies in anger that he can do no such thing, for he does not have the power to take his own life since he is only a fictional being. Augusto shows himself to be more animated and active in this tense interchange than previously, and asserts in his own defence several of Unamuno's favourite paradoxes. He asks Unamuno whether he can determine if the dream exists as fully as the dreamer, and quotes back to Unamuno the author's assertion that Don Quixote and Sancho are more real than Cervantes. Augusto goes further, declaring that it is even more difficult to know one's fictional characters than oneself. The fictional Augusto argues that all novelistic and dramatic characters have an internal logic that cannot be violated, for said transgression would contradict the reader's expectations. At this Unamuno attempts to defend his authority by bringing up the distinction between novelistic character and the *nivolesco*. Whereas novelistic characters have to conform to the reader's expectations, those in *nivolas* do not (155). Enraged, Unamuno claims that he will kill Augusto, to which Augusto threatens to kill Unamuno. Pleading for his own life (which he had just wanted to take), Augusto returns to Madrid. Augusto's death is as convoluted as his life. On the train trip home, he ponders his fate, only to decide that he is immortal for he shall live on in his reader's mind. Once home, he orders an enormous meal, and continues stuffing himself despite Liduvina's protests. Upon falling into his deathbed, he writes a message to Unamuno, informing him that he has won and that Augusto has died. In his final agony he repeats to himself the Cartesian *cogito ergo sum* until he dies. The doctor, who arrives too late, declares that perhaps if one did not believe in one's death, he or she would not die. Thus, Liduvina declares that Augusto's death was a suicide.

In *Niebla* the author Unamuno asserts his power of life and death over the hapless Augusto Pérez, only to be confronted in the final chapter by the character's ghost. The fictional tangle of the author's and the character's intentions is so enmeshed that one can for a moment savour the possibility that Augusto committed suicide, an act that would directly contravene authorial power. Of course, his suicide is yet another invention of Unamuno as flesh-and-blood author, to be distinguished from the fictional Unamuno within the text. Indeed, it is possible to read the representation of 'Unamuno' in the text as a parody of the nineteenth-century omniscient narrator and the attempt to create a unified text with a coherent message – all of which *Niebla* lacks (Øveraas 67). Never one to miss an opportunity for paradox, Unamuno ends up defending the justness of Augusto's complaint in the 1928 prologue to *The Life of Don Quixote and Sancho Panza*. Unamuno's *nivola*, however, only serves to confuse the issue of authorial control, particularly in reference to Cervantes and his characters, Don Quixote and Sancho Panza. The notion of authorial intention prevalent in literary criticism at the time re-enacted a version of literary scholasticism in which the creator became the prime mover plus the prime interpreter of the created work. Unamuno pokes fun at the godlike vision of the author in his novel *Niebla*, when the narrator Unamuno interrupts Víctor's and Augusto's conversation to snidely remark that all their attempts to justify their actions only justify their God, their author: 'And I am the God of these two poor *nivolesque* devils.'[42]

For Unamuno, the conundrum of the author/protagonist/reader triangle is the tragic conundrum of human existence. No one party holds complete power over another, nor is any one party completely powerless. At an ontological level, Unamuno even questions the existence of the split between the fictive and the real. By equating life to a dream, Unamuno deprivileges authorial intention. It is no accident that Augusto Pérez spits the following accusation at his creator: '[M]y master and creator don Miguel, you too will die, you too, and you will return to the nothingness from which you emerged ... God will stop dreaming you! ... Because you, my creator, my don Miguel, are nothing more than a *nivolesque* being, and your readers are *nivolesque*, just like me, Augusto Pérez, your victim.'[43] The *nivolesque*, as opposed to the novelistic, exists in the realms of both fiction and reality, and serves to unite the inhabitants of both realms. Augusto Pérez and Miguel de Unamuno, protagonist and author, share the same mortal fate: the descent into oblivion that can only be undone by the resuscitating work of the reader.

Niebla clarifies how Unamuno attempts to imagine the genre of the novel as a tragicomedy. The literary character Víctor Goti informs us in his prologue that Unamuno has long desired to write a tragic buffoonery or a buffoonish tragedy (*N* 101). According to Goti, the Spanish people want works of laughter to improve their digestion and take their mind off their troubles. To the contrary, Unamuno seeks a purgative kind of humour (*N* 102) – not humour for humour's sake, but rather committed to changing the lives and minds of the readers. In other words, it is a humour that operates a tragic critique of the human situation. In their conversation about the protagonist's possible suicide, Víctor and Augusto muse on Augusto's fictional being. Augusto claims to have begun as a mere shadow, but after having been ridiculed, he now feels real. To this Víctor responds that it is comedy, for in comedy he who represents the king believes or makes himself the king.[44] But what would truly render the comedy *nivolesque* in Víctor's opinion is that the reader might one day imagine himself as *nivolesque*, and thus, upon imagining his own ficticity, be redeemed or liberated. In short, Unamuno proposes that the purpose of the *nivola* is to raise the modern reader's consciousness of his own existential dilemma.

The philosopher's belief in the living text not only serves to justify his own reinterpretation of Don Quixote as hero but also his implicit rejection of a novelistics per se. Rejecting the image of the novel as a clock or a mechanism of fiction, Unamuno remarks in *How to Make a Novel* that the novel is a living organism.[45] As such, it is not a machine and cannot be examined by lifting its lid, for it contains nothing but 'entrails palpitating with life, warm with blood.'[46] Moreover, the relation between novelist and reader is also an organic one: '[T]he novelist doesn't have to lift [any lid] for the reader to feel the pulsation of the entrails of the live organism that is the novel, which are the very entrails of the novelist or the author and those of the reader who identifies with the author through the reading.'[47] To insist on peeling back the skin of the living novel, slicing it up to open it up, would constitute for Unamuno an unnecessary act of violence. Moreover, understanding the text as organism does away with the form and content distinction by dissolving the differentiation between internal and external, on which formalism as an analytic depends. A novelistic character, like an individual or an actor, 'carries his inner organs in his face. Or, to put it another way, his innards – *intranea* –, what is inside is his *extraña* – *extranea* –; his form is his depth [or background].'[48] The very living quality of a human being is the revelation of the internal psychological state through the face – a making transparent that calls into question the boundaries between the internal and the external. Unamuno relies on a number of puns and even a neologism here to complicate this insight. Whereas *entrañas* is a standard Spanish word for innards, the word *extrañas* forms through parallelism a neologism. The most common usage of *extraño/a* in Spanish is as an adjective to describe something strange, odd, disturbing, or alien. *Extraña* as a noun would normally mean a female stranger. Therefore, Unamuno seems to be suggesting a neologism parallel to *entrañas* that would name the external face of the internal. Ferrater Mora has analysed the way in which Unamuno strives to philosophize the 'within' by making it 'apparent *as* foundation. Or, to put it another way: the innermost is the "within" of things to the degree that it is deprived of a "without"' (116). The function of the literary character understood within the terms of the neologism *extrañas* is to make apparent or visible the foundation of its personality and trajectory in narrative.

The reference to the literary text as clock is, moreover, a direct allusion to an article published by Azorín in which he stated that in order to understand the mechanisms of a book one should write another book. This image is unacceptable for Unamuno, for it converts what he views as the living, organic text into a machine (La Rubia Prado, *Unamuno y la*

vida como ficción 52). The welding of the internal to the external face causes the dissolution of the distinction between external form and contained
depth or containing background. Unamuno concludes by stating that it
is for this reason that all expression by truly human beings – including
the novel – is autobiographical. As expression the novel must perforce
reveal the inner human, whether author or reader. Likewise, the reading
of the text as a living organism constitutes an ingestion of flesh – the
Word made flesh – similar to the Eucharist (*CHN* 170). For Unamuno,
aesthetic formalism is reductive and violent, because it defines the work
of art as a machine rather than a living being. Whereas the dyad of form
and function might serve well for the creation and use of a clock or a mill,
it is not capable of conceptualizing a text per se. The text exists for
Unamuno in the realm of the living, and when it exits that realm and
dies, is subject to resurrection by the reader.

Unamuno's assertion that Don Quixote and Sancho were born so that
Cervantes could write and that he, Unamuno, could read or comment
is not, strictly speaking, illogical. Literary characters do serve to identify their producers as authors, just as one can identify the saddle maker by his wares. Texts do shape and invoke their readers. It is the
assertion that readers are destined to read that is paradoxical. The notion that the reader has a destiny as a reader – that she is born to read a
certain text – flagrantly transgresses modern ontology, according to
which being does not proceed from texts, but rather texts proceed from
being. Unamuno obstinately returns to a pre-modern notion of text as
the Book of Life in order to ground his ontology of reading (Zubizarreta
138). Moreover, the ecstatic consumption of texts creates a madness that
is in itself existence (140). Thus, the maddened Don Quixote becomes
the model for the reader with a destiny, the reader that truly exists. But
we must not forget the purely modern face of this reader with a destiny:
the reader as poet, who, through reading, makes the self.

Unamuno, Cohen, and Ortega y Gasset

The tradition we are tracing in this book – up to and including Bakhtin
– is largely Kantian, with the exception of Unamuno. Perhaps what ultimately distinguishes Unamuno's thought from Kantianism and neo-
Kantianism is the Spaniard's assertion that philosophy rests not only
on Cohen's so-called three-legged stool of logics, ethics, and aesthetics,
but also on religion (leaving aside the fact that Cohen himself turns toward the incorporation of religion into philosophy in his final works).

In *On the Tragic Sentiment in Life*, Unamuno criticizes Kantian philosophy for having only three normative binary oppositions: true/false, beautiful/ugly, and good/bad (*UOC* 1:295). Omitted is the hedonic that determines the agreeable and the disagreeable, the pleasant and the bothersome.

There is reason to believe that Unamuno's concept of the *nivola*, as well as his novel *How to Make a Novel*, represents a rejection of the sort of novelistics proposed by Cohen and Ortega. One could explain the modern impulse to theorize texts as a response to the reordering of the relation between text and being. Unamuno's notes indicate that he viewed Hermann Cohen's philosophy in such a way. Cohen's characterization of medieval ethics particularly irked Unamuno, who called the philosopher's stance toward not only the Middle Ages, but also mythology, theology, mysticism, and Romanticism, 'stupid disdain.'[49] Referring to section 356 of Cohen's *Logic of Pure Knowledge*, Unamuno remarks that, for Cohen, medieval morality depends on religion. The German philosopher determined the medieval foundation of morality in God to be the source of weakness in its ethics (*LRE* 412). Unamuno disagrees, for he seeks to reground morality in faith as an antidote to the sterile common sense that he finds typical of his compatriots. Rejecting neo-Kantian standards of truth based on mathematics, Unamuno fumes: 'Life is the criterion of truth and not logical concord, which is only the criterion of reason. If my faith leads me to create or expand life, why do you want more proof of my faith? When mathematics kill, mathematics are a lie.'[50] Accordingly, will takes its place as the bedrock of faith.

It is thus that Don Quixote can become the model for heroic action, for he wills to believe in Dulcinea. Unamuno presents this defence of faith and will in response to chapter 31 of part I of *Don Quixote*, in which Sancho Panza lies about having delivered his master's letter to Dulcinea. Sancho paints the picture of a rustic, illiterate countrywoman, who smells like a man, tears apart the letter she cannot read, and gives him no gem in recompense upon parting. Don Quixote responds that Sancho must have been smelling himself, for he knows that Dulcinea smells like the rose among thorns. Moreover, as he knows that she is liberal to an extreme, Don Quixote believes that she offered no jewel because none was at hand. Unamuno pleads with his reader to reread this dialogue, 'for in it is encoded the intimate essence of Quixotism as a doctrine of knowledge. The elevated truths of Don Quixote's faith, based on fundamental, deep life, respond to the lies of Sancho, who feigns events according to his vulgar and shallow life.'[51] The next step is obvious – knowledge itself subsides before will as what makes our world ('la que nos hace el mundo'). Unlike Cohen, who sees in Sancho the embodiment of justice, Unamuno cannot accept the squire's pragmatic political stances. Most galling for Unamuno is Sancho's refusal to pass judgment upon the true identity of the barber's basin that Don Quixote sees as Mambrino's helmet (*VDQ* 123). Instead, our wily peasant coins a neologism and declares it a 'basin-helmet' (*baciyelmo*). For Unamuno this act epitomizes moral mediocrity, for through it Sancho tries to avoid the unhappy consequences of affirming his own values (Navajas 111).

Another point of contact between Cohen's and Unamuno's novelistics is their notion of the ethical working out of the self: for Cohen, the *Aufgabe*, and for Unamuno, the *obra*. It is doubtful, however, that Unamuno would have been directly influenced by or dialoguing with Cohen on this point. What seems to occur here is that both Cohen and Unamuno respond to ethical notions that converge. For Cohen, the concept of the task (*Aufgabe*) responds to his interpretation of the will in neo-Kantian terms. For Unamuno, the concept of the work (*obra*) springs from Cervantes' novel. Don Quixote serves as a model for Unamuno precisely because he epitomizes the creation of the self as envisioned and willed by the self; in this way, one is, in Cervantes' words, the son or daughter of his works (*hijo de sus obras*; Roberts 107). In other words, we are all a work in progress. Unamuno takes this definition of the self one step further than Cohen insofar as the Spaniard recognizes that the written text also exists as a work in progress. Perhaps it is the Spanish language itself that suggests this extension of the term, since one of the accepted meanings of *obra* in Spanish is the work as text, composition, or artwork. The fact that Unamuno picks out from *Don Quixote de la Mancha* this notion of the self as work-in-progress indicates how and why the text was attractive to a reader such as Cohen.

As the two leading intellectuals of early twentieth-century Spain, it is perhaps only natural that Unamuno and Ortega y Gasset were more rivals than colleagues (Marías, *Ortega. Circunstancia y vocación* 143). The younger of the two, Ortega wrote his *Meditations on Don Quixote* (1914) as a response to and rejection of Unamuno's *The Life of Don Quixote and Sancho* (1905) and *The Tragic Sentiment of Life* (1913; Hampton 47; Orringer, 'El Unamuno casticista en *Meditaciones del Quijote*' 37–54). Unlike Unamuno, who found in Cervantes an antagonist, Ortega sought in the author of *Don Quixote* an intellectual ancestor and mentor. The urgent search for a mentor forms the substance of an important letter, finally mailed in February 1907 after various drafts were penned, that Ortega addressed to Unamuno. In one version, Ortega writes of Cervantes as 'the only Castilian who, being a superman, knew how to ironize himself and his superiority as spectacle, surpass it, and thus manage, if not total-ly, at least theoretically, to become a Man.'[52] The vision of a virile Cervantes hinted at by this early date indicates the fundamental difference between Unamuno's reading of *Don Quixote* and Ortega's. Unamuno, much like Lukács, valued 'literature *because* of its alienated position within modern society,' a position that 'tends to create an unexpected and ultimately adverse alliance between literature's self-proclaimed defenders and those who would believe that the true measure of our modernity lies in the achievements of science and technology' (Cascardi, *The Subject of Modernity* 122). Reason too often for Unamuno represents the debased common sense of those who deride the hero.

On the other hand, Ortega seeks to rescue reason. That he does so through the figure of Cervantes and Cervantes' novel, rather than through the character of Don Quixote, is an indirect refutation of Unamuno. Unamuno views Don Quixote as a manifestation of Spain's *intrahistoria*, whereas Ortega views Cervantes and his novel as a decisive experience in the nation's history to be studied phenomenologically (Cerezo Galán, *La voluntad de aventura* 96). The difference is profound, for Unamunian *intra-historia* is not the object of detached observation – even from within – but rather a matter of feeling, will, and faith. Moreover, Ortega's denial of the Unamunian opposition of reason to life will result in the formulation of his own central concept: *raciovitalismo*. Whereas Unamuno proposes a tra-gic form of heroism that results from the individual's wilful vocation and deeds, Ortega proposes a sporting hero, whose deeds do not transcend the here-and-now but rather comprehend it (Cerezo Galán, *La voluntad de aventura* 122–3). Subsequently, laughter, humour, and joking take oppos-ing forms in Unamuno's and Ortega's respective interpretations of Cervantes (132–3). For Unamuno, the joking to which Don Quixote is sub-jected is destructive and degrading. To the contrary, for Ortega it is ironic and constructive.

Nor did Unamuno refrain from addressing his adversary Ortega through writings about Cervantes. Luis Fernández Cifuentes suggests that *How to Make a Novel* contains a veiled allusion to Ortega's failure to combat openly the Primo de Rivera dictatorship ('Unamuno y Ortega' 46). Ortega's distanced, cool approach to the politics of the period clear-ly rankled Unamuno, who considered all the Spanish intellectuals who did not speak out against Primo de Rivera as traitors and cowards. One wonders how much of *How to Make a Novel* represents a polemic with

Ortega. Certainly, Unamuno's assertion of the confluence between author and reader, novel and autobiography, stands in opposition to the delimitation of these concepts in Ortega's *Ideas on the Novel* from 1924 (48–53). The most succinct statement that Unamuno offers us on the nature of the novel in *How to Make a Novel* stipulates that the genre's purpose is to overcome the radical loneliness of the reader and the author: 'And why does one make oneself a novelist? To make the reader, to make oneself one with the reader. And only by making the reader and the novelist one are both saved from their radical solitude. When they are made one, they become real, and making themselves real, they become eternal.'[53] Ortega, however, presents the novelist as a painter who presents to the reader a virtual reality ready to engage the reader's phenomenological knowledge and experience of life. The ideal novelist would disappear behind the canvas, as the reader would lose herself in the text. For Unamuno, it is the novel that disappears as the author and the reader enter into communion. The most direct reference to Ortega in this quote is Unamuno's use of the concept of saving themselves. For Ortega, it is the object that is saved by the reader's contemplation; for Unamuno, the author and reader are saved in community through mutual resuscitation. Be it the vanishing text or the vanishing author? By opting for one or the other, our two Spanish theoreticians and rivals propound two radically different definitions of literature and the novel.

Possible, Compossible, and Virtual Worlds

Unamuno and Ortega do, however, share an insight into the nature of the boundary that separates the fictive from the real that has proven to be transformational in our own times: both not only acknowledge, but also explore the realm of the virtual. As we shall see in chapter 6, one of Ortega y Gasset's achievements in aesthetics is to name this virtual world and explain its relation to the planes of fiction and reality. Although Unamuno does not use the term 'virtual,' his notion of the theatricality of human life and self-consciousness is suffused with the experience of the virtual as textual embodiment. How else can one understand his insistence that the fictional characters are in fact the real entities that make use of flesh-and-blood authors to manifest themselves to us? (*VDQ* 274) By inverting the epistemological and ontological categories of reality and make-believe, Unamuno in effect creates a liminal zone between them that comprises the virtual. This third zone is implicit in Unamuno's thought when he asserts that the literary characters are more real than their authors, as they are resurrected through the resusci-tating power of the reader. The act of reading creates a virtual plane on which the real reader makes the literary real, and into which the literary infiltrates, shaping the reader. This is not a realm of physical substance, but rather of the idea and of the mind, or, in Unamuno's terms, the spiritual. Nonetheless, the literary can erect itself only upon the plat-form of the real author and the real reader. Just as the virtual worlds of our digitalized age are dreams projected through binary code, Unamuno's liminal world of literary self-consciousness (one that reflects the human condition itself) are dreams projected by human beings, arising from and constituting human realities.

The windmill episode links two key passages in Unamuno's private notebooks of the 1920s that reveal how his thought moved toward what we could now understand as the virtuality of fiction. In an entry labelled 'Dream and Waking' (*Sueño y vigilia*), Unamuno highlights the differ-ence between his and Ortega's definition of being. After asking how one distinguishes between sleep and waking, Unamuno alludes to the distinction between active looking (*mirar*) and passive seeing (*ver*) that Ortega established in the *Meditations on Don Quixote* (1914). Active look-ing, as Ortega shows, depends on wilfully paying attention. Unamuno repeats Ortega's assertion that active looking depends on differentiating the seen from the field of vision, making it individual, and thus, for Unamuno, making it real. At this point, Unamuno diverges from Ortega's thought. Ortega interprets the windmill episode as illustrative of two different realities, one material, the other cultural. For Unamuno, the windmill/giant dilemma represents not a difference between two dissimilar substances, but rather two different wills: 'Don Quixote cre-ated the giants in an awakening looking that overcomes the weak vi-sion of the windmills' (*CHN* 103).[54] In the first instance, Unamuno figures Don Quixote's vision in antagonistic relation to a weaker-willed vision, but then he couches it in ontological terms: 'The subject creates its object ... The object creates itself in the subject, and creates itself and recreates or preserves itself, its existence. Thus the object exists, the dream.'[55] Subject and object are intertwined in a relationship of interdependence that seems to erase the subject/object boundary. Such an erasure of the self and the object characterizes reading and dreaming, and thus Unamuno quips: 'Knowledge is not passive but active. If I have known Don Quixote, it is by making him in me, mak-ing a Quixotic work.'[56] Finally, Unamuno moves into the realm of the absolute, recalling the creation of the universe by God, *ex nihilo nihil fit*. This same power to create something from nothing provides Unamuno with a new definition of humanity as the animal that dreams, just as God dreams and creates the universe (*CHN* 104). The implications of this chain of thought are various: firstly, the creative, poetic act of dreaming is to be preferred to the instinctual, stupid, inattentive vision of the awake. Don Quixote's vision of giants triumphs over windmills. Secondly, it raises the world created in the dream to the same level as the world created by God; that is to say, it asserts the reality of the poetic.

Unamuno also manages to wrest from Cohen's idealism support for his own notion of poetry as self- and world-making through the notion of the thinkable and the unthinkable. In a note compiled in the *Manual de Quijotismo*, Unamuno writes the following: 'The real world and the ideal. Don Quixote does not believe that windmills are giants, he wants them to be so. V. Cohen 353. Matter is the absolute possibility of the passive (Stuart Mill) and God the absolute possibility of form=consciousness. The verisimilar and the truthful. The possible and the compossible. V. Cohen.'[57] The problem of will must involve the difference between the real and the ideal, for the will seeks to work out the ideal in the real. Unamuno's nod to John Stuart Mill seems to echo the latter's assertion that matter 'may be defined as a Permanent Possibility of Sensations' (183), postulating the continuous existence of the external as evidenced by visual and tactual sensation even when these sensations are not present. In this case, matter is subsumed into mind and, by extension, art, through reference to verisimilitude. The reference 'Cohen 353' sends us to the section in *Logic of Pure Knowledge* where Cohen echoes theological speculation that God is absolute substance, only to observe that humankind cannot be certain of this (*LRE* 408). To what reality does the human being refer, to that of things or one closer to his own being? Cohen names this second reality the thinkable, and defines it dialectically as everything that is not unthinkable. The thinkable, a concept found in Aristotle and medieval metaphysics, inserts itself, according to Cohen, into modernity as a shadow in Cartesian light. Cohen then introduces Leibniz's distinction between the possible and compossibility, which determines which possible things can coexist in any given world. Cohen further suggests the importance of this notion of compossibility for aesthetics, especially given that Leibniz introduces the distinction between possibility and impossibility with reference to a novel, Honoré D'Urfé's *L'Astrée*.

Unamuno transposes Cohen's questions into literary terms by introducing the notion of the verisimilar. Even in Aristotelian poetics, the verisimilar can be understood as a function of compossibility, for the reader determines the verisimilitude of a work through the coherence, or lack thereof, of given elements in the novelistic framework. In this vein Cohen notes that compossibility serves as a control through which to orient the literary towards the real world in the novel (*LRE* 410). Unamuno, on the other hand, goes much farther in the next note as he jots the following: 'Humanism (personalism) versus idealism and realism versus spiritualism. The idea for the human, not the human for the idea. Don Quixote the idea made man. The Word became flesh and dwelt among us. The man made idea.'[58] Compossibility is now associated with incarnation, as the human being makes the idea and is made by the idea. From this juxtaposition one can explain Unamuno's frequent quip that the individual must make of him/herself a novel. Life is fiction, and fiction is life. The individual makes herself, and the idea or novel she makes of herself will return in the way others see and make her.

Perhaps the deepest tragedy in Unamuno's thought is the one he himself lived. Already in the 1920s exile in Paris, he was aware that the public persona he had created had taken on a life of its own, independent of and freed from its creator. In journalistic writings and public speeches of the last decade of his life, he repeatedly told the story of a trip to an insane asylum, where one of the patients asked to meet him. When he presented himself, the man merely said that he had wanted to see if he was the real Unamuno, and then walked away. Unamuno had achieved immortality through his image, and yet he realized in this man's dismissive gesture that the Unamuno he had created did not correspond to himself. As we shall discuss in chapter 8, the tragedy of the public Unamuno became intricately entwined with the tragedy of Spain in his death. His thought became his reality.

6 Form Foreshortened: Ortega y Gasset's *Meditations on Don Quixote*

'Is *Don Quixote*, perchance, only a silly romp?'[1] With this quotation from Hermann Cohen, the Spanish philosopher José Ortega y Gasset begins his first major work, *Meditations on Don Quixote* (1914).[2] The question posed by the German philosopher is clearly rhetorical, since the interpretation of Cervantes' parody of chivalric romances as an ultimately serious endeavour had firmly taken root in both the German intellectual and popular traditions. For both philologists and philosophers, the humour of Don Quixote's mishaps belied the ultimately profound critique of modernity offered by the novel. For the lay reader, Don Quixote was the noble fool, and Cervantes' novel was, as so aptly described by Heinrich Heine, the greatest satire on human enthusiasm ('Einleitung zum Don Quixote'). Nonetheless, when the Spanish philosopher repeats his mentor's question, it takes on a different context (or circumstance, as Ortega would put it) and, hence, connotation. It is nothing less than Ortega's call for the modernization of Spain. Ortega's rejection of the philology of his day would have considerable impact on later Cervantes specialists, the most notable and controversial being his colleague Américo Castro. Assumptions put forth by Ortega y Gasset have shaped the research of both Spanish and international Cervantes scholars: the inescapable presence of the comic in both *Don Quixote* and the novel as a genre; the definition of Quixotism as a means Cervantes used to explore life in all its facets; the enigmatic nature of Cervantes and his creation as a key to unlocking the destiny of Spain; and the pessimistic recognition of the limitations of culture revealed by Don Quixote's madness (Navarro 74–5).

Ortega's Search for a Mentor

Like Unamuno, Ortega viewed turn-of-the-century Spain as a culture isolated from mainstream Europe, insofar as Europe represented modernity based on scientific reason, the secular state, and mercantile capitalism. Unlike Unamuno, Ortega championed science and reason as the means to reform Spain and to move beyond modernity, which he saw as hopelessly anachronistic in the twentieth century. Cervantes would never be for Ortega an impotent man of letters, but rather a model for thought *and* action: in short, a model for the man young Ortega wanted to be. For Ortega, Cervantes' universality is a function of his devotion to ideas. Curiously enough, this is precisely the explanation he offers in a letter he finally sends to Unamuno. Referring to the older man's assertion that the ambition for glory characterizes Don Quixote, and by extension, Spain, Ortega replies that Spaniards have not achieved immortal renown precisely because they have not served the immortal and universal Ideas; the only one to do so was Cervantes (*Epistolario completo Ortega/Unamuno* 59).

In the spring of 1905 Ortega left for Germany, in order to compensate for what he considered the inferior education available in Spain. Steeped in Kant and inclined to sympathize intellectually with Cohen, the young philosopher eventually arrived in Marburg (Cacho Viu, 'Prologue' 24). The intellectual affinities between Ortega and Cohen appear already in the former's musings upon *Don Quixote* in a letter addressed to Unamuno of February 1907. Central to Ortega's reading of Cervantes' novel are pivotal concepts from Cohen's thought, including the Idea and infinity. But perhaps more importantly, Cohen offers the young Spaniard a vision of philosophy as an enterprise based on the heightened, critical awareness of problems (what Ortega called *nivel*) and on the systematic analysis of logic, ethics, and aesthetics (Morón Arroyo, *El sistema de Ortega y Gasset* 53–62). Ortega's letters written during his first stay in Marburg paint a picture of Cohen as an ebullient, impassioned teacher and thinker. The young Spanish student was thrilled to be repeatedly invited, along with other favourite pupils, to the Cohen residence for meals and discussion, and boasted in letters to his parents of his triumphs in gatherings at the homes of both the Natorps and the Cohens (*Cartas de un joven español* 285–7). After years of isolation, the young man had finally found a group of peers as well as a mentor figure.

According to Ortega's accounts in his letters, Cohen felt empathy for his young Spanish student based on his own identity as a German Jew.

When Cohen invited Ortega to remain for another semester to take his course on logic, the latter responded that he would like to but could not tolerate the Germans any longer. Clearly, Ortega believed that he shared with Cohen a marginalized position vis-à-vis German culture: 'Cohen thinks likewise of his semicompatriots, and I say semi – because he is Jewish, and as his name indicates the most Jewish of the Jewish.'[3] In a similar vein, the student also told his fiancée how his teacher would throw his arms around him every time the young Ortega mentioned a Sephardic or Arabic book, and would pepper him with questions about Spain (563).[4]

The young Ortega returned from Marburg to Spain in 1907 to throw himself into an active life as 'a publicist, a professor, and a polemicist' (Abellán 42). Ortega's politics at the time were clearly leftist although uniquely his own, as he strove for a conception of socialism that would not exclude the distinctions of merit.[5] Like Cohen, Ortega sought the engine of socialist change in culture rather than in the economy. Like Unamuno, he called for the general education of the Spanish public and saw fulfilling that need as a political act. Indeed, in a time and place where illiteracy rates hovered around 60 per cent, education was a political concern and a political action (Dobson 17). In a speech from 1910 titled 'Social Pedagogy as a Political Program,' the young man equated political socialist action with pedagogical action. With a quotation from Paul Natorp, the young Spaniard describes the relation between society and education as one of reciprocal influence: each shapes the other. Thus, Ortega defines politics as social pedagogy and the Spanish problem as a pedagogical one (*OC* 1:506).

His personal notes reveal that Ortega understood Cohen's notion of *Aufgabe* as not only the productive interchange of the individual with the world, but also, like Natorp, the creation of the self: 'The person creates himself in the unity of action. Action is always *Aufgabe* (a doing, not a having or a having known). The person or the *Selbst* is always an *Aufgabe*, not an intellectual content.'[6] When Ortega states that culture is work, the work involved is both that of making the nation (Spain) and making the individual (*OC* 1:507). Society itself is bettered by this activity, since individuals form cooperatives, setting aside their differences in order to pursue common goals and ideals. We glimpse here the link between socialism and idealism for the young philosopher: the work through the real toward the ideal creates community by dissolving individual interests into a common purpose. Ortega further diagnoses the Spanish problem, then, as one of excessive alienation and individualism: 'Our nation at this time disjointed into atoms, our activity is reduced to the negation of one person by another, of one group by another, of one region by another.'[7] In this sense, he directly contradicts Unamuno's pedagogical politics, in which the older philosopher calls for an intensification of individuality and a diminution of 'group think.' Echoing Cohen's call for a community that transcends tribal and parochial identification, Ortega's prescription for the Spanish problem is, simply but yet not so simply, Europeanization to counter what he considers the trivialization of its culture.

The young Ortega y Gasset's encounter with Hermann Cohen represented for the Spaniard nothing less than his encounter with Europe. The most important visit for Ortega's development of his theory of the novel took place in 1911. There Ortega belonged to a 'group of young men of 1911' who would become leading philosophers of their generation, including Nicolai Hartmann and Heinz Heimsoeth. Three general philosophical tendencies united them: (1) the desire to verify philosophical theory against fact (veracity); (2) the appetite for system, admittedly difficult to reconcile with the first tendency; and (3) the need to move beyond idealism (Marías, *Ortega. Circunstancia y vocación* 337–40). Moreover, his intellectual companionship with Cohen deepened into the contradictions typical of the moment when a student begins the salutary process of gaining intellectual independence from the mentor. The move beyond idealism that he and his contemporaries sought was explicitly a move away from what they perceived as Cohen's and Natorp's rigid defence of their own ideas against all attackers – including the philosophers they sought to study and the reality that surrounded them.[8] Nonetheless, Ortega in 1934 acknowledges a very profound debt to Cohen: his dramatic manner of teaching in which intellectual lessons are transformed into tragic performances for the students (*OC* 8:34). Part of this tragic effect Cohen achieved through what Ortega described as his muscular speech: 'I felt every one of his phrases like a blow to the back of my neck.'[9]

The significance of the summer of 1911 for the theory of the novel should not be underestimated, since the two scholars read *Don Quixote* together as they elaborated their respective theories of the novel. Ortega described the intellectual dialogue as an ideal dispute (*contienda*) between equals. According to Ortega, Cohen, who at the time was writing his *Aesthetics*, responds to his student's mention of Cervantes by re-reading *Don Quixote*. Ortega, for his part, not only reinterprets *Don Quixote*, but also begins to develop his own philosophy working out of the dispute with Cohen. The description of this exchange that Ortega offers in his essay 'Meditations on the Escorial' (1915) serves to identify the two sides of Ortega's own heritage as a thinker.[10] The Escorial, Philip II's countryside retreat that also housed a massive library, and Gothic Marburg juxtapose themselves in the young man's thought and imagination. According to Ortega, he owes at least half of his hopes and almost all of his discipline to Marburg. He remembers the small Gothic city as ringed by trees and embanked by a dark, placid river, a vague warp against his image of the Escorial. In contrast, the Escorial represents for Ortega not only the solidity and reality of God for the realistic Spaniard, but also the historical sense of incompleteness and frustration that characterizes sixteenth- and seventeenth-century Spain and Europe. Europeans began to doubt whether their own existence was as complete or perfect as that of earlier times. In other words, they began to feel modern, conscious of their historical separation from antiquity and of the emptiness or decadence of their own times. Ortega describes this sense of loss with figurative language that recreates the weight and solemnity of the Escorial; human desires are energies held captive in the prison of matter, and human strength is wasted resisting the force of gravity upon us (*OC* 1:549). The Spaniard responds to this sense of impotency by striving ever harder to impose his own will on reality in a furore epitomized by both the Escorial and Sancho Panza.

As we have seen in Cohen's theory of the novel, Sancho Panza receives more attention than Don Quixote, in part because the squire, in his time as governor of Barataria, serves as a model for the ideal statesman. Ortega y Gasset, in his memories of the summer of 1911, reveals that Sancho Panza was the nexus connecting his quite different theory of the novel to that of his mentor. Silhouetted by the restless, trembling stars of a Marburg summer's night, Ortega would walk to Cohen's home, where he would find him leaning over the Ludwig Tieck translation of Cervantes' masterpiece. Cohen frequently greeted the young Spaniard with the telling observation that Sancho used the same word on which Fichte founded his philosophy (*OC* 1:558).[11] This word is in German *Tathandlung*, and in Spanish *hazaña*. *Hazaña* is frequently translated into English as *deed*, and yet such a translation fails to express the bold wilfulness and heroism of the individual who takes on a deed normally beyond his or her capacity that flavours the Spanish word. Often *hazañas* pertain to the actions of knights errant, and it is thus ironic that in *Don Quixote* this term 'fills the mouth' (to borrow Ortega's meaty phrase) of the squire rather than the master. Furthermore, as both Cohen and Ortega insist, *hazaña* understood as *Tathandlung* founds modern philosophy. Kant acknowledged the importance of the will by juxtaposing ethics to logic. Fichte goes one step further by privileging the will, seeing it as prior to logic. As Ortega explains, 'Prior to reflection there is an act of bravery, a *Tathandlung*; this is the origin of his philosophy.'[12] For Cohen and Ortega, Sancho preceded German idealism in his insistence on the priority of will to reason. Ortega provides us, then, with yet another image of overlapping Spanish and German cultures, as the philosophy of Sancho shines through that of Fichte.

The implications of this interpenetration between the Spanish novel and German philosophy are of great significance for Ortega's vindication of the Spanish intellectual tradition. Cervantes can now occupy the place of a great philosopher, a transformation of the novelist that not only lets Ortega insert his fellow countryman into the philosophical canon, but also permits him to ground his own philosophical thought in aesthetics. In this 'Meditation on the Escorial,' we find the most succinct statement of Cervantes' role as a philosopher: 'Cervantes composed in his *Don Quixote* the critique of pure force.'[13] One can place Cervantes' *Don Quixote* on the philosopher's bookshelf, next to Kant's *Critique of Pure Reason*, *Critique of Practical Reason*, and *Critique of Judgement*, as well as Cohen's *Logic of Pure Knowledge*, *Ethics of Pure Will*, and *Aesthetics of Pure Feeling*. The notion of force is related to Natorp's ideas about the consciousness of the self, in which force and sentiment characterize the relations between the self and the content of consciousness – in Ortega's words, the circumstances (Orringer, *Ortega y sus fuentes germánicas* 89). Cervantes is envisioned as a philosopher and, moreover, the one who problematizes most completely the complex relations between the self and the exterior world.

The tragedy of Spain, however, is that pure force leads nowhere except to melancholy. Significantly, Ortega opts for the term *esfuerzo*, referring more directly to power or imposition, rather than *voluntad*, or will. For Ortega at this point, Don Quixote, like Don Juan, is a man of little intelligence propelled forward by a few empty, simple ideas to impose his desires on his surroundings. Even though he converts his environs into a pretext for exercising his will, grave doubt begins to besiege him (*OC* 1:553). The would-be knight errant, exemplar of pure force, suffers at the end not only from disillusionment and frustration, but also from a lack of purpose. Observing that Don Quixote desires death by the end of the novel, Ortega ends this essay with a personalized quote: 'Above all, there is this anguished confession of the forced one [*el esforzado*]: the truth is that "I do not know what I conquer by the force of my works," I do not know what I achieve with my force.'[14] Turning the word *fuerza* on its head into *esforzado*, Ortega highlights the way in which the power of the outside world ends up imposing its reality upon Don Quixote. Such a turn of events results in and from the protagonist's ignorance; neither does he have knowledge of the world that he seeks to transform, nor does he acquire knowledge from his activity.

Ortega, after quoting Don Quixote's confession of ignorance, paraphrases a similar confession using the first person. Insofar as Ortega attempts to characterize the tragedy of the Spanish nation, there is no doubt that he expresses melancholy over his own identity as a man of force. Referring both to the imposition of will implied in Philip II's construction of the Escorial and Nietzsche's characterization of Spaniards as those who have desired too much, Ortega asserts that the force of will defines his nation's history: 'Against the extremely wide backdrop of universal history, we Spaniards were a gesture of boldness. That is all our greatness; that is all our misery.'[15] The tragic flow in this forcefulness lies in its disassociation from the realm of the idea, resulting in a lack of direction. Echoing Cohen's notion of activity directed toward an ultimately unrealizable goal, the Spaniard asserts that the end of action does not interest the man of force so much as the difficulty and willpower required by action: 'The forced one is not interested in action; only the wilful deed [*hazaña*] interests him.'[16] Not only does the man of pure force fail to act ethically according to the norms of Kantianism for disinterested action, he even fails to act ethically according to the norms of utilitarianism. The end of the action has no import whatsoever; all that matters is the amount of force used up in the process. This melancholic vision of Spain proffered by Ortega represents what he considers to be Cervantes' critique of pure force, and by extension the novelist's critique of his nation. It stands as a rejoinder to Unamuno's exaltation of individualistic will, and as a call for the moderation of Spanish character through reason.

Meditations on Don Quixote as Philosophy

Ortega's *Meditations on Don Quixote* (1914) generally occupies pride of place as the young man's first major philosophical treatise. The work has been treated as Ortega's 'discourse on method,' in which the philosopher transforms himself into a spectator presenting points of view to his audience who will, in turn, find their own way to the truth (Carpintero 32). Ortega shows in this text how he will use language and metaphor to pursue philosophical truths. First, he treats Spanish as German philosophers treated German, that is to say, by playing with prefixes, suffixes, and etymological roots to reveal meaning (Tierno Galván, 'Ortega y la metafísica' 60). Second, he makes full use of metaphors to render his theory visible and to reveal how thought relies on imagery (F.J. Martín, *La tradición velada* 149). The famous quip that will shape all of the thinker's subsequent work, 'I am I and my circumstances,' represents for Ortega's students, Julián Marías and Antonio Rodríguez Huéscar, the overcoming of both idealism and realism. Ortega surpasses Fichte, for instance, by positing an I that does not posit the not-I, but rather is composed with it in the circumstances.[17] The first I of the equation is not abstract, but rather a *position* in reality (Marías, *Ortega. Circunstancia y vocación* 381). Ortega's postulation of the I and its circumstances as a basis for metaphysics constitutes a '"radical" reality [that] is, originarily speaking, both a duality and a mutuality; it is an originary and active interdependence that cannot therefore be located either outside or inside the self' (Rodríguez Huéscar, *José Ortega y Gasset's Metaphysical Innovation* xxxi).[18]

Many commentators take at face value Ortega's statement in 1934 that by 1911 he was no longer a neo-Kantian, but neither was he strictly speaking a phenomenologist. Phenomenology could not offer him a philosophical system in neo-Kantian terms, that is to say, dealing with logic, ethics, and aesthetics. His conception of the 'I' as a position from which agency and effect emanate contradicts the phenomenological reduction of the self to pure conscience, eliminating the relation of subject, action, and object (Marías, *Ortega. Circunstancia y vocación* 394; Rodríguez Huéscar, *José Ortega y Gasset's Metaphysical Innovation* 65). There is no doubting the impact phenomenology had on his thought, and one must agree with Philip Silver that the Marburg School's lack of interest in the sensorial and sensual verification was by this time off-putting for Ortega (46). Nonetheless, like many others, Ortega did not so completely move beyond his mentor Cohen's thought as he would have wanted others to believe (Orringer, 'Ortega, psicólogo y la superación de sus maestros' 186–8). Holmes notes a structural debt to neo-Kantian metaphysics in Ortega's mature thought: 'Ortega replaced Cohen's logic with his notion of "human" life. That is, Ortega's generalized view of existence contains human life in place of human logic as the underlying unifying principle of reality' (28). Aspects of Cohen's thought that Ortega does not reject include his notion of present action oriented toward future goals and the figuring of the other as an equal

Tú (80, 95). He also clearly takes from Cohen the commitment to 'conceptual, "schematic" thinking and theorizing,' his notion of the unity of thinking with knowing and being, and his practice of philosophizing through writings on art, literature, and science (Graham, *A Pragmatist Philosophy of Life in Ortega y Gasset* 108–11). Morón Arroyo summarizes the issue of Ortega's debt to Cohen in this way: the unifying point of system becomes humanity rather than mathematics, and the ideal is to 'save' things by respecting and contemplating their plurality (*El sistema de Ortega y Gasset* 101).

By 1914, when he publishes his *Meditations on Don Quixote*, Ortega has moved toward the notion of *aletheia*, in which truth reveals itself (245).[19] This stance is consistent with his notion of the self as existing in reciprocal relation with the circumstances, for the circumstances act upon the self just as the self acts upon them. Ortega emphasizes that the hero is authentic in his striving to be himself, but that this striving is limited by the circumstances. In order to achieve self-actualization, the human being must return to the circumstances, reabsorb them, and give them meaning; moreover, it is precisely this activity that creates culture, and culture implies the realm of ideas. Nonetheless, the hero suffers the tragedy of his reabsorption into circumstances, for they also make a claim upon him (Cerezo Galán, *La voluntad de aventura* 127). In Ortega's thought, then, neo-Kantian insistence on human agency and early phenomenological work on the constructive aspect of perception combine to propose an interactive, reciprocal, and even conflictual relation between the self and her surroundings. In order to appreciate the self and the object within their circumstances, Ortega will propose in the *Meditations on Don Quixote* a new method of knowledge based on circling the object of study rather than penetrating it in a direct assault. My own analysis of Ortega's text will follow the circuitous path he uses to structure these meditations. In this circling path we will see doubled metaphors and images as *Don Quixote* is contemplated from different standpoints.

The Circumstances of *Meditations on Don Quixote*

The year 1914, the date of this work's publication, is normally considered of particular importance in Ortega's life not only because it marks a philosophical turning point, but also because of his political speech 'New and Old Politics,' given in March, which served to galvanize the so-called Generation of 1914 (Marías, *Ortega. Circunstancia y vocación* 333). This speech inaugurated the League of Political Education (La Liga de Educación Política), an association composed of young, upcoming figures as well as established ones from Spain's intellectual, cultural, and political elites. Most notable among them were Manuel Azaña, later to become the president of the Spanish Republic, the literary writers Ramón Pérez de Ayala, Pedro Salinas, and Antonio Machado, and the intellectuals Ramiro de Maeztu, Américo Castro, and Salvador de Madariaga. All rejected what they considered the 'official' Spain – that of the Restoration – and would go on to consider 'the problem of Spain' in their own ways (Fernández Sanz 59–62). For these young cultural leaders the Restoration government, based on a tripartite distribution of power between the urban oligarchy, provincial strongmen (*caciques*), and civil government, was corrupt and led to the disenfranchisement of the people and the weakening of Spanish character. The league itself dissolved as its members joined regular political parties, perhaps in part due to Ortega's reluctance to step into a leadership role for the group (Massó Lagó 280–1). Nonetheless, this meeting of likeminded individuals would plant the seeds for Spain's future as they sought the nation's modernization through democratization and education. One wonders how this meeting affected the course of Cervantes studies, as three of Spain's most influential interpreters of *Don Quixote de la Mancha* – Ortega, Salvador de Madariaga, and Américo Castro – met in that room. Certainly, the final destiny of the different members of the group speaks to the coming tragedy of Spain. Those associated with the Republic (1932–6) would enter into exile from Francoist reprisal. The poet Antonio Machado would die in France in exile in 1939, and Manuel Azaña, president of the Republic, would die there one year later. Américo Castro would pursue his academic career in the United States, founding American Cervantism, only to be harshly criticized by colleagues in Spain. Salvador de Madariaga, in addition to his academic career, would work tirelessly for the causes of European unity and pacifism. Ramiro de Maeztu, whose vision of a modernized Spain inspired Ortega and the other members of the League of Political Education, would become a reactionary ideologue in the 1930s and die in an extrajudicial execution by leftist forces in 1936.

Ortega's *Meditations on Don Quixote* was published on 21 July 1914, just days before the start of the First World War, and was written from a room with a view of the Escorial (Gray 91). Spain remained officially neutral during the war, but was split from within (Romero Salvadó 5–26). In general, the Conservative party, the monarchy, and the Church supported the Axis powers, whereas leftist intellectuals, politicians, and artists supported the Allied powers. France and Germany represented for the Spanish left reforms they so desired: democratic government, modernization of industry and education, and civil freedoms. Ortega, as a member of the Spanish Francophile left but a student of German philosophy, must have found himself in a bind, caught between the Escorial and Marburg. To that effect he noted in August of 1914 that a world conflagration had started, in which Germany's isolation would render it the terrible hammer of Thor (Molinuevo, 'Fichte y Ortega III' 226). Ortega's anonymous portrait of Cohen in an unsigned description of the philosopher (*España*, 16 August 1915) insists on the need to distinguish between German politics and science, and labels Cohen's initial defence of German bellicosity a contradiction of his philosophical work (Massó Lagó 298). Critics have speculated as to various causes for the hasty publication of the incomplete *Meditations on Don Quixote*, but the coming war might have contributed to Ortega's decision to publish. In spite of its official neutrality, Spain suffered economically during the war, as the demand for its raw materials fuelled inflation to levels that caused great dislocation of rural populations as well as general deprivation.

Indeed, the writing of the *Meditations on Don Quixote* can only be understood as a fully integrated act of philosophy *and* politics. Marías outlines the six logical steps that lead to the concatenation of theory and national critique in this most curious and important of essays: (1) the goal of philosophy is to know how to live; (2) one can know how to live only by leaving oneself and attending to one's circumstances (in Ortega's case, Spain); (3) Spain becomes intelligible through certain essential elements, one of which is *Don Quixote*; (4) in order to understand *Don Quixote* and Cervantes, one must understand their connection to the real and intelligible; (5) this sort of analysis can only be done through looking at ultimate connections, i.e., through the work of philosophy; and (6) looking at the novel's connections is in itself a foundational work of Spanish philosophy, since it circumstantializes the same (*Ortega. Circunstancia y vocación* 347–9). Other writers find a European political context for the work. Francisco José Martín argues convincingly that the coming world war raises a new question for Ortega: what is the problem of Europe? ('Hacer concepto'). Cervantes, as the most revered Spaniard in Europe, serves to meditate on the Spanish problem within the European problem, understood by Ortega as a crisis in political ideology. Ortega, by refusing to take sides in the current conflict, will be the most European of all, standing for the ideals of Europe (Marías, *Ortega. Las trayectoria* 61). For Ortega, neither traditional liberalism, limited by its strongly individualistic streak, nor socialism, marked by its dogmatic utopism, was sufficient any longer for actually describing the political problems of the age, let alone addressing them (Molinuevo, 'Fichte y Ortega II' 353). John T. Graham puts Ortega's dilemma this way: 'Long before Husserl realized it in Nazi Germany, however Ortega saw in his *Meditations on Quixote* ... that Western man was in transit through a gray area between two antagonistic value systems – the old one founded on culture and science, the new one on life and its enhancement – and that a sharp crisis was inevitable' (*Theory of History in Ortega y Gasset* 223).

The fragmentary nature of the *Meditations on Don Quixote* is not particularly unusual in Ortega's oeuvre, which one critic has called a *disiecta membra* constituted by variable surface arrangements of fragments atop a deep structure (Carpintero 9). Ortega had in mind a series of meditations on Spanish authors, including his friend Pío Baroja, his contemporary Azorín, the baroque playwright Lope de Vega, the Romantic journalist Mariano José Larra, and Goethe.[20] Although one is tempted to imagine and analyse the non-existent complete text, I would argue that it is necessary to approach this work as is. Perhaps Ortega changed his mind and decided the work was complete. He certainly could have published more, but even manuscript versions of the promised chapters on Cervantes ('How Cervantes Was Accustomed to Seeing the World' and 'Cervantes as a Halcyonic Figure') have never been found.[21] In a notebook he describes the existing essays as 'of a constructive rebelliousness,' and it is this rebelliousness – perhaps in the final instance against the systematic impulse of his mentors at Marburg – that could explain the work's incompletion (Molinuevo, 'Sobre Cervantes y *El Quijote* desde el Escorial' 36).

Ortega figures the essays as *salvaciones*, works of salvation. The concept of the *salvación* brings together neatly both sides of Ortega's intellectual persona: the philosopher's attempt to introduce a new methodology focused on the thing itself, the surface, and its surroundings; and the public citizen's obligation to analyse and reform his nation's situation. Writing of this genre, Ortega affirms that one takes 'a matter of fact,' be it an individual, book, painting, landscape, error, or pain, to its fullest meaning. This process hinges on rescuing the materials of all kinds that life casts at our feet like the useless flotsam of a shipwreck (*MQ* 14). Elsewhere Ortega affirms that to save a classic (such as *Don Quixote*), one must make it contemporary again by submerging it in the reader's existence (García Alonso 195). This redemptive action is for Ortega one of intellectual love (he borrows the term *amor intellectualis* from Spinoza),²² and thus involves radiating the small and trivial with a light that links it to the intellectual and ethical problems of human existence. Platonic dimensions adhere to this love, for it is erotic (a desire that searches) and contemplative (Cerezo Galán, *La voluntad de aventura* 100–2). Perhaps most importantly, love does not possess the object (Rodríguez Huéscar, *Perspectiva y verdad* 63). Intellectual love is the opposite of hate, the latter characterizing for Ortega the modern Spanish spirit. Hate separates us from the object, effectively eliminating all its intrinsic value except for that small part touching on our own self-interest. Subsequently, Ortega claims that the universe is dry, rigid, and desert-like for the Spaniard. Love, on the other hand, leads one to a further investigation of the loved one, drawing the viewer on to new connections and eventually creating a relationship of mutual absorption. As Ortega concludes, love expands the individual and allows for the absorption and unification of others within the self (*MQ* 16).

The Jericho Hermeneutics, Perspectivism, and the Concept

Directing these meditations to his younger readers, Ortega proposes a two-pronged change in attitude. On the one hand, Spaniards should undertake an intellectual reform involving a different sort of hermeneutics, one in which the text in question is circled rather than invaded: in short, what some critics have called the 'method of Jericho.'²³ Ortega rejects the philology practised by such Spanish literary critics as Marcelino Menéndez Pelayo and Juan Valera, whom he criticizes for their 'lack of perspective' (*MQ* 55). Moreover, the sort of literary criticism undertaken in *Meditations on Don Quixote* is clearly a form of philosophy as Ortega understands the term. He describes the difference between erudition and philosophy thus: 'Erudition occupies, then, the surrounding countryside of sciences, because it is limited to the accumulation of facts, whereas philosophy constitutes its centralizing aspiration, because it is pure synthesis.'²⁴ Unlike erudition, which creates a disconnected mass of facts, synthesis reduces the facts to their vital essence (*vigor esencial*). The moment of illumination understands (*comprender*), and takes on the temporal form of an epiphany. Referring to Hegel's *Logic*, which culminates in the grand epiphany that 'The Idea is the absolute,' Ortega describes the power of philosophy thus: 'When we think about it as we should, this whole treasury of signification explodes in one burst, and in this burst we see illuminated the enormous perspective of the world.'[25] The motions toward Hegel function partially as Ortega's effort to overcome Kant by engaging his antithesis (Villacañas Berlanga 76), but they are also an attempt to overcome Hegel's linking of reason to spirit. Ortega recognizes this moment of sudden discharge in three levels of human experience: sexual pleasure as a discharge of nervous energy, aesthetic fruition as a discharge of emotion, and philosophy as a discharge of thought.

The link between perspective, an encircling hermeneutics, and theoretical epiphany appears when one imagines the movement of gradual approach to a text figured in the following image: 'A work on the order of *Don Quixote* has to be taken like Jericho. In broad circles, our thoughts and emotions have to slowly expand, resounding in the air like ideal trumpets' (*MQ* 38).[26] As one shifts from point to point around the text, the perspective will also necessarily shift. The text will appear under different lights and from different vantage points. Indeed, the work of the literary critic is nothing less than completing the work itself by completing the reading. What does Ortega mean by this statement (now almost a cliché but revolutionary in its time)? Rather than sitting as a judge upon the correctness or worth of the work, the critic should accept the validity of the reader's viewpoint (García Alonso 247). This she does by introducing any manner of ideological or sentimental context that might intensify and clarify the text. Encircling the text constitutes a *salvación*, insofar as it provides a means of restoring the things to be studied to what Ortega terms their fullness, which he figures as the atmosphere of light enveloping objects in a Rembrandt painting. It also reinserts them into a network of relations, the connective tissue of love that is Plato's divine architect. Moreover, the circling motion embodies an active search that brings about the revelation of truth, the moment of *aletheia* sought by Ortega. Things present themselves to the self in an 'action exercised by instancies, an action which consists in their genuinely encircling or "besieging" me' (Rodríguez Huéscar, *José Ortega y Gasset's Metaphysical Innovation* 105).[27] A strange and never-resolved tension underlies this image of a siege hermeneutics: that between war and love.

In Ortega's terms, the *Meditations* are an act of presentation. Ortega's circular methodology does not oppose but rather juxtaposes competing points of view. There is no moment of Hegelian *Aufhebung*, in which the dialectical pair would be subsumed and suspended in synthesis. Insofar as he focuses on juxtaposition and division rather than overcoming and integration, Ortega conceives of dialectics in Platonic rather than Hegelian terms (Orringer, 'Ser y no-ser en Platón, Hartmann y Ortega' 78). Nor is there a moment of phenomenological reduction, when, through the exclusion of perceptual moments, original consciousness springs into view. What there is is a movement through multiple, different points of view until a moment of transcendent vision appears, in which there is a sudden panoramic outlook on the conceptual topology. The first three steps of the meditation hinge on different perspectives on truth. In the preliminary meditation, nymphs lead us deep into a forest. It follows that truth is a function of desire; desire belongs to the realm of the imagination; the imagination pertains to the literary and the fictional as well as to the erotic. The philosopher loves truth, and pursues it just as the lover pursues the beloved. The second step of the meditation turns toward the dialectical pair of profundity (or depth) and surface upon which Ortega elaborates the supposed difference between 'deep' northern European and 'superficial' Mediterranean thought. The Spaniard seizes upon the symbiotic relationship of the superficial to the deep, for the deep would not exist without the presence of the surface that hides and defines it. Moreover, surface and depth combine to form the third dimension of objects. One could continue slicing an object into infinitesimally small parts, and yet the surface would always need the depth to exist and vice versa. Surface and depth are not a dialectical pair in opposition to each other, but rather intimately connected and dependent on each other for their very existence.

In the third step, following the 'dialectical faun that chases the nymph into the forest,' Ortega considers the problematics of consciousness. The sounds of the stream and the chirping of a golden oriole form an undifferentiated surface if no consciousness intervenes to give them order and meaning: 'Without needing to deliberate, as soon as I hear them I envelop them in an act of ideal interpretation and I cast them far away from me: I hear them as distant.'[28] As Ortega clarifies, the conscious self maintains the sounds in a virtual distance, thus distinguishing them and placing them in a system of relations; likewise, the self imposes distance and depth on visual sensation and presumably any other patent sensations to collaborate in the creation of a background world [*trasmundo*] constituted by structures of impressions. Ortega uses the term *trasmundo*, literally speaking, 'the world beyond,' in order to emphasize both the reality of this deep world and its relational distance from the surface.[29] In the fourth step of this journey, entitled 'Trasmundos,'

Ortega expounds upon the necessary activity involved in viewing and maintaining the depth behind the surface of things. Noting that the only real truth is that which is found, he briefly returns to his concept of epiphanic illumination, this time referring to truth (*aletheia*) or apocalypse. 'Whoever wants to teach us a truth, let him place us in such a position that we discover it ourselves' – this is Ortega's pedagogical method as well as his justification for considering literature capable of transmitting philosophical reflection (*MQ* 50).[30]

Ortega's ocular-centrism carries the metaphor of the eye as vehicle of knowledge to the extreme of equating vision with ideas. In so doing, he makes a fundamental distinction between passive sight and active looking that evidences his intellectual connection to phenomenology. For Ortega, every act of looking involves an act of interpretation, an ordering of the sensation into significance: 'If there were nothing more than passive sight, the world would remain reduced to a chaos of luminous points. But there is above passive sight an active sight, one that interprets seeing and seeing interprets: a sight that is a looking.'[31] Moreover, Plato called these visions 'ideas.' This phenomenological approach to the idea represents a significant break with neo-Kantianism, as the idealist distinction between the sensorial and the mental disappears. Ortega connects this concept of an active looking that is in itself a creation of ideas with the relation of the surface to depth. Again, just as surface and depth exist in a mutually dependent relation rather than a dialectical one, so do sight and thought.

Another key concept of Ortega's life work to receive its first complete airing in the *Meditations on Don Quixote* is that of perspective. Ortega's perspectivism is not of the negative sort that negates appearances as mere illusions, but rather posits a way in which humankind can achieve access to the real and the true. Perspective participates in the creation of one's reality, and thus in the creation of reality itself. Searching for a new vocabulary with which to describe this relation of surface and depth – sight and thought – Ortega resorts to a visual term, 'foreshortening' (*escorzo*). Alluding to the artistic technique of foreshortening, Ortega asserts that the dimension of depth, be it spatial, temporal, visual, or auditory, always presents itself on a surface (*MQ* 52). Just as the artist uses the distortion of relationships of size and location in the picture plane to produce the illusion of depth, the thinking viewer applies profundity or depth to the surface. Reality is seen through foreshortening, both concretely (from a specific point of view) and intellectually (as an interpretation). Never does he question the reality of either the concrete or the intellectual, for reality exists on both planes, as surface and depth. Almost ten years later in *Ideas on the Novel*, Ortega will call the plane of depth the virtual. Writing here of the way novelistic characters attract the reader's attention, Ortega asks this question: 'How is it possible that their representation moves us? ... They, *the* realities, do not move us, but rather their representation, that is to say *the* representation of their reality. To my understanding, this distinction is decisive: the poetic aspect of reality is not reality as this or the other thing, but rather reality as a generic function.'[32] The generic function of reality is what constitutes the poetic (or virtual) plane as it represents reality. Moreover, foreshortening as an image explains the fundamental connection between the material and the virtual, as the virtual must extend from the material and vice versa. 'Foreshortening is the organ of visual profundity; in it we find a limiting case, where simple vision is welded together with a purely intellectual act.'[33]

In effect, the concept of a looking that is thinking justifies Ortega's philosophical approach to *Don Quixote*, as well as his lifelong intellectual engagement with the visual arts. The undoing of the idealist opposition between the sensorial and the intellectual serves to undermine the dogmatic denial, typical of some strains of Kantianism, that the arts, understood as sensorial, are capable of containing and transmitting knowledge. In addition, within his own national circumstances, it provides the Spanish philosopher with a native canon of world-class thinkers, including Cervantes, Velázquez, and Goya. It is no accident that Ortega declares with his next breath Cervantes' *Don Quixote* to be the 'book/ foreshortening par excellence.' Conceiving of the novel in this manner allows the philosopher to claim a national predecessor: Cervantes. For Ortega, the reading of Cervantes' masterpiece as a mere book of jokes not only denies the novel of its depth, but it also strips Spain of its intellectual heritage. Depth constitutes for Ortega theory, and without theory scholarship declines into mere erudition. Finally, returning to the concept of a vision that is simultaneously aware of surface and depth, Ortega proposes a similar form of reading: 'Just as there is a way of seeing that is looking, there is a way of reading that is *intelligere*, or reading from within, a thoughtful reading. Only thus does the profound meaning of *Don Quixote* make itself visible.'[34] This manner of reading joins the sensorial and the intellectual, and leads the reader on a journey of ideas as well as emotions and pleasure.

Dividing the world into sensualists and contemplators, Ortega y Gasset argues that the senses and the concept serve similar functions for both groups as organs for knowing reality. The senses of sight, touch, taste, hearing, and smell allow for knowledge of the surface, whereas the concept allows for knowledge of the depth. Knowledge, be it sensorial or intellectual, consists of an ordering of reality, by setting the various parts into relation with each other. With reference to the recent advances of optics, Ortega uses vision as an example for this structuring of reality. Upon opening our eyes, objects penetrate our visual field; only little by little is order bestowed on them as the eye quiets and fixes them, first attending to those in the centre and then those in the margins. Borders and limits are set between them, serving to set them in a network of relationships. 'If we continue attending to an object, it will progressively become more fixed because we gradually find in it more reflections of and connections to the surrounding things. The ideal would be to make of everything a centre of the universe.'[35] Just as the eye orders and affixes the objects in the visual field, in so doing granting them both identity and significance, so does the mind order and affix concepts. A double activity takes place: first, boundaries appear, establishing the particularity and unity of objects by differentiating them from others; second, the individual overrides the same boundaries by placing the objects within a larger web of relationships. An object's identity depends on the first step of division, whereas its meaning (its conceptual force or existence) depends on the second step of connection.

Given this primarily visual explanation of the conceptual process, the role of the limit or boundary takes on special significance. The limit both grants the thing identity and must be superseded when the thing is put into relationship with others. Although Ortega's concept of this process of establishing and overcoming the boundary cannot be equated to the Hegelian process of *Aufhebung*, the Spanish philosopher does acknowledge a debt to Hegel's concept of the limit (*die Grenze*). Hegel remarks that the limit cannot be the thing it limits, nor can it be the exterior substance on the other side of the thing (*Hegel's Logic* 136).[36] In other words, when objects A and B are given in juxtaposition but separate from each other, the limit cannot be the same as either A or B. Ortega describes the logical consequences of this observation thus: since the limit is neither A nor B, it is a virtual entity that is interpolated or injected within matter and whose nature is that of a schema that both differentiates and brings together the very objects it defines. It is none other than the concept – and we must hasten to remember that the virtual world of the concept as depth linked to surface is real for Ortega.

Nonetheless, the concept itself is not a separate substance; although Ortega's notion of the concept springs from both the Platonic notion of eros and the Hegelian notion of the limit, it does not grant the conceptual its own reality above and beyond the material. Here Ortega moves past idealism, as the concept adheres to vision rather than a realm of thought separate from the perceptual. Referring once again to the eye that divides and orders as well as the etymological root of *concept* as to catch or trap, the Spanish philosopher insists that '[e]ach concept is literally an organ with which we capture the objects.'[37]

The Novel as a Foreshortening Genre

The 'First Meditation,' subtitled 'A Brief Treatise on the Novel,' addresses the larger question: what is a novel? After referring briefly to the modern quality of *Don Quixote* experienced by contemporary readers and rejecting Benedetto Croce's denial of the existence of literary genres, Ortega sets off on a conceptual journey through various literary genres: epic, rhapsody, myth, chivalric romance, lyric, tragedy, and comedy. His final resting point will be to associate the novel with *tragicomedia*, the mixture of tragedy and comedy typical of not only *Don Quixote* but also of Fernando de Rojas's *La Celestina* (1498). Nonetheless, it is worth noting from the outset several elements of Ortega's novelistics common to other authors encountered in this study. First, the novel, like all genres, is essentially historical, and represents modernity. As such, the novel stands in opposition to the epic, the genre representing the past. Up to this point, Ortega offers nothing unique in his definition of the novel, referring to what are now the old chestnuts first offered up by Schlegel and popularized by Hegel. Indeed, even Ortega's supposedly chauvinistic declaration that the novel was born in Spain is, by now, a mere cliché. Nonetheless, in 'Adam in Paradise' (1910), generally held to be one of his works most influenced by Cohen, Ortega is perhaps the first to assert in so many words that *Don Quixote*'s primacy as the first novel rests upon its unique composition as an assemblage of dialogues (*OC* 1:485). From this follows Ortega's definition of the novel as the category of the dialogue, the only pre-classical predecessors of which are the Platonic dialogues and, to a certain extent, comedy.

Ortega y Gasset establishes his whole notion of genres on another relationship of foreshortening, namely, that of form (*forma*) and background (*fondo*). Contrary to ancient thought, genres are not rules or paradigms to follow into which inspiration is deposited. As Ortega states, '[F]orm and background are inseparable and poetic background flows freely without the imposition of abstract norms.'[38] The image of a liquid background contradicts the modern propensity to merge background, theme, and form (MQ 96–7). Theme, understood as fluid, gives rise to the structure of the form, but the two cannot be understood as one and the same. Ortega recasts the relation using Flaubert's image of form emitted from theme as heat is from the flame. The mutable and protean quality of fire underscores the fluidity of form, and further underlines the relation of surface and depth between form (heat) and theme (flame). The nature of literary genres as manifestations of a foreshortened relation between form and background grants them an almost organic capacity to evolve and adapt within time, as the fluid base moves and transforms itself.

As revealed by his use of mathematical language, Ortega recalls once again Cohen's notion of infinitesimal progress. The Spanish philosopher writes, for example, that '[l]iterary genres thus understood are poetic functions, directions toward which esthetic generation gravitates.'[39] Function is defined mathematically as 'a relation that uniquely associates members of one set with members of another set' (Eric Weisstein's World of Mathematics, http://mathworld.wolfram.com/Function.html). When graphed, a function takes the form of a curve that within differential calculus extends toward a limit never actually reached. Such a curve corresponds to what Ortega terms the direction, differentiated essentially from the path: 'To take a direction is not the same as to have walked a path to the goal that we proposed for ourselves. The rock that is thrown carries with it the predisposed curve of its area of excursion. This curve becomes the explanation, development, and execution of the original impulse.'[40] In short, the curve is the graphed relation of the two sets, in this case the theme and the form, which becomes the literary genre. Take the example of tragedy described as 'the expansion of a certain fundamental poetic theme and only of it; it is the expansion of the tragic.'[41] Cohen's concept of infinitesimal movement leads toward Ortega's notion of tendency, the motor of action in general, and ethical action in particular. The literary form is none other than the working out of the theme's tendency – and thus we see how Ortega welds his notion of foreshortening on to his mentor's image of a differential calculus of ethical behaviour and development.

By associating inverisimilitude with the Italianate *novella* form seen in Cervantes' *Exemplary Novels*, Ortega rejects Romantic claims that the epic was a faithful representation of life in antiquity. The type of foreshortening that constitutes the epic as a genre arises from the juncture between the theme of the ideal past and archaic form, in the case of ancient Greece the rhapsody. Since the theme remains the past, perfected and closed off from the present, the epic poet does not even conceive of inventing new stories (*MQ* 107). In terms of Ortega's opposition of depth and surface, the epic exists only in the profound, since it is essentially ungrounded in the actual. One could go so far as to say that the epic is the most virtual of the genres – a supposition that perhaps explains the predominance of epic themes and modes in contemporary technologies of virtual reality, among them movies, computer games, and television. This vision of the epic as unreal is highly modern since, as Ortega reminds us, reality resided for the ancient Greek in the ideal, whereas we seek reality in appearances. Indeed, the value of the epic from the point of view of the ancients was that it was the actualization of the unique, heroic beings of myth – semi-divine in that they lived in a world composed of different rules. Epic brings Achilles and Helen nearer to earth, but they still represent a sphere other than earth. This explains the continued existence of the epic in other guises – what Ortega calls the literature of imagination, including the literature of knight-errantry and adventure stories. The philosopher speaks of the transforming power of these genres as a fire that consumes the historical and the actual (in other words, the possible) only to recast it according to the impossible laws of the mythic (*MQ* 113).

The de-actualization of the real undertaken by the literature of the imagination serves the often salutary purpose of breaking, at least momentarily, the chains of reality that bind and limit us. A lifelong preoccupation for Ortega was the capacity of art to suspend reality and allow the individual space to play and create. Consequently, Ortega's most detailed analysis of a scene from *Don Quixote* centres on the episode of Maese Pedro's puppet play (2, chaps. 26–7), providing a perfect example of the spectator's escape from reality through fictional suspense. An itinerant player and con artist, Maese Pedro, whom Don Quixote had previously met in the persona of the picaresque criminal Ginés de Pasamonte, puts on a puppet play based on the well-known chivalric tale of Melisendra, a young Christian noblewoman taken captive by the Moors, only to be rescued by her lover Gaiferos. The puppeteer's creative task is remarkably similar to that of the epic poet – he must present a mythological tale already familiar to his audience. Elaboration, rather than invention, and artifice, rather than originality, are the instruments of his artistic technique. The audience follows the show in rapt attention. Chief among them is Don Quixote, who repeatedly interrupts the performance to correct the telling of this standard tale, until he loses sight of the limit between his world and the artistic world. In that moment, he takes the puppet play to be real and attacks the Moorish puppet in aid of Gaiferos. In a sense, Maese Pedro has succeeded too well in his representation of the virtual world of knight-errantry, resulting in the very real economic loss of his artistic apparatus, the puppets. The scene, as analysed by Ortega, represents two worlds, that of the fantastic sphere of the impossible and the imaginary, and that of the real, in which impoverished, naive men try to escape for a moment from the difficulties of life.

We, as readers, can also escape for an instant, moving into a trajectory of suspense. Ortega's description of this phenomenon bears up to scrutiny, for it ultimately returns us to the image of the mathematical function, the notion of a calculus of human experience inherited from Cohen. As the trajectory of adventure unfolds, one experiences growing emotional tension. Reality grasps at the reader, and so she requires a new burst of energy to continue on her way. 'We are flung into the adventure as if within a projectile, and in the dynamic fight between this force, advancing on the tangent and now escaping, and the centre of the earth that aspires to subject it, we take the side of the former.'[42] In each step and each instant we take adventure to be reality. One could easily graph the reader's voyage: the X (or horizontal) axis is reality, like gravity pulling the individual toward it, whereas the Y (or vertical) axis is imagination, pulling the reader up into new spaces of possibility. The narration itself is the motor of the movement, pushing the reader forward in time and up into a state of rising suspension above the horizon of the actual until he reaches a moment of suspended disbelief, mistaking the adventure for reality. The reader is no different from Don Quixote, a minor gentleman rendered a fool by a small cerebral abnormality (MQ 119). As Ortega continues, we enter the book's scene, filled with people like us. In effect, we enter the book, a theatre even larger than that directed by Maese Pedro: 'If we stepped into this room, we would have put our foot into an ideal object; we would move into the concavity of an aesthetic object.'[43] One could argue that Don Quixote's intrusion into the puppet play is nothing more than the step taken by all theatre-goers further down the aesthetic foreshortened line, away from the actual and toward the virtual world of fiction.

Concerning the relation between the inn and the puppet theatre, the realm of the actual and the virtual, Ortega remarks that the osmosis and endosmosis between them is of most importance. His introduction of biological terms describing the movement of substances across the cell wall implies that the actual and the virtual share an environment, and that the relation between them is mutual and cooperative.[44] The imaginary fourth wall of the theatre metamorphoses into the permeable membrane of the cell. Only a few months earlier Ortega used the terms 'osmosis' and 'endosmosis' in his speech 'Old and New Politics' to the League of Political Education. Here he reveals how these terms describing cell function relate to social and political relations: throughout the nineteenth century, the Spanish Restoration had remained vital – that is to say, alive and functioning, if not exactly healthy – through 'an activity of osmosis and endosmosis between parliamentary Spain and non-parliamentary Spain, between the somewhat artificial organisms of the political parties and the spontaneous, diffuse, and all-encompassing organism of the nation' (*OC* 1:271).[45] Once this mutually sustaining activity ceased, the system died. It follows, then, that the transgression of the boundary between life and art exemplified by Don Quixote's attack on the puppet play is essential to the continuing vitality of both art and life.

The puppet play represented by Maese Pedro, as well as the spectators's reactions to it, exemplifies the aesthetics of the epic, the literature of imagination, and the adventure tale. The reader is swept away from the actual toward the ideal. In contrast, the novel is, for Ortega, 'actuality as actuality.' Instead of giving reality to the heroes and heroines of myth, the novel typifies the human beings of the present. Ortega insists that Madame Bovary is a type, that of the provincial adulteress, whereas Helen of Troy is unique. The novel's foreshortening appears at first glance to be the opposite of that of the epic (*MQ* 102). Whereas the epic moves the protagonists from the plane of the profound or ideal toward that of actuality, the novel transfers the persons from the plane of actuality toward abstraction. For Madame Bovary to be a type, she must lose whatever concrete, idiosyncratic characteristics that would not contribute to her exemplification of a certain sort of adulteress. Hence we arrive at the paradox of modern realism: in our preference for the appearance of reality, we actually make it virtual. This is due to the very dynamics of art or poetry: 'Art is the technique – it is the mechanism of actualization in the face of which the act of creating beautiful objects appears as the primary and supreme function of poetry.'[46] Returning to the notion of function, Ortega insists that making art actual, that is to say, creating or bringing it about, is, in the aesthetic sense, making beautiful objects. It follows that realist art would involve the harmonization and simplification of the irregularity and idiosyncrasy of the real, in this case creating types rather than uniquely beautiful objects. Thus, even realist art can only present us with the typical.

If this characterization of the novel as the genre of the actual and the typical seems simplistic to us today, that is because it arises from Ortega's (perhaps simplistic) examination of nineteenth-century novels. We must remember that the nineteenth century in general represents for Ortega a period when perspective is lost and when depth and profundity wane before a bourgeois and self-satisfied attraction for the superficial.[47] As he proceeds step by step through his novelistics, the Spanish philosopher moves toward Don Quixote, the book that typifies foreshortening, the conjoining of surface and profundity. Like Velázquez's Las meninas and Las hilanderas, Cervantes' Don Quixote is an art object in which the real and the virtual come into coexistence. This means that the classical definition of the real or the actual as non- or even anti-poetic no longer holds sway. A new foreshortening is formed, in which the real adds another dimension to the plane of the poetic. One should imagine the superficial plane of ideal beauty being deepened by the transposition of the actual. Indeed, this is precisely the image that Ortega offers: 'The epic plane where imaginary objects burst forth was until now the only one, and the poetic could be defined only with the same traits that constituted it. But now the imaginary plane gives way to become the second plane. Art enriches itself with another term; to put it this way, it augments itself with a third dimension, and conquers esthetic profundity, which, like geometric depth, supposes a plurality of terms.'[48] Regarding Don Quixote, the implications of this vision of a new plane of reality being transposed onto the old plane of the epic are obvious. Ortega protests against considering Cervantes' novel purely realistic because the real must be poeticized in order to become the stuff of art. This is the problem of Sancho Panza and Maese Pedro, who represent the anti-poetic over and against the world of the puppet play. How can these dirty, rough, and base characters be made interesting, if not quite beautiful? By the same token, Ortega objects to overlooking Don Quixote's parodic function with relation to the literature of knight-errantry. By so doing, one fails to see the epic plane of the novel, its foundation on adventure.

Don Quixote: Foreshortened Figure of the Epic and the Real

Significantly, it is the figure of Don Quixote that provides the juncture between the plane of the epic and the real. An impoverished country gentleman, typical of sixteenth-century rural Spain and thus 'real,' brings the epic and ideal world of chivalric romance into being on the dusty roads and in the flea-ridden inns of La Mancha. In this sense Don Quixote is an artist of sorts, making the imaginary real and inaugurating the novel as the genre in which the ideal and the real coexist in a foreshortened relationship. Indeed, it is impossible to place Don Quixote on either the side of the real or the imaginary: 'It would be forced to decide for one continent or the other. Don Quixote is the intersecting line where two worlds slice into each other, forming an oblique cut on the border.'[49] Ortega has now switched from the mathematical imagery of the graph, defined as the two dimensions of the X and the Y axes, to the three-dimensional imagery of solid geometry. Two solid bodies intersect, making an oblique cut. The oblique cut indicates their three-dimensionality, since such a cut can only occur in depth. This cut serves as both border and juncture, and takes on the function that Ortega earlier assigned to the limit – that is to say, to divide and unite. Don Quixote divides and unites the realms of the epic and the actual, giving rise to the genre – or concept – that is the novel. Moreover, he manages such a feat through the force of his will, precisely his will to adventure.

Next Ortega establishes the difference between the novel and the literature of imagination based on Don Quixote's will to adventure: 'Don Quixote, who is real, really wants adventures. As he himself says, "The enchanters can perhaps take from me my good fortune, but it is impossible to take from me my force and spirit".'[50] Don Quixote, who brings the world of the chivalric into sixteenth-century Spain, stands for all human beings involved in bringing into being their own imagined self. For Marías this passage is tragic, for it highlights the hero's will to be himself through ambitious aspiration or self-projection (*Ortega. Circunstancia y vocación* 404). Thus, Ortega can make the claim that Don Quixote occupies a liminal state (*MQ* 121). Indeed, it is the extreme life that is perhaps most authentic and thus most revealing of human nature, for the tragic hero is the one who most fully lives life in both the real and the imaginary spheres. In other words, the hero who dares to be who he or she wants to be lives in the cleft formed by the foreshortened relation between the real and the imaginary. Residing between two worlds, Don Quixote creates his own.

Through his will to adventure Don Quixote not only engenders the novel, but also vindicates the Spanish character and typifies the ideal of humanity. Ortega's assessment of the Spanish character as one of pure force in the 'Meditation on the Escorial' here takes a less melancholic and more productive turn as he links Don Quixote's will to adventure with the creation of culture itself. First he situates Cervantes within his circumstances, the Renaissance understood as the period in which adventure seen as self-sufficient and individual experience becomes unviable. Science renders adventure impossible, for the possible now depends on the physical realm; that is to say, the marvellous and fantastic deeds of the hero can no longer be conceived of as really possible. In addition, the Renaissance discovers psychology, opening up to sight the interior workings of the individual and revealing the power and the secrets of the subjective. Although Ortega does not elaborate, it follows that the modern hero is no longer transparent and idealized but rather riddled with darkness and frailties.

The novel *Don Quixote* 'saves' the adventure, making it possible by realizing it in the mind of a madman. This salvation is perforce ironic, for adventure is saved only in the psychological realm as mental vapours (*MQ* 123). Ortega explores the negative side of this salvation by comparing the novel to a mirage, the imaginary oasis cast by the burning sun on the dry plains of La Mancha. Such a mirage is none other than a foreshortening, composed of the barren reality of burnt-up earth and the ideal vision of cool waters. The mirage can be experienced in two ways, one naive and rectilinear, according to which the water is real, and another oblique, by which we see the dryness of the earth as real (*MQ* 124). The naive, direct way of *living* the imaginary is through the adventure novel, the story, and the epic, whereas the realist novel is the oblique way. Moreover, the realist novel needs the first naive vision in order to allow us to see the mirage (*MQ* 124). Not only does this symbiotic relation of the realist and the adventure novel exist in *Don Quixote*, but it also does so in all novels. In short, reality is poeticized when the poetic is looked at from an oblique point of view – in other words, that of irony. This ironic perspective implies the destruction of myth through its critique and entails the aggressive movement of reality against the ideal. In effect, the destruction of the ideal takes place in every novel (*MQ* 124).

After establishing the ironic, corrosive power of the novel, Ortega then moves to one of the most commented sections of the work, 'The Windmills,' in which he injects his notion of the concept into his interpretation of *Don Quixote*. First, Ortega invites the reader to join him in the countryside of La Mancha, more specifically Montiel, imagined as an ideal space with shimmering, unbounded horizons in which things are exemplary. This gesture of invitation, ironically undoing the cleft between the imagined world of the meditation and the real one of the reader, also places him or her beside Don Quixote and Sancho Panza, who glimpse ahead the infamous windmills. Unlike the two novelistic characters, who see the objects respectively as giants and windmills, the reader will share Ortega's point of view. Significantly, this point of view is doubled, encompassing both the knight errant's and the squire's different identifications of the machines, but in such a way that Ortega's careful foreshortening of the ideal and the real begins to fall apart. It is important to note carefully Ortega's exact words: 'Walking along [the plain] with Don Quixote and Sancho Panza, we come to the understanding that things have two vectors. One is the "meaning" of things, their signification, what they are when we interpret them. The other is their "materiality," their positive substance, what constitutes them before and beyond all interpretation.'[51] This passage, along with the subsequent reference to all culture as a mirage, including justice and truth, has been interpreted by various critics as the young Ortega's final rejection of neo-Kantian idealism. Culture, the cornerstone of Cohen's ethics and aesthetics, would seem to be a mere giant, ideal arms imagined over the windmill's sails just as Ortega sees Marburg's Gothic skyline juxtaposed against the weightiness of the Escorial. But before charging forward with such a reading, one must acknowledge Ortega's gestures toward the reader. Firstly, he places the supposedly opposite concepts, meaning and materiality, in quotation marks, thus inserting an ironic inflection around them. Strictly speaking, these are not his words, but those he cites from discourses other than his own. In traditional Romantic readings of *Don Quixote*, meaning understood as the ideal is associated with Don Quixote, and the material understood as the real with Sancho. In such a reading of the novel, interpretation as a cognitive activity only pertains to the madman. Ortega indicates that this is *not* his reading by again using quotation marks: 'These windmills have a meaning: as "meaning" these windmills are giants.'[52]

Windmills Are Giants: The Problem of Meaning

'These windmills have a meaning: as "meaning" these windmills are giants': Ortega offers us a sentence that approaches a chiasmus, the rhetorical trope in which two phrases bound together and separated by a pause mirror each other. The chiasmus as a linguistic structure resembles foreshortening, given that they are each composed of opposing elements joined by a central space that functions both as absence in its lack of content and presence in its unifying function. The chiasmus, by highlighting the mirrored elements of the two conjoined phrases, calls attention to the differences between them. The second phrase clearly expresses Don Quixote's perspective on the windmills as giants. As Ortega adroitly acknowledges, the problem of the windmill-giant is not that of the madman, but that of all culture, the 'ideal vector of things.' The fact that culture veers toward the ideal does not, however, discredit its creation, as long as one recognizes its ideal tendency. The word Ortega chooses for 'meaning' (*sentido*) also means 'direction' in Spanish, and this sense of direction gives rise to the movement typical of the ideal in both Cohen's and Ortega's thought. When Ortega writes of culture as a mirage, then, he refers to the trajectory of infinitesimal movement figured by differential calculus in Cohen's notion of movement toward the ideal: 'Culture – the ideal vector of things – intends to establish itself as a separate and self-sufficient world to which we could transfer our guts. This is an illusion, and culture is only put in its rightful place when seen as an illusion, when placed as a mirage against the earth.'[53] The illusion, however, is not to be rejected; indeed, the Spanish word for mirage (*espejismo*) indicates the relation of culture to the real. Deriving from the word for mirror (*espejo*), the mirage exists in a foreshortened relation to the reflected. One could imagine a chiasmus as a sort of relation between a mirror or a mirage and what is reflected. The ideal reflects the real, and exists only in relation to it.

The significance of the first part of the chiasmus comes into view: 'the windmills have a meaning.' A limited reading of *Don Quixote* attributes the act of interpretation only to the deluded knight errant and not to his 'realistic' companion, Sancho Panza. Such a reading is impossible for Ortega, given his interest in phenomenology and his insistence upon the conceptual activity of the eye. Seeing the objects as windmills is also giving them meaning, and it is no accident that the following section, 'Realist Poetry,' repeats both Platonic and phenomenological assertions of the interpretive nature of vision. Moreover, windmills are not natural phenomena, but man-made objects, the very stuff of culture: products of cultural knowledge that produce the material conditions of culture. Upon identifying the objects as windmills, the 'realist' Sancho acknowledges their cultural production and significance. Thus, we are already and always in the realm of culture, the concept, and the ideal.

Ortega's critique of realist poetry (i.e., the novel) and mimesis follows the vector of the windmill. Realism cannot show us the real in and of itself because the real is self-sufficient, a mere presence. It can only show us the comic underside of the ideal – its insufficiency – and thus serves as a critique of culture. Realist poetry, in its comic nature, makes the illusion visible, and is a descendent of the Greek mime and comedy. The windmills make us laugh upon making visible Don Quixote's folly. But it is also the descendent of the Platonic dialogue, where the real is not only made fun of but also described. Writing of this genre, Ortega notes that the comic maintains an extrapoetic interest linking it to science: 'We will never find the poetry of the real as simply real.'[54] The realist vector thus unites comedy with science, both understood as ways of capturing the real, although never completely as itself. Ortega's harking to the Kantian notion of the irremediable otherness of the *Ding an sich* could not be clearer, nor could his linking of poetry and science fail to recall the neo-Kantian attempt to ground the human sciences in the natural sciences. In addition, a certain ethical value accrues to realist poetry or the novel, as its function of critique serves to pursue the real.

The mixed nature of the novel arises from its comic representation of a hero. Insofar as it presents comically or realistically an individual who wills adventure and seeks to impose his ideal on the world, it is a novel. This is Ortega's final and most definitive statement on the genre. Because the world corresponds to their desires, epic protagonists are not novelistic heroes (*MQ* 132). The novelistic hero, in contrast, breaks away from the past and tradition by willing to be herself. Her modernity, however, does not correspond to that of determinism or Darwinism, for only the will to resist reality and to be oneself constitutes modern heroism (*MQ* 135) The modern hero's resistance to the environmental forces limiting and restraining the struggle to become one's own self echoes Cohen's notion of the ethical self. By categorizing the modern individual as a morally incomplete and undifferentiated self, it is Cohen who anticipates Ortega's critique of the modern man of the masses. In fact, Cohen suggests the mixed nature of the novel when he analyses its comic aspect in a quote that bears repeating: 'That is the grace of humour, that contrary to the solemnity and elevated rhetoric of high art, it lowers its gaze toward the baseness and conceit of human life, and claims indulgence for it.'[55]

In the penultimate section, 'Comedy,' Ortega returns to examine the reader's experience of the novelistic plot.[56] The tragic vector causes us to identify with the hero, to revive the 'atrophied' heroism inside ourselves (*MQ* 139). The comic vector absorbs the hero's idealism, pulling him down from his heavenward trajectory toward the earth (*MQ* 141). Ortega describes the difference between the comic and the tragic as a chasm, and in so doing defines the space of the novel: 'From wanting to be to believing that one already is – that is the distance from the tragic to the comic. That is the step from the sublime to the ridiculous. The transference of the heroic character from the will to perception causes the reversal of tragedy, its dismantling, its comedy. The mirage appears as such – a mirage.'[57] Once the novelistic hero begins to believe that he is indeed a hero, and like Don Quixote begins to see the world according to the template of his own idealism, then irony must insert itself to undercut his hubris and arrogance. The virtue of modesty propounded by Cohen, the awareness of one's own limitations that is the ethical counterpart of the neo-Kantian critique of the limits of reason, has been transgressed. Yet, realism in the novel could not exist only with comedy, for comedy itself is a function of tragedy. Once again Ortega uses the language of mathematics to graph the symbiotic relationship between the two poetic modes: 'The upper line of the novel is tragedy: there the muse hovers following the tragic in its fall.'[58] The tragic fall of this Icarus is due to the 'force of inertia, reality,' as the would-be flier plunges toward the axis of comedy. Ortega finishes his definition of the novel as *tragicomedia* (borrowing the term Fernando de Rojas coined for his *La Celestina*) by recounting the episode from Plato's *Phaedrus* to which Cohen referred when he wrote of the novel in his *Ethics of Pure Will*. The men lie sleeping around the banquet table at dawn when Aristodemos awakens and overhears Socrates telling Agathon and Aristophanes that the tragic and the comic poets should be one person.

Now that we have clearly identified the idealist component to Ortega's *Meditations on Don Quixote*, the critique of the nineteenth-century novel with which he finishes this essay takes on fuller significance. The novel should take a foreshortened form, embodying the juncture between the tragic and the comic. *Don Quixote*, as the novel par excellence, is none other than a foreshortening par excellence. The aesthetic and even ethical weakness of the nineteenth-century novel is the shallowness of its tragic vector, as the overwhelming interest of the age in the real, the material, the economic, and the deterministic weakened and diminished the vector of the ideal. Life is mere survival dependant on adaptation to the circumstances, and thus Darwin has swept the heroes off the face of the earth (*MQ* 148). The environment becomes the protagonist as it moulds the hapless human characters, and verisimilitude exists only as a function of the real. Ortega cannot help but object, precisely because such a deterministic attitude has left his generation with a legacy of cynicism and bitterness. The answer is to be found in a renewed consideration for the ideal and the virtual, not at the expense of the real, but rather as a process of attaining the balance necessary for foreshortening. 'But doesn't tragedy have its own internal, independent verisimilitude? Isn't there an aesthetic *vero* – the beautiful? And isn't there a similarity to the beautiful?'[59] To respond in the negative to these questions is to revert to positivism. Thus Ortega answers Cohen's question ('Is Don Quixote perchance only a fool?') in the negative. As a being living in the foreshortened fold between the real and the ideal, he is more than just a fool, for he exemplifies the human condition.

Ortega's *Ideas on the Novel*: The Novel as Virtual Reality

Ortega's *Ideas on the Novel* (1924–5) represents a more tightly focused examination of the literary form. As a response to his ongoing polemic with the Spanish novelist Pío Baroja, Ortega adopts a pragmatic and even prescriptive stance toward the definition of the novel. Whereas Baroja maintains that the novel has no definition, and can include the sociological and ideological, Ortega argues that the novel, although open to these discourses, cannot become them (Salas Fernández 130–3). In effect, Ortega seeks to understand the novel *qua* novel, just as he seeks to understand the visual arts *qua* visual arts in *The Dehumanization of Art*. Contrary to the many misinterpretations of his thought at the time, Ortega does not employ the word 'pure' to mean uncontaminated by reality, but rather uses it in almost neo-Kantian terms: that is to say, art is pure when it is viewed in its most essential, purified forms. In effect, Ortega y Gasset in the 1920s espouses a high form of formalistic modernism present in other thinkers of the time, although he eschews the wilful experimentation of writers such as James Joyce (curiously enough, he is more open to experimentation in the visual arts). Finally, references to *Don Quixote*, unsystematically scattered throughout the essay, indicate that Ortega still considers Cervantes' novel to be one of the genre's classics.

It has been customary among Ortega scholars to read this aesthetic essay from 1924–5 in conjunction with the philosopher's other major work of the period, *The Dehumanization of Art* (1925). Such an approach has led to the erroneous assumption that Ortega predicted the end of the novel as a genre and promoted the 'dehumanization' of the novel. Spanish novelists of the period even joked among themselves about the distinction between art and life that Ortega found in the visual arts of his time (R. Johnson, *Fuego cruzado* 203–5). Nevertheless, this assumption overlooks the fact that *The Dehumanization of Art* treats exclusively of the visual arts, and is an attempt to explain the abstracting tendencies of artists such as Picasso. Far from dehumanizing literature and rendering it abstract, Ortega claims that the novel plays to the faculties of the human mind in order to submerge the reader in a virtual experience.

Moreover, Ortega suggests that his present might provide the most propitious circumstances for the novel as a genre. As a time of decadence, the early twentieth century provides a setting in which experience and progress have refined creative nerves and set them on edge (*IN* 197). More precisely, the novel as a genre depends on a psychological understanding of humanity. Psychology, understood both as a science and as a general comprehension of the human mind by Ortega, has advanced so much that it is inevitable that the novel in its representation of human psyches would also improve. Ortega does not deny the importance of plot, but rather sees dramatic interest as nothing more or less than psychologically necessary to the novel (*IN* 178).[60] Far from calling for a dehumanized novel, Ortega actually states that for the novel of his time 'the important part is not *what* one sees, but *that* one sees well something human, whatever that might be.'[61] To see something human is to see characters being themselves, living out their lives in accordance with the parameters of their respective psychologies and in relation to their circumstances. The fact that psychology is now more interesting than adventure indicates for Ortega that his contemporaries boast a more refined way of reading.

Far from presaging the death of the novel upon pronouncing the lack of new themes, Ortega proclaims the progression of the genre toward its *ideal* form. To suggest a latent idealism in the philosopher's work in the 1920s is perhaps anathema, and yet *Ideas on the Novel* reveals how idealism and phenomenology converge in novelistics. Ortega's insistence on vision as the overriding dimension of the reading process allows him to link literature to art. In the case of the twentieth-century novel, the closest relative to the novel is Impressionist painting. Writing of the novel, Ortega affirms his preference for description over definition, linking definition to the sciences and description to art. The sciences use definitions to point toward the world of objects, whereas the arts make objects present. The reader of the modern novel, like the viewer of the Impressionist painting, does not merely think the art object, but actually experiences it. Ortega asks of the novelist not that he merely state that Pedro is bilious, but that he present visible actions that the reader will interpret as signs of Pedro's character. In this showing the novelist is like an Impressionist painter (*IN* 159–60). It is in this sense that the philosopher believes the form of the novel to be descriptive and presentational. Not only does the novelist allude to another world, but she also makes it present for the reader. The reader makes meaning from the novelistic world in the same way that she makes meaning of her own world.

Dostoevsky's manner of presenting a character and then allowing the character to act in ways that seem to contradict the initial impression exemplifies how a novelistic world becomes present to the reader. The reader's very frustration upon encountering individuals, albeit literary characters, that defy simple definition and conceptualization mirrors our reaction to those around us. After our first impression of the character, we have a second one in which we view him as if directly, unmediated by the author. A third moment entails an inevitable reaction, for the reader begins to worry that she might not see the character in the tangle of contradictory facts. Finally, and unintentionally, the reader 'mobilizes in pursuit of the character,' struggling to make from the opposing signs and symptoms a unified image (*IN* 173–4). The hermeneutical process of interpreting the character's meaning converges with the phenomenological insofar as the reader confronts the literary character with the same tools and strategies one would use upon meeting a person of flesh and blood (García Alonso 158). In other words, the literary character is not understood conceptually, that is to say, as a system of signs or ideas, but rather phenomenologically, cloaked in all the vagaries and paradoxes of reality. The literary character, like the person we meet in daily life, escapes mere conceptualization. It is precisely this 'excess,' to borrow Bakhtin's term, that constitutes Dostoevsky's realism. For Ortega, the realist element of literature is not the author's imitation of reality, but rather the reader's interpretation of the work according to the same mental patterns used to make sense of reality.

Moreover, Ortega modifies the traditionally passive image of the reader by splicing the classical concept of contemplation to the phenomenological one of attention. Recuperating the notion of interest, seen within the Kantian tradition as pertaining to the realm of action and inappropriate to the uncluttered, unselfish clarity necessary for contemplation, the Spanish philosopher insists that disinterested contemplation cannot exist. On phenomenological grounds is it impossible that there be disinterested contemplation, for the eye must fix on some spot. Without stopping to focus, the individual would confront only a surrounding cloud of blurred images. With no centre, the whole field of vision would remain formless and undifferentiated like that of the periphery. In the work of paying attention, interest enters the process of contemplation (*IN* 180). The truth of 'new psychology,' or phenomenology, is that knowledge always depends on desire, and therefore takes place in a midpoint between pure contemplation and the realm of interest or action. It follows that the novel, representing the modern sensibility for psychology, focuses less on action and more on interested contemplation. Not only does the reader attend to the novel, but the author also attends to the reader by immersing her in fictive horizons. For Ortega, it is mistaken to assume that literature broadens horizons; to the contrary, it submerges the reader in small, provincial worlds similar to villages in the reduced cast of characters and circumstances. Referring to Henri Poincaré, whose ideas subsequently inspired Einstein's notion of relativity, Ortega repeats that our world, made smaller, would still have the same dimensions. Such is the world of the novel, bound by smaller horizons but still filled with interest for the reader who passes through as a transitory provincial (Salas Fernández 54). As Ortega explains, 'The author's tactic should consist of isolating the reader from his real horizon and imprisoning him in a small, hermetic, and imaginary horizon that is the interior ambience of the novel.'[62]

We now glimpse the profile of a novelistics of the virtual. The novel's attention to character over plot, density of detail, slow rhythm, and hermetically sealed atmosphere – all of these are necessary elements for the creation of a new horizon of experience that does not have to reflect reality. The novelistic process coincides with lived experiences and becomes the expression of psychological mechanisms we use for interpreting reality (A.M. Fernández 94). In other words, the novel works by 'turning on' the mental functions humans use to process and interpret their everyday world. The fundamentally non-transcendental nature of the novel for Ortega does not imply that he denies social, scientific, or ideological content to the genre, as has often been assumed. To borrow an adjective that the philosopher himself used, it may be thought of as a 'virtual' presence, or even a virtual reality.[63] As Ortega writes in *The Dehumanization of Art*, the role of the poet and the artist is to 'make the world grow, adding to the real – that was already there for itself – an unreal continent.'[64] A painting, a poem, a novel – all are alike insofar as they are unreal. A novel's presence to the reader is, of course, imaginary, and depends upon two efforts of the imagination: firstly, the author's creation of an engulfing, detailed, and dense world of fiction, and secondly, the reader's recreation of this world in her own imagination. Through this second act of recreation, the work of art becomes an actual event, a deed performed by the reader or viewer (*IN* 178). The novel is vital not as the presence of the author's imagined creation or intention, but as the presence of the reader's phenomenologically structured instillation (or distillation) of meaning in the work.

Although Ortega makes few direct references to *Meditations on the Quixote* and employs a different vocabulary, his novelistics of 1924–5 does not substantially differ from that of 1914 in its basic assumption that the novel exists as a form of the frontier between the real and the ideal. That is to say, the pleasure of reading stems from the invention and imagination of the ideal, now figured as the virtual. Ortega poses the problem of the reader from Seville who, never having known such chaotic and turbulent souls, encounters the exoticism of Dostoevsky's characters: '[n]o matter how insensitive [he] might be, the psychological mechanism of these souls seems as forceful and self-evident to him as the functioning of a geometrical proof dealing with ten-thousand-sided forms never before guessed at.'[65] To play a bit with Ortega's own vocabulary, the provincial reader confronts hitherto unknown strangers that would seem to be other in the strongest sense of the term. Nonetheless, following both Kantian epistemology and the 'new psychology' of phenomenology, one cannot recognize or understand the completely unknown. This problem leads Ortega to a Kantian solution: the assertion of a psychological *a priori* by which the *sevillano* is able to understand the Russian literary character (*IN* 200). This psychological *a priori* postulated by Ortega serves as a law or a limit for the imagination, and in this sense fulfils the same function as the concept does in 1914: dividing, ordering, and giving identity to the external. Its regulative function allows both the novelist and the reader not only to participate in imaginative construction of literary characters, but also to communicate with each other using more or less the same models and forms for human psychology and behaviour.

Moreover, Ortega asserts that literature is the place where these *a priori* forms reveal themselves. We can now appreciate Ortega's sweeping claim that history and the novel, in addition to philosophy, will provide the strongest 'intellectual emotions' in the near future (*IN* 198). Given the care with which Ortega uses language, we must accept the oxymoron, intellectual emotions, as intentional. Having established the essential connection of interest to contemplation through the phenomenological model of attention, Ortega hints at a radical undoing of traditional epistemology. Reason and sentiment combine. Indeed, such a pairing of strange (or estranged) bedfellows is necessary to rescue literature from the banishment to the realm of sentiments it suffered in the Enlightenment (not to mention the banishment of mythical thought to the realm of sophistry that took place in ancient Greece). If the novel is to reveal psychological truths in the form of psychological *a priori*, poetry must somehow be capable of disclosing knowledge, and that implies explaining how emotions can disclose knowledge.

Ortega limits himself here to a description of the phenomenon of reading, reprising two notions from his earlier work, that of the *salvación* and the survivor of a shipwreck (*náufrago*). Indeed, the salvation and the shipwreck are two sides of the same coin, and describe the fate of famous older novels, or 'classics,' from whom few have been saved from the shipwreck of boredom (*IN* 155). Shipwreck signifies not mere destruction, but being cast away, isolated, and forgotten on distant, unknown shores. The work of rescuing brings the lost one back into community, and thus to communication. In the case of the classical novels, as in the case of all literature, the rescuing of the work takes place in the reader's mind. The shipwrecked one falls off the face of the earth, going over the edge into unmapped territories; she falls out of the field of vision. It is contemplation, understood as attention, which brings the castaway back into sight. Ortega reprises the figure of the circling steps of meditation from *Meditations on Don Quixote* in *Ideas on the Novel* when he describes the historical development of human knowledge through seeing the universe step by step and piece by piece (*IN* 182–3). Contemplation understood as movement involves a gradual, cumulative knowing as well as an interested and emotional one; thus Ortega can consider certain interests, feelings, and necessities to be instruments of knowledge. With these instruments the individual saves the shipwrecked, pulling them back into their native context and giving them meaning.

With his analysis of the reader's experience, Ortega counteracts the instrumentalization of human life implied in viewing literature only as the work of the author (who uses her characters as instruments). According to Ortega, absorbed readers, immersed in their environment and in their experiences, join the literary characters. The literary world must remain totally distinct from the real world in order to preserve the reader's experience, for in the next moment she finds herself back in her reality. The key to Ortega's analysis, however, is the transition from one world to the other, a moment of indecision and vacillation – that is to say, a moment caught between worlds: 'Perhaps the sudden brush of a memory's wing submerges us suddenly once again into the universe of the novel, and with some effort, as if stroking through a watery element, we must swim toward the shore of our own existence. If someone looks at us, they will discover in us the rapid blink of the castaway.'[66] The reader of the novel becomes none other than the lost and forgotten one, caught outside the limits of the map, separated even from her own existence. She vacillates between her own reality and that of the fictional reality created by the bubble. The excess froth of details in those books Ortega considers great novels, including ones by Cervantes, Stendhal, Dickens, and Dostoevsky, constitutes their virtual reality. Because there are more details than the reader can possibly attend to, she is under the impression that there are even more underlying the visible surface. Ortega chooses the figure of the coral reef, composed of millions of separate but interdependent creatures, to describe the luxurious detail of the novel: 'The greatest novels are coral islands formed by myriads of miniature animals, whose apparent weakness stops the onslaught of marine waves.'[67]

It is this very experience of being castaway, landing upon the coral island of the novel, and then returning to our reality with the dazed, perplexed look of the stranger that defines the novel for Ortega: 'I call a novel the literary creation that produces this effect.'[68] His previous definitions of the novel as tragic comedy or foreshortening, both based on the work's form, now cede to a definition based on the reader's experience. Any work that does not create this effect is a bad novel. Nonetheless, there is an important conceptual connection between the formal definition of the novel in *Meditations on Don Quixote* and this phenomenological definition of the novel in *Ideas on the Novel*. In the first work, the novel as exemplified by *Don Quixote* is a mixed genre, a crossbreed of tragedy and comedy that shows in the trials of its hero the mixed nature of humanity, caught between the real and the ideal. In this later essay, the emphasis switches to the reader, who actually experiences this same mixed nature through the sensation of being shipwrecked far from home in another sphere. This experience, disorienting as it might be, serves on all levels to create new horizons for the reader and thus multiplies existence (*IN* 189).

Ultimately, the conceptual link between *Meditations on Don Quixote* and *Ideas on the Novel*, as well as the central figure for Ortega's novelistics, is the literary character Don Quixote. By positing an ecstatic reader that crosses the boundary (if only for a moment) between the real and the imagined, Ortega repeats the image of Don Quixote. The episode recounting his assault on Maese Pedro's puppet play is only the most emblematic representation of this transgression. Don Quixote, upon abandoning his identity as Alonso Quijano the Good and becoming Don Quixote de la Mancha, is the most exemplary reader – and the worst example of one. Insofar as Ortega y Gasset posits reading as an activity linked to cognition and perception, Don Quixote is also an epistemological figure. He stands for the problems of knowing and interpreting the circumstances that stand in relation to and define the self. Seeing windmills as giants is not so different from seeing them as windmills. By probing the opposition between imagination and knowledge, fiction and science, Ortega articulates one of the central intentions behind modern theories of the novel: the vindication of art and literature as forms of knowledge in the face of science.

Curiously enough, one must turn to *The Dehumanization of Art* to find mention of irony, another key component of the modern theories of the novel. Elusive as ever, Ortega buries any reference to Schlegel's Romantic irony at the end of the essay when he mentions the proclamation of irony as the highest aesthetic category by the Schlegel brothers and their companions. This they did, according to Ortega, for the same reasons that he critiques traditional notions of mimesis and authorial intentionality: 'Art cannot justify itself or limit itself by the mere reproduction of reality, duplicating it in vain. Its mission is to incite an unreal horizon.'[69] By associating Romantic irony with the 'unreal' horizon of art, Ortega finally acknowledges the conceptual links between his perspectivism and novelistics. What else are the hermeneutic circles and their corresponding points of view but Romantic irony as figured by Schlegel in Athenaeum Fragment 116? Moreover, the distinction that Ortega has drawn between hate and love as hermeneutic attitudes is undone by irony: 'Rancour approaches art as seriousness; love approaches victorious art as a farce that triumphs over everything, including itself, in the manner of a system of mirrors reflecting themselves one in the other indefinitely. No form is the ultimate, for all are ridiculed and rendered pure imagery.'[70] Ortega, unlike Schlegel, sees the uncanny nature of the unreal and the virtual elements in art. Note his discomfort before wax figures: 'When we perceive them as living beings, they make fun of us by revealing their cadaverous secret as dolls, and yet if we view them as fictional they seem to flutter in irritation. There is no way to reduce them to mere objects ... The wax figure is pure melodrama.'[71] This is the irreducible problem of the character Don Quixote; he cannot ultimately reconcile the vitality of the puppets with their ideal signification and their reality as dolls. It is also the irreducible problem of the novel, its authors, its readers, and most certainly those who would make philosophy from it. How can one reconcile philosophy – the love of the truth – with this unreal, virtual form? It is precisely the uncanny irreality or virtuality of literature and the representative arts in general that has rendered the novel a problem for philosophers.

7 *Don Quixote* in Bakhtin

The figure of Mikhail Bakhtin offered to Western academics in the last half of the twentieth century a *tabula rasa* upon which to inscribe almost any image they desired. Ignored by Soviet authorities when his work was not actually being censored, he was largely unknown during his lifetime outside of the Soviet Union. Among the first to bring to the West Bakhtin's ideas were Tzevtan Todorov and Julia Kristeva, who, in accordance with their own intellectual profiles, presented him as a precursor of post-structuralism. Nonetheless, many contemporary Russian academics tend to reject facile characterizations of a 'postmodern' Bakhtin, and insist instead on his Russian intellectual heritage and identity (Emerson 3–28). Nor has the issue of Bakhtin's relation to Marxism been clarified. On the one hand, Bakhtin was sentenced to exile in 1929 for his supposed involvement in Orthodox Christian groups, a fact that certainly signals a dissident attitude toward the standard Marxism of the Stalinist USSR. Couple this fact with the neo-Kantian cast of his writings from the late 1910s and early 1920s, and it becomes hard to maintain an identity for Bakhtin as a Marxist thinker. But yet again Bakhtin presents as the Janus of twentieth-century thought, for such a work as *Marxism and the Philosophy of Language* has been attributed to him.

There is no doubt that the image of Bakhtin has been up for grabs, so to speak, since before his death. Bakhtin himself did not contradict the myth circulating in the USSR during his lifetime that he was descended from nobility, nor did he ever declare whether he was in fact the author of works such as *The Formal Method in Literary Studies.* Bakhtin seems to have conceived of himself as a thinker (*myslitel'*), in other words, an intellectual with varied and interdisciplinary interests who tended to philosophize (Emerson 73). Recently, scholars have taken on the task of demystifying his legacy through the study of the sources and influences in his work. In contrast to the previous Western image of Bakhtin as an isolated genius, what is emerging is a portrait of a thinker submerged in the Western and Russian intellectual debates of his day. Bakhtin personally approved of the description of his work offered by his disciple, Vadim Kozhinov, according to whom Bakhtin's project was to wed the systematic, objective character of German thought with the creative, spiritual heritage considered native to Russia (Emerson 125). As Galin Tihanov sums up the current debate over Bakhtin, 'is he a thinker emerging from Western, mainly German, philosophical culture, or an exclusively Russian (Orthodox) philosopher?' (*The Master and the Slave* 5).

Among literary critics, Bakhtin is most often read for his commentary on the novel as a genre. The juxtaposition of the concepts of the carnivalesque, the epic, and the novel in Bakhtin's writings on the novel and his monumental work on Rabelais makes it very difficult not to draw connections between them. Couple this with contradictory uses of the terms 'novel' and 'epic,' and a kaleidoscopic presentation of the possibilities of the novel, rather than its definition, emerges. Is the novel a modern phenomenon or a literary form unlinked to historical consciousness? In 'Epic and Novel,' Bakhtin assumes the modern genesis of the novel, writing that it 'is the only genre that was born and nourished in a new era of world history and therefore it is deeply akin to that era' (*DI* 4), only to contradict the genre's modern origins in 'Forms of Time and Chronotope in the Novel' by proffering quite adept characterizations of the ancient novel. What is the relation of the novel to parody? In 'Epic and Novel' the genre emerges from the struggle with other genres, constituting self-critique based in the parody of other literary forms (*DI* 5–6). Yet in 'From the Prehistory of Novelistic Discourse,' Bakhtin maintains that the Roman novel evinced much greater parody than works of our time in which '[p]arody has grown sickly, its place in modern literature is insignificant' (*DI* 71). Is the novel opposed to or allied with the epic? In 'Epic and the Novel,' the completed, past nature of the epic is clearly distinguished from the open, becoming nature of the novel. But in *Problems of Dostoevsky's Poetics*, Bakhtin asserts that the novel is rooted in the carnivalesque, the rhetorical, and the epic (*PDP* 109). How does one account for such discrepancies, and how does one draw a notion of Bakhtinian novelistics from such a mass of contradictions?

Only of late have scholars begun to focus on the very inconsistency of Bakhtin's writings on the novel. Karine Zbinden explains these contradictions as a function of Bakhtin's wavering understanding of the novel's relation to society – in her words, its sociality: '[O]n the one hand sociality is presented as all-pervasive and always already there, while on the other hand it consists in the conjunction of the right factors for the birth of the novel' (*Bakhtin between East and West* 59). She suggests that this historical notion of the novel is Hegelian, and thus acceptable in 1930s USSR (66). Tihanov, also, has struggled with the inconsistencies of Bakhtin's theory of the novel. To date, his work on the sources of Bakhtin's thought is by far the most comprehensive and thoughtful. As Tihanov notes, four features clearly distinguish the epic for Bakhtin in 'Epic and Discourse': its subject is 'the heroic national past'; its source is 'national tradition'; its memory is based on 'totemic veneration of the predecessors'; and its plot depends on 'repetition and familiarity' ('Bakhtin, Joyce and Carnival' 72). In addition, carnival as understood by Bakhtin steps into the cultural space of the epic: 'Like the epic, carnival is about the maintaining of traditional practices, but in an open and charitably "insecure" way' (80). *Gargantua and Pantagruel* allows for the continued existence of the epic, as understood in the Schlegelian tradition as the repository of communal identity and national tradition. The inconsistencies in Bakhtin's novelistics are extremely important for the contextualization of Bakhtin's thought, as they provide us with a structure of references in which to situate the Russian. When read together with the double-voiced allusions to Schlegel and Cohen, the inconsistencies give evidence that Bakhtin was writing in a muted dialogue with various thinkers. According to Michael Holquist, Bakhtinian dialogism should be understood in the context of early twentieth-century neo-Kantianism, a movement that sought to adapt epistemology to the new notions of mind and the world emerging in the natural sciences (17). In a similar vein, I would suggest that Bakhtin's novelistics should be understood in the context of the novelistic tradition traced in this book, with Hegel's appropriation of thought about the novel already present in earlier German writers such as Schlegel and Cohen serving as a useful cover for Bakhtin's reading of these less-favoured authors.

It has been remarked that *Don Quixote de la Mancha* is surprisingly absent from Bakhtin's writings on the novel when compared to the predominance afforded Dostoevsky and Rabelais (W. Reed 29). Notwithstanding this objection (one based largely on the number of references to the respective authors), the centrality of *Don Quixote* to Bakhtin's novelistics becomes obvious when one considers its place in relation to two central axes of his thought: the novel understood as an essentially dialogical genre, and its genetic connection to carnivalesque culture. The texts of most importance for Bakhtin's interpretation of Cervantes' masterpiece count among his best-known works, for in them he sets out lucidly and neatly his understanding of dialogism and the carnivalesque. These include *Problems of Dostoevsky's Poetics* (1929), 'Discourse in the Novel' (1934–5), and *Rabelais and His World* (1940, 1965). Due largely to his prestige as a theorist, Bakhtin's interpretation of *Don Quixote de la Mancha* has received broad airing, at times in an unquestioning mode, among literary scholars.[1]

Where, then, does this place Cervantes? The short answer is that it places *Don Quixote de la Mancha* in two positions: within the diachronic narrative of the evolving novel as a pivotal work of modernity, and within the synchronic description of aesthetic forms as a supreme example of heteroglossia. In the diachronic narrative, it keeps parody alive and re-embodies the carnivalesque at a crucial time when the medieval cedes to the modern. In the synchronic plane, it epitomizes heteroglossia in many levels: the character of Don Quixote himself, the parody of chivalric romance, and the all-pervasive textual heteroglossia.

Notes on Reading Bakhtin

Bakhtin's concepts of dialogism, double-voicing, and heteroglossia are often manifest in Bakhtin's academic writing, most obviously when he deals with thinkers such as Kant, Schlegel, and Cohen, all of whom were anathema in his time and place. The difficulty of double-voicing becomes even more complicated in the issue of authorship surrounding the three texts at times attributed to Bakhtin. The disputed texts include the above-mentioned *Marxism and the Philosophy of Language* plus *Freudianism: A Marxist Critique,* attributed in English translation to Valentin N. Vološinov, and *The Formal Method in Literary Scholarship*, attributed in English translation to Pavel N. Medvedev and Bakhtin. The three men met in the 1920s in Vitebsk, and formed a circle of young thinkers now referred to as the Bakhtin Circle. Authorship of these works was never attributed to Bakhtin until the Russian semiotician Vyascheslav Ivanov publicly claimed in the 1970s that these works were authored by Bakhtin, with only minor insertions by his 'students,' Vološinov and Medvedev. This assertion was at first accepted at face value by Western scholars and is still current in Russia, although the majority of Western scholars now generally doubt the claim for Bakhtin's authorship. As tended to happen in Bakhtin scholarship, the authorship became more an ideological question than a philological one, with members of the two sides accusing the others of basing their beliefs about attribution on a preference for a liberal or a Marxist Baktin.[2] Bakhtin himself refused to sign a document with the Soviet copyright agency by which he could have claimed authorship of the three texts (Clark and Holquist 147). The strategy for explaining away this fact corresponds to what Zbinden criticizes as 'enactment,' in which Bakhtin is viewed as acting out his concepts of double-voicing or dialogism by ceding away or muddying authorship (*Bakhtin between East and West* 53).

Nevertheless, the authorship of the works most closely related to the theory of the novel is not contested. *Problems of Dostoevsky's Poetics* was published by Bakhtin in 1929, and again in a version he revised in 1963. The essays, 'Epic and Novel. Toward a Methodology for the Study of the Novel,' 'From the Prehistory of Novelistic Discourse,' 'Forms of Time and the Chronotope in the Novel,' and 'Discourse in the Novel,' appeared in print for the first time in 1975 (the year of Bakhtin's death), although they are generally dated to the 1930s. Bakhtin wrote *Rabelais and His World* circa 1940, and finally published it in 1965. There is no doubt, then, that we are presented with Bakhtin's theory of the novel, or that he was deeply invested in the theory of the novel as an intellectual enterprise.

Before entering into my analysis of Bakhtin's place within the novelistic tradition traced in this book, it behooves me to make some remarks about the way the Russian thinker quoted and alluded to Kant, Schlegel, and Cohen. Kant, neo-Kantianism, idealism, Romanticism – all of these were anathema for Soviet materialists. Let us not forget that in his 1908 work, *Materialism and Empirio-Criticism: Critical Comments on a Reactionary Philosophy*, Lenin twice harshly attacked Hermann Cohen as a triumphal spokesperson for the ascendancy of idealism over materialism (chapter 5: section 5, 'The Two Trends in Modern Physics, and German Idealism,' and section 8, 'The Essence and Significance of "Physical" Idealism'). Reading Kant – as Bakhtin and his circle did – in the 1920s Soviet Union was an act of political rebellion (nor were references to Christianity such as those in *Art and Answerability* any more welcome). Yet Bakhtin manages to riddle his works with allusions to such objects of opprobrium in a way that typifies double-voicing with ironic intent – using the words of the other to contradict them. In that sense, Bakhtin can be considered a master of academic irony. The double-voicing is probably not 'enactment,' in which Bakhtin's first priority would be performing his theory, but a strategy for writing and speaking about what was forbidden to be written and spoken. Therefore, it is necessary to analyse references to Kant, Schlegel, and Cohen in specific, and Kantianism and Romanticism in general, as examples of double-voiced discourse that cannot be interpreted merely at face value. Bakhtin's references to Cohen, as well as other thinkers condemned by official discourse, offer an interesting example of a form of double-voicing in which the other's discourse is respected in one phrase and then undermined in the next. These contradictory references and re-marks tend to take place in apparently marginal textual spaces such as parentheses or footnotes. Here we have a good example of the power of the centrifugal vis-à-vis the centripetal, a guiding juxtaposition in Bakhtin's thought by which the centrifugal undermines centralizing forces. It is an interesting strategy for dealing with the political reality of his time, a sort of self-censorship that unmasks itself, and should not lead the twenty-first-century reader astray.

Let us take a concrete example in which Bakhtin simultaneously criti-cizes Cohen and yet hints that he is building upon the neo-Kantian's thought. In the opening pages to 'Author and Hero in Aesthetic Activity,' Bakhtin expresses his dissatisfaction with aesthetics based on simplistic notions of expression and empathy (*Einfühlung*), in which the text is considered a direct expression of the author's consciousness and the reader's responsibility is to feel with the author through the text. Nonetheless, Bakhtin attempts to recuperate the notion of aesthetic love. Upon mentioning aesthetic love, he names in parentheses two theorists, Jean-Marie Guyau and Hermann Cohen: '(cf. Guyau's idea of social sympathy and, on an entirely different plane, Cohen's idea of aesthetic love)' (*AA* 11). Indicating already in parentheses that Cohen, in fact, rises above Guyau, Bakhtin hastens to criticize them both: 'But these two [undecipherable] conceptions are too general, too unspecific in character, both with regard to the particular arts and with regard to the special object of aesthetic vision – the hero (in Cohen there is more specific differentiation).' By praising Cohen's better definition of the hero, Bakhtin hints that he is building upon the neo-Kantian despite criticizing him.

Evidence in the text of Bakhtin's double-voicing of Cohen is strength-ened by biographical information. Matvei Isaevich Kagan, a neo-Kantian mathematician and Bakhtin's close friend, had taken refuge from anti-Semitic pogroms in Russia by journeying to Marburg, where he began to study philosophy with Cohen. His return to Russia in 1918 fanned the interest in Cohen's ideas that already existed among Bakhtin's circle of friends and colleagues (Holquist 5).[3] Cohen's importance for the Bakhtin Circle in the 1920s is evident in the book attributed to Bakhtin and Medvedev, *The Formal Method in Literary Studies* (1928). Here the two theorists openly adopt Cohen's understanding of art and the aesthetic realm in general as a superstructure that rules other ideologies. In other words, art incorporates in its expression reality as already conceived through logic and evaluated ethically (*The Formal Method in Literary Studies* 24). It follows that art as an object of study offers the researcher a privileged perspective on reality, given that art itself conceives of and judges reality. Indeed, Cohen's insistence on defining the world not as something already give (*gegeben*) but rather as something constructed and conceived (*aufgegeben*) became a slogan for Bakhtin's circle (*Mir ne dan, a zadan*).[4] Bakhtin did distance himself from Marburgian neo-Kantianism, however, in his rejection of Cohen's notion of universality (*Allheit*), necessary to the German philosopher for the unification of his system (Holquist 6). Bakhtin's interest in the concrete circumstances of communication – which at times brought him close to phenomenology – distanced him even more from Cohen (Bernard-Donals 22–32). Thus, by analysing double-voiced references to Cohen in conjunction with his biographical context, one can argue that Bakhtin both draws from and moves beyond Cohen's thought.

Authority and Intersubjectivity

Although Bakhtin does not refer specifically to *Don Quixote de la Mancha* or even to the novel as a genre until his works of the later 1920s and 1930s, his reception of Cervantes' masterpiece can only be completely understood in the light of his early works from the period of 1919–24, in particular the long essay 'Author and Hero in Aesthetic Activity.' Probably because of its neo-Kantian orientation, Bakhtin never sought to publish it, nor did he mention it to friends until the end of his life. Nonetheless, the fact that he carefully guarded the notebook in which it and other early manuscripts were found indicates the importance he attributed to these works (*AA* xviii). Moreover, his notes from 1970–1 reveal a return to this early work, in particular referencing 'philosophical anthropology,' the study of the self in relation to the world and the other (*Speech Genres* 146–7). In the essay 'Author and Hero in Aesthetic Activity,' Bakhtin offers the reader an account of aesthetic creation and interpretation as an ontologically distinct activity, differentiated from both the ethical and the epistemological insofar as it deals with a different plane of experience, but linked to both cognition and ethical activity through the notion of tasks to be achieved.[5] As such, Bakhtin's essay provides an important and illuminating reworking of Cohen's assertion that aesthetics forms the third leg of the neo-Kantian stool (the other two legs being epistemology and ethics). In this essay the Russian bases his thought on Cohen's notion of *Aufgabe* as unending, future-oriented ethical action, but also moves beyond the German philosopher's characterization of the aesthetic impulse toward the other as empathy (*Einfühling*). By the same token, Bakhtin rejects the definition of aesthetic creativity as expression found in Cohen and others, and replaces it with the notion of consummation.

In order to define the aesthetic as a unique mental category, Bakhtin distinguishes it from both epistemology and ethics. As one knows from Kant, epistemology originates in logic, and is concerned with rational knowledge of the world. For Bakhtin, writing in the early twentieth century, epistemology or the '[t]heory of knowledge has become the model for theories in all other domains of culture' (*AA* 88). Epistemology posits the single, unified consciousness typical of science – in other words, the transcendent self that does not allow for the outside to be understood as subject. Bakhtin's moral disgust at this scientific, unified consciousness is evident in the way that he describes the epistemological self as contravening the Kantian moral imperative and turning the other into an end, in this case a mere reflection of the self. 'Any unity is its *own* unity; it cannot admit next to itself any other unity that would be different from it and independent of it (the unity of nature, the unity of another consciousness), that is, any sovereign unity that would stand over against it with its *own* fate, one *not* determined by epistemological consciousness' (*AA* 89). Indeed, understanding consciousness only according to the epistemological notion of the unified self does not explain lived experience. As Bakhtin writes, 'Our concern is rather with the concrete lived experience of our subjectivity and the impossibility of its – of our – being exhaustively present in an object, in contrast to the object-status of any other human being' (*AA* 38–9).

Viewing art according to an epistemological paradigm based on unity of consciousness results in a serious distortion of the very nature of the aesthetic: '[T]he unity of the event's performance is displaced by the unity of one's consciousness, one's understanding of the event, and the *subiectum* who was a participant in the event itself is transformed into the *subiectum* of a nonparticipant, purely theoretical cognition of the work' (*AA* 88). Unlike the unitary consciousness of epistemology, aesthetic consciousness is plural. This plurality occurs in the 'author's (the *I*'s) consciousness of the hero's (the *other*'s) consciousness' (*AA* 89). By couching the distinctiveness of aesthetic consciousness in the I-other relation, Bakhtin links it to the ethical. Indeed, for Bakhtin as for the neo-Kantians, the boundary between the aesthetic and the ethical blurs in spite of their protestations to the contrary.

Implicit in Bakhtin's early thought, although never clearly enunciated, is the notion that the aesthetic belongs to another ontological plane – what Ortega terms the virtual. The ethical, then, occurs in what Bakhtin calls lived life, and ethical action occurs when we interact with others in the same plane of lived life. The aesthetic event arises when, from our positions in this lived life as author or spectator, we create and experience an other in the virtual realm. Curiously, Bakhtin expresses the difference between the ethical and the aesthetic by means of a thought experiment remarkably similar to the episode of Maese Pedro's puppet play in *Don Quixote*, in which the would-be knight errant loses sight of the fact that he is watching a theatrical representation and intervenes violently. The Russian invites us to imagine a naive spectator of a play who warns the protagonist of coming danger and is ready to leap to his defence. In ethical terms, the spectator's response is correct – he jumps to the aid of another. It is in the aesthetic realm that he can be considered mistaken: '[h]e stepped across the footlights and took up a position *beside* the hero on one and the same plane of life lived as a unitary and open ethical event, and, in so doing, he ceased to be an author/spectator and abolished the aesthetic event' (*AA* 79). To be aware of the aesthetic, then, we must juxtapose it to the ethical and the epistemological. As Bakhtin makes very clear, the good spectator does not suspend ethical judgment, but rather holds it in suspension in relation to the aesthetic plane. Otherwise, we would all be leaping to the aid of mere figures.

The ontology of the aesthetic raises interesting issues that Bakhtin addresses in his formulation of the author-hero relationship. The problem of the aesthetic realm is that it presupposes two different sorts of being: the lived being of the author in our shared world of life, and the represented being of the literary character in the created world. It is useful to remember Unamuno's novel *Niebla* (*Mist*), in which the protagonist confronts the author. As Unamuno reminds Augusto, he the character depends on the author for existence, but the dependence is not mutual. Unamuno exists quite happily without Augusto. Although

Unamuno ironizes the obvious parallel between God and humanity implicit in this understanding of the author-hero dyad, Bakhtin takes it seriously in the 1920s. Writing of tragedy, he remarks that 'it is the author/contemplator who is active, whereas the heroes are passive; *they* are the ones who are saved and redeemed through aesthetic salvation' (*AA* 71). In other words, the traditional authority of the author over the protagonist is preserved in 'Author and Hero in Aesthetic Activity.' Nonetheless, at the end of his life, after having developed further his notion of dialogism, Bakhtin will violate the ontological difference between the author's world and the fictional world. In notes for revising his Dostoevsky work written in 1961, Bakhtin minimizes the role of the author as participant and organizer of the dialogue that is the hero's story (*PDP* 296–7).

The reference to salvation moves us once again to the ethical, and highlights the obvious parallel between ethical and aesthetic activity: both involve the leaving of one's own self to enter into the place of the other. For Bakhtin, this movement of exiting the self and projecting into the other constitutes a necessary step of both ethics and aesthetics. The ethical response to the suffering of a fellow human being is action, but the aesthetic takes place only with the return into the self. 'Aesthetic activity proper actually begins at the point when we *return* into ourselves, when we *return* to our own place outside of the suffering person, and start to form and consummate the material we derived from projecting ourselves into the other and experiencing him from within himself' (*AA* 26). To remain in the other would result in a psychotic loss of boundaries and cognitive disorder, but it would also constitute an ethical violation of the other's unique identity and render the self incapable of clear judgment or action. Consummation, then, occurs only in the exiting of the other, when he or she is again seen from outside. This seeing from the outside constitutes what Bakhtin calls the 'excess of my seeing, volition, and feeling' (*AA* 27). It is excess in that it is inaccessible to the other, available only to the self by virtue of being outside the other. Moreover, this excess is aesthetic: 'The clear blue sky that enframes him becomes a pictorial feature which consummates and resolves his suffering' (*AA* 27).

Cherishing the Body

It may come as a surprise that Bakhtin's much-touted notion of the carnivalesque body could have roots in German Romanticism, neo-Kantian philosophy, and the Christian concept of incarnation and grace. None-theless, a careful reading of 'Author and Hero in Aesthetic Activity' leaves no doubt about this, in spite of (or perhaps because of) the in-complete allusions. One of the sketchier sections of the manuscript, 'The Value of the Human Body in History,' clarifies Bakhtin's sources of inspiration. Contrasting it with a neo-Platonic trend in Christianity, Bakhtin highlights an alternative that rehabilitates the flesh through divine grace. The allusions to Schlegel and Cohen are even briefer, yet unmistakable and noted in the Liapunov translation. In reference to the German Romantic affirmation of sexual love epitomized in Schlegel's novel *Lucinde*, Bakhtin jots: 'Rehabilitation of sexuality in Romanticism' (*AA*58). The text follows immediately with a reference to Cohen's no-tion of the ethical state and the Talmudic injunction to treat the other as Thou: 'The legal idea of man: man-as-the-other,' a direct reference, as Liapunov notes, to Cohen's *Ethics of Pure Will* (*AA* 245).

Bakhtin moves beyond these strains of thought in order to propose the beginnings of a new ethics and aesthetics of the body based on the distinction between the inner and outer body. The inner body corres-ponds to ourselves and is a given (*Gegeben*); the outer body corresponds to the other and is 'not given but *set as a task*: I must actively produce it' (*AA* 51). In our lives, the body of the other, then, exists in the realm of *Aufgabe*, meaning that our interaction with the other is ethical. Bakhtin draws on several images for this ethical care for the body of the other, including the maternal embrace and loving sexual relations. With re-gard to love, Bakhtin again quotes and unquotes Cohen twice (*AA* 11, 81) in a manner that reveals that he is, in fact, expounding on the neo-Kantian's definition of love as '*sympathetic* co-experiencing' (*AA* 81). In this co-experience of love, we do not merely feel the other's self-love, but rather experience the other as other, and thus alive.

For Bakhtin, this co-experiencing can and should take place on the aesthetic plane. 'Sympathetic co-experiencing of the hero's life means to experience that life in a form completely different from the form in which it was, or could have been, experienced by the *subiectum* of that life himself' (*AA* 82). As such, we do not strive to merge with the other, but rather return to ourselves in the aesthetic act. Moreover, this re-turning to ourselves allows us to see the other in his or her environment and trajectory. In literary terms, we see the setting and the narrative arc of the other. For Bakhtin, only the aesthetic point of view can produce this image of a 'whole, integral human being,' for it alone can give value to the human being at the same time that it remains separate from the human being (*AA* 83). Aesthetic form arises from this 'aesthetically productive sympathy or love that *comes to meet* the co-experienced life from outside.' As such, the aesthetic form is the expression of the author's external vision of the hero. In Bakhtin's words, form expresses the author's activity, but the hero remains passively expressed. Indeed, the author's *task* is to express the protagonist. In other words, aesthetic form manifests on the boundary between author and hero. It 'operates at those points where this life is turned *outward*, where it comes to an end (in space, time, and meaning) and *another* life begins, that is, where it comes up against a sphere of self-activity beyond its reach – the sphere of *another's* self-activity' (*AA* 85). The aesthetic form itself, then, can be considered a boundary or a threshold between two worlds, an image for the novel that Bakhtin will explore further in his later work.

It is perhaps tempting to associate the realm of the aesthetic with the unreal or imagined, and yet it is very real for Bakhtin insofar as it completes or consummates the lived experience of the individual with the lived experience of the other. This relation is clearly reciprocal in the social realm. In one of his most evocative images, Bakhtin writes, 'As we gaze at each other, two different worlds are reflected in the pupils of our eyes' (*AA* 23). Much of Bakhtin's subsequent work explains how these two different worlds, seen from two different sets of eyes, can coexist, and be co-perceived and co-experienced in literature and language. Nor can the moment of projecting oneself into the other be clearly separated from the exiting, for they are intertwined in lived experience. This intertwining reveals itself in literature in the dual nature of the word. 'In a verbal work, every word keeps both moments in view: every word performs a twofold function insofar as it directs my projection of myself into the other as well as brings him to completion, except that one constitutive moment may prevail over the other' (*AA* 27). Here Bakhtin makes explicit the link between neo-Kantian ethics and what he will later call polyphony or heteroglossia in language. The special attribute of the word is its ability to hold within itself both the self and the other. This grants to the word a privileged position in ethical action, just as it grants to literature a privileged position in society.

Moreover, this ability to hold simultaneously the vision from within of the other and the vision from without typifies the relation of the author to the hero, one that is figured with the neo-Kantian notion of *Aufgabe*, or in Bakhtin's translation of the German word, *zadannyj*. 'That is, the author must move the very center of value from the hero's existence as a compelling *task* into his existence as a beautiful *given*; instead of hearing and agreeing with the hero, the author must see all of him in the fullness of the present and admire him as such' (AA19). Thus, Bakhtin understands the author's work as consummating the hero. Nor is it wrong to link this notion of the author-hero relation with a religious understanding of the God-human relation. The excess of knowledge that the author has of her character is parallel to the complete knowledge God has of creation. Moreover, it is a model for the ethical relation between the self and the other: 'What I must be for the other, God is for me. What the other surmounts and repudiates within himself as an unworthy given, I accept in him and that with loving mercy as the other's cherished flesh' (AA 56).

Dostoevsky's Copernican Revolution

Bakhtin's first serious foray into the theory of the novel occurs in his *Problems of Dostoevsky's Poetics* (1929). Although this work is often read only in conjunction with the later writings, it clearly springs from Bakhtin's earlier essay, 'Author and Hero in Aesthetic Activity.' In short, it represents the Russian thinker's attempt to transfer his exploration of the cognitive, ethical, and aesthetic lived experiences of the self (his 'philosophical anthropology') to a more detailed analysis of the relation between author and protagonist in the modern novel, specifically that of Dostoevsky. For Bakhtin, Dostoevsky has achieved a 'small-scale Copernican revolution' by upsetting the traditional relation between the authoritative author and the malleable hero (*PDP* 49). The author, instead of directly showing us the situationality of the character, reveals it through showing us the character's inner life and self-consciousness. In other words, the protagonist is conscious of the way he is seen by others, and of his own striving for completion.

This Copernican revolution of the author-protagonist relation has several consequences, some glimpsed by Bakhtin. Other consciousnesses (characters) inhabit the narrative plane, and see the hero from their own points of view. This multiplicity of consciousnesses within the narrative world contributes in part to what Bakhtin considers the polyphony of Dostoevsky's novels, for the protagonist is aware of the perspectives of the others that would serve to delimit him, and struggles against them (*PDP* 104). In this sense, the narrative world and its multiplicity of perspectives, defining the other from outside yet struggling for the unfinished, internal self, mirrors Bakhtin's earlier description of lived experience. The novelistic protagonist faces the same challenges as the living individual: to be seen by the other, to see the other, to enter the other, to exit the other, to complete the other, to continue his own quest to be incomplete. He is a work in progress. In this way, the novel is mimetic, reflecting the very conditions of capitalistic modernity that have cast the individual into profound solitude (*PDP* 288).

The same ethical relation that should exist between two selves in lived experience and two characters in the novel – one in which the other is completed by the self even though the self remains incomplete – should now also exist between author and hero. In *Problems of Dostoevsky's Poetics*, this ethical relation is referred to as dialogic, yet it is clearly quite similar to what is described in the earlier writings and springs from the same intellectual influences. As such, it involves Kantian respect for the other as a free and worthy individual, Cohen's notion of the ethical life as an unending task oriented toward completion but never arriving, and even the Talmudic I-Thou relation referenced by Cohen and later Buber: 'Thus the new artistic position of the author with regard to the hero in Dostoevsky's polyphonic novel is a *fully realized and thoroughly consistent dialogic position*, one that affirms the independence, internal freedom, unfinalizability, and indeterminacy of the hero. For the author the hero is not "he" and not "I" but a fully valid "thou," that is, another and other autonomous "I" ("thou art")' (*PDP* 63). Because this dialogic relation exists between author and protagonist, the discourse between the two must allow for the protagonist to respond, for response is essential to dialogue.

In spite of – or because of – the ontological impossibility that a protagonist would respond to his or her author, Bakhtin insists that this is the very foundation of the novel: 'By the very construction of the novel, the author speaks not *about* a character, but *with* him' (*PDP* 63). Since Bakhtin (unlike Unamuno) acknowledges that literary characters cannot be free from the author and do exist in another ontological state, he must focus on form as the liminal stage or threshold between the author's world and the hero's world. It is in the form of the novel that the author's power over the protagonist gives way to his or her freedom: 'The characters' freedom we speak of here exists within the limits of the artistic design, and in that sense is just as much a created thing as is the unfreedom of the objectivized hero' (*PDP* 64–5). Bakhtin offers several structural devices by which the author can cede freedom to the protagonist: making the protagonist aware of others's viewpoints; not holding on to an excess of information unavailable to the protagonist; and making all elements of the created world provoke and incite the hero.

Irony, Parody, and Cervantes

When Bakhtin maintains in 'Author and Hero in Aesthetic Activity' that lived experience confronts daily the aporia of otherness – the unified consciousness challenged and limited by the subjectivity of the other – he argues for a 'materialist' re-evaluation of aesthetics and ethics through none other than the concept of Romantic irony. In an extremely important footnote to this sentence, Bakhtin makes clear the Schlegelian origins of this insight: 'This point was thoroughly understood and assimilated in the aesthetics of Romanticism (cf. Schlegel's theory of irony)' (*AA* 39). It is probably no accident that this reference to Friedrich Schlegel occurs in a footnote, disguised as an offhand remark and yet central to Bakhtin's thought. After all, Romanticism and idealism were considered excretions of bourgeois decadence. Bakhtin does with Schlegel what he does with Cohen: he names a theorist to discredit him in his text, only to name him again in a seemingly parenthetical aside that reveals how central that thinker actually is. Likewise, Bakhtin's assertion that his notion of lived experience is materialist rather than idealist is far from convincing, and yet another ruse. What is Bakhtin's point here about Schlegel's theory of irony?

For Bakhtin, irony manifests the aporia of knowing the other as well as being known by the other. We are each excess to the other's knowledge of us, just as they are excess to ours. Our consummation of the other from the outside can be compared to the Schlegelian notion of the hovering viewpoint of irony:

> It is impossible for me to experience convincingly all of myself as enclosed within an externally delimited, totally visible and tangible object, that is, to experience myself as coinciding with it in every respect. Yet that is the only way in which I can represent the other to myself. Everything inward that I know and in part co-experience in him I put into the outward image of the other as into a vessel which contains his *I*, his will, his cognition. For me, the other is gathered and fitted as a whole into his outward image. My own consciousness, on the other hand, I experience as encompassing the world, as embracing it, rather than as fitted into it [indecipherable]. In other words, the outward image of a human being can be experienced as consummating and exhausting the *other*, but I do not experience it as consummating and exhausting *myself*. (*AA* 39)

Bakhtin enunciates here the conundrum central to Romantic irony: one experiences the external as complete and consummate, but the self remains incomplete and inexhaustible. If one accepts that the other should not be viewed as mere object, then he or she also enjoys an inexhaustible self. One then achieves consciousness of the other's consciousness: a sort of potentialized consciousness similar to the Schlegelian notion of the multiplying mirrors of irony. The author-hero relationship typifies this consciousness of consciousness: 'The author's consciousness is the consciousness of a consciousness, that is, a consciousness that *encompasses* the consciousness and the world of a hero – a consciousness that encompasses and *consummates* the consciousness of a hero by supplying those moments which are in principle transgredient to the hero's consciousness' (*AA* 12).

Nonetheless, in *Problems of Dostoevsky's Poetics*, Bakhtin will move beyond Romantic notions of irony to associate it with the social phenomenon of the carnivalesque and with dialogism. Positing here the notion of the carnivalesque (which will be much further fleshed out in *Rabelais and His World*), Bakhtin defines carnival laughter as a renewing laughter directed against something higher and more powerful, be they gods or leaders. Although carnivalesque laughter finds expression in all periods, its apogee is the Renaissance, when it rings through the works of Rabelais, Cervantes, and Shakespeare. Subsequent to the Renaissance, it occurs as the 'reduced laughter' present in eigtheenth-century and Romantic irony (*PDP* 165). Even Socratic irony, the basis of Friedrich Schlegel's notion of irony, is for Bakhtin 'reduced carnival laughter' (*PDP* 132). What has been reduced? Bakhtin hints at this loss in his 1961 notes on the Dostoevsky work when he argues that the nineteenth-century Russian writer approaches the 'depths of the human soul' from without, whereas Romantic irony only approaches it from within (*PDP* 277–8). What is lost in Romantic irony, with its emphasis on the individual, is the social, dialogical setting in which we all live.

Indeed, the ironic utterance can only occur within the social dialogical relation – even if Schlegel might have lost sight of this fact. Quoting Leo Spitzer's work on spoken Italian, Bakhtin notes that irony is speaking the words of the other (*PDP* 194). As such, it is a prime component of what Bakhtin calls 'discourse with an orientation toward someone else's discourse (double-voiced discourse)' (*PDP* 199). Irony is analogous with parody, for parody also speaks the words of another only to give them a different semantic intention (*PDP* 193). Indeed, parody tends to function in Bakhtin's thought as extended discursive irony, or as the literary genre of irony. It is through the conjunction of irony and parody that Cervantes enters into Bakhtin's thought as an essential precursor to Dostoevsky and the polyphonic novel. The influence that Cervantes – as well as Shakespeare – exercised over Dostoevsky came not through ideas or themes, but through the carnivalesque form: 'a *carnival sense of the world itself*, that is, the influence of the very *forms* for visualizing the world and man, and that *truly godlike freedom* in approaching them which is manifest not in the individual thoughts, images, and external devices of construction, but in these writers' work as a *whole*' (*PDP* 158). On the one hand, Cervantes provides the parodic, multi-voiced, and subversive discourse of the carnivalesque to Dostoevsky; on the other hand, he models 'godlike freedom'! We find ourselves once again in the presence of the hovering freedom of Romantic irony.

Dostoevsky's own remarks on Cervantes oriented Bakhtin's interpretation of *Don Quixote de la Mancha*. Fyodor, in a diary entry dated September 1877, claimed for Cervantes' masterpiece the dubitable honour of being the saddest book in the world. Upon commenting on Don Quixote's explanation of the marvellous deeds performed by knights errant, Dostoevsky highlights the universal human capacity for self-deception (2:1127–31). Bakhtin argues that Don Quixote is 'born in the bosom of parody [as] one of the greatest and at the same time most carnivalistic novels of world literature' (*PDP* 128). To bolster that argument, he quotes Dostoevsky: 'There is nothing more profound and powerful in this world than this work. It is the ultimate and greatest word yet uttered by human thought, it is the most bitter irony that a man could express, and if the world should end and people were asked there, somewhere, "Well, did you understand your life on earth and what conclusions have you drawn from it?" a person could silently point to Don Quixote: "Here is my conclusion to life, can you judge me for it?"' For Dostoevsky, *Don Quixote* embodies the irony of the human condition, an irony understood as the limitations of human capability. Parody is the generic vehicle of that life-defining irony. Bakhtin leaves the quote largely uncommented, with one exception: 'It is characteristic that Dostoevsky structures his evaluation of *Don Quixote* in the form of a typical "threshold dialogue".' The threshold, along with the public square constitutes one of two typical spaces for Dostoevsky. It is the place of crisis and transition, where death and life meet, and thus deeply carnivalesque.

Don Quixote, Heteroglossia, and Irony

Arguably the most innovative aspect of Bakhtin's thought is his assertion that dialogue is the essential condition of language. The word, generally considered the origin of language, springs from dialogue. Indeed, its essential condition is to respond to dialogue; that is to say, the enunciated word is always a response to what has already been said (*DI* 279). In his work of the 1930s, Bakhtin expands his notion of double-voicing in linguistic utterances to explain the co-existence of different languages in heteroglossia. Caryl Emerson and Michael Holquist define dialogism in a glossary as 'the characteristic epistemological mode of a world dominated by heteroglossia' (*DI* 426). Heteroglossia as understood by Bakhtin comprises the 'social diversity of speech types' (*DI* 263). As an essentially dialogical genre, the novel is distinguished by the plurality of discourses that it contains. Bakhtin lists the following five discourses as relevant to the novel: '(1) Direct authorial literary-artistic narration ...; (2) Stylization of the various forms of oral everyday narrative ...; (3) Stylization of the various forms of semiliterary (written) everyday narration (the letter, the diary, etc.); (4) Various forms of literary but extra-artistic authorial speech ...; (5) The stylistically individualized speech of characters' (*DI* 262). It follows that the novel as a site of heteroglossia manifests in its unity the diversity of the culture from which it springs, a diversity it presents through the multiplicity of narrative forms, types of social speech, written genres, and even distinct languages. Novelistic language also has at its disposal three stylistic categories with which to give form to heteroglossic plurality: hybridization, the dialogical interplay of languages, and dialogue itself (*DI* 358). Hybridization, perhaps because it problematizes the limits of dialogue, has been of most interest to Bakhtin's readers. The Russian defines it as a mixing of two different social languages representing two different mentalities or perspectives in one enunciation. Among the hybrid forms one finds two central to modern readings of *Don Quixote*: parody and irony.

Bakhtin states the heteroglossic nature of Cervantes' masterpiece: 'Of such a sort is the classic and purest model of the novel as genre – Cervantes' *Don Quixote*, which realizes in itself, in extraordinary depth and breadth, all the artistic possibilities of heteroglot and internally dialogized novelistic discourse' (*DI* 324). He subsequently defines novelistic heteroglossia as the incorporation of *'another's speech in another's language*, serving to express authorial intentions but in a refracted way.' The reference to authorial intention reminds us that Bakhtin does not assume the death of the author in heteroglossia, but rather the refraction of voice. The notion of authorial refraction is central to the understanding of parody, also constituent of Cervantes' work. Parody, of course, links the novel to other literary discourses, but it also injects into the novel a reflexive, mirroring structure. Referring to both Don Quixote as hero of the novel and the parodic sonnets that preface the novel, Bakhtin states in 'From the Prehistory of Novelistic Discourse' that they are 'simultaneously represented and representing' (*DI* 45). The author engages with the character or the sonnet 'in a zone of *dialogical contact.*' Both the figure of Don Quixote and the parodied sonnets represent the 'image of another's language and outlook on the world,' and thus involve the author in a dialogical relation with another. On one level, the parody represents this point of contact. On another level, it can represent only a representation of the other. As Bakhtin notes concerning Cervantes' parodic sonnets, 'in any case, what results is not a sonnet, but rather the *image of a sonnet*' (*DI* 51).

Bakhtin figures this representation of representation in other works as the mask, again associated specifically with Cervantes. In 'Epic and Discourse,' he links masks to the laughter that undoes epic distance to render a more authentic image of humanity: 'Laughter destroyed epic distance; it began to investigate man freely and familiarly, to turn him inside out, expose the disparity between his surface and his center, between his potential and his reality' (*DI* 35). This it accomplishes through the use of 'durable popular masks – masks that had great influence on the novelistic image of many during the most important stages of the novel's development (the serio-comical genres of antiquity, Rabelais, Cervantes)' (*DI* 36). In 'Forms of Time and Chronotope in the Novel,' Bakhtin notes the power of the mask in the figures of the rogue, clown, and fool, who enjoy 'the right to be "other" in this world" (*DI* 159). The laughter they elicit is doubled, for they too laugh at themselves. Parody and the mask acquire a revelatory and even investigative power in Bakhtin's thought, because they make man visible in new ways and allow for new knowledge.

It is in this investigative function of the mask and parody that Friedrich Schlegel's notion of irony as an instrument for expanded knowledge emerges. At the beginning of 'From the Prehistory of Novelistic Discourse,' Bakhtin hints at the Romantic presence in his thought through a footnote in the usual 'but-and' style: 'The Romantics maintained that the novel was a mixed genre (a mixture of verse and prose), incorporating into its composition various genres (in particular the lyrical) – but the Romantics did not draw any stylistic conclusions from this. Cf., for example, Friedrich Schlegel's *Brief über den Roman*' (*DI* 41). As we have seen in chapter 2, the mixed nature of the novel for

Schlegel is a function of Romantic irony. Irony, for Bakhtin, is the intonational valence of parody and hybridization: 'Every type of parody or travesty, every word "conditions attached," with irony, enclosed in intonational quotation marks, every type of indirect word is in a broad sense an intentional hybrid – but a hybrid compounded of two orders: one linguistic (a single language) and one stylistic' (*DI* 75). The linguistic hybrid is the uttering of the language of the other, while the stylistic hybrid engages the other's utterance in the author's intention through what Bakhtin calls directional bias.

In other words, Bakhtin recuperates the notion of Romantic irony, in which the author hovers over the creation in an especially privileged position of knowledge, through his concept of parody. His self-proclaimed advance over Schlegel is his analysis of the effect of parody and irony on language itself and the effect of irony and parody on the reader through language – hence, his claim for a stylistics of the mixed genre. Once again, Cervantes proves exemplar in the Bakhtinian analysis of heteroglossic style. Parodic stylization of the type seen in the comic novel depends on the posited author, the Cide Hamete Benengeli who refracts the authorial voice (*DI* 312).

Schlegel's Arabesque and Bakhtin's Dialogism

As we have seen, Bakhtin's relation to Romanticism and idealism is likewise complicated and contradictory. Nonetheless, his reading of *Don Quixote de la Mancha* participates fully in the tradition of Romantic interpretation of this novel. Friedrich Schlegel's ideas on the novel as a genre and Cervantes (as well as those of Heinrich Heine, Ivan Turgenev, and Lord Byron) would have been accessible to Bakhtin both in a book by C. Derjavin (*Cervantes and Don Quixote,* Leningrad, 1933) and in an article by Krzhevsky (Turkevich 208, 218). For example, in his essay 'Epic and Novel,' Bakhtin refers to Schlegel's Lyceum Fragment 26, where the Romantic posited that novels were the Socratic dialogues of modernity given that within them practical know-how sought refuge from scholastic knowledge (*KA* 2:149). Bakhtin, admitting that he is paraphrasing Schlegel, includes Socratic dialogues in his history of the ancient novel (*DI* 22). Again, echoes of Schlegel are clearly audible when Bakhtin writes about incomprehensibility in the novel, especially in the case of Cervantes. Schlegel's well-known essay 'On Incomprehensibility' explored the link between irony and the lack of understanding; moreover, in Lyceum Fragment 81 he commented on the need to write polemical fiction by playing out the contrast between vulgar stupidity (*Dummheit*) and educated foolishness (*Narrheit*; *KA* 2:157).[6] According to Bakhtin, stupidity or lack of understanding plays a polemical role in the novel by unmasking through dialogic interaction a haughty, but false sort of intelligence (*DI* 403). From this follows the novelistic use of dialogically opposed pairs, among them the fool and the poet, the fool and the scholastic, the dolt and the saint, and the dolt and the politician. Said oppositions occur frequently in *Don Quixote*, especially in the episodes when Sancho serves as governor of Barataria.

To what extent can the form of the arabesque so preferred by young Friedrich be linked to Bakhtin's thought? As we have seen in chapter 2, Schlegel associated dialogue with one of his own favourite genres, the fragment, from which he would weave a chain of fragments to create a whole that was simultaneously subjective and objective (Athenaeum Fragment 77, *KA* 2:176). The fragment allowed Schlegel the freedom to juxtapose contrary ideas, to put forth provocative concepts, and yet leave them unfettered and uncompleted by system. The fragment could participate in a larger organization, the arabesque, in which contraries were juxtaposed but not resolved or dissolved. In other words, the arabesque could offer an alternative to the dialectic. Bakhtin's discomfort with the Hegelian dialectic as methodology (even though he incorporated a dialectic notion of history into his thought) is clear. As he sharply quips in his notes from 1970–1, 'Dialogue and dialectics. Take a dialogue and remove the voices (the partitioning of voices), remove the intonations (emotional and individualizing ones), carve out abstract concepts and judgments from living words and responses, cram everything into one abstract consciousness – and that's how you get dialectics' (*Speech Genres* 147). In other words, dialectics is dead dialogue – the muted, gutted, and inert object of a single consciousness similar to the epistemological consciousness he criticized so harshly fifty years earlier.

To the contrary, Bakhtin finds in Schlegel's arabesque a manifestation of the carnivalesque, albeit weakened into the form of the grotesque. The Russian considers the Romantic grotesque a rejection of classicism and official authoritarianism that was based in the rediscovery of the carnivalesque in Shakespeare and Cervantes: '[I]t was a rejection of that which is finished and completed, of the didactic and utilitarian spirit of the Enlighteners with their narrow and artificial optimism' (*RW* 37). By making the world alien again to human reason, the Romantic grotesque referred back to the carnivalesque values of the body and the mysteries of birth and death. Its weakness was the absence of transformative, regenerative laughter. Referring to Schlegel's *Dialogue on Poetry*, Bakhtin asserts that Friedrich 'usually calls [the grotesque] "arabesque" and considers it "the most ancient form of human fantasy" and the "natural form of poetry." He finds the grotesque in Shakespeare and Cervantes, in Sterne and Jean Paul' (*RW* 41). Moreover, Bakhtin understands the link between the arabesque and the grotesque in Schlegel's thoughts in terms that reveal an understanding of the arabesque as a form or a genre: '[Schlegel] sees [the grotesque's] essence in the fantastic combination of heterogeneous elements of reality, in the breaking up of the established world order, in the free fancy of its images and in the "alternate succession of enthusiasm and irony".' In effect, Bakhtin recognizes in Schlegel's notions of the grotesque and the arabesque forms of dialogism, where the images mix freely and fantastically heterogeneous elements of reality with social patterns of order. One last thought: can it be an accident that Bakhtin refers to Schlegel's *Dialogue on Poetry*, in itself a dialogue between friends?

Don Quixote: Carnivalesque Masterpiece and Heteroglossic Novel

Among the cacophony of different languages and speech types in dialogic discourse, the carnivalesque rings out. In *Rabelais and His World* Bakhtin maintains that Renaissance works such as *Gargantua and Pantagruel* and *Don Quixote de la Mancha* occupy a liminal space between the traditional, popular carnivalesque culture and the official culture typical of modern institutions, among them – one assumes – the Stalinist state. Bakhtin signals three medieval cultural manifestations of the carnivalesque: (1) ritual spectacles of a ludic nature, including those accompanying the carnival and religious festivities (*festa stultorum, risus paschalis*) and those taking place in the marketplace and city square; (2) comic works of literature, be they oral or written, in Latin or the vernacular; and (3) the transgressive language of oaths, curses, and foul language (*RW* 5). Drawing from various conventions of the carnival, including the subversion or inversion of official roles and the transgression of sexual and corporal taboos, Bakhtin argues that the carnivalesque represents a discourse alternative to officially sanctioned culture. The carnivalesque values what is normally downplayed, if not prohibited or repressed. This includes an alternative concept of the human body that valorizes body parts and functions: eating, defecation, fornication, sexual reproduction, and even death. Insofar as it celebrates the universal, creative power of the body, this so-called grotesque realism differs from bourgeois discourses that attempt to control and hide the corporal. In this manner the carnivalesque degrades the abstract, spiritual, and elevated, for it brings these discourses down to earth in sexual, reproductive, and digestive bodily functions (*RW* 19). Carnivalesque laughter serves to sustain and unify the community instead of denigrating and excluding those who do not observe its official norms. Therefore, medieval carnivalesque laughter holds a key position in carnivalesque culture, where it includes all individuals in its embrace and revitalizes rather than destroys the community. Although in the Renaissance this laughter enjoys philosophical significance as a way to access truth, in later centuries it loses prestige, a change that resulted in Cervantes' *Don Quixote* being judged a mere work of entertainment (*RW* 65).

In spite of the fact that *Rabelais and His World* deals mainly – and obviously – with Rabelais, Bakhtin refers many times to Cervantes' *Don Quixote de la Mancha* in order to bolster his analysis of the carnivalesque. Sancho Panza, for example, exemplifies the carnivalesque body through his stomach, his physical appetites, and the way in which he regularly degrades and parodies the disembodied idealism of his master, Don Quixote (*RW* 22). When both protagonists are viewed as one entity, they form what Bakhtin calls a comic pair, an ancient convention that continues to be reproduced in modern times in comic spectacles and the circus (*RW* 434). Indeed, the comic pair perpetuates carnivalesque duality within modernity by undoing what modernity tends to conceive of as dualities: life and death, the upper body and the lower body, purity and earthiness. In other words, Sancho brings down to earth the abstract pretensions of Don Quixote (*RW* 22). Moreover, Sancho's corrective function serves to signal *Don Quixote*'s place as a Renaissance work, the Renaissance understood as a liminal time bridging the Middle Ages and modernity that constituted a significant stage in the historical development of the novel (Gómez 47–54). Sancho's carnivalesque body serves to insert the carnivalesque in the novel, where it doubles with the modern, bourgeois notions of the body represented not only by Don Quixote, but also by the characters of the interpolated sentimental novels (*RW* 23). Likewise, Sancho's carnivalesque laughter doubles with the individualized, bourgeois laughter of the new modernity.

Bakhtin's notion of the carnivalesque is not completely unstained by neo-Kantian thought. One of the links between Bakhtin and Hermann Cohen is the latter's student and defender, Ernst Cassirer. Poole has definitively demonstrated that the Russian either appropriated without citation entire paragraphs of Cassirer's *Individual and the Cosmos in*

Renaissance Philosophy or plagiarized the text (although one notes that citing Cassirer in that moment would have been dangerous for Bakhtin; 542–3). The material in question consists of Cassirer's delineation of the spatial hierarchy of the elevated to the low typical of medieval cosmology. The importance of Cassirer's analysis of this cosmology for Bakhtin's notion of the carnivalesque is obvious since the carnivalesque turns on its head the traditional hierarchical order. In addition, Cassirer employs *Don Quixote* as an example of the dialectics on which Renaissance humour depends, for Cervantes destroys (albeit lovingly) the chivalric ideal at the same time that he conserves its form (*Platonic Renaissance in England* 171–2; Brandist, 'Bakhtin's Grand Narrative' 11–30).

According to Bakhtin's history of the novel, *Don Quixote de la Mancha* occupies an intermediate position between the so-called First Line of novelistic development and the Second. Novels from the First Line acknowledge social heteroglossia, but try to organize and order it. A good example of this phenomenon is none other than the literature of chivalric romance, which opposes an ennobled, literary language to vulgar speech (*DI* 384). Bakhtin draws on *Amadís de Gaula* as an example of such ordering; clearly he considers both chivalric and sentimental romances of the period to belong to the First Line. Second Line novels, among which Bakhtin numbers the works of Rabelais and Cervantes as well as picaresque novels such as *Lazarillo de Tormes*, confront the elevated language of the First Line with a multitude of other discourses. This confrontation, in turn, makes Second Line novels ripe for parody, sociopolitical critique, and autoreflexivity. The example of *Don Quixote* is typical: the parody of the romances of knight-errantry becomes a parody of that genre's language. Bakhtin hastens to clarify that to see *Don Quixote* as a parody only of that decadent genre – as Charles Sorel saw it – is to interpret Cervantes' novel according to an overly narrow and bourgeois perspective (*RW* 103).[7] For Bakhtin, Cervantes unfolds and develops in the novel, especially in Sancho's dialogues with the representatives of various official positions, the whole variety of discourses and languages typical of his time (*DI* 384).[8] There is no doubt that Bakhtin conceives of this linguistic plurality as a preferred form of mimesis, for he goes so far as to accuse the chivalric romances of avoiding encounters with crude, vulgar reality.

By intensifying the hybridization of language, Second Line novels open up to what Bakhtin calls the self-criticism of discourse. Once more *Don Quixote* steps to the head of the class due to its testing of literary discourse in various levels. Firstly, the character Don Quixote is himself a literary man who sees the world through a literary discourse (*DI* 413). His failure to confront reality constitutes in itself a critique of the sentimental and chivalric romance genres of his time. It is not only the protagonist Don Quixote who lives the conflict between literary discourse and reality, but also, according to Bakhtin, the author Cervantes. From this lived conflict springs the metafictional level of Cervantes' novel in all its authorial ambiguity and narrative complexity. Moreover, Bakhtin argues that *Don Quixote de la Mancha* resides in a liminal space between simple parody, in which the author merely proposes to parody the discourse in play, and Romantic irony. For Bakhtin, Romantic irony involves the author's own identification with the parodied discourse to the extent that he himself runs the risk of adopting the parodied perspective (*DI* 413). In other words, as far as Bakhtin is concerned, Cervantes was fighting off a bad case of Quixotism.

Moreover, Cervantes' novel exists for Bakhtin within several temporal registers, including the diachronic register of the history of prose and the synchronic register of the chronotope. *Don Quixote de la Mancha* represents for Bakhtin, then, a parodic hybridization of the chronotope of chivalric literature and the chronotope of the picaresque. Given that the former represents a marvellous, distant world, and the latter represents the journey through one's homeland, Cervantes' novel brings together these two quite disparate chronotopes in common juxtaposition of the fantastic to the everyday (*DI* 165).

Modern Russian Reception of *Don Quixote*

Several Russian scholars of our times have rightly insisted on reading Bakhtin within his own intellectual context – that is to say, they choose to view him as a specifically Russian thinker. Concepts central to Bakhtin's theory and history of the novel already circulated among his contemporary compatriots: for example, the understanding of the novel as a literary genre based on everyday life rather than official discourse, and the notion that the novel evolved over the centuries in opposition to the epic. V.G. Avsyenko suggested in 1877 in 'The Origin of the Novel' that parallels existed between Rabelais and Cervantes as representative figures of the French and Spanish Renaissances (Turkevich 91–4). Toward the end of the nineteenth century, Aleksandr Veselovskii traced the history of the novel back to ancient times, where he saw it as emergent from a society experiencing a profound conflict between a public, cosmopolitan form of life and another more domestic and private (Tihanov, 'Bakhtin's Essays on the Novel' 32–4). A specialist in the ancient Greek novel, Olga Friedenberg maintained that social differences as portrayed in the novel constituted a form of heterogeneity (40). By the 1920s Iuri Tynianov and Viktor Shklovsky both believed that the novel introduced different types of non-literary speech into literature, and posited that this process took place in the margins and peripheries of what was considered literary (38). Tihanov sums up three theoretical ideas about the novel as a genre that Bakhtin learned from other Russian literary critics: 'the concept of the social (class) determination of the novel that had been defended by the sociological method; the idea that the novel is born in the process of exceeding the narrow limitations of a single nation was Veselovskii's bequest; finally, the notion of the impact of one language on other languages as a factor of evolution and change was first formulated by the Formalists' (49).

Likewise, parallels exist beween Bakhtin's interpretation of *Don Quixote de la Mancha* and those of important compatriots. Russian readers often felt sympathy for Don Quixote, whom they revered as an eloquent, refined idealist destined to failure. Indeed, many Russian literati identified with Don Quixote precisely because they felt they shared the same fate (Turkevich 223). Don Quixote's exaltation by Ivan Turgenev is the best-known case of such affection for the mad protagonist. The Russian writer saw in the Cervantine character an aspect of highly prized humane idealism: faith in something outside the self. Hamlet's lack of faith, to the contrary, represented for Turgenev human egoism. Nor did Turgenev overlook the would-be knight errant's comic countenance, but rather believed that the laughter Don Quixote evoked in his readers had a salutary effect that only heightened their love for the madman (Turgenev 16). To the contrary, Sancho did not enjoy such popularity among nineteenth- and early twentieth-century Russian readers. The most notable exception to this general rule was Viktor Shklovsky, who found in Sancho a representation of popular wisdom that contrasted with his master's lettered erudition (Turkevich 220, 224). Bakhtin quotes another exception, Boris A. Krzhevsky, a Marxist critic who argued that the Renaissance laughter that rang through the pages of Cervantes' novel accompanied the disappearance of the medieval feudal system (*RW* 99). Krzhevsky saw in Sancho a sympathetic picaresque figure, and thus *Don Quixote de la Mancha* represented for him a generic and psychological mixing of the picaresque and the carnivalesque (Turkevich 210–11).

Bakhtin's and Shklovsky's Interpretations of *Don Quixote*

The parallels between Shklovsky's interpretation of *Don Quixote de la Mancha* in his *Theory of Prose* (1925) and Bakhtin's are so numerous and striking that they make one wonder whether the latter, either consciously or unconsciously, based his interpretation of Cervantes' novel on that of the former. This similarity in readings is even more curious given the critique of Shklovsky voiced in *The Formal Method in Literary Scholarship*. Whether it be authored by Medvedev alone, Bahktin alone, or Medvedev and Bakhtin together, the charge that formalism failed to understand the social essence of language and literature certainly reflects Bakhtin's position. In addition, the assertion that 'the basic tendency of the formalist concept of material is the abolition of content' would also coincide with Bakhtin's thought (*The Formal Method in Literary Studies* 110).

One way of understanding Bakhtin's notion of the carnivalesque, for instance, is as the recuperation of a content-based analysis. Nor does content-based analysis consider plot as the stringing together of interchangeable events, a sort of syntax in which slots can be filled by different semantic units. The shortcomings of such an approach are seen in the case of a travel novel such as *Don* Quixote: 'If the narrative is about the travels of a hero, as in *Don* Quixote, these travels only serve to motivate the device of "stringing together" [*nanizyvanie*]. Thus every element of the story, i.e., of the event being related, is only significant to the extent that it motivates some constructive device, some object of the tale itself, which is taken as a self-valuable whole independent of the event being narrated' (*The Formal Method in Literary Studies* 107). As an antidote to such formalistic reduction of the plot, it is recommended that the novelist see life in terms of *fabula*, a function of 'the wider and deeper relationships of life on a large scale' (*The Formal Method in Literary Studies* 134). This call for the novel to engage the grand scale of life appears in other writings on the novel, such as 'The *Bildungsroman* and Its Significance in the History of Realism (Toward a Historical Typology of the Novel),' in which Bakhtin claims an epic scope for the novel that 'should reflect the *entire* world and *all* of life' (*Speech Genres* 43). In the case of Rabelais and Cervantes, this epic scope results in a condensation of reality against the backdrop of history. Certainly, the carnivalesque constitutes one way of refocusing analysis on the *fabula* by positing such a backdrop.

Another main objection against formalism voiced in *The Formal Method in Literary Scholarship* concerns the construction of literary characters. For

Shklovsky, Don Quixote emerges as a type from the narrative. This Bakhtin and/or Medvedev cannot accept, for it contradicts the vision of the novel as 'organic' and 'in the process of formation' (136). The novel emerges from 'the struggle for a new genre,' a struggle which involves the emergence of a new vision of reality. Likewise, the character of Don Quixote must emerge as an integral whole in order to respect the Bakhtinian notion of the ethical relation between author and protagonist. Don Quixote cannot be a mouthpiece for the author, or a 'motivation' in Shklovsky's terms, for this would transform him into a means and violate the moral imperative: 'the figure of Don Quixote is not motivation for anything – not for wise speeches or insane situations. It is an end in itself, as are all essential constructive elements of the work' (138).

Given the definition of the novel as emergent whole and the ethical relation of author to character, the two main bones of contention concerning Cervantes' novel that appear in *The Formal Method in Literary Studies* are the problem of the interpolated stories and the emergence of the character of Don Quixote. Medvedev and/or Bakhtin mention the problem of explaining the interpolated tales in *Don Quixote* as a theoretical issue, requiring that the reader 'perceives connections and relationships which break open the novella and force its subordination to the higher unity of the work' (137). Their conceptualization of the novel as an organically emerging genre requires that the particular be subsumed to the whole. They do not, however, offer an actual interpretation. It is Shklovsky who, because of his notion of the stringing together of plot, questions such issues as the purpose of the interpolated tales. It is in the arena of actual textual analysis rather than theorization that, with regard to certain important issues specific to *Don Quixote de la Mancha*, Shklovsky examines the text in a much more detailed manner than does Bakhtin.

One can argue that in *The Formal Method in Poetics* Shklovksy is being double-voiced in the same ironic way that we have seen Bakhtin double-voice Schlegel and Cohen. For some reason, perhaps in this case the need to establish a distinct intellectual identity for the Bakhtin Circle against the prestige of the Formalists, Shklovsky's reading of *Don Quixote de la Mancha* is derided and accepted in the same breath. Bakhtin's later comments on Cervantes' novel, as well as his novelistics, reveal clear parallels to Shklovsky's reading of the text. Given his understanding of the character as a function of plot, Shklovsky offers in many ways a more exact account of Cervantes' text. According to Shklovsky, Don Quixote emerges at first as a fool, but by the end of the book serves as the mouthpiece of wisdom (73). To the contrary, Sancho manifests folkloric wisdom in his voicing of proverbs and popular sayings as well as his weighty performance as the good governor of the island Barataria (77). By voicing his own ideas through Don Quixote, Cervantes realizes halfway through the book that he has created a duality in the character, and decides to exploit said duality in order to achieve his own aesthetic ends (80). One hears echoes of Bakhtin's notion of heteroglossia here, although the formalist Shklovsky conceives of the voice doubled in the literary character as belonging to the author. In addition, Shklovsky identifies in the interpolated tales another type of doubling present in Cervantes' novel, one dependent upon the motif of the trip in which the road and the inn serve as vehicles for the encounters between Don Quixote and the characters involved in the interpolated tales (99). Again one notes the echo of the Bakhtinian concept of the chronotope. For Shklovsky, the integration of these episodes into a unit forms a kaleidoscopic image, and represents a step toward the modern novel (99). Upon ascribing the physical fights in *Don Quixote* to the world of the circus and the sphere of fairy tales, the Formalist even suggests, albeit in negative terms, the carnivalesque aspect of Cervantes' humour (85).

In short, Bakhtin's innovation with respect to Shklovsky does not reside in his reading of *Don Quixote de la Mancha*, since both theorists focus on more or less the same aspects of the text. To the contrary, his innovation depends on the interpretive twist he gives to the elements of Cervantes' text already signalled by Shklovsky: the parody, the duality of Don Quixote's voice, the popular violence and wisdom, and the chronotope of the inn and the road. Bakhtin places these elements into his own global theory of language and literature, and thus effects a reevaluation of them. Indeed, one can characterize Bakhtin's takings from Shklovsky as heteroglossic but not naive: he adopts the Formalist's words and dubs them with new meaning.

Bakhtin, Cohen, and Lukács on Cervantes and the Novel

Hermann Cohen's reading of *Don Quixote* parallels Bakhtin's ideas in telling ways. Cohen maintains that Cervantes' text serves as a foundational form for the modern novel insofar as it contains not only all the literary styles, but also the intellectual and spiritual cosmogony of modernity. Cervantes' humour has, for Cohen, an essentially mundane aspect, for it represents the lack of faith the author had in the redemptive power of the Catholic Church (*ARG* 2:119). In addition, upon describing Sancho as the ideal figure of a governor, Cohen also underlines the political facet of *Don Quixote de la Mancha*. Cervantes' novel, then, forms an archive of the documents of love, and incorporates into the novel a dimension to love inaccessible to the epic (*ARG* 2:121). The similarities between Bakhtin's and Cohen's interpretations of Cervantes are easily drawn: both understand the novel to be an example of the modern novel, and contrast it with the epic; both find a level of political signification implicit in its parody of the chivalric code; both see Sancho as a figure that critiques (if not condemns) the official discourses of the age; and both view the novel as a vehicle for an erotic (in the Platonic sense) knowledge of the multiple, heterogeneous experiences that define modernity. Finally, Cohen and Bakhtin privilege love in their aesthetics as an ethical activity equal to artistic expression, for in both activities the individual dedicates herself to a fuller faith and hope oriented toward the creation of a better future (Emerson 221–2).

Likewise, there are telling similarities and discrepancies between Bakhtin's and Lukács's interpretations of *Don Quixote*. As he does with Schlegel's ideas, Bakhtin makes heteroglossic, if not polemical, use of Lukács's thought. Georg Lukács, a loyal member of the Communist Party, participated as a plenary speaker in a debate on the nature of the novel that took place during 1934–5 at the Communist Academy in Moscow. By this time Lukács had largely rejected his *Theory of the Novel*, yet this is his work that exercised the most influence over Bakhtin. Tihanov has established beyond a doubt that Bakhtin knew this early work by Lukács as well as other writings. As we have seen in chapter 3, the young Lukács, under the influence of liberal or socialist thinkers such as Georg Simmel, already attributed devaluation and reification of the individual to the evils of capitalism, and viewed the modernity manifest in the genre of the novel as devoid of values, fragmenting society and leaving the individual without a sense of purpose or community. For this reason he views both Cervantes and Rabelais as engaged in a fight against medieval slavery as well as modern degradation (Tihanov, *The Master and the Slave* 117). Don Quixote provides Lukács with a figure for formulating his notion of the abstract idealist. Like Don Quixote, novelistic protagonists of this type manifest a 'narrow soul.' In short, abstract idealists project their ideals over an indifferent world as they refuse to conform to modern realities. By presenting this novelistic figure of the existential problem of the individual's destiny in the modern world, Lukács distinguishes between the novel as a genre and the epic. The novel reproduces the split between the individual and society that defines modernity for Lukács, for whom the modern individual is condemned to a meaningless life. In contrast, the epic belongs to ancient culture, which Lukács understood as unified. The epic hero does not experience the alienation typical of the novelistic hero's situation, since he is believed to live in complete communion with the forms and values of his society.

The parallels between Bakhtin's and Lukács's notions of the epic and the novel are obvious – what differs between them is their judgment on the genres. For both thinkers, *Don Quixote de la Mancha* occupies a crucial moment in Western history. The epic, seen as monological, is totalizing in its generic sweep. Whereas Lukács expresses regret for the passing of the unified society the epic expresses, Bakhtin judges epic unity in negative terms. In the same way, the novel, seen as dialogical, is heterogeneous. Whereas Lukács considers the heterogeneity represented by the novel to be modern humanity's tragic destiny, Bakthin grants to the genre's plurivocity a critical power and even a greater capacity for mimesis. Both Bakhtin and Lukács reveal a largely unacknowledged debt to Schlegel and Hegel, as they all subsume literary history into a larger historical trajectory. Neither the epic nor the novel is a simple literary genre; to the contrary, they represent a stage in the development of human mentality (Tihanov, *The Master and the Slave* 114; Holquist 73–4). Unlike Hegel and Lukács, who both see in the novel's history the disappearance of the epic and a teleological finality, Bakhtin conceives of a continuous struggle between monologism, including the epic, and dialogism, where the novel resides (Holquist 77). Unlike Lukács, but akin to Cohen, Bakhtin conceives of the novel as a genre oriented toward the future but founded in the present.[9] Therefore, it must remain incomplete and open.

Although Dostoevsky and Rabelais enjoy marquis roles in Bakhtin's novelistics, gracing the titles of two major works, Cervantes plays a role that, in fact, serves to provide continuity and stability to Bakhtin's evolving thinking. Was Bakhtin personally drawn to Cervantes? Certainly not as the great friend or rival that we see in the cases of Unamuno or Ortega. Cervantes is more an inescapable presence for Bakhtin as he negotiates the terrain already charted by Friedrich Schlegel and Hermann Cohen. Bakhtin conceives of language not as an instrument of reason or a unified system of signification, but rather as a product of society and as a producer of society. One of the most innovative aspect of his thought – and one that pertains directly to Cervantes – is the notion of the carnivalesque as an alternative cultural mode that participates in double-voiced discourses such as the polyphonic novel, and that serves as a subversive counterweight to official cultures and discourses. Moreover, Bakhtin situates his notion of polyphony and the novel in an analysis of subjectivity that underlines intersubjective exchange. For Bakhtin, both language and the novel come into being as participants in dialogue between subjects. In this sense, Don Quixote and Sancho Panza stand as the very figures of novelistic dialogism.

8 Revolutions and the Novel

No action can be performed without renouncing something, and he who
performs an action can never possess universality.
  Georg Lukács, 'On the Romantic Philosophy of Life. Novalis' (*SF* 50)

One way to define modernity is as a time of permanent revolution. This
oxymoronic assertion poses the question: how can revolution be permanent? Revolutions work in forward motion, radically severing the
present from the past and redirecting it toward an imagined future.
Revolutions do not go into reverse (although someone of the opposition might find a revolution reactionary), nor do they themselves represent a desired state of social and political affairs that one would wish
to sustain. Revolutions are teleological, aimed toward an ideal future.
According to Hannah Arendt, both the idea of freedom and a desire for
(or an experience of) a new beginning combine in the modern definition of revolution (29). Nonetheless, as demonstrated by Agnes Heller's
logic of modernity, the foundation of modernity on the concept of liberty or freedom, the foundation that does not ground, propels individuals into a state of constant change, hence constant revolution.
According to Heller, the dynamics of modernity depend on the constant negation of previous assertions. The questioning proceeds thus:
'If nothing is taken for granted, everyone can ask why. Why should I
agree to do this and not that? Why should I believe in the truth of this
rather than the truth of that?' (*A Theory of Modernity* 41). Rational systems are deployed to answer these questions; modern revolutions tend
to claim reason on their side, and from reason seek to start society anew.
Rational system, however, can soon become tyrannical.

Perhaps nowhere can this spiral of revolution, the self-fuelling need for change for its own sake, be more clearly seen than in the avant-gardes of elite literature and art. It would not be amiss to speak of our theorists as high modernists, for a belief in the possibility and the inevitability of change underlies their most basic assumptions about history, society, and literature. None of them consider their theories of the novel to be only aesthetic; they intend them to be political. As such, Schlegel makes reference to the French Revolution, and Cohen, Lukács, Unamuno, and Ortega situate their thinking in relation to the social and political upheavals of the first half of the twentieth century. Even the forms they use to imagine and analyse the novel involve revolutions. The Schlegelian arabesque embraces entwining and intricate turns and flourishes as the whole manages to include and contain opposition and struggle. The novel functions as a literary arabesque in which genres mix, ideas contradict each other, and irony abounds. Lukács imagines the novel as occupying the suffocating cleft between the individual and society. Having denied the possibility of reform, only revolution will beckon as a way to break through the narrowing chasm. Cohen opts for reform rather than revolution; his image of the tangential curve of the differential equation, one based on the gradual accumulation of small changes, rejects the possibility of a radical break with the past. The beginning orients the movement toward the future, and the infinitesimals build slowly toward it, but the tragic separation between ideal and actual cannot be undone. Likewise, Ortega prefers reform to revolution. His image of foreshortening offers a way to reformulate images of depth and surface by introducing into them the aspect of perspectives. By imagining a plurality of points of view, one can sidestep the absolute break necessary for revolution. Bakhtin combines multiplicity and future-oriented ethical action in his respective notions of heteroglossia and the self-other relation. Even Unamuno, whose idea of revolution can be generally summed up as obstinate disagreement with all parties, considers the modern tragedy to be the isolated individual.

The notion of an intellectual, rather than a political, revolution stems from Kant's 'Copernican' revolution, by which he claimed to have radically recentred philosophical discourse to the same degree that Copernicus recentred cosmology. In the case of the Copernican revolution, the discovery that the earth revolved around the sun had the effect of removing humanity from the centre of the cosmological order. Mankind was no longer the mediating point, the being situated between the divine and the corporal. The long-term effect of the Copernican revolution was to plant humanity firmly on the ground of the corporal, the here and now. Kant's contribution to this development was to attempt to ground philosophy within the human realm, thus disengaging it from the theological. Recourse to the non-human or the supernatural as bases for philosophical analysis and logical critique were now illegal moves according to Kant's ground rules (so doing, he hoped to save religion from reason). As Copernicus sought to situate the earth in its rightful place in the universe, Kant sought to situate reason within the confines of its existence, namely, the human mind. Moreover, Kant's politics for his time and culture were surprisingly progressive. He advocated for republican causes, and initially sided with the French revolutionaries; he imagined a universal organization of states that would work for peace over war; he encouraged non-sectarian education (van der Linden 11).

Subsequently, Continental philosophy focused on the limits of human knowledge: the nature and possibility of knowledge, the relation of the self to the outside world, and the structure of just societies. Nineteenth-century neo-Kantians tended to be socialists, for they saw in the creation of a just democracy the only means to fulfil the Kantian categorical imperative of treating humans as ends and not means. The desire that analysis be pure, understood as freedom from contamination by mysticism, superstition, and tradition as well as plain old illogic, does not characterize only idealism, but also phenomenology and existentialism. Following the lead of Kant, who displaces the notion of inutility with disinterestedness, Schlegel, Lukács, Cohen, Unamuno, and Ortega y Gasset all attempt to revalue art, in part by presenting it in the modern guise of revolution. To a surprising extent, their notions of modernity, revolution, and art are reactions to Kant. In Ortega's words, 'Copernicus limits himself to substituting one reality for another in the cosmic centre. Kant turns against all reality, throws off his mask of the *maestro*, and announces the dictatorship.'[1] The dictatorship is that of modernity: the founding of thought and culture in doubt, and the rendering of life and humanity to the service of the idea.

How did modernity, dedicated to and founded on the liberation of the individual, devolve into a form of tyranny? Perhaps the life struggles of Schlegel, Lukács, Cohen, Unamuno, Ortega, and Bakhtin can illuminate the dark side of modernity – its tendency to cheapen human life, fracture communities, and create oppressive totalitarian systems based on instrumental reason. Although each sought shelter from modernity in the life of the mind, politics impinged upon them, forcing them to live their ideals – or not live them – in the midst of modernity's messy upheaval. Their responses run the gamut of possible reactions: from Lukács's active involvement in violent Marxist revolution to Ortega's passive impotence before Franco's Fascist regime, we see lived out the dilemma of modernity.

Schlegel: Revolution, Republicanism, and the Novel

The political event of Friedrich Schlegel's day was the French Revolution. The young man's political leanings corresponded to those of his sister, Caroline Bödmer, who had been an active participant in the failed Mainz Revolution, and never gave up her radical support of the French Revolution. In one letter of 1796, Friedrich called his conservative brother August Wilhelm a counter-revolutionary, and in another he boasted of his desire to revel in republican politics (Weiland 21). In this same year, he wrote his essay *Republikanismus*, and soon won from Novalis the epithet of a revolutionary rigorist. The essay in question is a critique of Kant's *On Eternal Peace*, which maintains that necessity leads individuals into society in order to ensure peace. Schlegel considers Kant's position only a minimal step in the historical progression toward freedom and peace, and insists upon the necessity of historical situations propitious to the establishment of peace and freedom (150–9). In the years 1798–1802 – those most important for his theory of the novel – Schlegel finds himself forced by the atheism controversy (in which Fichte lost his university chair) to hide his political views from the prying eyes of the censors. This is the period of his great production of fragments, and one wonders if he adopts this broken, discontinuous form in order to disguise through rupture the totality of his thought, including its political basis. Indeed, Novalis recommended the reading of the Athenaeum Fragments for their revolutionary content (22). Schlegel's political position by the turn of the century reflects his disillusionment *not* with the ideals of the French Revolution but rather with its reality (Peter 144). Such disillusionment appears in Schlegel's reference to revolution as the 'tragic arabesque' of the time (Polheim 96–7).

The young man began to look for the site of revolution in literature, just as he later looked for it in Catholicism.[2] By the same token, revolution becomes a universal metaphor for historical change, and stands in opposition to the classical preference for completion and stasis (Behrens 145). This transformation also takes place at the social level through the process of educating the people (*Bildung*), an attitude toward revolution influenced by Schiller (Mennemeier 38). Schlegel repeatedly refers to republicanism in the fragments of the period 1797–1801, where political reflection coincides with literary. This fragment (Athenaeum Fragment 118) follows almost immediately upon the famous fragment (Athenaeum Fragment 116) that defines Romantic writing as a universal progressive poetry:

> It's not even a subtle but actually a rather coarse titillation of the ego, when all the characters of a novel revolve around a single figure like the planets around the sun. And this central character usually turns out to be the author's own naughty little darling who then becomes the mirror and the flatterer of the delighted reader. Just as a cultivated human being isn't merely an end but also a means both to himself and others, so too in the cultivated literary work all the characters should be both ends and means. The constitution should be republican, but with the proviso that some parts can choose to be active and others passive. (*PF* 32)

If one reads this fragment as Novalis advises, looking for its revolutionary content, the first figure to emerge is the egotistical sun around which the planets revolve, a possible allusion to the French monarchy in which Louis XIV figured himself the sun king. From this metaphor of the absolutist main character emerges a caution for both the reader and the writer. As long as the reader focuses on only one character, the reading will be an egotistical reflection of his own self-image. The others, in the forms of the literary characters, are to be freed from their subjection as mere means for self-glorification. Good writing is to be republican, recognizing that all characters are subjects, and granting them the sovereignty to choose their own activity or inactivity.

A logical problem presents in this formulation, and yet it is the paradox of fiction. The literary characters are not subjects acting according to free will, but rather creations of the author. Neoclassical criticism, which emphasized the sovereignty of the writer, never lost sight of the artificial nature of the novel, and thus consistently viewed literary characters and content as the author's instruments. Typical of this rationalistic understanding of fiction is Johann Jacob Bodmer: 'Don Quixote is, then, nothing other than a symbolic person, through which is fashioned a special and noteworthy trait of the Spanish national character to be acted out before the eyes of the whole world; the author takes into account that for the masses it is often not necessary to go any farther to free a person from a moral fault than to mimic the same foolishness before his eyes.'[3] Don Quixote is Cervantes' means by which to achieve his end of enlightening his compatriots. Such an interpretation of the novel can be found in many eighteenth-century sources, and illustrates how the fictive world of the novel and its characters is subsumed to the author's real-life world (that this was, in fact, the flesh-and-blood Cervantes' intention we do not know). The author employs his characters as means to an end, and that end is to reform the readers of his world. Schlegel explodes the use of the fictive world merely as a means to improve this one by insisting on the paradoxical status of the literary character as subject and the autonomy of the reader.

In his review of Ludwig Tieck's translation of *Don Quixote* (1799), Schlegel summarizes how Cervantes' novel exemplifies this artistic freedom. Firstly, Cervantes is the only modern writer whose prose can be compared to that of Tacitus, Demosthenes, or Plato. The literary significance of the ancients for the young Schlegel is linked closely to his political stance as a republican; indeed, in his *History of Greek and Roman Poetry* (1798), he doubts whether it can be determined which revolution, that of Greek lyric poetry or Hellenic republicanism, came first (*KA* 1:555–6). Poetry is republican discourse in Lyceum Fragment 65: 'Poetry is republican speech: a speech which is its own law and end unto itself, and in which all the parts are free citizens and have the right to vote' (*PF* 8). Turning to the concept of Socratic dialogue, which Schlegel associates with Romantic irony and literature in Lyceum Fragment 26, we see the political overtones of his definition of the novel: 'Novels are the Socratic dialogues of our time. And this free form has become the refuge of common sense in its flight from pedantry' (*PF* 3). Written at the height of Schlegel's revolutionary fervour in 1797, this fragment describes the novel as a popular form in which common sense finds refuge from elitist book learning. But the political significance of this equation between the novel as a genre and Socratic dialogue goes deeper: the great Greek philosopher, to whom Schlegel often refers as Plato's Socrates, establishes a literary form, a sort of republican discourse, in which all are autonomous, free to participate and to abstain. As in a republic, the individuals make up the whole, and are yet individual subjects within the whole.

That this ideal of dialogue informs Schlegel's theory of the novel is underscored by the 'Letter on the Novel' in the *Dialogue on Poetry*. Calling for a theory of the novel that would be a novel, the character Antonio fantasizes: 'The things of the past would live in it in new forms; Dante's sacred shadow would arise from the lower world, Laura would hover heavenly before us, Shakespeare would converse intimately with

Cervantes, and there Sancho would jest with Don Quixote again' (*DP* 103). Dialogue is such an important element of this fantasized theory of the novel that it is not only duplicated but tripled: first, in the dialogue between two great modern authors, Shakespeare and Cervantes; second, in the dialogue between the two great literary characters, Don Quixote and Sancho Panza; and finally, in the dialogue Antonio shares with his friends. The novel is dialogical in a republican sense, that it is to say, it is a literary genre in which different points of view are freely embodied and expressed. Schlegel ends his review of Tieck's translation of *Don Quixote* with this exhortation to his contemporaries: 'Let us forget the popular scribbling of the French and the English, and strive after this model!'[4]

One hears echoes of the revolutionary cry for 'Liberté, egalité et fraternité' in Schlegel's theory of the novel. The concept of equality and fraternity are to be found in his call for a novel that is a dialogue, a stance that explains why he refers to the dialogue between Sancho Panza and Don Quixote as a parody of Socratic dialogue. Socratic dialogue is the basis for what Schlegel terms a philosophical friendship, one in which understanding and misunderstanding alternate. As Schlegel proposes, it is the process of trying to comprehend each other that makes for a philosophical friendship (*KA* 2:164). Certainly the conversation between Don Quixote and Sancho Panza in Cervantes' novel exemplifies a revolutionary exchange, if one focuses on the class differences between the master and his servant. Let us not forget that in part II, chapter 60, Sancho defeats Don Quixote in a physical fight, and declares that he, the peasant, is his own master. In addition, in part II, chapter 71, Don Quixote, calling Sancho friend, releases him from the obligation to disenchant Dulcinea in order that the peasant might look after his own family.

The presence of *liberté* in Schlegel's literary thought is more elusive. It is assumed that the freedom of the Romantic artist is boundless, and constitutes a transposition of aristocratic privilege to the creative class – indeed, this sort of freedom comes close to Schlegel's beliefs in his later years. Nonetheless, the young Friedrich champions a different concept of freedom, in which individual liberty is bound to and limited by the other. Athenaeum Idea 143 summarizes this notion in a nutshell: 'There is no great world but the world of artists. They live nobly, though they still lack a proper sense of decorum. But decorum would develop wherever everybody expressed themselves openly and cheerfully, and felt and grasped the value of others completely' (*PF* 108). This concern for the freedom of the other is not only the basis of art, but also of morality, as Athenaeum Fragment 86 makes clear: 'Real sympathy concerns itself with furthering the freedom of others, not with the satisfaction of animal pleasures' (*PF* 28). Given the young Schlegel's interest in a literature that would address the needs of the whole society, he coined a new meaning for classicism, one that would certainly include *Don Quixote* (Mennemeier 304). Defending Georg Forster's writing for a popular audience, Schlegel insists that freedom consists of expressing the interest of the whole through the individual voice of the author (189).

Nonetheless, Schlegel's republicanism seems at times totalitarian, expressing the absolute will of the cultured (Behrens 152–3). In Athenaeum Fragment 214, immediately before his renowned reference to the French Revolution as a great tendency of the age, the young Romantic expounds on his vision for the future. This republican utopia would be not merely democratic, in the words of Schlegel, but also aristocratic and monarchic in the sense that, through freedom and equality, the educated would prevail over the uneducated and lead them to become part of the whole (*KA* 2:198). This conservative tendency of the young Schlegel's political musings might originate from the very progressive nature of his conceptualization of the self. Romantic thought about reflexivity implies a decentring of the subject since there is no longer a fixed, static position for the self or the other (Behrens 131). By invalidating the legitimacy of sense perception for understanding, Schlegel casts into crisis not only the relation of the self to the outside world, but also the notion of a unified self. The young man counteracts these radical ideas by positing the necessity of God to fill the world of appearances with meaning (Zeuch 92–3). The Romantics reject the notion of an immutable human nature, and indeed of unchanging nature understood through reliable perception, and thus question the Enlightenment notion that human nature, through rational analysis and the institution of means to improve it, might in time be perfected (Behrens 254).

This decentring of the subject leads to a re-evaluation of history as heterogeneous rather than homogeneous (255). Revolution in human history, and perhaps even in human nature, is possible because of historical discontinuity. Revolution, particularly when viewed through the optics of the French Revolution, has two aspects: it is both constructive and destructive. It can provide the opportunity to repair society, art, and the individual (Mennemeier 36), but it also entails inevitable loss and homelessness.[5] Schlegel could offer us a means to understand the relativity of truth beyond nihilism, if the young German Romantic proffers a concept of the absolute that embodies both the search for truth and its relativity through interrelations between error (Bowie 77–9). Here we glimpse once again the figure of the arabesque, with its never-ceasing folds and convolutions, as well as the simultaneously chaotic and systematic creation of the novel.

Friedrich Schlegel, after having converted to Catholicism and adopted a conservative political stance as a supporter of the Hapsburgs, monarchs of the Austro-Hungarian Empire, returned to Cervantes' *Don Quixote* in his *History of Ancient and New Literature* (1812), only to undo his exaltation of this novel as the model for modern writers. He stands by his earlier characterization of the work, noting that '[w]hat I have said on another occasion about poetic works of wit, that the poet in this genre, through a rich bestowal of poetry in the secondary action, in the representation, in the form and speech, must confirm his calling and his right to all liberties that moreover he takes into safekeeping – here it is used fully.'[6] The artistic freedom of the Romantic author is exemplified by Cervantes. Nonetheless, by 1812 Schlegel cautions against using the Spanish author as a model: 'Cervantes' novel has been heedless of its noble internal excellence, and has become a dangerous and error-inducing example of imitation for other nations.'[7] He continues to accuse *Don Quixote* of having inspired unsuccessful attempts to represent reality among the French, English, and German. These would-be imitators are bound to fail because they are of another time and place in which the sort of freedom Cervantes enjoyed, one more benign for literature, is not to be found: 'Real life in Spain was then even more chivalric and Romantic than in any other European land. The very lack of an all too strong, completed bourgeois order, combined with the freer and wilder life in the provinces, managed to be more propitious for poetry.'[8] Schlegel has clearly applied his new idealistic vision of the Middle Ages to Cervantes' *Don Quixote*, with a result that would have seemed sadly ironic to his younger self: he has lost sight of the parody. Cervantes is viewed as a champion of chivalric values – in this belief, the older Schlegel reveals himself to be the forerunner of another modern stream of interpretation of *Don Quixote*. We are confronted with the Cervantes of Gustave Doré, Hollywood, and Broadway, who represents conservative bourgeois values by championing the past rather than the present or the future. In this approach to both Cervantes' novel and the novel as a genre, past freedom is idealized, and present freedom is a dangerous thing.

Lukács: Revolution and Terror

Georg Lukács lived in troubled times when political decisions carried grave consequences. In a sociohistorical context defined by polar splits, first between the opposing camps of the First World War, later between Fascist Europe and Stalin's USSR, and finally between Communist Eastern Europe and capitalist Western Europe, politically engaged intellectuals were faced with a particularly thorny dilemma. Should they devote themselves above all to the work of critical enquiry, submitting even their own political parties and causes to the scrutiny of reason and analysis? Or should they bow before the demands of *Realpolitik*, adopting an uncomfortable orthodoxy in order to shore up the political goals and ideological claims of their group? Lukács was no stranger to this dilemma; to that effect, his legacy continues to trouble both Marxist and non-Marxist scholars. Were his *Blum Theses* of 1928 sufficiently critical of Stalinism, or did he capitulate when he allowed himself to be called to Moscow and silenced? Did he betray the Hungarian Revolution of 1956 when he stepped down from Imre Nagy's cabinet shortly before Russian troops moved in? Did he act tyrannically when he sanctioned the execution of deserters during the Hungarian Revolution of 1919? Our generation of scholars is enamoured of rushing to political judgment on our predecessors, and Lukács has not escaped attention. Some see Lukács's willingness to debate Marxist texts and dogma as a virtue that counterbalances whatever political mistakes he might have made (Sim xix–xxvi); others are not so sure.

The young Lukács as a Hungarian Jew lived a peripheral life in the geographical centre of Europe, caught between Germany and Russia, and thus had an outsider's view of his times (Gil Villegas M. 102). In his essay from 1910, 'Aesthetic Culture,' Lukács toys with the allure of socialism as an antidote to the turn-of-the-century ennui. Revolution attracts the young man as a force that will sweep away the peripheral, the inessential, and the inauthentic, but he rejects it at this point based on the grounds that socialism fails because it requires the soul-breaking submission of the individual to the greater good. 'Tragic singularity' marks the lives of great individuals, and thus, for a bit of promised peace and solace, they betray their own souls by turning away from the engagement of their individual interests in activity toward socialism: 'Anatole France's "conversion" to socialism is just as sad a turning away from life as Friedrich Schlegel's or Clemens Brentano's escapes to the quietism of the only true faith' (376). In other words, the older

Schlegel betrayed Lukács's beloved younger Schlegel by abandoning Romantic revolution for Catholic orthodoxy and Austro-Hungarian imperial politics.[9]

Nonetheless, upon adopting Marxism, Lukács recognized a twelve-year path of progression from his neo-Kantian and Romantic self to communism (*Record of a Life* 63). In his essay 'Bolshevism as an Ethical Problem' (1918), he affirms that '[t]hat ethical idealism which broke all its earthly bonds, and which Kantian-Fichtean thought utilized in its attempt to lift the old world off its hinges – metaphysically – that idealism became a deed in Marxism' (218). In addition, Lukács demonstrates how Schlegel's notion of Romantic poetry as permanent transformation could be transferred to the political realm. In another essay from 1918, 'Conservative and Progressive Idealism,' he observes: 'Ethical idealism is a permanent revolution against what exists, simply because what exists does not measure up to its ethical ideal. And being permanent revolution, absolute revolution, it is capable of defining and correcting the course of true progress that never finds a point of equilibrium' (Löwy, *Georg Lukács* 127).

The outbreak of the First World War in the summer of 1914 marked a turning point for Georg Lukács. His heart-wrenching question, who will save us from Western civilization, would eventually lead him to Marxism (Grauer 67–82; Löwy, *Georg Lukács* 111–12). As Ferenc Fehér explains, for Lukács 'the war was nothing but *concentrated capitalism driven to the extreme*' ('The Last Phase of Romantic Anti-Capitalism' 148). In a fictional dialogue of 1916, Paul Ernst imagines a speaker, presumably Lukács, who argues that modern warfare turns men into servants of machines: 'From these servants one will demand more performance than from earlier warriors; this will be possible only through the subordination of personality to performance in all essentials. The result of the war will be on the one hand a further development of the capitalist economy, on the other, the emergence of a socialism of officials' (Arato and Breines 61). By 1917, Lukács describes the Russian Revolution to Paul Ernst as the first step away from capitalist mechanization and bureaucratization of life toward freedom (Grauer 79). Nonetheless, his difficult search for a justification of violent revolution, a problem that apparently plagued him until 1918, prevented him for years from becoming a Marxist (*Record of a Life* 54). Béla Kún, leader of the Hungarian Communist Party and a close colleague of Lukács at the time, expressed the justification for violence thus: 'Unless we annihilate the counter-revolution, unless we wipe out those who rise up with guns against us, then it will be they who will murder us, massacre the proletariat, and leave us with no future at all' (Löwy, *Georg Lukács* 140).

How many literary critics who dare dream of revolution actually participate in one? After joining the Hungarian Communist Party in 1918, Lukács became a key player in the short-lived Hungarian Revolution of 1919. In March 1919, following the collapse of Károlyi's moderate government, the Social Democratic Party joined with the Hungarian Communist Party to lead what they viewed as a proletarian dictatorship.[10] The intellectual son of a rich banker, Lukács became the Deputy Commisar of Public Education in a government that lasted only 133 days (the Hungarian Soviet Republic fell on 1 August 1919 to Rumanian troops backed by the Allied powers of the First World War). Ironically, the German academic post he had long sought was offered to him simultaneously at the University of Marburg; he turned it down in favour of revolution. During this short and volatile period, Lukács proved himself surprisingly decisive and even cruel, enacting a number of extreme measures. Although he was only deputy commisar, Lukács admitted to wearing down his more moderate boss, Zsigmond Kunfi, in long discussions into the night; on other occasions, he would claim Kunfi was absent, and sign decrees on his behalf. His political aim was to reconstruct Hungarian culture only after eradicating its bourgeois institutions. To that effect, he suspended professors from the university, closed down the Hungarian Academy of Sciences, advocated for censorship, and organized the confiscation of thousands of art objects from private collections for an 'Art for the Masses' exhibition in June 1919.

Insofar as Lukács did not hesitate to undertake reform through force, he became a complete revolutionary. In 'Law and Terror,' he attacked the social democrats of the coalition government as too soft, and labelled parliamentary government cretinism: 'We know and proclaim that the new world order – like all social orders – is founded on force. We also know that capitalism, under the death sentence, will fight back with every means at its disposal' (Kadarkay 213). With these words Lukács advocates for violence as the only means to the end of establishing the communist order. Likewise, he rejected reason; according to his friend Ervin Sinkó, Lukács proclaimed, 'Let's be clear about it: there is no rational tragedy, because all heroism is irrational' (Kadarkay 203). In 'Tactics and Ethics' (1919), Lukács argues that there is no escaping responsibility for the bloodshed that follows necessarily from the historic rise of the proletariat through revolution. Whether capitalist or communist, '[e]veryone ... is therefore obliged to bear the same *individual* responsibility for each and every human being who dies for him in the struggle, as if he himself had killed them all' (*Political Writings* 8). Lukács's desire for heroism led him out of the university lecture halls and commisariat offices into the trenches where he volunteered to serve as the political commisar for the Red Army's fifth division. Jószef Lengel recounted a speech he gave to soldiers in the trenches: 'We must take full responsibility for the blood that is to be shed. We must also provide an opportunity for our blood to be shed … In short, terror and blood-shed are a moral duty, or, more plainly, our virtue' (Kadarkay 222). Lukács did not shirk from what he viewed as his duty when the twelfth Red Army battalion deserted from a battle. In the town square of Porszló on 1 May 1919, he ordered a hasty proceeding that resulted in the death sentence for eight soldiers (one escaped, one was pardoned, and six were executed). Lukács never repented of this act, and recounts it cool-ly as necessary to 'restore order' (*Record of a Life* 65).

What are we to make of the blood Lukács knowingly spilt in the 1919 Hungarian Revolution? How does this brief moment of violent revolu-tion square with his writings, both prior to and after the fact? In 'The Old Culture and the New Culture' (1919), Lukács expressed his dis-satisfaction with the proletariat, who were not ready to accept revolu-tion. When faced with resistance to his ideas, Lukács retreats into a stance of alienation. The similarities between the revolutionary Lukács, philosopher-warrior, and Don Quixote, the alienated knight errant, are obvious.[11] In spite of Lukács's admiration for Dostoevsky's troubled protagonists, it may have been Cervantes' Don Quixote who was his closest alter ego. Even in his later years, the split between individual and society that Don Quixote enacts remains a constant in Lukács's thought about the novel. For example, when writing about the histor-ical novel in 1936–7, he notes that persons living in relation to modern society do not often have a specific aim for individual action, and cites Don Quixote's aim to seek adventure and resuscitate knight errantry as a merely general one (*The Historical Novel* 148). One assumes that if Don Quixote – as seen by Lukács – were to wander into twentieth-century Europe, he would have lent his services to the Marxist cause. Already in 1910, the young Lukács conceives of the heroic individual pursuing his soul's destiny in Quixotic terms: 'For the person of action learns … that his own inner necessities are still necessities; he knows that even if his actions do not result in anything outwardly, they are still necessary. Recognizing that illusions are but illusions can only affect the direction of actions; it only makes one select different paths for realizing the same idea' ('Aesthetic Culture' 375).

Cohen: The Utopics of Revolution

Of the figures herein studied, it is Hermann Cohen whose controversial political stances have resulted in his erasure from memory, even though his misdeeds look tame compared to Lukács's or even Ortega's. The son of a cantor, Cohen was the first Jew to take a university chair in Germany without converting to Christianity, and was opposed to religious assimilation (Novak 267). In retrospect, his German nationalism and his devotion to stalwarts of German culture, such as Kant, have caused a revulsion in large part responsible for his rejection by many Jewish thinkers. Yet Ortega y Gasset, writing in 1915, describes Cohen as the most energetic and courageous intellectual of the time in the fight against imperialism, capitalistic exploitation of labour, and Bismarck's and Kaiser Wilhelm II's triumphalist politics (*Kant, Hegel, Scheler* 129). Nor was independent political activity encouraged in German universities at the time: '[A]ll academic production – particularly that of a progressive socialist such as Cohen – was subject to both informal censorship, largely through the influence of the cultural ministry, and, as an even more pervasive consequence, self-censorship' (Moynahan 39). As a socialist, he represented political perspectives unfavourable to the Prussian bureaucrats who controlled German universities. Moreover, as a Jewish academic, Cohen struggled his entire life against institutional anti-Semitism.

Neo-Kantianism served to give a philosophical foundation to much socialist writing in the last decades of the nineteenth century. Friedrich Albert Lange's socialism had a deep influence on the young Cohen. Lange posited that economic change was not sufficient to improve the workers' lot; in addition to organization in unions, they needed education. At the end of his *History of Materialism and Criticism of its Present Importance* (originally published 1866), Lange writes: 'One thing is certain, that man needs to supplement reality by an ideal world of his own creation, and that the highest and the noblest functions of his mind co-operate in such creations' (3:342). As Cohen summed it up in the introduction to Lange's book of 1898, 'Kant is the true and actual creator of German socialism' (Moynahan 59). Neo-Kantianism provided the intellectual sphere within which to work through the problems of societal reform and improved personal education because '[t]he Kantian tradition put the question "For what may I hope?" on the agenda of modern philosophy' (Mittleman 43).

Cohen, like many neo-Kantian socialists, echoes Marx in his disapproval of the capitalistic notion of value that hides the labour required for the production of goods: 'The worth of a thing is clearly for all modern men the worth of the labour required to produce it.'[12] The philosopher's dry prose becomes vivid as he continues: 'The worker's sweat sticks thus to worth and glues up the flaming sword that separates culture from paradise.'[13] For the neo-Kantian, the damage done by capitalistic reification is not only material, but also cultural, for it limits human value to economic value, and obscures the realm of the ethical. Cohen fumes about the apparent neutrality of the term 'worth,' noting that '[w]orth itself cannot be conceived of independently from monetary worth, if the entire problem of value, in which modern socialism has founded its science, is not simultaneously considered.'[14] Moreover, since the person's work belongs as property to someone else, the ancient condition of the slave merely metamorphoses through medieval serfdom into that of the modern worker (*ERW* 605). Work remains the property of someone else even though the person in other aspects might be free – a condition that causes the isolation of the individual, and denies her ethical agency. From his critique of capitalism, Cohen reformulates Kant's categorical imperative in a manner that becomes 'almost a slogan of neo-Kantian socialism': 'all individuals become colegislators in the social, economic, and political institutions in which they participate' (van der Linden 223, 225).

For Cohen, Hegel's failure to distinguish *Weltgeist* from *Volksgeist* relegates world history to a dialectical movement of concepts, and has thus not considered the state as an ideal, that is to say a heuristic fiction with which to ground ethics. This leads to the political danger of defining the state as an ethnic people: 'With regards to the nation understood as a *Volk*, the identity of the people depends upon circumstantial differences experienced as historical but claimed to be natural.'[15] The naturalistic genealogy of the nation state, which represents community as an organic development, presents the fatherland as proceeding from the people, the clan, the family, and ultimately the couple (*ERW* 240). The nation's family tree obscures its ideological bent by presenting itself as natural, and thus 'naturalizes' racism and ethnocentricity. To the contrary, it falls upon the state to establish a sense of the nation inclusive of all and freed from the poisons of nationalism and racism; in short, the state should set forth an ethical culture (*ERW* 255). After the Nazi regime, such a faith in the state seems particularly wrong-headed on Cohen's part. Nonetheless, we should remember that, as Zygmunt Bauman explains, nineteenth-century European Jews could not acquire the rights pertaining to citizenship without the active intervention of the state (51). Cohen's attempt to ground socialism in the juridical relation between state and individual leads him to posit the state as 'the self-legislating unity of individuals, the ethical foundations of which rest on the science of legal concepts: jurisprudence' (Brandist, 'The Hero at the Bar of Eternity' 210). In this sense, the method of jurisprudence, in which the particulars of actual life are measured and judged against the principle of justice, serves to create the heuristic fiction of the transcendental ethical actor. Socialism becomes the favoured political form because it applies the same law to all groups, and democracy the favoured function because it 'guarantees the equal use of power' (211).

Moreover, even Cohen's rigorous demystification of the scientific method can be understood as a response to a broader social movement in which science and biology were being used to serve political and social aims. As Ernst Cassirer explains, '[f]or Cohen, Kant's system answers the truly fateful question of philosophy in general: the question of the relation between philosophy and science' ('Hermann Cohen and the Renewal of Kantian Philosophy' 95). The Kantian 'revolution of thought' problematizes science and the perception of objects on which science is based (97). By problematizing science and perception, Cohen attacks two forms of dogmatism: the first, a naive faith in science as an objective vehicle of truth; and the second, antirationalistic, impressionistic, and intuitive judgments about people and society from which racism springs (Moynahan 61–2). Cassirer also reveals that Cohen considered his ethics revolutionary insofar as he rejected using historical events and precedent as the basis for determining right or wrong action (101). Moreover, Cohen's notion of infinitesimal calculus as a model for ethical change figures incremental reform rather than abrupt revolution, at the same time that it frees up hope for the future from the concrete histories of a tribe or a people.

Another original insight is Cohen's notion of the relation between the 'I' and the 'Thou,' in which he anticipates Martin Buber and Emmanuel Levinas. Alterity serves as a guiding concept for Cohen's thought, appearing in his logics as well as his ethics and writings on religion. His logic of the origin depends on alterity, for it is nothingness (*Nichts*) that makes possible the identification of the being (*Sein*). His ethics depends on the correlation of the self and the other, in which, importantly, the self does *not* sublate the other, but rather coexists with the other. In Cohen's writings on religion, focusing on the existential rather than the transcendental self, he argues that the self evolves only by serving the other (Munk 251–65). Most importantly for our purposes, Cohen even configures the aesthetic self as fundamentally tied with the other through intersubjective dialogue and tragic catharsis. The enactment of suffering through drama creates fear and compassion in the spectator, who must then ask: 'Who is Hecuba to us?'[16] The exchange between tragic figure and spectator is, for Cohen, action (*Handlung*), that is to say, action that creates a form of unity (*Allheit*) linking them in body and soul. Again, the echoes of Jürgen Habermas's notion of ethical communication and action as *Handlung* clearly resound.

When Cohen attempts to reconcile his critical philosophy with the Jewish religion, the concept of social justice underpins his thought. In a speech given to the Fifth International Congress of Free Christians and Other Religious Liberals (Berlin, 1910), Cohen commended the practice of the Sabbath as a day of rest as the most important contribution of Judaism to the world because '[s]lavery is, at least conceptually, annulled by this institution' ('The Significance of Judaism for the Religious Progress of Humanity' 50). Note, for example, Cohen's praise of the Sabbath as the day of rest and religious education for all in his *Religion of Reason out of the Sources of Judaism*: the Sabbath brings joy into the world and alleviates human suffering because it serves to figure a future when all will have equal opportunities in the workplace and in education (Kaplan 20).

Cohen's socialist and idealist messianism looked terribly naive after the horrors of the First World War and the even greater horrors of the Second World War and the Holocaust. Too often Cohen, who died in 1918, has been interpreted in hindsight as a pseudo-Nazi, but how could he have known of the horrors to come that would take the life of even his own wife, who died in Auschwitz?[17] In his own time and place, Cohen consistently spoke out against abuses of power in the German universities. Moreover, he sought to create a philosophical underpinning for socialist thought that would lead to the abolition of the ills that were to explode in Germany within decades: a racist definition of the state that excluded minority ethnic and religious groups; the capitalist degradation of the worker; and the capitulation of the intellectual class to the powers that be.

More concerning is his early support for the Germans in the First World War, a stance not uncommon among his intellectual peers. Of particular worry to post-Holocaust Jewish readers has been Cohen's tract written during the First World War, 'Germanness and Jewishness,' in which he repeated his assertion that Judaism (along with ancient Greece) roots German culture in its finest, i.e., neoclassical and idealist, manifestations.

No less a scholar than Emil Fackenheim defends Cohen against charges of 'assimilationist cowardice. On the contrary, the publication was an act of Jewish courage, as was proved when the nationalistic critics did not praise him for his German patriotism but rather accused him of Jewish presumptuousness' (45). Cohen's initial pro-Teutonic position has been attributed to a confluence of several historical factors: the paralysis of German politics in 1912 by a conservative umbrella party aiming to stop the German Socialist Party in its tracks; the beginning of a worldwide recession in 1913; and the brief silencing of German anti-Semitism in 1914 when the majority of German Jews expressed support for the war (Schmid, *Ethik als Hermeneutik* 297–9). In a letter to Paul Natorp of 1914, Cohen expressed his hope that the war would have a salutary effect on internal German politics. Nonetheless, by 1916, Cohen, like so many of his fellow intellectuals, was thoroughly disillusioned with the war and hoped for its quick end. By this point he turned to his Jewish heritage for solace, because only religion seemed to offer the true compassion and love for the other necessary to bring about economic, social, and ethical reform.

In retrospect, Cohen's attempt to win a place for Jews and Jewish culture in early twentieth-century German culture could only end in tragedy. It is a tragedy foreshadowed by his philosophy; the ideal can never be achieved fully in this world, for then it would no longer be the ideal. It is doubtful that Cohen identified with the figures of Don Quixote or Cervantes, as the others (Schlegel, Lukács, Unamuno, and Ortega) surely did. Unlike those who were inspired by Cervantes as young men, Cohen approaches *Don Quixote de la Mancha* as a mature, established scholar who has not only won for himself a worldwide reputation as one of the most important philosophers of his time, but has also worked out his own system encompassing logic, ethics, and aesthetics. Cohen merely moulds Cervantes' novel to this system, and focuses on several aspects that correspond to the philosopher's own take on politics and ethical action. Sancho Panza, the man of the people, represents the socialist hope for democracy by and for all the people. His wisdom as a ruler embodies this future goal. Don Quixote serves to parody epic heroism, and in this works a strong critique of the cult of national heroism that Cohen sees menacing modern Europe. Finally, Don Quixote's love for Dulcinea figures Cohen's belief in the necessity to bring ideal love for the other as a true Thou into actuality through literature. Perhaps Cohen did not pay enough attention to the beatings Don Quixote receives in return for his efforts.

Unamuno: A Life Framed by Revolutions

To an uncanny degree, Miguel de Unamuno's life and death (1864–1936) were defined by revolution and civil war. As he would muse upon commemorating the First Spanish Republic, he was born on 29 September 1864, the day that Marx and Engels signed the International Pact (Mezquita 149). As he remembered in 1930, while campaigning for the institution of the Second Spanish Republic, the defining moment of his boyhood and the origin of his civil consciousness was the bombardment of Bilbao by forces loyal to Carlos de Borbón on 21 February 1874 (94). His death on 31 December 1936, only weeks after his final public act – the denunciation of Franco's uprising during an official commemoration of the Día de la Raza (12 October) – brought to a painful close his lifelong struggle for the liberalization of Spain. Indeed, during the long Fascist dictatorship to follow, Unamuno's timely protest and his – unhappily – timely death took on mythical significance as the philosopher who claimed to speak for Spain's destiny seemed doomed to share in its death.

None of the other thinkers covered in this book identified themselves with Don Quixote so completely as Unamuno. At each turning point in his eventful life, he appeared on the public stage wearing the mask of the mad knight errant. His friend, the poet Antonio Machado, described him as Quixotic, the strong Basque wearing the grotesque armour of the good Manchegan (Cerezo Galán, *Máscaras de lo trágico* 313). For Unamuno, Don Quixote was a solitary figure who fought for individual experience against the collective, and thus he, like Don Quixote, would provide a model for individual integrity and freedom of conscience to the Spanish people (Roberts 169). The identification with Don Quixote strengthened during Unamuno's exile in the 1920s, and while in Fuerteventura in the Canary Islands, Unamuno proposed a never-written book, *Don Quijote en Fuerteventura* (Urrutia Jordana 60, 119). Moreover, the critique of the Primo de Rivera dictatorship that landed him in exile was, for Unamuno, the realization of his Quixotic *imitatio* (Zubizarreta 43–4). Nevertheless, shortly before his death in 1936, when he already saw how his own thought was appropriated in the cultural battles leading to the Civil War, he renounced his identification with Don Quixote: 'They named me the Knight of the Sad Countenance, trying to honour me with that courtesy. I lament that I cannot accept it. In order to emulate Don Quixote, one must comply with the essential trait of his person, one must never succeed. I have been successful.'[18]

In keeping with his notion of the agonistic intellectual, Unamuno's political stance was that of opposition to whichever governor, government, or ideology was predominant in any given moment. Tendencies that characterize his lifelong political views include antimilitarism, his view of the Spanish Catholic Church as an illiberal institution, the need for secular education, and the defence of individual liberty and freethinking against the conformist thought typical of herd mentality (*PP* 620; Cerezo Galán, *El mal del siglo* 111; Marichal 174). As such, his views combine liberalism, socialism, and republicanism in variable degrees according to the given situation. Unamuno's version of liberalism constitutes a way of life, in which the individual enjoys freedom of conscience but also recognizes the responsibility of working in community with other free individuals (Ouimette, *Los intelectuales españoles* 1:94). Indeed, Unamuno's repeated critiques of Spain's parliament hinge upon his taking seriously the etymology of the word; the 'parlamento' should be a place of speaking dialogues, and yet in Spain it too often housed monologues (*PP* 474). Unamuno 'coined the term "alterutrality" (*alterutralidad*) as against neutrality to qualify his position as being, not so much detached from any side, but with one side and another, as they appealed to him or repelled him' (Nozick 115–16).

After he was removed in 1914 from the rectorship of the University of Salamanca at the orders of the Liberal prime minister, Romanones, (probably due to a personal conflict and his promotion of agrarian reform), Unamuno resorted to the press as his lectern. Between 1914 and 1924, he published articles for magazines and newspapers at the rate of one every two or three days, and thus became the most prominent voice in the Spanish press (Roberts 189). He also knew how to spin controversy within Spain to better his own reputation in foreign media. In 1920 he was sentenced to sixteen years in prison for speaking out against King Alfonso XIII, whom he considered personally responsible for promoting destructive factionalism (the sentence was never served). Upon his exile in 1924, he became a figure galvanizing the cause of free press and freedom of expression. International intellectuals who championed Unamuno included H.G. Wells and Gabriele d'Annunzio (Gullón, *Autobiografías de Unamuno* 268), and Spanish figures who lamented publicly or privately his absence included Américo Castro, Antonio Machado, Gregorio Marañón, and Ramón del Valle-Inclán (Zubizarreta 195). Upon his return to Spain on 9 February 1930, he declaimed the motto *Dios, Patria y Ley* ('God, Country, and Law') instead of the traditionalist *Dios, Patria y Rey* ('God, Country, and King'; Nozick

111). Unamuno had the honour of proclaiming the establishment of the Second Republic from the balcony of the Salamanca courthouse, and became an elected deputy in Parliament. Fiercely opposed to party orthodoxy and firmly committed to an agonistic understanding of politics, Unamuno quickly became disillusioned (Roberts 227–9). When the Second Republic enacted the Law of the Defence of the Republic, a de facto institution for censorship, Unamuno reacted with the same defiance and horror that earlier governmental censorship had provoked in him.

By presenting himself as a figure of and for Spain, Unamuno made himself a spectacle for his compatriots (Zambrano 104). Among his many roles was that of heretic. As a self-proclaimed political heretic, he could not subscribe to party discipline, and even stated that he was his own party (Mezquita 23). He died labelled a religious heretic by Franco's Dirección de Prensa (Trapiello 45), and both *The Tragic Sentiment of Life* and *The Agony of Christianity* ended up on the index of books banned by the Spanish Catholic Church (Luby 17). He had a special regard for famous Spanish heretics such as Miguel Servet, and liked to believe himself descended from a Juan de Unamuno, burned at the stake in 1442 (Mezquita 244). In his own version of Spanish history, heresy was as essential as orthodoxy, and the Reformation stood as the counterpart to the Counter-Reformation. In a speech on the destiny of Spain that he gave to the Colegio de España in Paris in 1935, he likened the relation between heterodoxy and orthodoxy to a surface that appears concave or convex according to the viewer's perspective: 'To those who looked at the Reformation from within the Catholic Church it seemed concave, and to the reformers, the Protestants, the Counter-Reformations seemed convex. But they were the same, by dialectical necessity.'[19] To preach liberty of thought and speech was, for Unamuno, to call for a return to what he considered one of Spain's formative values.

Unamuno even claims that it is spiritual civil war within Spain that defines its *intrahistoria*, for from this civil war sprang subsequent events such as the establishment of the Cortes de Cádiz and the Latin American wars of independence. The phrase 'civil war' peppers his writings, and generally refers to a civil war as precisely civil: concerned with ideas and spiritual issues, held between brothers without physical violence through discourse, and at its deepest level occurring within the self. As such, civil war could take place within the individual or within the body of the nation, and could even contribute to the 'civilization' of a nation (*PP* 568). For example, when Unamuno called for Spaniards to follow Don Quixote in 1905, it was a challenge to both the conservative institutions of the Church and the military and the liberal Europeanizers (Cerezo Galán, *Máscaras de lo trágico* 318–26). It is in the vein of internal self-scrutiny and open dissent that Unamuno could claim that his own politics were those he proclaimed in *The Life of Don Quixote and Sancho* (*PP* 575). In a conference given at King's College, Oxford, in February 1936, Unamuno diagnoses Spain's problem as a lack of internal, spiritual revolution: 'Spain … lives in a permanent state of civil war because the Spaniard shies away from the true and holy civil war, that which each one wages – or should wage – within himself with his other "I".'[20] Here Unamuno succinctly stated what one could call his politics of the civil war: the difference between political, external civil war and spiritual, internal civil war; his political calling to stir up the consciences of his countrymen; the use of paradox to unsettle thought; and his ultimate failure.

Even before 1936, actual political revolutions were problematic for Unamuno. His childhood experience of the siege and bombing of Bilbao in the final Carlist war (December 1873–May 1874) served as an ambiguous touchstone in his personal story and his personal history of Spain. On the one hand, it has been argued that his notion of the ethical civil war sprang from the sublimation of the childhood trauma, and created a dangerously romanticized notion of civil struggle (Azaola 25–31). On the other hand, Unamuno consistently expressed horror at physical violence and war, and thus the term 'revolution' could be either negative or positive. Unamuno wrote of the necessity of agrarian reform in 1914 as a form of revolution, but with rhetorical questions that indicate that he applied his convex/concave image to the matter. Referring to possible acts of violence against large landowners, he asks whether these are brutal and revolutionary, or are the acts of the landowners themselves not just as revolutionary (*PP* 454). His criticism of the Bolshevik Revolution, in which he follows the argument of Bertrand Russell, is that it is not a Marxist revolution because it is being carried out by utopian men, rather than the material circumstances (*PP* 584). As he muses in the 1930s, men make revolution in order to make themselves and gain power. But revolution is more than a deed controlled by human beings, and thus sweeps up the individuals in its own wake: 'A revolution is never a deed; a revolution is always an unending project. Because a revolution revolves around itself, it revolts against itself. It is the mythical serpent that devours itself, chewing itself by the tail.'[21] Likewise, Unamuno refers to revolution as a whirlwind sweeping up its own, the revolutionaries (*PP* 734).

The metaphors of the whirlwind or the snake eating its own tail correspond tragically to the events of 1936 leading up to Unamuno's death. In a speech given to the Madrid Ateneo in November of 1932, Unamuno already expressed his fear at the growing violence unleashed during the Second Republic. Fearing a sort of Jacobin backlash, he criticized the confiscation of Jesuit properties, arguing that, according to revolutionary logic, cadavers have no heirs (Mezquita 297). In a speech from December 1932, he asserts that the supposed novelties of revolution are anything but new, for all are involved in revolution from birth to death (291). Here he equates Marxism and Fascism as tyrannical regimes opposed to individual liberty, and thus establishes the thrust of his subsequent political discourse. By 1935, he is highly critical of Spain's youth, and comments that they seem to be using his words in ways that render them unrecognizable to him (365). Having always identified himself as a teacher, this alienation from the youth of Spain must have been particularly painful, and probably contributed to his controversial attendance at a Falange youth rally in 1935 (Cerezo Galán, *Máscaras de lo trágico* 822–4). When Franco's uprising began in the summer of 1936, Unamuno first welcomed it as a means to save Spain's civilization. It is probable that he viewed the military uprising in the light of nineteenth-century Spanish coup d'etats, which had been essentially bloodless.

The climax of this tragedy takes place on 12 October 1936, the Día de la Raza, when a public act was held at the University of Salamanca attended by Franco's wife and other Fascist dignitaries. By this time Unamuno had received news of the arrest and assassination of friends and colleagues by the Fascist forces. As the rector of the university, Unamuno apparently did not intend to speak. He was moved to do so as he listened to the violent, overblown rhetoric directed by the professor Francisco Maldonado against the Catalans and Basques (Rudd 297), and began to write notes on the back of a handwritten letter pleading for help from the wife of his soon-to-be-murdered friend, the Protestant minister Atiliano Coco (C. Rojas 72–3). Maldonado was followed by General Millán Astray, who described Catalonia and the Basque country as cancers requiring extirpation, and called for the death of all socialists, republicans, and communists. At some point the cries '¡Viva la muerte!' and '¡Arriba España!' rang through the auditorium.

Unamuno's heroic rebuttal before a room full of enraged Fascists was widely reported in the international press and has become the stuff of myth. Several versions of his speech exist, but they all contain the phrase 'to conquer is not to convince' (*vencer no es convencer*). By all accounts,

Unamuno confronts the distortion of his own thought. In one account, Unamuno calls the events an uncivil war rather than a civil one; in another, recounting his own use of paradoxes, he calls the paradox '¡*Viva la muerte*!' perverted and repelling (C. Rojas 73–8). After a moment of pandemonium and then silence, he was led from the room by Franco's wife, Carmen Polo, to prevent violence. That night he was snubbed and insulted at the casino by acquaintances and friends, and two days later he was removed from the rectorship of Salamanca as well as the city council. In 2006, a motion to reinstate Unamuno to city council in honour of the seventieth anniversary of his death was defeated.

In the short time remaining before his death on 31 December, Unamuno lived as a broken man, vanquished in part by his own mythology. In a letter to a friend, he attributed his own initial support of Franco to his innocence and instability (Azaola 108). In a private notebook, he tried to make sense of what had happened to himself and to Spain. The Civil War represented Spain turning against itself, and caused him to rethink his own work (Unamuno, *Resentimiento trágico de la vida* 31). Remembering his political battles with Alfonso XIII, Primo de Rivera, and even the leaders of Second Republic, he remarked that he was not the one who had changed, but rather the others (47). He labelled Bolshevism and Fascism the two forms, one concave and one convex, of the same collective mental illness (51), plus he interpreted the conflict between Fascists and Marxists as the outcome of the Copernican revolution, noting that both suffered from the desperation caused by their lack of belief (55). A manifesto written between 23 October and 21 November ends with the following observation: 'It would be a sad thing to want to replace the barbarous, anti-civil, and inhumane Bolshevist regime with a barbarous, anti-civil, and inhumane regime of totalitarian servitude. Neither the one or the other, for, ultimately, they are the same.'[22] A letter addressed by Unamuno to a 'socialist of good faith' was published posthumously in Caracas. Therein Unamuno took responsibility for his country's collapse into civil war: 'And I, who believed I was working for the health of my country, also bear responsibility for this catastrophe. I was one of those who wanted to save the human race without really knowing mankind.'[23] Upon his death, members of the Fascist Falange carried Unamuno's coffin to the cemetery, and Franco's propagandists began reworking his image into one of their own (Urrutia Jordana 14).

On 12 October 1936, Unamuno turned for what seems to be the first time in his life towards Cervantes, not Don Quixote, as a model. An unnamed Salamancan journalist described Unamuno in this moment as grimacing with contempt beneath his 'Quixotic' beard (Rudd 299). Facing the General Millán Astray, whom the same journalist described as emaciated and mutilated, Unamuno called him a war cripple that would reproduce Spain in his own image (C. Rojas 77). He then compared him to Cervantes, also crippled by war, but who 'was a man – not a Superman – virile and complete in spite of his mutilations.' Millán, not given the 'superiority of spirit' seen in Cervantes, would only 'find comfort watching the number of cripples around him grow.'[24] In all his lifetime of praising Don Quixote, it is now that Unamuno speaks his greatest praise of his rival, Cervantes, who as a man – and not a heroic, Nietzchean superman – refrained from inflicting his wound on others. An entire vision exalting the individual will crumbles, and the General, overcome with fury at Unamuno's insurrection, cries, '¡Muera la inteligencia!' (Rudd 301).

Ortega y Gasset: The Critical Revolution

To write of Ortega's politics is deeply problematic. Ortega's political life and thought exemplifies in an almost eerie manner his philosophical principle that 'I am I and my circumstances.' In addition to serving briefly in the Republican parliament, he lectured widely to lay audiences on political and philosophical themes, and published opinion pieces on current events in Spanish periodicals at an astounding rate; fully one-third of his completed works (numbering a million words) deal with politics (Marichal 179). Like Unamuno, Ortega understood that the Spanish intellectual must be involved in politics, and that the most effective political action open to the intellectual was to educate the country. He founded Espasa-Calpe, the first publishing house in Spain devoted to the translation and publication of major literary and intellectual works in well-edited and financially affordable editions widely accessible to an expanding reading public (which to this day remains a major publishing house in the Spanish language). He also founded the *Revista de Occidente*, the first major academic periodical in which cutting-edge international thinkers were introduced to the Hispanic world (also to this day a premier academic journal in the Spanish language). Through the publishing house division of the *Revista de Occidente*, he was responsible for introducing many of Spain's avant-garde poets and novelists, especially those from the Generation of 1927. In addition, he periodically gave lectures to diverse publics on contemporary philosophy as well as serving as a professor at the University of Madrid until his exile in 1936. In spite of the disappointment he aroused in contemporaries for his perceived failure to stand up to Franco, Ortega's death in 1955 was a galvanizing experience for many students, and has been linked to the student demonstrations of 1956, the first overt expression of resistance to Franco's regime in almost twenty years. Ortega's works were never banned, and thus for two generations of university students Ortega's was one of the few critical voices available to them.[25]

For Ortega, Spain is the problem of *Don Quixote de la Mancha*, and the crux of the problem of Spain is the nature of modernity, or, more precisely, the absence of modernity within its borders. For Ortega, liberalism and conservatism as understood within Spain are alike insofar as they both spring from a Spanish aversion to modernity. And yet, the most salient aspect of Cervantes' novel for Ortega is its essential ambiguity. Nowhere does Cervantes clarify whether his text is built on a joke, and if so, what the butt of the joke is. Nor does he explain what it is to joke, or if joking is itself perforce only negation: 'Far away and alone in the open plains of La Mancha, the long figure of Don Quixote doubles in on itself like a question mark; it is as a guardian of the Spanish secret, the ambiguity of Spanish culture.'[26] The image of Cervantes' crazed protagonist as Spain's question mark most fully expresses Ortega's own struggle to understand his and his nation's destiny. If Don Quixote's heroism is completely foolish, then what of Spain's identity as a nation of individuals possessed and driven by the force of pure will? Are there grounds for vindicating Don Quixote's will for adventure and heroism? Are there grounds for vindicating Spain? Cervantes himself, according to Ortega, offers no clues for the interpretation of his text, but perhaps that is his greatest gift. Instead, in Ortega's imagery Cervantes soars as the swallow that, according to legend, builds a nest during the calm days of stormy times as a sign of new life and hope.[27]

Ortega's influence in contemporary democratic Spain can be linked to two factors: his drive to include Spain within Europe as a liberal democracy, and his understanding of *convivencia*, in which separate entities (be they objects, persons, or ideas) coexist without threatening each other's integrity. One critic even suggests that we can only understand Ortega's notion of liberal democracy by seeing it as *convivencia* (Flórez Miguel 132). In contrast to the combative image of the relation between self and the exterior world, Ortega strove to offer a more pacific image for social relations. In his work *Invertebrate Spain* (1921), Ortega articulates the political implications of *convivencia* by contrasting it with particularism (*particularismo*), the malady infecting the Spain of his time (*OC* 3:56–71). Whereas *convivencia* links disparate groups through a shared purpose, *particularismo* prevents different groups from feeling a part of the nation, and leads to a lack of understanding of the rest. *Convivencia*, understood as the juxtaposition of the distinct into an overarching whole, provides an apt concept for a reformist view of Spain as composed of separate but unified elements.

The concept of *convivencia* is most famously associated with Ortega's colleague Américo Castro, who reformulated Spanish national historiography according to a lost period of *convivencia* between Christians, Jews, and Muslims in the Middle Ages. For Castro, Cervantes' *Don Quixote* contains traces remaining from this period, and reflects the spiritual, economic, and intellectual impoverishment that Spain suffered upon expelling its Jewish and Muslim populations (*Cervantes y los casticismos españoles* 17–143). The political connotations of Castro's thought are obvious: once Ferdinand and Isabel, the so-called Catholic monarchs, expelled the Jews and defeated the Moorish Kingdom of Granada, Spain was doomed to decline because it lost the intellectual vitality and economic importance provided by the Hebrew and Islamic sectors of its culture. Two important pieces of the Spanish cultural mosaic were missing, and indeed one could aptly apply Ortega's metaphor to the situation of Spain after 1492: 'If from a mosaic we tear one of its pieces, its profile remains for us in the form of a hole, limited by the surrounding pieces' (*MQ* 77).[28] Not only have Castro's ideas (which were vilified by the official discourse of Franco's Spain) served to enliven the study of Spain's history and culture by reintroducing the issue of medieval Iberia's cultural and religious diversity, they have also contributed to contemporary debates about Spanish identity and nationhood.

Ortega clearly understood his own time as one of flux and political change, and wrote throughout his lengthy career about the problems of crisis and revolution. Modernity was for him already long gone; he associated it with the failures of the nineteenth century. Perhaps his description of the change that took place throughout Europe in Cervantes' times serves to reflect his sense of his own time, for he dates a sense of uneasiness and dissatisfaction with life to around 1560 (*OC* 1:549). In *The Twilight of Revolution*, Ortega postulates a three-stage historical development typical of Europe from 1500 on, but which is also present in other societies. First, traditionalism based on group values and identity prevails. As the individual begins to feel himself or herself separate from the group, rationalism, understood as freedom from social considerations and received wisdom, begins to flourish. Modernity, for

Ortega, begins with Descartes's rationalism, in which 'pure reason' rather than life serves as the founding principle for thought. This results in the creation of a modern mentality that disdains the spontaneous and direct in favour of rational constructions (*El tema de nuestro tiempo* 26). The modern individual despises historical political institutions insofar as they do not conform to pure reason. By the same token, the modern philosopher or intellectual lives behind the scenes of revolution, making it possible (Ouimette, *Los intelectuales españoles* 2:176).

Although the young Ortega expressed a certain longing for revolutionary change understood through neo-Kantianism as progression toward the ideal ethics (Elorza 36, 48–9), he grew ever more disenchanted with the concept of revolution. By the 1920s, Ortega maintains that the imperative to turn away from the past should not take the form of a revolution. Ortega would pepper his lectures on revolution with Cohen's quip that revolutions were periods of ethical experimentation (López Frías 90). Even more damning is the way modern revolutions subject the individual to principles by putting life at the service of ideas (*El tema de nuestro tiempo* 90). Utopic thinking leads to the imposition of a new social order obeying abstract laws; when this fails, as it inevitably does, a counter-revolution takes place. But both revolution and counter-revolution depend on rationalism. The final stage of historical evolution is from that of the revolutionary to the disillusioned soul who has lost faith in reason and tradition. According to Ortega in the 1920s, the transition to the stage of disillusionment had already begun in the Mediterranean, and would progress gradually into northern Europe (*El tema de nuestro tiempo* 95). Nonetheless, Ortega held out hope for the historical transition from modernity in the form of a sort of United States of Europe (Graham, *Theory of History in Ortega y Gasset* 287).

Ortega's politics, particularly during the Spanish Civil War and the subsequent Franco era, have been an issue of much debate in post-Franco Spain. For the philosopher, despite his political involvement in Spanish socialism as a young man, the politics of democracy were always somewhat troublesome, although democracy itself represented the only viable political system at the moment (Dobson 65–8). Like Unamuno, he avoided political affiliation with parties and would not saddle himself with the strictures of party discipline. Already in his twenties Ortega expressed distaste for both the German and the Spanish masses, a visceral reaction that would later be transformed into his well-known critique of modern Spanish, and ultimately European culture, expressed in *Invertebrate Spain* (1921).[29] Like Cohen, Ortega experienced German *Volkskultur* as an artificial, debased form of popular culture that forged a sense of national identity based on alienation and exclusion of minorities. His book *The Rebellion of the Masses* has been widely misread as an elitist attack on the lower classes, yet he understands the mass-man not as the prole or the redneck, but rather as the member of any group who does not choose or desire to rise above social norms and engage his own freedom (Ouimette, *Los intelectuales españoles* 2:209). The interest of the man of the masses is to create stasis and stifle reform. His fear of mass action tempered his support for the Second Republic, and he quickly resigned from the Spanish parliament. In response to anticlerical violence in May 1931, Ortega published a condemnation of the violence written by the Group at the Service of the Republic (Agrupación al Servicio de la República), of which he was a founding member. According to Ortega, too many millions of Spaniards had voted for the Republic for it to be endangered by the chaotic, theatrical actions of a few (Zamora Bonilla 330).

Although he participated in the Republic and fled Spain after Franco's triumph, Ortega had ties to Franco's movement that have tainted his political legacy. Madrid in the summer of 1936 descended into violent chaos, with extremist bands from the left engaging in violent street attacks. In June of that year, Ortega's son, Miguel, was shot at in Madrid, apparently for being of the upper class as evidenced by his attire in a jacket and tie (Dobson 34). Although Ortega fled to France, his two sons joined Franco's army, one serving as a medic and the other as a soldier (Morán 57–8). By this time Ortega hoped for Franco's victory in the ensuing Civil War. Ortega spent the next ten years in exile, much of it in Argentina and Portugal, before returning to Spain on 8 August 1945. After fleeing Spain in 1936, the philosopher criticized Spanish communists for having forced him and other intellectuals to sign public statements of support for their cause. This, coupled with his return to Spain in 1945 in an ill-fated attempt to reinsert himself into his home country's cultural life, has occasioned harsh criticism from certain leftist corners that continues to this day.[30] Moreover, the Falangist leader José Antonio Primo de Rivera seems to have been inspired in his nationalism in part by Ortega's *Invertebrate Spain,* although Dobson successfully shows the limitations of arguing from this fact that Ortega would have been a Fascist thinker. *The Rebellion of the Masses* contains a succinct statement of the mature Ortega's political beliefs, all of which distinguish his politics from Fascism: 'a defence of the achievements of liberal democracy …; an attack on the "mass-man"; an attack on excessive state power, and an implicit favouring of individualism' (Dobson 102).

If one were to look for a defence of Ortega's return to Franco's Spain in his own thought, it could be found in his equation of political with pedagogical action. To return to Spain to teach, even during Franco's regime, was perhaps Ortega's attempt to continue his own political agenda of modernizing the country through philosophy. According to his brother Eduardo's account (who served in the Madrid city government during the Republic as a member of the socialist party and was a close friend of Unamuno), Ortega believed that the end of the Second World War would provide Spain an opportunity to normalize, and that he himself could contribute to that process (Abellán 149). Nonetheless, all biographers agree that Ortega had very little, if any, influence in the last decade of his life (1945–55) within Spain. He never returned to teach at the University of Madrid, although he might have received a pension corresponding to his tenured chair of metaphysics, which had been turned over to an Integrist Catholic.[31] His attempt to found an institute of humanities failed, and he was prevented from starting up again the *Revista de Occidente* – an order that might have proceeded directly from Franco (Ouimette, *José Ortega y Gasset* 34). Depression and ill health plagued him, and Ortega repeatedly expressed his dissatisfaction with Franco's Spain and his sense of alienation in letters to friends. His silence in these years has angered many Spaniards, and continues to cause debate within the nation. Of late, Jordi Gracia has defended Ortega's silence as an implicit recognition that rational discourse in Franco's Spain was impossible (192).

Perhaps as a function of Ortega's intellectual and political impotence, his image became fodder for political propaganda. On the one hand, his thought was routinely castigated as atheistic and anti-Catholic by members of the Integrist right who even suggested that his books be banned (Abellán 232–5). On the other hand, certain persons, including his own student Julián Marías, claimed that Ortega's presence in Spain demonstrated the nation's cultural health. Ortega replied with anger and exasperation to Marías that he had *tried* to be in Spain, but that that attempt had failed when Marías published such a false assertion (Abellán 172). Even Ortega's death provided grist for the propaganda mill. There are extant two versions of orders sent from the government concerning how newspapers should cover the philosopher's death; among other details, it would be necessary to mention his political and religious 'errors' and avoid calling him *maestro*.[32] Having defined himself as *acatólico* – acatholic – throughout his life, it would have provided a major propaganda coup for Franco and the Integrist Spanish Catholic church if he would have converted on his deathbed. His wife, a practising Catholic, called a priest, Félix García, to his bedside to perform absolution. García claimed upon Ortega's death in 1955, and repeated the claim in 1975, that the philosopher had converted on his deathbed. Nonetheless, Ortega's children responded repeatedly that their father had remained resolutely 'acatholic' at least until the last moments when he began to lose lucidity. Witnesses of his death reported that his final words expressed consternation and anxiety about his growing confusion (Abellán 211–17).

Like Schlegel, Lukács, Cohen, and Unamuno, Ortega's life experiences changed his political positions through time. Seen from the twenty-first century, his life seems tragic, as he succumbed in the last decade of his life to the problems he had diagnosed in his youth and maturity: the malaise of the alienated Spanish intellectual, and the passivity of the disillusioned soul living after the epoch of revolutions. Certainly his support for Franco during the Civil War and his failure in 1945–55 to oppose the regime actively, despite his own disgruntlement, are historical facts that cannot be denied. But to what extent does a thinker's historical legacy depend on the influence of his thought rather than the efficacy and correctness of his actions? Ortega glimpsed and worked toward possibilities for Spain that have come to pass in the three decades since Franco's death: democracy, albeit within a parliamentary monarchy; complete participation in the European Union; and an increasingly vibrant academic community. Should Ortega be judged by the same criterion as Cervantes – that is to say, by his writing? To what extent is Ortega, like Don Quixote, a figure for the cipher that was twentieth-century Spain?

Bakhtin: Writing from within a Revolution

Scholars turn to metaphor when trying to explain the difficulties inherent in Bakhtin's life for good reason. Trying to 'capture' Bakhtin is like trying to catch a fish barehanded. Just when you think you've got him, he wriggles right out of your hands. The slipperiness of Bakhtin is, in large part, due to the difficult circumstances under which he worked as a heterodox thinker in the USSR, but one also wonders whether he was by nature a trickster. To this day, key elements of his biography remain obscure.[33] The fact that he actively misrepresented himself (for example, he did not attend university in Saint Petersburg nor did he have aristocratic roots) renders suspect the testimony of those who knew him and were convinced by the man's own legend-making (Brandist and Shepherd 9). He appropriated events from the life of his brother, Nicolai, and claimed falsely that he, like his friend Matvei Isaevich Kagan, had studied in Marburg (Hirschkop, *Mikhail Bakhtin* 142). Apparently, he told his friend Kagan, who was complaining of academic 'adventurists,' that they too had no choice but to be the same (Poole, 'From Phenomenology to Dialogue' 124).

What becomes clear upon comparing Bakhtin to Ortega and Unamuno, for example, is the profound opacity of his life. Unlike the Spanish intellectuals, who lived in the public sphere and whose political opinions were actively sought and published on an almost weekly basis, Bakhtin lived in the shadows of Soviet culture. Without a free press or a public sphere, the publication of dissident ideas took place in the quiet of parlours, where Bakhtin gave private lectures, or in closely guarded manuscripts, that might or might not have been read by a few trusted friends. Double-voicing seems as much a strategy for dissident communication in a totalitarian state as a linguistic or philosophical principle. Revolution as a word scarcely enters his writing, except for the mention of Dostoevsky's minor Copernican revolution in the novel. Perhaps that is apt, for Bakhtin's only recorded memory of the Revolution of 1917 was going to the library when the heat was turned on (Hirschkop, *Mikhail Bakhtin* 145). Even in his understanding of the resistant qualities of the carnivalesque, he describes revolt rather than revolution (Pechey 28). There is no system to this resistance of the powerless, and revolution, understood in either its Enlightenment or Marxist manifestations, is nothing if not system: systematic destruction and systematic reconstruction.

There is no doubt that Bakhtin led a life on the margins of Soviet academic and cultural life, in large part because he would not toe the party line. Although one can make an argument that he was sympathetic to certain aspects of Marxist thought, it is impossible to present him as an orthodox Soviet Marxist. Several key and undisputed events of his life flatly contradict such a possibility: his early interest in Kant and neo-Kantianism; his arrest and exile in 1929 under accusations of participating in Russian Orthodox circles; and his unsuccessful bid to receive the degree of Doctor of Philological Sciences. He suffered great physical pain and deprivation as a result of his marginalization. The man who theorized the carnivalesque lower body, dedicated to the joys of eating and regeneration, was no stranger to hunger. According to Valerii Yakovlevich Kirpotin, the Deputy Director of the Institute of World Literature at the time, Bakhtin sought to defend his Rabelais work in order to receive more food coupons. He reportedly pleaded with Kirpotin, "'I need a higher degree so as to get ration coupons,'" and "'If the dissertation doesn't get through, then I won't get any coupons'" (Pan'kov 44). Nor was he a stranger to physical deformity and bodily imperfection. After years of suffering from osteomyelitis, a leg was amputated in 1938, so that he required the use of crutches for the rest of his life (Clark and Holquist 261).

Given that the influence of Kantian and neo-Kantian philosophy on Bakhtin has been widely discussed as of late, there remains no doubt that traces of Kant's and Cohen's thinking underlie several key concepts in Bakhtin's novelistics. Lenin had characterized Kant as an idealist thinker, and thus anathema to Marxists. Bakhtin was an active member of a group of young intellectuals that formed in Nevel in 1918 and then moved several years later to Vitebsk. This group assiduously studied Kant's *Critique of Pure Reason* and sponsored debates on the work in which Bakhtin took part (Clark and Holquist 43). Moreover, many were interested in questions of religion, be it mystical Russian Orthodoxy, Judaism, or syncretism. Although the general intellectual atmosphere was open and unrestrained in the first years after the Soviet Revolution, it became ever more constricted and rigid until the first round of purges took place in 1929. Around 1927 the group began to make concessions to Soviet Marxism, but all were imperiled in 1929 (Clark and Holquist 117–19). By that time, Bakhtin and his friends, with their wide-ranging philosophical and spiritual interests, considered themselves to be engaged in transgressive intellectual activity. Furthermore, they innocently believed that their dedication to the contemplation of philosophical 'ultimate questions' would be a more effective way of confronting the social crisis of their time than actual political action (Hirschkop, *Mikhail Bakhtin* 160). The daughter of Bakhtin's friend and collaborator M.I. Kagan, Judif' Kagan, describes the destinies that awaited those in the group: regardless of their stances, they were arrested, exiled, assassinated, or disappeared (4). Even Pavel Medvedev, who entered the party and sought to further his career, was shot in the 1938 purges of party apparatchiks and intellectuals.

Bakhtin's lectures given in 1924–5 reveal to what extent these young thinkers wrestled with Kant and Cohen in order to move beyond them. Indeed, in his desire to ground a philosophy based on lived experience rather than the transcendental self, Bakhtin coincided with Ortega. Whereas Ortega moved toward phenomenology in the quest to overcome Kant and his personal mentor, Cohen, Bakhtin moved toward aesthetics – a movement he made in the 1920s via Russian Orthodoxy. Like religion, aesthetics offered for Bakhtin the notion of two consciousnesses in relation, one that judges and forgives, and the other that is only completely known and seen through grace. Notes from Bakhtin's lecture of 1 November 1925 reveal that the young Russian consciously adheres to the Orthodox notion of Incarnation, in which the coexistence of spirit and body 'destroyed the unity of the Kantian person' (Pumpiansky 220).[34] Even more, he hints at Cohen's own attempt to Judaize Kantianism as a 'kind of cultural immanentism that contemporary neo-Judaism, fearing the personal God,' set up in order to avoid the personal orientation to God. The mixture of Kantianism and Russian Orthodoxy was potentially incendiary by 1929. Whereas Bakhtin did not publish texts that contained open theological musing, such as 'Author and Hero in Aesthetic Activity,' neither did he attempt to erase evidence of Kant's influence on his thought. For example, Bakhtin recognized his debt to Kant in the conceptualization of the chronotope, and noted that the German philosopher had affirmed that time and space served as the forms essential for any type of cognition. Bakhtin, of course, differentiates the chronotope from the Kantian concept of time, for the chronotope is not transcendent but rather constitutes a representation of reality. Nonetheless, the influence is real and acknowledged by Bakhtin, an act of considerable courage in his time and place.

Following his arrest in 1929 for forbidden intellectual activities and his ties to religious groups associated with Russian Orthodoxy, Bakhtin was sentenced to exile for the same crime for which Socrates was condemned to death: the corruption of youth through his teaching (Clark and Holquist 138–42). The primary charge was that he was a member of the group Voskresenie (Resurrection), a religious group also interested in revolution. Other charges include the inclusion of his name on a list of persons who could potentially form a non-Communist government, and that he was a member of the tsarist Brotherhood of Saint Serafim (this charge was eventually dropped). The arrest occurred shortly before his publication of *Problems of Dostoevsky's Poetics* (1929). Rumours circulated at the time in Russia to the effect that Anatoly Lunacharsky's positive review of the book contributed to the commutation of the original sentence, one which would have sent Bakhtin to a Siberian concentration camp – effectively, a death sentence (Emerson 75). One assumes that Soviet authorities disapproved of Bakhtin's predilection for the ideas of Hermann Cohen, whom Lenin had harshly criticized for his neo-Kantian idealism (Clark and Holquist 58).

During his time in Kazakhstan in the 1930s, Bakhtin witnessed the rigours of Stalinist collectivization, which, due to the destruction of the traditional lifestyle of the local nomads, resulted in the death of more than 1.5 million people (256). Consequently, there are now Western and Russian scholars who interpret Bakhtin's novelistics and notion of the carnivalesque as a veiled critique of Stalinist policy. In it they find not only an exaltation of individual liberty but also a denunciation of the Stalinist practice of appropriating popular traditions for political ends (Pechey 23; Emerson 169–71). Even the puritanical Stalinist censorship of literary and artistic representations of the human body and sexuality can be seen as a subtext to Bakhtin's defence of the carnivalesque body in all its sexual and digestive glory (Clark and Holquist 305–20). Are his other writings of the 1930s on language similarly informed by his experience of the Stalinist purges, the Five-Year Plans, and the enforced collectivization of the rural USSR? Both his emerging notions of language and time could be read Aesopically, that is to say, according to the custom of the time of looking for hidden meanings (Fitzpatrick 188). For example, his characterization of the collective life of the land in the section on the Rabelaisian chronotope in 'Forms of Time and Chronotope in the Novel' could be read as an indictment of the Five-Year Plans. Nothing could be farther removed from the enforced, rationalized timelines of Stalinism than Bakhtin's description of a time 'not separated from the earth or from nature' (*DI* 208).

It is hard not to read his defence of language's subversive powers through carnivalesque laughter and joking in relation to the stunted, stuttering kinds of discourse that emerge in a totalitarian society. Jokes circulated widely, and constituted one of the few forms of verbal dissidence available (Fitzpatrick 166). Denouncers and spies abounded, so private conversation was never really private. Public 'confessions' and self-criticism made a mockery of the confessional forms studied by Bakhtin in his writings on Augustine and other ancient writers. Since 'unmasking' spies and traitors was encouraged, Bakhtin's defence of the mask could even be read as political resistance. Bakhtin probably at times employed a mask for self-protection in his writings in such a way that he cloaked original thoughts in party mandates. For example, his notion of heteroglossia might respond to the call for a socialist realism that would be accessible to the people, and his attack on Formalism, itself under fire, could have served to mask his interest in parody and irony (Clark and Holquist 271). Because the stigma of having once fallen afoul of the authorities could not be erased, it is not surprising that Bakhtin was again accused in 1937; perhaps more surprising is the fact he escaped un-harmed, his accusers being purged (Clark and Holquist 260).

Rabelais and His World (1940) is fundamental to an understanding of all of Bakhtin's thought, and harks to his exile in Kustanai in Kazakhstan. Bakhtin's defence of the material as a doctoral thesis presented to the Gorky Institute of Universal Literature in 1946 resulted in an academic scandal. Before seeking a defence of the manuscript, Bakhtin had failed to get it published in Paris. His concerns about the political dimensions of the defence are revealed in the care with which he and M.V. Yudina tried to find jurors who 'were good and "non-standard" people, that is, people who did not have ulterior motives, and who were able to turn a blind eye to departures from Marxist dogma' (Pan'kov 31). The defence apparently lasted seven hours, and had a public of twenty-five or thirty people who expected controversy to arise in the proceeding. Whether or not Bakhtin broke into a cry of 'obscurantists' directed at his jury remains disputed, particularly since tales and myths of public outbursts were rampant under Stalin (Fitzpatrick 186). Some jury members took him to task for not situating Rabelais in relation to Engels's vision of the Renaissance as an overcoming of medieval society, and for not suffi-ciently highlighting the issue of class struggle (Pan'kov 49). The jury re-quired that the dissertation be rewritten to eliminate both its ideological depravity as well as its explicit treatment of the sexual and the bodily. Although some colleagues did defend Bakhtin by proclaiming the panel's decision to be excessive and unjust, Bakhtin finally had to accept the less prestigious title of candidate rather than doctor (Emerson 91–3).

Bakhtin lived to experience the stirrings of vindication. In the 1960s his work started to gain notice in Russia, and soon thereafter in the West. He was offered a professorship, which he turned down, apparently saying '"I cannot take the title upon myself ... A philosopher, and I am a phil-osopher, must be no one, because once he becomes someone he starts to adapt his thinking to that position"' (Rzhevsky 438). The question of his possible authorship of *Freudianism, The Formal Method in Literary Scholarship*, and *Marxism and the Philosophy of Language* continued to haunt him. When arrested in 1929, interrogators had offered to keep se-cret his writing the three books, saying they knew he knew Marxist methods (Clark and Holquist 144). In 1975 he refused to sign an official affidavit claiming authorship for the three disputed books, but also ap-parently on the threshold of death referred to them as his sin. According to his executor, V. Kozhinov, 'Only, on his death bed so to say, he told two men, me and Sergei Bocharov, his other executor, that "This is, after all, my sin, and I should acknowledge it"' (Rzhevsky 432). For Kozhinov, the sin implied was the Marxist mask Bakhtin would have had to adopt had he written these books. One wonders, though, if Bakhtin's sin might have been something else. Pavel Medvedev was executed in 1938, and Valentin Vološinov died in 1936 of tuberculosis. It is impossible to say what Bakhtin's sin would have been: survivor guilt for outliving his friends and intellectual companions? Guilt at having fostered the legend that he had written their works? Guilt at having attributed to them works that were his? Guilt at having collaborated with them? In the absence of a true deathbed confession, Bakhtin took his sin to the grave.

In the last decade, Bakhtin scholars have accused him of the more mundane sins of plagiarism and not citing sources. The discovery by Brian Poole of sections copied from Ernst Cassirer, followed by further investigations into his methods of working with German texts and not always fully citing sources, led to a period of disillusionment among Bakhtin scholars at the end of the 1990s, although textual criticism of his manuscripts and published works has recently shown that some names such as Cassirer and Leo Spitzer were removed from the published versions (Hirschkop, *Mikhail Bakhtin* 123). The disappointment in the fallen idol rings clearly through comments such as Poole's confession that '[w]e've swallowed the legends – hook, line and sinker' ('From Phenomenology to Dialogue' 124) or David Shepherd's admission of 'the possibility that the man was a charlatan' (Hitchcock, 'The Bakhtin Centre and the State of the Archive' 757). The question that remains to be answered is: why did Western Bakhtin scholars feels so betrayed? As Charles Lock remarks, 'His "sorrowful" confession to Sergei Averintsev, *"Ya byl ne luchshe svoego vremeni"* ("I was no better than my time"), strikes no note of shame, but reaches down to a fine dignity. In the present climate, it is too easily forgotten how few individuals endured the Soviet regime so untainted: in that context it is no wonder at all that younger scholars might have wanted to learn "how to live so that we might become like you"' (97–8).

Heroic Criticism

It is curious that the thinkers covered in this book conceived of the novel as a political genre, and understood their theories to be a form of political action. For all of them, modernity was a problematic historical reality. Humanity, whether figured as Lukács's alienated individual, Cohen's devalued worker, or Ortega's mass-man, lives subject to, rather than as a subject of, society. Society, which should be humankind's creation, becomes its oppressor. Literature in general, and the novel in particular, were valued by these philosophers for providing a space freed (at least in part) from social control. In a period defined by rationalized social mechanisms that threaten individual autonomy, literature and the novel create a space where imagination has free play. Imagination is a word that appears rarely in the writings of these theorists. And yet its absence is but a sign of its overwhelming presence as the unseen backdrop for the critique of modernity. For Schlegel, imagination conceived of as entwining fantasy and reality has a clearly positive potential. By the second decade of the twentieth century, early Romanticism and its open embrace of the imagination has been co-opted by cheapened forms of Romanticism based on nationalistic, if not xenophobic or racist, paradigms. Deterministic ideologies, either social Darwinist or Marxist, further devalue the imagination by denying to it the power to change reality. Extreme forms of capitalism degrade the individual into a cog in the great economic machine. Reality, be it genetic, social, or economic, precedes the imagination, shapes it, and renders it impotent. Literature would seem to be of no use whatsoever.

The uselessness of literature turns it into an attractive vehicle for cultural critique. To begin with, art, unlike science, seems freed from the instrumentality condemned by Kantian ethics. When Cohen reasserts the future as an orienting ideal for reality, when Lukács views the abstract idealist in a tragic light, or when Ortega attempts to reground philosophy in the whole of human life – these are moments in a trend to vindicate the imagination and individual agency. Ultimately, the attack on imagination results in a denial of human agency. Images that exist outside actual reality are necessary, these thinkers would claim, to form and motivate actual change in life as it is lived. Ortega explains best the capacity of art to expand human understanding and experience. The work of culture appears in relation to the work of building a whole from various parts. The old topos of nature as the book of God is transformed in such a way that culture and life take on a relationship of foreshortening: 'Life is the eternal text, the burning bush at the edge of the road where God cries out. Culture – art, science, or politics – is the commentary, that mode of life in which life, refracting itself within itself, acquires refinement and ordering.'[35] It follows that literature not only exemplifies the multiplicity of life, but also orders and comments upon it. Literature can be and is a theoretical point of view on life. The novel provides a space both for theorizing upon life and imagining new forms.

Many wars and revolutions fall as enigmatic backdrops to these theories of the novel – the French Revolution, the First World War, the Hungarian Revolution, the Soviet Revolution, the Spanish Civil War. Can it be an accident that Lukács and Ortega write their theories of the novel on the eve of the First World War? Do war and violent revolution represent a failure of the imagination that these thinkers felt the need to address? Had twentieth-century Europeans lost the ability to imagine themselves as separate from the corporate identities of state, political party, or nationality? Was going to the front a way to regain a cheapened form of individual agency or heroism? Hannah Arendt has observed that 'violence itself is incapable of speech' (19). Does the return to the novel present a return to speech?

Nineteenth- and twentieth-century philosophy seemed to offer a new form of heroism – criticism – and a new form of hero – the critic. Unflinching examination of the limits and determinant conditions of human existence would offer access to the truth about humankind. Criticism would reveal the enslaving chains of prejudice, superstition, and irrationality that hinder individual and communal development. Indeed, this belief in the reforming, if not revolutionary, power of criticism persists in certain corridors of academe to this day. Habermas presents three types of philosophical critics who are '[u]nited in their goal of enlightening the Enlightenment': 'critical critics,' who promote a vision of themselves as an avant-garde leading the way to future enlightenment; 'metacritics,' who criticize the danger in 'a new priestly domination' by other critics; and Nietzchean critics, who criticize 'betrayal by the intellectuals,' including themselves in this treacherous class (57). Of the theorists studied in this book, Schlegel clearly belongs to the group of critical critics, and, in his notebooks, writes of criticism as philosophy and literature. Part of Bakhtin's sentimental appeal for us today might be that he also seems to be sincerely and fully engaged in his own theoretical vision. By the twentieth century, cultural criticism is tinged with metacriticism; Cohen, Unamuno, Ortega, and Lukács intend their enlightening activities to counteract the ill effects of other intellectuals. By the end of their lives, Cohen, Unamuno, and perhaps even Ortega begin to question the efficacy and results of their own thought.

All of these thinkers – Schlegel, Lukács, Cohen, Unamuno, Ortega, and Bakhtin – evidence a deep and perhaps unconscious belief in the political power of their ideas. Theories of the novel will somehow effectively critique and reform, if not revolutionize, society. There is a strong strand of heroism underlying their notion of the intellectual life.

That is to say, they see critics as capable of heroism. There is also a not so deeply hidden fear of the non-intellectual masses. As Ortega quips: 'What a thing is man? The great philosophers have passed this question down through the generations, and whenever it has slipped from their hands, either through carelessness or on purpose, into the people's possession, a revolution has erupted.'[36] In fact, such an unspoken and largely unconscious vision of the critic as hero founds our general idea of what a good intellectual is. If we did not see these thinkers as heroes, why would we be so disappointed in their failures? The list of fallen intellectuals is long, and grows ever longer, as we uncover hidden weaknesses: Paul de Man's and Martin Heidegger's Nazism, Hannah Arendt's love for Heidegger, etc. In point of fact, we in the Western world (with the possible exception of Hispanic societies) must consider these thinkers to be more powerful and important than artists, for do we really get so worked up about a poet's collusion with unsavoury political forces? By highlighting the human flaws in the lives of Lukács, Cohen, Unamuno, and Ortega, it is not my intention to discredit their intellectual work. To automatically expel from the forums of civil academic discussion all thinkers upon discovering their failings is to pretend to an intellectual and ideological purity that none of us can claim.

To the contrary, their cases can reveals to us the limitations of our own construction of the heroic critic. Lukács submits himself completely to the idea, and lives with blood on his hands. Cohen, blinded by his deep desire to be incorporated into German society, fails to see the corrupt underbelly of the German war machine even when his own critique of nationalism would have shown it to him. Unamuno attempts to educate through paradox, to find his paradoxes have slipped out of his control only to stand for what he most abhors. Ortega y Gasset, after a lifetime of working for the general education and democratization of the Spanish people, contributes either wittingly or unwittingly to the imposition of a Fascist regime that will stifle the public sphere for four decades. Bakhtin survives a series of Stalinist purges, hunger, and physical distress, but seems to plagiarize and obscure quotes and allusions in the process. In the final analysis, they were excellent critics, but failed prophets and heroes.

The centrality of Cervantes' *Don Quixote de la Mancha* to these theories of the novel should no longer surprise us. Don Quixote is the personification of the heroic critic. He recognizes modernity and seeks to change it. In a time marked by the emergence of the modern army, based on professional soldiers drawn from the lower classes and using the advanced technology of gunpowder to avoid hand-to-hand combat, Don Quixote tries to revive the practice of medieval knighthood. Revolutions do not only run forwards, but also look back to the past for lost models that will condemn present practice. A true revolutionary, Don Quixote not only thumbs his nose at the judicial and police officers of the monarch to enact his own justice. He also – and more importantly – attempts to give birth to himself. In an extreme bid for autonomy, he creates a new identity. Alonso Quijano becomes Don Quixote, who fashions a helmet and armour for himself, renames his broken-down nag Rocinante, transforms the peasant Sancho Panza into his squire, finds an ideal love in Dulcinea, and manages to get himself knighted, albeit by an innkeeper. He proclaims a new beginning, one based on his freedom to determine his identity and circumstances that will found his future.

As much as we might try, we moderns do not seem capable of only laughing in derision at such arrogance. This was the prevalent, if not exclusive, reaction of Cervantes' contemporaries to *Don Quixote*, and proof that they still lived in a transitional age. But Don Quixote's radical self-fashioning strikes to the core of modern identity to such an extent that we cannot help but identify with that aspect of his folly. For this reason, all attempts by philologists to change popular 'romantic' readings of *Don Quixote* are doomed to fail. We might not try to make ourselves into knights errant, but we will try to make ourselves into the image of something. Even those readers, such as Cohen and Bakhtin, who prefer the model of Sancho Panza are still enchanted by the transformation that the illiterate peasant undergoes. The great contradiction of modern identity, of course, is that precisely at the same time that the individual fights for autonomy and liberty, she perceives the weight of social forms bearing down on her. It is but a short step, then, to read Don Quixote's conflicts with those around him as a result not of his insanity or delusion, but rather as an example of the state of the modern individual in constant struggle against societal determinants. Free to imagine a different future for ourselves, we are locked in combat with our circumstances.

Cervantes beckons as a nuanced, contradictory figure. Indeed, the problematics of his life resemble the existential dilemmas of the twentieth- or twenty-first-century individual. A professional soldier, he was maimed at the battle of Lepanto against the Ottoman navy. A minor bureaucrat, he had the unsavoury task of collecting provisions for the Spanish Armada. An accounting problem landed him in jail. His desire for literary fame was thwarted in his lifetime as younger generations found him old-fashioned. Cervantes believed that he was creating something new in his fiction, and to this effect he boasted that he was the first to '*novelar*' in Spanish (*Novelas ejemplares* 1:64). Although he would have understood the *novela* as the Italian genre of *novella* practised by Boccaccio, there are points of contact between his claim and what subsequent theorists of the novel have claimed for him. He was interested in taking for literature the stuff of the everyday, the sentimental, and the humorous. He was interested in the vagaries of the human individual as grist for fiction.

The very structure of *Don Quixote*, evolving as it did over time, reveals that Cervantes became aware of key elements of his novel. Already by the windmill episode, Cervantes realizes that the fictional conceit of a would-be medieval knight errant in Hapsburg Spain raises questions of interpreting and knowing reality. At some point in part I, he sees that, in Don Quixote and Sancho Panza, he has stumbled onto a comic pair whose spoken interchange would change each other. By the beginning of part II, he realizes that Don Quixote and Sancho Panza are effecting the other people around them, involving them in their imaginative adventures. Moreover, he realizes that they exist on a metafictional plane as characters of a book, and that readers of that book would seek to enter into the fiction, be it through interpretation of the plot, identification with the characters, or actually crossing the same threshold between literature and reality that Don Quixote has violated. To give only one example, the university-educated Bachelor Sansón Carrasco, who originally disguises himself as a knight errant to defeat Don Quixote and lure him back home, actually becomes angry when Don Quixote beats him, and seeks revenge. Cervantes represents this transgression of the boundary between fiction and non-fiction in the episode of Maese Pedro's puppet play, when Don Quixote, at first an attentive, respectful spectator, loses sight of the fictional fourth wall of theatre and attacks the puppets in order to protect them.

One is left transgressing the same boundary and asking to what extent our modernity might be Cervantes' creation – or at the very least, our understanding of modernity might be, in part, Cervantes' creation. I close with Don Quixote's remarks to Sancho as they leave the palace of the Duke and the Duchess where they have been subject to much humiliation (2: chapter 58). Exercising their traditional seigniorial rights, the aristocrats have treated the pair as their feudal lieges, and subjected them to courtly machinations only to laugh at them. In short, they have treated Don Quixote and Sancho as means to their own ends (in Kantian terms) or as slaves (in Hegelian terms). Don Quixote clearly yearns for freedom, and will no longer live by the traditional system, in which the lower classes trade autonomy for material well-being:

> Freedom, Sancho, is one of the most precious gifts heaven gave to men; the treasures under the earth and beneath the sea cannot compare to it; for freedom, as well as for honour, one can and should risk one's life, while captivity, on the other hand, is the greatest evil that can befall men. I say this, Sancho, because you have clearly seen the luxury and abundance we have enjoyed in this castle that we are leaving, but in the midst of those flavorful banquets and those drinks as cool as snow, it seemed as if I were suffering the pangs of hunger because I could not enjoy them with the freedom I would have had if they had been mine; the obligations to repay the benefits and kindnesses we have received are bonds that hobble a free spirit. Fortunate is the man to whom heaven has given a piece of bread with no obligation to thank anyone but heaven itself! (*DQ* 832)[37]

Notes

Preface

1 Curiously, Cervantes scholars are the most willing to consider *Don Quixote* as something other than a novel. Take, for example, Parr's assertion that Cervantes' text is prenovelistic, composed of diverse genres such as Socratic dialogue, Menippean satire, and anatomy as defined by Northrop Frye (135–58).
2 McKeon considers Jameson and Watt as revisionists of the 'grand theory' because they continue to situate the novel in periods of historical change (355–9).
3 See also Kristeva's *Revolution in Poetic Language*, 59–60.

1. *Don Quixote* and the Problem of Modernity

1 Toulmin, writing in 1990, argues that our modernity better resembles the tolerant humanism of the sixteenth century rather than the rigid dogmatism of the seventeenth century. One wonders if he would make such an assertion now.
2 Philip II constructed El Escorial not only as a place for devout retreat, but also to house his massive library and laboratories for alchemical and scientific experimentation. Unhappily, many key works of botany and herbaria were destroyed in a seventeenth-century fire (Goodman, 'Science, Medicine, and Technology in Colonial Spanish America' 15).
3 On Vesalius and the study of anatomy in Spain, see O'Malley and López Piñero. The former recounts that the Spanish physicians in Philip II's court expressed considerable jealousy toward the foreigner (138–9). On the other hand, it should be noted that Vesalius had a positive influence on the study of anatomy in Valencia (López Piñero). On metallurgical advances and the Americas, see Barrera-Osorio 65–72.
4 The popularity of Spanish literature in other European nations of the time has long been noted (Chartier 129–50). What is only now being documented

is the widespread diffusion of non-literary Spanish texts at the time and their influence on scientific thought outside Iberia (Portuondo 52, Cañizares-Esguerra 14–45, 112–38).

5 The Spanish Inquisition in its modern form (1478–1834) extended throughout the empire and was most active in its first decades, becoming practically inactive in the eighteenth century. It prosecuted charges of blasphemy, heresy, and sexual crimes, and became more focused on the latter in its last two centuries. The total death toll of the Spanish Inquisition is not known, although ten thousand executions is now considered the upper limit (Pérez 423). In terms of the number of executions, it is not so different from other European judicial systems of the period, although its focus on heresy and crypto-Judaism as well as its highly bureaucratic structure are unique.

6 Américo Castro is the most famous proponent of this version of Spanish early modern history, in which the expulsion of the Jews and the Moors is seen to damage the overall well-being of the nation. Certainly the Inquisition gradually quelled the open publication of religious dissent, but Spaniards continued to get around the banning of books by publishing and acquiring books published abroad. Kamen has suggested that up to 25 per cent of books used by Spaniards between 1550 and 1700 were published abroad ('Censura y libertad' 114). Nonetheless, two sixteenth-century Spaniards, Pedro Nuñez and Juan Mariana, report that the Inquisition had stifled free expression and caused widespread distrust, turning all into potential spies. For a meticulous examination of the effect of Inquisitorial censorship on the dissemination of scientific books, see Pardo Tomás.

7 *Lazarillo de Tormes* was published anonymously, and its authorship has been undetermined throughout the centuries. There is currently a heated debate raging among Spanish philologists in which several authors have been put forth. Mercedes Agulló, basing her argument on documents from the period, has proposed Diego Hurtado de Mendoza as the author. Mendoza, a high-ranking noble, wrote and published *Historia de la guerra de Granada*, an account of the battles against the *morisco* uprising in 1568 in the Alpujarras. Rosa Navarro, based on a lexical concordance with reference to other works, has proposed Alfonso de Valdés as the author. Brother of the famous humanist Juan de Valdés, who penned the influential *Diálogo de la lengua*, Alfonso died in 1532, a fact that makes Navarro's attribution difficult for many to accept. Francisco Calero, using a method similar to Navarro's, has proposed Juan Luis Vives as the author. One of the leading humanists of his age, Vives is well known for his humanistic writings in Latin and his correspondence with Erasmus. For a balanced assessment of all three attributions, see Fernando Rodríguez Mansilla's review article 'A vueltas con los autores del *Lazarillo de Tormes* (a propósito del libro de Mercedes Agulló).'

8 'Dichosa edad y siglos dichosos aquellos a quien los antiguos pusieron nombre de dorados, y no porque en ellos el oro (que en esta nuestra edad de hierro tanto se estima) se alcanzase en aquella venturosa sin fatiga alguna, sino porque entonces los que en ella vivían ignoraban estas dos palabras de *tuyo* y *mío*' (*DQM* 1:169).

9 '[S]ólo me fatigo por dar a entender al mundo en el error en que está en no renovar en sí el felicísimo tiempo donde campeaba la orden de la andante caballería' (*DQM* 2:35).

10 'Mas agora ya triunfa la pereza de la diligencia, la ociosidad del trabajo, el vicio de la virtud, la arrogancia de la valentía, y la teórica de la práctica de las armas, que sólo vivieron y resplandecieron en las edades del oro y en los andantes caballeros' (*DQM* 2:35).

11 Don Quixote encounters the power of the printing press in book II, as he meets readers of the first part. On Cervantes and the technology of print, see Martín Morán 122–44, and Scheunemann 135–48. On reading and metafiction in Cervantes, see Brito Díaz 37–54, and Fuentes, *Cervantes o la crítica de la lectura*.

12 'Bien hayan aquellos benditos siglos que carecieron de la espantable furia de aquestos endemoniados instrumentos de la artillería, a cuyo inventor tengo para mí que en el infierno se le está dando el premio de su diabólica invención, con la cual dio causa que un infame y cobarde brazo quite la vida a un valeroso caballero, y que, sin saber cómo o por dónde, en la mitad del coraje y brío que enciende y anima a los valientes pechos, llega una desmandada bala, disparada de quien quizá huyó y se espantó del resplandor que hizo el fuego al disparar de la maldita máquina, y corta y acaba en un instante los pensamientos y vida de quien la merecía gozar luengos siglos' (*DQM* 1:461–2).

13 For information on how the need for gunpowder fuelled technological research and innovation in early modern Spain, see Goodman, *Power and Penury* 109–41. Trained artillery men and gunners were in such demand that artillery schools were expanded. Engineer training was also promoted, in part to facilitate the construction of fortifications.

14 '[T]odavía me pone recelo pensar si la pólvora y el estaño me han de quitar la ocasión de hacerme famoso y conocido por el valor de mi brazo y filos de mi espada, por todo lo descubierto de la tierra' (*DQM* 1:462).

15 The phrases are 'con cuatro cepas y dos yugadas de tierra,' and 'aquellos hidalgos escuderiles que dan humo a los zapatos y toman los puntos de las medias negras con seda verde' (*DQM* 2:43).

16 Cervantes, *Don Quixote de la Mancha*, trans. J.M. Cohen 627. 'A la guerra me lleva/mi necesidad;/si tuviera dineros,/no fuera, en verdad' (*DQM* 2:211).

17 'Ésta es cadena de galeotes, gente forzada del rey, que va a las galeras' (*DQM* 1:270).

18 '¿Es posible que el rey haga fuerza a ninguna gente?' (*DQM* 1:270).

19 'Advierta vuestra merced – dijo Sancho –, que la justicia, que es el mesmo rey, no hace fuerza ni agravio a semejante gente, sino que los castiga en pena de sus delitos' (*DQM* 1:272).

20 'La chusma izó la entena con la misma priesa y ruido que la habían amainado, y todo esto, callando, como si no tuvieran voz ni aliento' (*DQM* 2:507–8).

21 'Tan albarda es como mi padre; y el que otra cosa ha dicho o dijere debe estar hecho uva' (*DQM* 1:532).

22 My translation. Cohen's and Grossman's translation of *bellaco villano* as 'base villain' does not sufficiently capture the very clear class identification of a *villano*. '– Mentís como bellaco villano' (*DQM* 1:532).

23 '… don Fernando tenía debajo de sus pies a un cuadrillero, midiéndole el cuerpo con ellos muy a su sabor' (*DQM* 1:532).

24 Jehenson and Dunn have observed that class relations, despite Don Quixote's wilful avoidance of them, re-emerge in the text upon carefully reading, and are often voiced by secondary characters (36, 87, 98, 111).

25 'Es, pues, el caso que los cuadrilleros se sosegaron, por haber entreoído la calidad de los que con ellos se habían combatido, y se retiraron de la pendencia, por parecerles que, de cualquiera manera que sucediese, habían de llevar lo peor de la batalla …' (*DQM* 1:534).

26 '… entre algunos mandamientos que traía para prender a algunos delincuentes, traía uno contra don Quijote, a quien la Santa Hermandad había mandado prender, por la libertad que dio a los galeotes, y como Sancho con mucha razón había temido' (*DQM* 1:534).

27 Cervantes, *Don Quixote de la Mancha*, trans. J.M. Cohen translation 408–9. '… quiso certificarse si las señas que don Quijote traía venían bien …' (*DQM* 1:534).

28 '–¡Favor a la Santa Hermandad! Y para que se vea que lo pido de veras, léase este mandamiento, donde se contiene que se prenda a este salteador de caminos' (*DQM* 1:534).

29 '¿Quién el que ignoró que son esentos de todo judicial fuero los caballeros andantes, y que su ley es su espada, sus fueros sus bríos, sus premáticas su voluntad?' (*DQM* 1:535).

30 For a discussion of money in *Don Quixote*, particularly Sancho's salary, see Carroll Johnson 15–36.

31 '¿Qué caballero andante pagó pecho, alcabala, chapín de la reina, moneda ferrera, portazgo ni barca?' (*DQM* 1:536).

32 As Heller makes clear, the modern critique of ideology, like ideology itself, is not necessarily either conservative or radical, but fluctuates between the two poles in what she terms 'the pendulum of modernity.'

33 For an analysis of memory in Cervantes' work within the Renaissance context, see Egido 93–135.

34 '… unos que traen y derivan su decendencia de príncipes y monarcas, a quien poco a poco el tiempo ha deshecho, y han acabado en punta, como pirámide puesta al revés; otros tuvieron principio de gente baja, y van subiendo de grado en grado, hasta llegar a ser grandes señores' (*DQM* 1:267).

35 '… que cuando se le antojase la pusiese como nueva, llamándola de villana, hija de destripaterrones y de la pelarruecas!' (*DQM* 2:62).

36 '[E]so que a ti te parece bacía de barbero, me parece a mí el yelmo de Mambrino, y a otro le parecerá otra cosa' (*DQM* 1:305).

37 For the Celtic roots of the literature of knight-errantry and their reemergence in *Don Quixote*, see Dudley.

38 Salillas (1905) and Iriarte (1947) suggested that Cervantes was influenced by Huarte de San Juan's *Examen de ingenios*, describing medical disorders arising from imbalances of the humours. García Gibert has reprised this view (98–9). For a review in English of what Cervantes might have known of anatomy and medicine, see Arráez-Aybar 690–4.

39 'La locura en la obra de Cervantes no debe tomarse, pues, de ninguna manera en un sentido médico, a modo de un padecimiento venido de donde viniere, sino como una construcción ficcional en la que muestra y describe la *trascendencia del error en la construcción de la vida propia por parte de cualquier ser humano en general* …' (Castilla del Pino 64).

40 '[E]l sujeto *dis*-loca, se sale de "su sitio," de su realidad de sí y su contexto. Y quien disloca paga, y muy caro, porque su dislocación tiene consecuencias, a veces tan graves como para no sobrevivir' (Castilla del Pino 65).

41 'La novela moderna nació como una contienda entre un *yo* y otro *yo*, no entre situaciones, o entre bondades y maldades, o entre ansias de amor, bien o mal correspondido, etc.' (Castro, *Cervantes y los casticismos españoles* 73).

42 In some ways this book is a response to Anthony Close's *The Romantic Approach to Don Quixote*. I offer it in the spirit of collegial polemic which I know that he intended upon publishing his controversial work.

2. Arabesques and the Modern Novel: Friedrich Schlegel's Interpretation of *Don Quixote*

1 'Ich würde nicht aus dem Kreise meiner Studien herausgehn, wenn ich den Don Quixote übersetzte. Der Roman wird mir gewiß einmahl eben so

sehr Hauptsache seyn als die Alten, in denen ich jetzt wieder bis oben an lebe und athme' (Mennemeier 304–5). The young Friedrich was also an assiduous reader of Cervantes' pastoral novel *La Galatea* (1585), which he termed the most delicate of novels and full of fantasy (Schmidt, 'Cervantes's *Galatea* and Friedrich Schlegel's *Lucinde*' 25).

2 It is important to note that in Schlegel's early writings, particularly in *On the Study of Greek Poetry* (1795), 'modern' is a pejorative term used to describe contemporary literature that is negatively disordered, reflecting the chaos of the times without achieving an internal unity that would cause it to transcend the problems of the epoch (Mennemeier 27–30). Nonetheless, the young man does hold out hope for a modern, that is to say contemporary, literature that would allow the writer to transcend modernity's chaos to create beautiful, ordered art.

3 'Revolutionen sind universelle nicht organische, sondern chemische Bewegungen. Der große Handel ist die Chemie der großen Ökonomie; es gibt wohl auch eine Alchemie der Art. Die chemische Natur des Romans, der Kritik, des Witzes, der Geselligkeit, der neuesten Rhetorik und der bisherigen Historie leuchtet von selbst ein' (*KA* 2:248).

4 Schlegel borrowed the seventeenth-century Spaniard Gracián's most famous book, *Agudeza y arte de ingenio*, from the Göttingen University library at the beginning of 1800 (Schanze 73).

5 'Die einzelnen Großen stehen weniger isoliert unter den Griechen und Römern. Sie hatten weniger Genies, aber mehr Genialität. Alles Antike ist genialisch. Das ganze Altertum ist ein Genius, der einzige den man ohne Übertreibung absolut groß, einzig und unerreichbar nennen darf' (*KA* 2:206).

6 'From Winckelmann, Schlegel acquired two fundamental beliefs: that the purpose of all art should be to portray beauty, and that imitation consists not in copying individuals in nature but in reproducing the ideal form behind nature' (Beiser 113).

7 Lacoue-Labarthe and Nancy believe that Ludoviko corresponds to Schelling, with Lotario being Novalis (89). Ernst Behler suggests that Lotario would be Schelling, but affirms that the discourse must be ultimately assigned to Schlegel (*Irony and the Discourse of Modernity* 138–9).

8 Not only does Schlegel's history of genres spring from his sense of historical separation from antiquity, but also from the awareness of language as a historical phenomenon present in the writings of Herder, for example (Bowie 63).

9 'Anders hat Cervantes nie gedichtet ...' (*KA* 2:336).

10 'Und doch kann auch sie am meisten zwischen dem Dargestellten und dem
Darstellenden, frei von allem realen und idealen Interesse auf den Flügeln
der poetischen Reflexion in der Mitte schweben, diese Reflexion immer
wieder potenzieren und wie in einer endlosen Reihe von Spiegeln verviel-
fachen. Sie ist der höchsten und der allseitigsten Bildung fähig; nicht bloß
von innen heraus, sondern auch von außen hinein; indem sie jedem, was ein
Ganzes in ihren Produkten sein soll, alle Teile ähnlich organisiert, wodurch
ihr die Aussicht auf eine grenzenlos wachsende Klassizität eröffnet wird' (*KA*
2:182–3). As indicated by the difficulty in translating *Darstellenden* (Behler
and Struc prefer to objectify the writer by translating this word as artist rather than the work), this personification of Romantic poetry grants it the status
of the creative subject. Nonetheless, I opt to read this description of a hovering point of view as more akin to the experience of the author (and perhaps the reader) who can adopt a hovering view of both world and work.

11 Schlegel's reference to reflection can be read in Kantian terms in relation to
the subject that reflects in the *Critique of Judgement* (Lacoue-Labarthe and
Nancy 105). The multiplication of reflections would entail a fragmentation
of the subject, an aspect crucial to the 'postmodern' visage of Schlegel.
Nonetheless, I agree with G.R. Thompson that Schlegel is 'committed to an
'expressive poetics': the author is the ultimate subject, and the text is an expression of the author's mind' (228). My interpretation of the fragmented
reflections as mimetic, reflecting the outside world and not the poetic subject, corresponds to such a notion of expressive poetics.

12 'Die Reflexion ist kein Anschauen, sondern ein absolut systematisches
Denken, ein Begreifen' (Benjamin I-1, 32). For a slightly different reading
of Kant's influence on Schlegel, see Parlej's argument that Schlegel problematizes self-presentation (19–20). *Don Quixote* is, in Parlej's reading, primarily an exploration of the problem of '*self*-sameness' (91).

13 'Die schaffende, die von der Freiheit, und dem Glauben an sie ausgeht,
und dann zeigt wie der menschliche Geist sein Gesetz allem aufprägt, und
wie die Welt sein Kunstwerk ist' (*KA* 2:192).

14 'Die Form der [Lyrik] originell, des [Dramas] individuell, des [Epos] uni-
versell. –Im Epos muß alles [Pathos] zu [Ethos] verschmelzen. Das *Moti-
virte* entsteht aus d[er] Durchdringung des [Ethos] und [Pathos] und hängt
zusammen mit d[er] Individualität. – [Epos] = objektive [Poesie]. – [Lyrik]
= sujektive/[Drama] = Obj.[ektiv-]Subj[ektive] –' (KA 16:271–2). I have
omitted Greek words from quote, as their meaning was added by the
editor in brackets in German translation. The same applies to footnotes 19,
21, 23, 26, and 31 of this chapter.

15 For reference to the first and second epochs of Romanticism, see note IX: 253 in *KA* 16:275.

16 Lacoue-Labarthe and Nancy remind us that the epic itself was not considered in ancient times a pure genre, but rather a mediating genre between diegesis and mimesis (96). Schlegel must redefine 'purity' and 'unity' in terms of content rather than form in order to argue that epic is an unmixed genre containing reflection of a unified culture. This fundamental instability in the subsumption of the category of the epic in modern novelistics might be responsible for the continual reformulation of the definition of the genre.

17 '*Stufen* des Rom[antischen] I) bei d[en] Alten: [Epos] und [Drama]. Anfang des Mischgedichts in *Prosa* und myst.[ische] sentim.[entale] Liebe [Erotika] 2) Das absolute mystisch Wunderbare, d.[as] eigentl[ich] Romantisch[e] 3) Don Quixote. –' (*KA* 16:91). The interpretation of Schlegel's abbreviation 'Rom' as Romantic is somewhat questionable, since it can also be read as 'Roman,' that is to say the novel. Nonetheless, 'romantic' and 'Roman' are practically interchangeable for Schlegel.

18 For a discussion of the misunderstanding of the Romantic notion of the absolute in the English-speaking world, see Bowie 75.

19 'Mathem[atik] ist Princ[ip] d[es] Chaotischen/ Die [mathematische] Form entsteht durch d[as] Irrationale, Potenzirte/ combinatorische Progress[ive] .' (*KA* 16:336–7). Schlegel ends this note by stating that Shakespeare is a thoroughly chaotic character, an attribution that does not contradict his characterization of Cervantes and the novel as chaotic, but rather highlights his understanding of the Romantic as transcending generic boundaries. In note IX 231 Schlegel writes that Cervantes could have easily been the truly great dramaturge of the Spanish stage (*KA* 16:273).

20 Schlegel's concept of chaos changed from viewing it as a negative aspect of modernity to understanding chaos as the natural stuff from which the artist creates his work (Mennemeier 30–5). For Lacoue-Labarthe and Nancy, Schlegelian '[c]haos is the state of always-already-lost "naivité" and of always-yet-to-appear absolute art and, in this sense, is also a definition of the human condition' (51).

21 '[Chaos] und [Epos] ist wohl die beste Erklärung d.[es] Romantischen–' (Note IX: 226, *KA* 16:272).

22 '[Absoluter Irrationalismus] das eigentl[ich] unterscheidende d[es] Rom[ans]' (*KA* 16:265).

23 'Dumm ist, wer nicht glaubt, was er sieht. Ein Narr ist, wer willkührlich dumm ist und es nicht glaubt, daß er es ist; er ist aus List dumm' (*LN* 248).

24 'Im Construiren liegt d[as] Wesen d[es] [Dramas]. In [Epos] wird deducirt; im Rom[an] combinirt' (Note IX: 712, *KA* 16:313).

25 '"Durch mich geht man zur ewgen Narrheit ein." – Sancho sinkt in immer tiefere Betrübniß und Sehnsucht nach s.[einem] Herren' (Note VI: 45, *KA* 16:198).

26 'Im Styl des echten Dichters ist nichts Schmuck, alles notwendige Hieroglyphe' (*KA* 2:193).

27 On Schlegel's references to Raphael's 'fantastic' painting, see Polheim 40–6. For an analysis of the arabesque in Persian carpets and Schlegel's notion of the term, see G.R. Thompson 170–81.

28 Behler argues that this movement between polar opposites is the most fundamental meaning of revolution for the early Romantics ('Die Auffassung der Revolution in der Frühromantik' 213). They even played with revolution in arabesque ways, opposing tyranny, for example, to spiritual counterbalance (204).

29 'Auch die Char.[akteristik] des D[on] Q[uichote] und Sa[ncho] behandelt Cerv[antes] durchaus [musikalisch] und spielend, ohne alle [Psychologie], Entwicklung ja gewöhnl[liche] Consequenz. Die Willkühr und das plötzlich.' 'Auffahrende im D[on] Q[uichote] und Sa[ncho]'s Donayres sind das feinste in ihrem Charakter. Der Dualismus zwisch[en] ihnen ursprünglich und notwendig' (*LN* 791, *KA* 16:211).

30 'Bildung und Verstand ist das Herrschende im II D[on] Q[uixote] und Parodie d[er] Bildung[,] d[es] verständigen Gesprächs, der ernsten Geschichte, der edlen Gesellschaft–' (*KA* 16:268).

31 Polheim has presented the most exhaustive analysis of this proposed novel/arabesque, and I will depend heavily on his analysis (313–68). The arabesque is transcribed in Polheim 315–16, and can also be found it *KA* 16:197–8, in a section entitled 'Zu den Arabesken.'

32 'Die Hölle äußerst lustig und possirlich genommen, mit Parodie d.[es] Klopstock' (*KA* 16:197).

33 '"Durch mich geht man zur ewgen Narrheit ein"' (*KA* 16:198).

34 'Sancho sinkt in immer tiefere Betrübniß und Sehnsucht nach s.[einem] Herren' (*KA* 16:198).

35 'Umgekehrte Sokrati[sche] Ironie von außen Anmuth' (*KA* 16:198).

3. The Emptiness of the Arabesque: Georg Lukács's Theory of the Novel

1 In the 1962 prologue, Lukács quips that *The Theory of the Novel* combines leftist ethics and rightist epistemology (16), a claim that led a whole generation of scholars to search for aspects characteristic of this antinomy in the work.

This approach can be useful, as in the case of Stedman Jones's analysis of Lukács's intellectual position relative to German *Lebensphilosophie* (24–30).

2 Lukács himself pointed to the novelty and validity of his analysis of time in the essay, a hint largely unheeded by scholars (TN 14).

3 On Budapest, see Congdon, 83–4; on Heidelberg, see the letter from Max Weber (*Selected Correspondence* 205).

4 Mészáros notes that Lukács intended it to be an introduction to a 'massive systematic work that has never been brought to completion. (Hundreds of pages of manuscript exist deliberately unpublished: Lukács once described to me this attempt of his at systematization as a "six-legged monster.")' (57). Mészáros adds in a footnote, 'In 1963, when I returned to him some three hundred foolscap pages of the manuscript that survived in Arnold Hauser's custody, though glad about the survival of an old document, he found that it would be a waste of his time reading it.' Ferenc Fehér and Agnes Heller found an outline for the proposed work on Dostoevsky, which Fehér contends proves that *The Theory of the Novel* was not incomplete ('The Last Phase of Anti-Capitalism' 140–3).

5 Lukács's reputation as an essayist and not a systematist contributed to the faculty vote against the young Hungarian in his unsuccessful *Habilitation* at the University of Heidelberg (*Selected Correspondence* 264).

6 Huhn reads Lukacs's refusal to let the essay settle into system as an example of his thorough neo-Kantianism: '[The essay] is instead the place in which reflective judgment is unsatisfied with itself – it is the place in which judgments made by reflection are once again submitted to reflection' (188).

7 Lukács first imagined *The Theory of the Novel* as a dialogue between friends, referring specifically to the storytellers of the *Decameron*, but also implicitly to the dialogical structure of Schlegel's *Dialogue on Poetry*. He remarks that it should have evolved out of a chain of dialogues (*TN* 11), a phrase that refers to Schlegel's Athenaeum Fragment 77, in which the young Romantic describes a genre not yet extant but that would be both subjective and individual, and objective and systematic (*PF* 27).

8 For Kadarkay, Vincent, the young Romantic, represents the young Lukács, whereas the sceptical Joachim represents a neo-Kantian naysayer, who finally insists that form and ethics must respond to an ideal. To the contrary, given the author's own engagement with Romantic thought and neo-Kantianism, both Vincent and Joachim represent facets of Lukács's self. Kadarkay does note that the essay serves as a satirical examination of Lukács' own thought and self as well as his erotic inadequacy (137–42).

9 'In fact, the concept of "totality" in Lukács, despite its later Marxist overtones, derives philosophically from the romantic belief – active in Hegel,

Hölderlin, and Schelling – in the existence of an ultimate unity or mystical *en kai pan* ("one and all")' (Miles 28). This notion of Romantic totality and the absolute looms large in Lukács, although it is largely absent in the other theorists of the novel.

10 The most complete investigation of Lukács's transformation of Kantian epistemological categories into ethical ones is found in Bernstein xviii–xix, 77–81.

11 'Diese Ironie ist die Selbstkorrektur der Brüchigkeit ...' (*Die Teorie des Romans* 65). This statement has caused much controversy in part due to translation problems. Derwin criticizes Bernstein for following Bostock's misleading translation in which the fragility is assumed to pertain to the world, only to assume that the fragility corrected by irony is that of the subject (187).

12 'Thus, while irony reveals the nonobjectivity of the novelistic representation, it also reveals the non-unity of the ironic, creating subject' (Derwin 27).

13 Bernstein argues that, for Lukács, '[t]he novel is the crisis of modern culture because it is the space, and the only space available to contemplative reason, where ethical reason and empirical reality can meet' (102–3). Krückeberg argues for the centrality of meaning-giving form due to the lack of meaning Lukács considers constitutive of modernity (76).

14 Bernstein notes that the centrality of history to Lukács's concept of form distinguishes it from Kant's atemporal notion of form, and thus links it to Simmel's influence (78).

15 The preference for the novel over tragedy also distinguishes Lukács's and Schlegel's aesthetics from Hegel's (Szondi 86).

16 There is found here the suggestion of Lukács's Marxist theory of reflection, by which the grotesque elements of Don Quixote correspond mimetically to the reification of experience created by modern capitalism (Királyfalvi 59).

17 Lukács was not advocating for Christian revival, but rather for a utopic vision of the pre-capitalist Middle Ages that he shared with Ernst Bloch 'of an inverted hierarchy inspired by Catholic doctrine, a hierarchy in which ascetic discipline and trials and tribulations (but not privileges) increase as one approaches the top of the ladder' (Löwy, *Georg Lukács* 54).

18 Lukács takes the image of the demonic from Goethe and links it to irony as a lack of fixed meaning and a becoming rather than a being (Derwin 22–3).

19 Bergson does write that 'we perceive duration as a stream against which we cannot go' (45). Nonetheless, he does not question that evolution is not in some way beneficial to humanity, its highest form.

20 Jameson posits the opposite conclusion, writing that the novelists are the true heroes of human freedom in *The Theory of the Novel*, a supposition he bases on the concept of the negative mysticism of modernity (173).

21 Jay links this moment of recognition to 'Hegel's Owl of Minerva flying only at dusk and Dilthey's idea of death as the sole moment of personal totalization' (106).

22 Congdon suggests that Lukács's reading of Dostoevsky is as doggedly wrong as his reading of Cervantes – and wrong in the same way: 'Contrary to what Lukács believed, [Dostoevsky] was not a utopian writer. If no one was more sensitive to this world's corruption, no one so loved corrupt men' (107).

4. Ideas and Forms: Hermann Cohen's Novelistics

1 Kagan wrote a dissertation, 'The Problem of Transcendental Apperception from Descartes to Kant,' at Marburg, and during his internment by the Germans during the First World War was personally defended by Cohen (Holquist and Clark 1:300).

2 The incorrect assertion that Cohen dealt only with Kant and the philosophy of science dates to Heidegger's 1929 debate with Ernst Cassirer. Although Cassirer defended his mentor from this simplification, Heidegger's reduction of Cohen's work has carried the day in standard histories of philosophy (Ferrari 7–9).

3 In the Marburg school, jurisprudence 'was regarded primarily as a science – in the broad meaning of the term – or a theory of legislating and of legal hermeneutics' (Coskun 309).

4 'Der Mensch ist ein schaffender Rückblick der Natur auf sich selbst' (*KA* 2:258).

5 Most current scholarship focuses on Cohen's logics and ethics, with little attention paid to his aesthetics. For an introduction to Cohen's system in English, see Holzhey, 'Cohen and the Marburg School in Context' 3–37. Dufour offers a helpful presentation of Cohen's *Aesthetics to Pure Feeling*, 101–11.

6 Lukács preferred Hegel's theory of origin, in which nothingness was linked to being. Heidegger attacked Cohen's concept of origin for being too analytical and displacing metaphysics from philosophy (Gordon 47–8).

7 For a discussion of the history of the logical and metaphysical notions of the infinitesimal, see Schultheis, 'Einleitung' 14–26.

8 In response to Heidegger's tendency to consider Cohen first and foremost a philosopher of science, Cassirer replied: 'So, for Cohen, the orientation to science does not imply any commitment to its temporal, contingent form. The "givenness" that the philosopher recognizes in the mathematical science of nature ultimately means the givenness of the *problem*' ('Hermann Cohen and the Renewal of Kantian Philosophy' 100).

9 'Die Realität aber ist – Bewusstsein; und zwar nicht materieller Inhalt des Bewusstseins, sondern eine gesetzliche Grundgestalt des wissenschaftlichen Bewusstseins, eine Art der Einheit des Bewusstseins, ein Grundsatz der Erkenntnis' (Cohen, *Das Prinzip der Infinitesimal-Methode und seine Geschichte* 162).

10 As Kluback reminds us, 'Purity is the only adjective which is proper for logic, ethics, and aesthetics because they must proceed from autonomy' (*The Legacy of Hermann Cohen* 4). The association of the word 'pure' with twentieth-century racism is a particularly painful historical irony.

11 *Allheit* should not be understood as totality, for Cohen contrasts *Allheit* to totality (Poma, *The Critical Philosophy of Hermann Cohen* 290).

12 *Ethics of Pure Will* is the linchpin of Cohen's whole system, for in it he proposes his notion of community (Philonenko, *L'école de Marbourg* 68).

13 'So lange er in einer Mehrheit schwebt, welche aus Einwirkungen auf ihn und Gegenwirkungen, die von der Mehrheit, die in ihm gelagert ist, ausgehen, ist sein Selbst noch gar nicht vorhanden. Erst die Einheit kann es ihm geben; kann ihn zum sittlichen Wesen machen' (*ERW* 81).

14 'Das Kapital wird selbst Arbeiter; es arbeitet, wie der Arbeiter; es erzeugt Werte, also Sachen' (*ERW* 609).

15 'Die Mythologie des Kapitals bringt selbst die Erlösung der arbeitenden Person herbei' (*ERW* 611).

16 'Das bleibt immer der treibende Gedanke: es gibt nichts Mächtigeres, nichts Evidenteres für Leben und Bewusstsein als Hoia, mir ist wohl; und sein Gegenteil. Daher müssen Lust und Unlust die Wertzeichen und Wertzeugen des Lebens sein' (*ERW* 160).

17 'In seinen sozialen Ständen bildet das Volk ein Aggregat von Besonderheiten, und bleibt somit selbst eine Besonderheit' (*ERW* 33).

18 'Es ist die Innerlichkeit des sittlichen Selbstbewusstseins, in aller Scheu und Ehrfurcht, aber auch in aller Zuversicht und allem Frohmut sittlicher Gewissheit, welche hier ihre Schwingen hebt' (*ERW* 301). Moses Hess, like Cohen, viewed the Lutheran Reformation as participating in liberation from the power of the Catholic church, and thus furthering secular ideas and freedoms (Liebeschütz 12).

19 'Die juristische Person entfernt sich von dem sinnlichen Vorurteil der Einzelheit und ihrem Charakter der Mehrheit; sie konstituiert sich auf Grund der Allheit als Einheit des Rechtssubjektes' (*ERW* 78).

20 More work on Natorp's and Cohen's respective concepts of *Aufgabe* would be helpful. Natorp understood *Aufgabe* as a doubled moment in knowledge: as both the moment when the subject structures perception of the object, and as the moment of the object (Holzhey, *Cohen und Natorp* 1:159–63). Natorp

explains that for Cohen, self-consciousness is not based on the internal whirring of the mind, but rather the continual work (*Aufgabe*) of the will ('Hermann Cohens philosophische Leistung unter dem Gesichtspunkte des Systems' 97).

21 The entire quote reads: 'Wir haben in der Logik den Begriff der Aufgabe auch für die allgemeine Charakteristik des Denkens im Urteil herangezogen; aber auch da für die Zusammenwirkung der Methoden, welche im reinen Denken sich ergänzen, so dass keine derselben ihren Lauf vollenden kann, sondern immer gleichsam halbwegs von der andern abgelöst werden muss' (*ERW* 143).

22 '[D]as Denken (der Theoretik) beruht auf der Sonderung, die Tendenz widerstrebt der Sonderung; es ist rastloser Fortgang, Fortstürmen, Antizipation, doch zugleich in strenger Kontinuität; *Aufgabe*' (Natorp, 'Hermann Cohens philosophische Leistung unter dem Gesichtspunkte des Systems' 97).

23 'Judgment is, thus, presented as a dialectical process, that is, as "correlation" ... of separation and unification. What did Cohen mean by correlation? ... In the present context, this term is used to avoid any distortion of the relationship between separation and unification in the sense of identity' (Poma, *The Critical Philosophy of Hermann Cohen* 86–7).

24 'Die Aufgabe widerspricht zunächst dem Gegebenen; sie enthält selbst das Gegeben; sie macht es aus' (*ERW* 143).

25 'Sein Dasein besteht nur in seiner Erzeugung; und seine Erzeugung nimmt kein Ende, sofern er ein echter Begriff ist. Das heisst: der Begriff ist Aufgabe' (*ERW* 170).

26 'Das Wollen dagegen bedarf des Gegenstandes, wenn die Handlung ihm nicht in Velleität und Impetuosität verfliegen und zerflattern soll' (*ERW* 175).

27 'Sie [die Handlung] bildet das Innere, dem gegenüber die ganze Aussenwelt zu einem schier Äusserlichen wird' (*ERW* 175).

28 'Ich kann nicht Du sagen, ohne dich auf mich zu beziehen; ohne dich in dieser Beziehung mit dem Ich zu vereinigen' (*ERW* 248)

29 'Der Vertrag ist ein Anspruch; ein Anspruch des Rechts, den ich an den Andern erhebe' (*ERW* 248).

30 'Der Vertrag macht nun aus dem Anspruch die Ansprache' (*ERW* 248).

31 'Es entsteht dann nämlich der Verdacht, als ob die Idee doch nur eine Idee wäre, der gegenüber und hinter der im Ding an sich der eigentliche und gediegene Vorrat des Seins sich eröffnete, oder vielmehr verberge und verschlösse' (*ERW* 26).

32 'Wahrheit bedeutet den Zusammenhang und den Einklang des theoretischen und des ethischen Problems' (*ERW* 89).

33 'Das Suchen der Wahrheit, das allein ist Wahrheit. Die Methode allein, mittelst deren Logik und Ethik, beide zugleich, nicht eine allein, erzeugbar werden, diese vereinigende, diese einheitliche Methode, sie vollbringt und verbürgt die Wahrheit' (*ERW* 91).

34 'Das Selbst ist keineswegs und in keiner noch so idealen Gestalt vorher vorhanden, bevor es sich darlegt, und es hat sich keineswegs nur darzulegen; sondern es hat sich erst zu erzeugen' (*ERW* 339).

35 'Wir fassen die Zeit nicht als Succession des Nacheinander, sondern als die Projektion gleichsam des Voreinander. Die Zukunft geht uns voran, und die Vergangenheit folgt nach' (*ERW* 106).

36 Cohen feared that Nietzsche's radical critique of morality would result in an annihilation of ethics rather than its renewal (Kluback, *Hermann Cohen* 29). According to Schmid, Cohen's ethics are neither Socratic nor Aristotelian, but '[r]ather he occupies an intermediate position in seeing virtue both as knowledge of principles and as practice of this knowledge' (236).

37 '"Handle so, dass du die Menschheit in deiner Person, wie in der Person eines jeden Andern jederzeit zugleich als Zweck, niemals bloss als Mittel brauchst." In diesen Worten ist der tiefste und mächtigste Sinn des kategorischen Imperativs ausgesprochen; sie enthalten das sittliche Programm der neuen Zeit und aller Zukunft der Weltgeschichte' (*ERW* 320).

38 'Und die Weisheit, wird sie nicht zum Dünkel, wenn sich sich nicht ihrer Grenzen bewusst macht? Und ist etwa der Don Quixote nur eine Posse? Oder ist Aristophanes ein Possendichter, indem auch hier die Tragödie unter die komische Maske einspannt? Plato hat er den richtigen Weg gewiesen, indem er in der tiefen Nacht, als alle dem Zechen erlegen und entschlummert waren, Sokrates es aussprechen lässt, dass der Tragiker allein auch der Dichter der Komödie sei' (*ERW* 487).

39 Jurisprudence depends, for Cohen, upon a category of pure knowledge: actuality (*Wirklichkeit*). Actuality is unlinked from physical reality, and instead connects to the realm of thought. The philosopher considers naive any supposition that actuality would exist in the here and now, or would be equivalent to reality. Instead, actuality is a category of critical thought that relates the category of the individual (*Einzelne*) to the category of magnitude (*Größe*) (*ERW* 478–9). In ethical terms, it problematizes in a critical and productive sense the relation of the individual person to her milieu (*LRE* 496).

40 'Sie erweckt den Sinn für die Lücken und für die Grenzen des Wissens. Und wenn die Lücken auch ausgefüllt werden; die Grenzen bleiben doch stehen' (*ERW* 531).

41 'Das scharfe, wohlwollende Auge für die Besonderheiten des Falles, für die Eigenart der Personen, die dabei in Frage kommen, gibt dem Blick

Umsicht und Umschau … Die Humanität wendet den Blick nach allen Seiten …' (*ERW* 631).

42 It would be interesting to read *Religion of Reason* as an outgrowth of Cohen's earlier ethics as many of his key concepts can be traced to Judaic thought. Funkenstein points out that Cohen's understanding of ethical action as *Aufgabe* 'speaks the language of the prophets and of the Jewish prayer-book – "to amend the world into the kingdom of God," *Le'taken 'olam be'malchut shaddai*. This, says Cohen, is the essence of ethical monotheism, the essence of Judaism, the essence of German idealism rightly conceived' (280–1). For readings that associate Cohen's rejection of the distinction between *Sein* and *Sollen* with Jewish Messianism, see Kluback, *The Legacy of Hermann Cohen* 135 and Fackenheim, 50–1.

43 'Der Laut ist der mächtigste und intensivste Ausdruck des Innern; das Zeichen dafür, dass das Innere innerhalb seiner Grenzen sich nicht einzuhalten vermag; dass es in das Äussere, in die Äusserung übergeht' (*ERW* 190).

44 According to Krois, the next step in neo-Kantian thought is taken by Cassirer and Peirce, who consider signs and symbols to be the embodiment of meaning in the sensual (66).

45 Novalis argues that language is reflexive, having meaning only through the relation of signs occurring through the weaving together of words in sentences (Bowie 211).

46 'Das präziseste Mittel, durch welches der Wille in der Handlung sich betätigt und sich bezeugt, das ist der sprachliche Ausdruck' (*ERW* 191–2).

47 'Zunächst bringt die Sprache freilich Mässigung und Ruhe in das Gewirr der Gefühle; das vulkanische Ungestüm wird gebändigt und beherrscht. Zugleich aber auch wirkt das Sprachgefühl, welches der Willenshandlung zu Grunde liegt, lösend und erlösend, indem es dem Abflusse des Affekts ein Bett bereitet und es eindämmt' (*ERW* 198).

48 'Indem der Wille, um Wille zu werden, in Worte nicht sowohl sich kleidet, als vielmehr in dieselben hineinwächst, so erwächst er aus den Wortgefühlen, mit denen die Begriffsworte der Sprache verwachsen bleiben' (*ERW* 198).

49 'Es gäbe keine Poesie, und keine Poesie, welche an Gedanken erblüht, wenngleich nicht in Gedanken, wenn diese Verwachsung nicht bestände und nicht unaufhörlich in dem gebildeten Bewusstsein sich erneute. Es ist ebenso das sittlich, wie das aesthetisch gebildete Bewusstsein, welches in diesen Pflanzungen sich ergeht' (*ERW* 198).

50 Cohen rejects Shaftesbury's sentimentalism on the grounds that ethics itself cannot be based on aesthetics (*ERW* 330).

51 'Die Poesie ist niemals ein Ersatz für Wissenschaft und Philosophie; sondern sie ist immer eine Gipfelung, eine Durchdringung, vor allem aber eine Aufsagung ihres tiefsten Gehaltes; nicht etwa die Abschöpfung ihrer Schlagworte' (*ERW* 509).
52 'Daher scheint unser deutsches Wort so bezeichnend: Kunst ist Können; das Vermögen zu schaffen und zu bilden. Bilder zu entwerfen und zu gestalten, welche im Scheine der Wirklichkeit mit der Natur wetteifern' (*ERW* 58). Gianna Gigliotti draws the inevitable conclusion that 'aesthetics – and therefore ... sensibility – [are] a *principle of itself and as such* constitutive' (99).
53 I have chosen to translate *Vollkommenheit* as 'fulfilment,' but it can also be translated as 'perfection' or 'completion.' By using fulfilment, I hope to avoid the sense of closure implicit in the other two terms.
54 'Die Vollkommenheit ist ein Augenblicksbild des Standpunktes; sie gibt dem Charakterbilde nicht Festigkeit und Sicherheit vor Schwankungen und vor dem Umfall ins Gegenteil' (*ERW* 542).
55 'Die Gestalt ist die Einheit von Seele und Leib' (ARG 1:191).
56 'Der Humor sagt: das soll ein Mensch sein, ein Ebenbild Gottes, diese Vogelscheuche der Menschheit!' (*ARG* 1:283).
57 Kluback reads this as an attack on Nietzsche rather than Friedrich Schlegel (*Hermann Cohen* 29).
58 For their respective metaphysical notions of the self, art, and history, Cohen rejected Fichte, Schelling, and Hegel (Poma, *The Critical Philosophy of Hermann Cohen* 72–7).
59 'Der ästhetische Unterschied der Weltalter möchte in dem Unterschied vom Epos liegen, den die neuere Zeit im Roman augesführt' (*ERW* 537).
60 Nervous about the notion of national heroes, Cohen proposes as an alternative the bravery of the prophets, who suffer for others and who fight for justice for the poor (*ERW* 559).
61 'Aber die Schwäche macht er zur Ursache des Schlechten; und Mängel und Schwachheiten hängt er daher auch der behäbigen Sittlichkeit an. So treten das Gute und das Schlechte in eine Verflechtung, und ebenfalls auch in ein Gewirr ihrer kleinsten Motive, so dass die Gutmütigkeit in alle Gegensätze und Widersprüche hineinscheint, und Harmonie und Versöhnung da hervorbringt, wo sonst der Gegensatz den einzigen Halt und Trost bildet. Das ist der Segen des Humors, dass er gegen die Feierlichkeit und Gehobenheit der höhern Kunst den Blick herabsenkt auf die Niedrigkeiten und Eitelkeiten des menschlichen Lebens, und für diese Indulgenz beansprucht' (*ERW* 538–9).
62 '[D]ie Poesie wird die prosa des Romans' (*ERW* 537).

63 'Von seiner Weite aus kann man vielleicht alle die Formen des Romans ableiten, welche die neuere Zeit hervorgebracht hat' (*ARG* 2:119).

64 'Denn sie alle sind Lehrgedichte großen Stils, geistige Kosmogenien, in denen die Schöpfung, die Umgestaltung, die Neubildung der Kultur des Geistes angestrebt wird' (*ARG* 2:119).

65 'Denn das ist der Sinn dieser neuen göttlichen Komödie, daß in ihr alle Heiligtümer der Kultur in Eitelket versinken' (*ARG* 2:119).

66 'Sancho Pansa wird das Ideal eines Statthalters. Das ist ein noch deutlicherer Gipfel in diesem Poetischen Gebirge, als daß Don Quixote der ideale Ritter ist' (*ARG* 2:119).

67 'Denn für das Epos ist die Liebe nur ein Kampfpreis, noch nicht ein Erlebnis, welches das Bekenntnis von der Begebenheit unterscheidet, und zu dem neuen Eigenwerte des individuellen Menschenlebens erhebt. Der Roman ist deshalb nur äußerlich die Fortsetzung des Epos, weil er innerlich vielmehr die Ausgestaltung der Lyrik ist' (*ARG* 2:121).

68 'Die Erweiterung des eigenen Selbst zum Mitgefühl für ein anderes Selbst, das allein sei der keusche Sinn dieser Nächstenliebe' (*ERW* 219). Significantly, the compassion or sympathy one feels for a literary hero can serve in the same way to broaden the confines of the self (220).

69 'Die Ewigkeit ist auch hier die Rastlosigkeit des Strebens und des Ringens' (*ARG* 2:132).

70 'Es gibt keine restlose Vereinigung für die sittliche Kultur zwischen Ideal und Wirklichkeit. In diese Kluft des Geistes tritt die Kunst ein' (*ARG* 2:128).

71 'Und so entsteht die Aufgabe des Romans: in der Liebesgeschichte der sterblichen Menschen die Ewigkeit der Liebe darzustellen, zu der das Menschenherz sich aufschwingt, vor der aber das arme Kulturwesen des Menschen in Elend vergehen muß' (*ARG* 2:128).

72 'Auch ihre Wechselfälle verdienen Entfaltung, ihr eigenes Auf und Nieder, und die Komplikationen, in die sie sich mit der umgebenden Menschenwelt verschlingen, fordern nicht nur Beschreibung, wie die Vermischten Nachrichten sie bieten, noch auch eine Untersuchung, wie in den Gerichtsverhandlungen, noch auch nur Mitberücksichtigung bei den diplomatischen Aktenstücken der Weltgeschichte: sie gehören in das Hausarchiv des Menschenherzens, das nicht erschöpft und erledigt wird durch die epigrammatischen Stoßseufzer der Lyrik' (ARG 2:121–2).

73 Cohen's notion of tragedy coincides in places with this description of the novel as a genre, particularly insofar as the spectator or reader is led toward action through his compassionate reaction to the hero's suffering. For Cohen's concept of tragedy, see Wiedebach, 'Aesthetics in Religion' 63–6.

74 The category of heuristic fiction provides a means by which one can consider the relation of the individual to the environment. In this sense,

Cohen legitimizes one of the most powerful methodological tools of the Marburg School, heuristic fiction (*Fiktion*) understood as a form of actuality (*Wirklichkeit*). For Cohen, the unity of mankind is a heuristic fiction, a foreshadowing or imagining of an idea located in the future, since current activity splits and separates humanity.

75 'Dios sabe si hay Dulcinea o no [en] el mundo, o si es fantástica, o no es fantástica; y éstas no son de las cosas cuya averiguación se ha de llevar hasta el cabo. Ni yo engendré ni parí a mi señora, puesto que la contemplo como conviene que sea una dama que contenga en sí las partes que puedan hacerla famosa en todas las del mundo ...' (*DQM* 2:273).

5. The Poetics of Resuscitation: Unamuno's Anti-Novelistics

1 Although the term was coined by Ortega to describe his own generation, children in 1898, it was appropriated by Azorín to describe the generation corresponding to Unamuno. Unamuno seems to have had little use for the idea (Cacho Viu, *Repensar el 98* 117–71).

2 For an overview of the nineteenth-century and early twentieth-century Spanish reception of *Don Quixote*, see Navarro 42–75 and Gutiérrez 113–24. The exposition catalogue by Reyero, *Cervantes y el mundo cervantino en la imaginación romantica*, offers a glimpse of the abundant visual representations of Cervantes' work from the period. García Sánchez has compiled a collection of writings on Cervantes from the era (*Visiones del Quijote*).

3 For information on the activities of the 1905 centenary of the publication of *Don Quixote de la Mancha* Part I, see Storm, 'El tercer centenario del *Don Quijote* en 1905 y el nacionalismo español,' and Schmidt, 'Beyond Words: Cervantes Iconography in the 1905 Centenary and the Following Decade' and 'Women in the 1905 and 1916 Cervantes Centenary Activities.'

4 For the correlation of Unamuno's interpretation of Don Quixote to major events in his life, see Catalán, and Blanco Aguinaga, 'De Nicodemo a Don Quixote.'

5 In 1913 Unamuno claims that his earlier call for Don Quixote's death was a blasphemy and that he wanted to say the exact opposite, an assertion that is difficult to accept at face value (*UOC* 7:290).

6 'Debe [la razón] su origen acaso al lenguaje. Pensamos articulada, o sea reflexivamente, gracias al lenguaje articulado, y este lenguaje brotó de la necesidad de trasmitir nuestro pensamiento a nuestros prójimos' (*UOC* 7:124). I have translated *acaso* as 'by chance or accident' given the evolutionary frame of this chapter, although it could also be translated as 'perhaps.'

7 It is ironic that Pascal, in his *Pensées*, calls the Cartesian method a novel of nature, similar to *Don Quixote de la Mancha*: '1008 Feu M. Pascal appelait

la philosophie cartésienne le roman de la nature, semblable à peu près à l'histoire de Dom Quichot …' ('Propos attribués à Pascal,' http://www .ub.uni-freiburg.de/referate/04/pascal/pensees.pdf).

8   Unamuno's notebooks on *Don Quixote* have been published, along with *Cómo se hace una novela*, as *Manual de Quijotismo*. Scholars differ on the dates of the notebooks, with Cerezo Galán sustaining that they are from the 1930s, although Vauthier believes that they are from the mid-1920s, when Unamuno was exiled in France and preparing his French edition of *How to Make a Novel*. The latter assertion seems more likely to me based on the parallels between the notebook's musings and the content of *How to Make a Novel*.

9   Olson notes the following possible translations of the title *Cómo se hace una novela:* 'How a novel *is made*,' 'How *one makes* a novel,' and 'How a novel *makes itself*,' and prefers the final translation (173). I prefer the second, because the identity and nature of the writing and reading 'I' is of utmost importance in Unamuno's thought. When he wrote of the death of the author, it was not in the postmodern sense of the absence of the author, but rather the actual mortality of the flesh-and-blood author.

10   See Vauthier, *Cómo se hace una novela*, 145–7, for a review of the various editions. This edition of the text indicates the various additions and censored portions, and constitutes the best critical edition currently available. *Comment on fait un roman* was published in the *Mercure de France*, tome CLXXXVIII, number 670, 15 May–15 June 1926, pp. 5–39, and included Cassou's 'Portrait d'Unamuno.' The Buenos Aires edition was published by Alba in 1927, containing an epigraph, a prologue, Cassou's portrait of Unamuno, Unamuno's commentary on the portrait, the translation of the French text, plus a continuation. It was retranslated into French by Cassou in a work titled *Avant et après la revolution* (1933) with even more additions.

11   The entire sentence reads: 'En el prólogo del *Quijote* – que como casi todos los prólogos (incluso éste) no son apenas sino mera literatura – Cervantes nos revela que encontró el relato de la hazañosa vida del Caballero de la Triste Figura en unos papeles arábigos con la que el bueno – ¡y tan bueno! – de Cervantes nos revela lo que podríamos llamar la objetividad, la existencia – *ex-sistere* quiere decir estar fuera – de Don Quijote y Sancho y su coro entero fuera de la ficción novelista y sobre ella' (*CHN* 172).

12   Unamuno attributes the lack of details given about Alonso Quijano's first fifty years of life to Cervantes' belief that everyone is a son of his own works, making himself through his life and work (*VDQ* 24).

13   See, for example, 'On the Reading and Interpretation of *Don Quixote*' (*UOC* 1:1230), *Cómo se hace una novela* 170, and *San Manuel Bueno, mártir* 3. Fernández Cifuentes links this eating of the text to the Spanish colloquial

phrase, 'devorar un libro' ('to devour a book'), and notes that the devouring is reciprocal: the writing devours the author and the reader, and vice versa ('Unamuno y Ortega' 51).

14 'Lo vivo es lo que yo allí descubro, pusiéralo o no Cervantes, lo que yo allí pongo y sobrepongo y sotopongo, y lo que ponemos allí todos' (*UOC* 7: 290).

15 '¿Seré como me creo o como se me cree? Y he aquí cómo estas líneas se convierten en una confesión ante mi yo desconocido e inconocible; desconocido e inconocible para mí mismo. He aquí que hago la leyenda en que he de enterrarme' (*CHN* 187).

16 'Lo que quiere decir que los entes que reputamos de ficción tienen una vida propia, independiente y siguen viviendo. Y todos los que al conocerlos los recreamos les damos vida' (*CHN* 133).

17 '"Para mí sola nació Don Quijote, y yo para él; él supo obrar y yo escribir," hace decir el historiador a su pluma. Y yo digo que para que Cervantes contara su vida y yo la explicara y comentara nacieron Don Quijote y Sancho, Cervantes nació para explicarla, y para comentarla nací yo …' (*VDQ* 276).

18 Death threatens the philosopher in part due to his philosophy. Since Unamuno defines life in a neo-Kantian manner as a continual self-creation, then death interrupts, if not obviates, this process (Blanco 149).

19 See Cerezo Galán, *Máscaras de lo trágico* 298–306, 322–4, 334, de la Fuente Ballesteros 249, and Regalado García, *El siervo y el señor* 115–20.

20 'La locura, la verdadera locura, nos está haciendo mucha falta, a ver si nos cura de esta peste del sentido común que nos tiene a cada uno ahogado el propio' (*VDQ* 97).

21 'Sólo el que ensaya lo absurdo es capaz de conquistar lo imposible. No hay más que un modo de dar una vez en el clavo, y es dar ciento en la herradura' (*VDQ* 126).

22 'En las entrañas de las cosas, y no fuera de ellas, están lo eterno y lo infinito. La eternidad es la sustancia del momento que pasa, y no la envolvente del pasado, el presente y el futuro de las duraciones todas; la infinitud es la sustancia del punto que miro, y no la envolvente de la anchura, largura y altura de las extensiones todas' (*VDQ* 201).

23 'Cacemos, pues, y traguémonos a las moscas ponzoñosas que, zumbando y esgrimiendo su aguijón, revolotean en torno nuestro, y Dulcinea nos dé el poder convertir esta caza en combate épico que se cante en la duración de los siglos por el ámbito de la tierra toda' (*VDQ* 201).

24 'El loco suele ser un comediante profundo, que toma en serio la comedia, pero que no se engaña, y mientras hace en serio el papel de Dios o de rey o de bestia, sabe bien que ni es Dios, ni rey, ni bestia' (*VDQ* 151).

25 'La razón es aquello en que estamos todos de acuerdo, todos o por lo menos la mayoría. La verdad es otra cosa, la razón es social; la verdad, de ordinario, es completamente individual, personal e incomunicable. La razón nos une y las verdades nos separan' (*CHN* 192).

26 '¿Qué es la vida? Un frenesí./¿Qué es la vida? Una ilusión,/una sombra, una ficción,/y el mayor bien es pequeño:/que toda la vida es sueño,/y los sueños sueños son' (Calderón, *La vida es sueño*, II: vv. 2182–7, p. 668).

27 '¡Pobre Don Quijote! A lindero de morir, y a la luz de la muerte, confiesa y declara que no fue su vida sino sueño de locura. ¡La vida es sueño!' (*VDQ* 261).

28 'Mejor que investigar si son molinos o gigantes los que se nos muestran dañosos, seguir la voz del corazón y arremeterlos, que toda arremetida generosa trasciende del sueño de la vida. De nuestros actos, y no de nuestras contemplaciones sacaremos sabiduría' (*VDQ* 272).

29 'Que haga del sueño, de su sueño, vida y se habrá salvado' (*CHN* 208).

30 'El que jugando a solitarios mira atrás ¡es la conc[iencia]!' (*CHN* 122).

31 'La duda metódica de Descartes es una duda cómica, una duda puramente teórica, provisoria; es decir, la duda de uno que hace como que duda sin dudar' (*UOC* 7:173).

32 'Y el alma, mi alma al menos, anhela otra cosa; no absorción, no quietud, no paz, no apagamiento, sino eterno acercarse sin llegar nunca, inacabable anhelo, eterna esperanza que eternamente se renueva sin acabarse del todo nunca' (*UOC* 7:260).

33 For the representation of Don Quixote as a Christ figure in various times and media, see Eric J. Ziolkowski, *The Sanctification of Don Quixote.*

34 '"¡He aquí el loco!", se dirían. Y la tragedia cómica, irracional, es la pasión por la burla y el desprecio. El más alto heroísmo para un individuo como para un pueblo, es saber afrontar el ridículo; es, mejor aún, saber ponerse en ridículo y no acobardarse en él' (*UOC* 7:293–4).

35 'Y el quijotismo no es sino lo más desesperado de la lucha de la Edad Media contra el Renacimiento, que salió de ella' (*UOC* 7:297).

36 When Unamuno states that Don Quixote was not 'modern in a modern sense – even less a modernist,' he means that Don Quixote was not fashionably avant-garde or 'snobbish' (*UOC* 7:300). This does not obviate what constitutes Don Quixote's true modernity for Unamuno: his conscious anachronism.

37 This leads Unamuno – paradoxically, given his own socialistic politics plus his valorization of heterodoxy and liberal Protestantism – to defend both the Counter-Reformation and the Inquisition. See Orringer, *Unamuno y los protestantes liberales* 178 and 220.

38 'Así nadie tendrá derecho a decir que deroga las leyes de su género … Invento el género, e inventar un género no es más que darle un nombre nuevo, y le doy las leyes que me place' (*N* 200).

39 'Mis personajes se irán haciendo según obren y hablen, sobre todo según hablen; su carácter se irá formando poco a poco' (*N* 199). It has been suggested that Víctor's novel is *Niebla* (Olson 79).

40 'Es el encanto de la conversación, de hablar por hablar, de hablar roto e interrumpido' (*N* 200).

41 The references to Cervantes and *Don Quixote* in *Niebla* have occasioned controversy as some scholars caution against reading the intertextuality as proof of parallels between Cervantes and Unamuno. The stance Unamuno takes toward literature in *Niebla* is the mirror opposite of Cervantes' critique in *Don Quixote*, for the twentieth-century author erases the distinction between art and reality that serves to occasion Don Quixote's many beatings and failures (Øveraas 41–4), and his approach should be considered Quixotic rather than Cervantine (Wyers 103).

42 'Y yo soy el Dios de estos dos pobres diablos *nivolescos*' (*N* 252).

43 'Pues bien, mi señor creador don Miguel, también usted se morirá, también usted, y se volverá a la nada de que salió … ¡Dios dejará de soñarle! … Porque usted, mi creador, mi don Miguel, no es usted más que otro ente *nivolesco*, y entes *nivolescos* sus lectores, lo mismo que yo, que Augusto Pérez, que su víctima …' (*N* 284).

44 The syntax of this sentence in Spanish is ambivalent. The phrase 'el que se crea rey' could be read in the indicative, in which it would be translated as he who makes himself king, or in the subjunctive, in which it would be translated as whoever believes himself to be king (*N* 275).

45 For a discussion of the organicism of Unamuno's work and thought and its relation to Romantic organicism, see La Rubia Prado, *Alegorías de la voluntad* 49–63.

46 The entire quote reads, 'Ante todo, porque una verdadera novela, una novela viva, no tiene tapa; y luego, porque no es maquinaria lo que hay que mostrar, sino entrañas palpitantes de vida, calientes de sangre' (*CHN* 220).

47 '[P]ero el novelista no tiene que levantar [ninguna tapa] para que el lector sienta la palpitación de las entrañas del novelista, del autor; y las del lector, identificado con él por la lectura' (*CHN* 220).

48 The entire quote reads, 'Pero ¿un hombre histórico?, ¿un hombre de verdad?, ¿un actor del drama de la vida?, ¿un sujeto de novela? Éste lleva las entrañas en la cara. O, dicho de otro modo, su entraña – *intranea* –, lo de dentro, es su extraña – *extranea*–, lo de fuera; su forma es su fondo' (*CHN* 220–1).

49 'II Edad Media. v. Cohen 356 Lo medieval es hacer depender lo moral de
la religión, lo renaciente la inversa, o acaso hacer depender la religión de la
estética. El romanticismo es a la edad media lo que el renacentismo es a
la edad clásica greco-romana. Estúpido desprecio con que Cohen habla
de la edad media, de la mitología, de la teología, de la mística, del romanticismo' (*CHN* 127).

50 'La vida es el criterio de la verdad y no la concordia lógica, que lo es sólo
de la razón. Si mi fe me lleva a crear o aumentar vida, ¿para qué queréis
más prueba de mi fe? Cuando las matemáticas matan, son mentira las
matemáticas' (*VDQ* 112).

51 'Ruego al lector relea todo este admirable diálogo, por cifrarse en él la
íntima esencia del quijotismo en cuanto doctrina de conocimiento. A las
mentiras de Sancho fingiendo sucesos según la conformidad de la vida
vulgar y aparencial, respondían las altas verdades de la fe de Don Quijote,
basadas en vida fundamental y honda' (*VDQ* 111).

52 'Sólo ha habido un castellano que siendo sobrehombre supo a fuerza de
ironizar e ironizarse tomar su sobrehumanismo como espectáculo, super-
arlo y llegar, si no totalmente, por lo menos teoréticamente a Hombre'
(*Epistolario completo Ortega-Unamuno* 161).

53 'Y ¿para qué se hace el novelista? Para hacer al lector, para hacerse uno con
el lector. Y sólo haciéndose uno el novelador y el lector de la novela, se sal-
van ambos de su soledad radical. En cuanto se hacen uno, se actualizan y,
actualizándose, se eternizan' (*CHN* 224).

54 'Don Quijote creaba los gigantes, era una miración de despierto sobre la
débil visión de los molinos' (*CHN* 103).

55 'El sujeto crea su objeto … Se crea el objeto a sí mismo en el sujeto, y
crearse y recrearse o conservarse, es existir. Así existe el objeto, el sueño'
(*CHN* 103).

56 'El conocim[iento] no es pasivo sino activo. Si yo he conocido a Don
Quijote es haciéndolo en mí, haciendo obra quijotesca' (*CHN* 103).

57 'El mundo real y el ideal. D[on] Quijote no cree que los molinos son gigantes, quiere que lo sean. v. Cohen 353 La materia es la absoluta posibilidad de lo pasivo (Stuart Mill) y Dios la absoluta posibilidad de la forma=la
conc[iencia]. Lo verosímil y lo verdadero. Posible y composible. v. Cohen'
(*CHN* 125).

58 'Humanismo (personalismo) contra idealismo y contra realismo espiritual-
ismo. La idea para el hombre, no el hombre para la idea. D[on] Quijote
idea hecha hombre. El Verbo se hizo carne y habitó entre nosotros. El hombre hecho idea' (*CHN* 125).

6. Form Foreshortened: Ortega y Gasset's *Meditations on Don Quixote*

1 The original quote, 'Und ist etwa der Don Quixote nur eine Posse?' (*ERW* 487), is translated by Ortega y Gasset as '¿Es, por ventura, el *Don Quijote* una bufonada?' (*MQ* 40).

2 For expositions of Ortega's philosophy in English, see Ouimette, *José Ortega y Gasset*, Dobson, and González.

3 'Cohen piensa análogamente de sus semicompatriotas y digo semi – porque él es judío y como indica su nombre de lo más judío de la judería' (*Cartas de un joven español* 285). Ortega hastened to add in his letter that he himself found Spaniards equally intolerable.

4 According to Ortega, Cohen attended the Sephardic synagogue on his trips to Paris in order to contemplate the gestures and movements of the Sephardim (Marías, *Ortega. Vocación y circunstancia* 202).

5 López Frías argues that Ortega was a liberal who supported socialism because it seemed to be the only viable option at the time (93). Elorza notes that Cohen's ethics, based on the Kantian moral imperative, make it possible for Ortega to juggle socialism and liberalism (41). For a discussion in English of the young thinker's socialism, see Dobson 45–57.

6 'La Persona se crea en la unidad de la acción – la acción es Aufgabe siempre (es un hacer, no un tener, un tener sabido) – La persona, el Selbst es una Aufgabe siempre, no un contenido intelectual' (Molinuevo, 'Salvar a Fichte en Ortega' 143). I understand Ortega's concept of *ejecutividad* (performance or execution) in terms of *Aufgabe*. 'Lo real' seems to refer to the German, *Wirklichkeit*. I will translate it interchangeably as 'the real' and 'the actual.'

7 '[H]e aquí nuestra nación en la actualidad disgregada en átomos: nuestra actividad se reduce a negarse unas personalidades a otras, unos grupos a otros, unas regiones a otras: nuestra actividad se reduce a negarse unas personalidades a otras, unos grupos a otros, unas regiones a otras' (*OC* 1:516).

8 Ortega's recounts this period in Marburg in 'Prologue for Germans,' where he uses the vivid image of Natorp holding Plato prisoner for eight years, feeding him only bread and water while he tried to submit the Greek's thought to his own template (*OC* 8:35–6). Silver points out that the image of 'fortress Marburg' that Ortega fashions in 1934 is not accurate, for he discussed Brentano with Cohen in 1911 and probably first read Scheler there (20).

9 'Yo sentía cada una de ellas [sus frases] como un golpe en la nuca' (*OC* 8:34).

10 First published in *El Imparcial* (22 May 1909), it was republished in the Argentine newspaper *La Prensa* on 29 April 1913 with the title 'Diario de

un español. Una meditación del Escorial. Febrero de 1913.' The 1915 version was presented as a conference paper at the Ateneo in Madrid (4 April 1915) and published with revisions in *España* (num. 11, 9 April 1915) (Massó Lago 390).

11 There are points in Ortega's writing when Cervantes seems to approach the German idealist tradition; take, for example, his 'Reflections on a Centenary (1724–1924),' written to commemorate the anniversary of Kant's birth. In this essay, Ortega distinguishes sharply between the reflective, solipsistic tradition of German philosophy and the externally motivated, socially defined philosophy of the Mediterranean, including the ancient Greeks. He argues that Fichte's idealist constructivism, in which the external is seen as a creation of the internal, springs from Kant. Moreover, this is philosophy understood as adventure: *'aventura, hazaña, empresa – Tathandlung'* (*Kant, Hegel, Scheler* 41).

12 'Antes de la reflexión, un acto de coraje, una *Tathandlung*: éste es el principio de su filosofía' (*OC* 1:553).

13 'Cervantes compuso en su *Quijote* la crítica del esfuerzo puro' (*OC* 1:553).

14 'Y, sobre todo, está esta angustiosa confesión del esforzado: La verdad es que "yo no sé lo que conquisto a fuerza de mis trabajos," no sé lo que logro con mi esfuerzo' (*OC* 1:554).

15 'Sobre el fondo anchísimo de la historia universal fuimos los españoles un ademán de coraje. Esta es toda nuestra grandeza, ésta es toda nuestra miseria' (*OC* 1:552).

16 'No le interesa al esforzado la acción: sólo le interesa la hazaña' (*OC* 1:552).

17 Ortega's rejection of Fichte's postulation of the other as the Not-I parallels Cohen's postulation of the other as the Du rather than the Not-I (Molinuevo, 'Salvar a Fichte en Ortega' 128).

18 Other key elements of Ortega's mature philosophy to be found in the *Meditations on Don Quixote* include the supposition 'that the basic reality is "human life", a dialectic of striving and resistance, of "Being-from-within" (or *Zuhandenheit*) and "Being-from-without"(or *Vorhandenheit*), of *aestheisis* (Be-ing) and *logos* (Having), and hence its name, *vital* or *historical reason*' (Silver 149).

19 The fact that Ortega posited *aletheia* already in 1914 led to his claim that he had beat Heidegger to the idea by some thirteen years. See Marías, *Ortega. Circunstancia y vocación* 428–37, for a defence of this claim.

20 For a reconstruction of this project, see Fox's edition of Ortega's *Meditaciones sobre la literatura y el arte (La manera española de ver las cosas)*. Fox considers the essays therein ('Pío Baroja. Anatomía de un alma dispersa,' 'La voluntad del Barroco,' and 'La agonía de la novela') to be the continuation of the *Meditations on Don Quixote*.

21 In working notes, Ortega suggested 'El sentido monadológico del *Quijote*,' only to replace it with 'Cómo Miguel de Cervantes solía ver el mundo' (Molinuevo, 'Sobre Cervantes y *El Quijote* desde el Escorial' 42).

22 Intellectual love is associated with intellectual altruism, the openness to dialogue not only with other human beings, but also to contemplate things. Ortega attributed this phrase to Hartmann, who, one day in Marburg, interrupted his playing of the violincello to remark that Ortega was gifted with intellectual altruism (Marías, *Ortega. Circunstancia y vocación* 303–4).

23 Ortega claimed to use the same methodology in his essay on Kant, 'Reflexiones de centenario (1724–1924),' and described it as a circular approach to Kant, followed by an unavoidable moment of penetration and invasion (*Kant, Hegel, Scheler* 37). Basdekis notes the 'obvious reference to the predilect phenomenological hermeneutic' in the 'Jericho method' (22). Bergson's assertion that knowing a thing requires two steps, the first revolving around it to take a point of view and the second immediate knowledge by intuition, seems to echo Ortega's approach. Nonetheless, it is radically different since the Frenchman denies the representation of the inner life by images or concepts (Marías, *Ortega. Circunstancia y vocación* 98–100). Cleveland's interpretation of the Jericho method parallels in many ways my own (83–98).

24 'Ocupa, pues, la erudición el extrarradio de la ciencia, porque se limita a acumular hechos, mientras la filosofía constituye su aspiración céntrica, porque es la pura síntesis' (*MQ* 22–3).

25 'Y al pensarla debidamente, todo este tesoro de significación explota de un golpe, y de un golpe vemos esclarecida la enorme perspectiva del mundo' (*MQ* 23).

26 'Una obra del rango del *Quijote* tiene que ser tomada como Jericó. En amplios giros, nuestros pensamientos y nuestras emociones han de irla estrechando lentamente, dando al aire como sones de ideales trompetas' (*MQ* 38).

27 The neologism coined by Rodríguez Huéscar, 'instancing,' depends on the combination of the Spanish verbs 'estar' (to be in place, to stand) and 'instar' (to insist or invite).

28 'Sin necesidad de deliberar, apenas los oigo los envuelvo en un acto de interpretación ideal y los lanzo lejos de mí: los oigo como lejanos' (*MQ* 48).

29 The definition of the term remains ambiguous. Earlier editions of the dictionary of the Real Academia Española define 'trasmundo' as meaning a world of fantasy or delusion, but the twenty-second edition refers to it as the world beyond this life.

30 'Quien quiera enseñarnos una verdad, que nos sitúe de modo que la descubramos nosotros' (*MQ* 50).

31 'Si no hubiera más que un ver pasivo quedaría el mundo reducido a un caos de puntos luminosos. Pero hay sobre el pasivo ver un ver activo, que interpreta viendo y ve interpretando; un ver que es mirar' (*MQ* 51).

32 '¿Cómo es posible que su representación nos conmueva? … [N]o ellos, no *las* realidades nos conmueven, sino su representación, es decir, la representación de *la* realidad de ellos. Esta distinción es, en mi entender, decisiva: lo poético de la realidad no es la realidad como esta o aquella cosa, sino la realidad como función genérica' (*MQ* 128).

33 'El escorzo es el órgano de la profundidad visual; en él hallamos un caso límite, donde la simple visión está fundida con un acto puramente intelectual' (*MQ* 52).

34 'Del mismo modo que hay un ver que es un mirar, hay un leer que es un *intelligere* o leer lo de dentro, un leer pensativo. Sólo ante éste se presenta el sentido profundo del *Quijote*' (*MQ* 56–7).

35 'Si seguimos atendiendo a un objeto éste se irá fijando más porque iremos hallando en él más reflejos y conexiones de las cosas circundantes. El ideal sería hacer de cada cosa centro del universo' (*MQ* 73).

36 Hernández Sánchez maintains that Ortega's reference to the Hegelian concept of limit comes from the *Prologue of the Phenomenology of Spirit*, in part because Ortega is concerned in this passage with the relation of concepts to system (145–50).

37 '[C]ada concepto es literalmente un órgano con que captamos las cosas' (*MQ* 78).

38 'La forma y el fondo son inseparables y el fondo poético fluye libérrimamente sin que quepa imponerle normas abstractas' (*MQ* 96).

39 'Pues bien, los géneros literarios son las funciones poéticas, direcciones en que gravita la generación estética' (*MQ* 96). Orringer outlines all the issues in which Cohen and Ortega differ in their novelistics, such as the relation of the novel to the epic or the lyric, and the concept of adventure, but does not notice Ortega's incorporation of Cohen's notion of the infinitesimal function (*Ortega y sus fuentes germánicas* 168–205).

40 'Tomar una dirección no es lo mismo que haber caminado hasta la meta que nos propusimos. La piedra que se lanza lleva en sí predispuesta la curva de su área excursión. Esta curva viene a ser como la explicación, desarrollo y cumplimiento del impulso original' (*MQ* 97).

41 'Así es la tragedia la expansión de un cierto tema poético fundamental y sólo de él, es la expansión de lo trágico' (*MQ* 97).

42 'Nosotros vamos lanzados en la aventura como dentro de un proyectil, y en la lucha dinámica entre éste, que avanza por la tangente, que ya escapa, y el centro de la tierra, que aspira a sujetarlo, tomamos el partido de aquél' (*MQ* 118).

43 'Si entráramos al aposento, habríamos puesto el pie dentro de un objeto ideal, nos moveríamos en la concavidad de un cuerpo estético' (*MQ* 119).

44 Ortega was influenced by Jakob von Uexküll, who asserted that the environment itself functioned as an organism. Individual organisms existed in reciprocal relation with the environment, as they themselves exercised influence over it (J. Varela 203–4).

45 The quote reads: 'una actividad de ósmosis y endósmosis entre la España parlamentaria y la España no parlamentaria, entre los organismos siempre un poco artificiales de los partidos y el organismo espontáneo, difuso, envolvente, de la nación' (*OC* 1:271).

46 'El arte es la técnica, es el mecanismo de actualización frente al cual aparece el acto creador de los bellos objetos como la función poética primaria y suprema' (*MQ* 111).

47 Ortega's critique of verisimilitude understood in nineteenth-century terms is a constant throughout his lifetime; what is lacking for him in this sort of literature is poetic tension (A.M. Fernández 78–82).

48 'El plano épico donde se deslizan los objetos imaginarios era hasta ahora el único, y podía definirse lo poético con las mismas notas constituyentes de aquél. Pero ahora el plano imaginario pasa a ser un segundo plano. El arte se enriquece con un término más; por decirlo así, se aumenta en una tercera dimensión, conquista la profundidad estética, que, como la geométrica, supone una pluralidad de términos' (*MQ* 120).

49 'Sería torcido decidirse por uno u otro continente. Don Quijote es la arista en que ambos mundos se cortan formando un bisel' (*MQ* 121).

50 'Don Quijote, que es real, quiere realmente las aventuras. Como él mismo dice: "Bien podrán los encantadores quitarme la ventura, pero el esfuerzo y el ánimo es imposible"' (*MQ* 121).

51 'Caminando a lo largo de él con Don Quijote y Sancho, venimos a la comprensión de que las cosas tienen dos vertientes. Es una el "sentido" de las cosas, su significación, lo que son cuando se las interpreta. Es otra la "materialidad" de las cosas, su positiva sustancia, lo que las constituye antes y por encima de toda interpretación' (*MQ* 125).

52 'Estos molinos tienen un sentido: como "sentido" estos molinos son gigantes' (*MQ* 125).

53 'La cultura – la vertiente ideal de las cosas – pretende establecerse como un mundo aparte y suficiente, adonde podamos trasladar nuestras entrañas. Esto es una ilusión, y sólo mirada como ilusión, sólo puesta como un espejismo sobre la tierra, está la cultura puesta en su lugar' (*MQ* 126). Morón Arroyo notes that these lines are a transliteration from Cohen's *Aesthetics* (*El sistema de Ortega y Gasset* 382). However, Ortega's placement of this unacknowledged quote within this section undercuts Cohen's idealism.

54 '[J]amás encontramos la poesía de lo real como simplemente real' (*MQ* 130).

55 'Das ist der Segen des Humors, dass er gegen die Feierlichkeit und Gehobenheit der höhern Kunst den Blick herabsenkt auf die Niedrigkeiten und Eitlekeiten des menschlichen Lebens, und für diese Indulgenz beanspruch' (*ERW* 538–9).

56 For the influence of Bergson on Ortega's notion of comedy, see Orringer, *Ortega y sus fuentes germánicas* 194–201, and P.H. Fernández, 173–82.

57 'De querer ser a creer que se es ya, va la distancia de lo trágico a lo cómico. Este es el paso entre la sublimidad y la ridiculez. La transferencia del carácter heroico desde la voluntad a la percepción causa la involución de la tragedia, su desmoronamiento, su comedia. El espejismo aparece como tal espejismo' (*MQ* 142).

58 'La línea superior de la novela es una tragedia; de allí se descuelga la musa siguiendo a lo trágico en su caída' (*MQ* 143–4).

59 'Pero ¿es que la tragedia no tiene su interna, independiente verosimilitud? ¿No hay un *vero* éstetico – lo bello? ¿Y una similitud a lo bello?' (*MQ* 148).

60 Although at one point in *Ideas on the Novel* Ortega opines that a crisis in the form ensues due to a lack of themes, he contradicts himself in the same work when writing that themes are not important to the novel (Salas Fernández 78–9).

61 '[L]o importante no es *lo que* se ve, sino *que* se vea bien algo humano, sea lo que quiera' (*IN* 159).

62 'La táctica del autor ha de consistir en aislar al lector de su horizonte real y aprisionarlo en un pequeño horizonte hermético e imaginario que es el ámbito interior de la novela' (*IN* 187).

63 García Alonso writes of the 'irrealization' produced by art as the habitual world is submitted to will and intellect, rendering it ideal (140–1).

64 'El poeta aumenta el mundo, añadiendo a lo real, que ya está ahí por sí mismo, un irreal continente' (Ortega y Gasset, *La deshumanización del arte* 72).

65 '[A] poco sensible que sea, el mecanismo psíquico de estas almas le parece tan forzoso, tan evidente como el funcionamiento de una demostración geométrica en que se habla de miriágonos jamás entrevistos' (*IN* 200).

66 'Acaso el brusco aletazo de un recuerdo vuelve de un golpe a sumergirnos en el universo de la novela, y con algún esfuerzo, como braceando en un elemento líquido, tenemos que nadar hasta la orilla de nuestra propia existencia. Si alguien nos mira, entonces descubrirá en nosotros la dilatación de párpados que caracteriza a los náufragos' (*IN* 188).

67 'Las máximas novelas son islas de coral formadas por miríadas de minúsculos animales, cuya aparente debilidad detiene los embates marinos' (*IN* 195).

68 'Yo llamo novela a la creación literario que produce este efecto' (*IN* 188). Gullón suggests that Ortega anticipates reader reception theory in his notion of novelistic structure and form ('Ortega y la teoría de la novela' 106–7).

69 'Éste [el arte] no se justifica ni se limita a reproducir la realidad, duplicándola en vano. Su misión es suscitar un irreal horizonte' (Ortega y Gasset, *La deshumanización del arte* 87).

70 'El rencor va al arte como seriedad; el amor, al arte victorioso como farsa, que triunfa de todo, incluso de sí mismo, a la manera que en un sistema de espejos reflejándose indefinidamente los unos en los otros ninguna forma es la última, todas quedan burladas y hechas pura imagen' (Ortega y Gasset, *La deshumanización del arte* 87).

71 'Cuando las sentimos como seres vivos nos burlan descubriendo su cadavérico secreto de muñecos, y si las vemos como ficciones parecen palpitar irritadas. No hay manera de reducirlas a meros objetos … La figura de cera es el melodrama puro' (Ortega y Gasset, *La deshumanización del arte* 70).

7. *Don Quixote* in Bakhtin

1 Bakhtin's ideas have stimulated many worthwhile projects among Cervantes scholars. Given the sheer number of these studies, I will mention only a few. Among those exploring the carnivalesque dimensions of Cervantes' works, Redondo's stand out, given that he supplements Bakhtinian thought with the historical findings specific to the Spanish context of Julio Caro Baroja (153–81). Hutchinson explores the Bakhtinian concept of the chronotope (155–60), as does Deffis de Calvo (99–108). Forcione links the carnivalesque to Erasmian notions of humour and folly (204–26). Piskunova explicates summer festival imagery in *Don Quixote*. Bakhtin's ideas have even been used to indicate Cervantes' theatrical works (Cory Reed). Iffland examines both Cervantes' use of humour and his characterization of madness through the lens of Foucault and Bakhtin (155–82).

2 In 1984, Clark and Holquist drew on the comments of family members and others to bolster their argument that Bakhtin wrote the three books (146–7). In 1990, Morson and Emerson, following up on I.R. Titunik's scepticism, dismantle this claim for authorship (101–19). Although Western scholars tend to side with Morson and Emerson, denying Bakhtin authorship of the

three works, in 1993 Thomson and Wall questioned Morson and Emerson's political motivation as an argument for a liberal and non-Marxist Bakhtin (63). Unlike most Bakhtin scholars, Vauthier posits a materialist rather than an idealist Bakhtin, one influenced more by Dilthey and Marx than by Kant and Cohen, and uses Bakhtin's reading of Cervantes as evidence for her argument ('Bajtín en la encrucijada de las ciencias humanas europeas "en crisis"' 73–4). Nonetheless, as I hope to show, Bakhtin's use of *Don Quixote de la Mancha* in his theory effectively highlights the links between Bakhtin and idealism.

3 Bakhtin also shared with Cohen an interest in reconciling the tension between the human experience of God and the conceptualization of the divine according to idealist philosophy (Holquist and Clark 308–9).

4 This saying became so well-known that Konstantin Vigonov used it in a novel to satirize the Bakhtin Circle (Clark and Holquist 59).

5 The translator, Vadim Liapunov, notes that he has translated *zadannj* and *zadonnist'* in different ways throughout the work, using phrases such as 'what is yet to be accomplished or achieved' or 'what is set as a task (to be accomplished)' (AA 235). As he explains, '*zadannyj* is equivalent to the German *aufgegeben* (set as a task to be accomplished). The world of cognition is not a world that is *given*, but a world that is to be methodically determined. The distinction goes back to Kant, for whom Noumena and Ideas are *aufgeben* in contrast to what is given (*gegeben*).' Bakhtin, like Cohen, extends the notion of the task to be done to the ethical and the aesthetic, and the concept of *Aufgabe* is present in the work of both men. Unlike many translators, Liaponuv has alerted his reader to the references to German philosophical terms, but this has not been the general case. For analysis of the problems translating Bakhtin and the way French and English translations have skewed our understanding of his thought, see Zbinden, 'Traducing Bakhtin.'

6 We know from Schlegel's notebooks, which would not have been accessible to Bakhtin, that the German Romantic associated vulgar stupidity and educated foolishness with the comic pair of Sancho Panza and Don Quixote (see chap. 2; *Literarische Notizen* 85–6, 148–9, and 206–7).

7 Nonetheless, Bakhtin recognizes that Sorel's own writings, such as *Le Berger Extravagant* and *Francion*, incorporate carnivalesque elements.

8 Morson offers a Bakhtinian theory of parody in which he carefully analyses the relation between parody and utopianism in *Don Quixote* (63–86).

9 Tihanov states that Bakhtin's understanding of the novel as an open-ended form is innovative when compared to Hegel's closed system (*The Master and the Slave* 145). This would be true with respect to Hegel, but it is an

innovation already noted by Cohen, who speaks of the novel as the narration of immediate and unmediated present circumstances (*ARG* 2:118).

8. Revolutions and the Novel

1 'Copérnico se limita a sustituir una realidad por otra en el centro cósmico. Kant se revuelve contra toda realidad, arroja su máscara de *magister* y anuncia la dictadura' (*OC* 4:46).

2 For a discussion of the connections between the young and the older Schlegel's political thought, based on the same notion that revolution is essentially moral, see Peter (147–9).

3 'Denn Don Quixote ist nichts anders, als eine symbolische Person, welche erfunden worden, eine besondere und merckwürdige Eigenschaft in dem Character der Spanischen Nation vor den Augen aller Welt zu spielen, massen der Verfasser in den Gedanken stuhnd, daß es öfters nichts weiters brauchte, jemand von einem moralischen Fehler zu befreyn, als die Thorheit desselben vor seinen Augen nachzumachen' (Bodmer 518–19).

4 'Laßt uns die populäre Schreiberei der Franzosen und Engländer vergessen, und diesen Vorbildern nachstreben!' (*KA* 2:283).

5 Mennemeier believes that Schlegel limits the concept of revolution to the cultural realm of *Bildung* (42). Given the young Romantic's insistence on connecting everything to everything else, such a limiting of revolution to only one sphere, divorcing it from politics, seems to me to be a misreading.

6 'Was ich schon bei einer andern Gelegenheit von poetischen Werken des Witzes sagte, daß der Dichter in dieser Gattung um so mehr durch eine reiche Mitgabe von Poesie in den Nebenwerken, in der Darstellung, in der Form und Sprache, seinen Beruf, und sein Recht an alle Freiheiten, die er sich übrigens nimmt, bewähren müsse, das findet hier seine volle Anwendung' (*KA* 6:272).

7 'Der Roman des Cervantes ist seiner hohen inneren Vortrefflichkeit ungeachtet, ein gefährliches und irreleitendes Beispiel der Nachahmung für die andern Nationen geworden' (*KA* 6:274).

8 'Das wirkliche Leben in Spanien war damals noch mehr ritterlich und romantisch, als in sonst irgend einem Lande in Europa. Selbst der Mangel an einer allzustreng vervollkommneten bürgerlichen Ordnung, das freiere und wildere Leben in den Provinzen konnte für die Poesie günstiger sein' (*KA* 6:274).

9 With reference to Lukács's many writings about the German Romantics, Fehér notes that Lukács 'slanders the young radicals' ('Lukács in Weimar' 76).

10 I base this section on Kadarkay 202–31. For a concise description of the larger political picture, see Arato and Breines (92–6).

11 Bela Balász, Lukács's bosom friend and fellow revolutionary, clearly identified with Don Quixote and 'self-revealingly translated the chapter on Don Quixote from Lukacs's *Theory of the Novel*' in 1921 (Kadarkay 241).

12 'Der Wert einer Sache, das ist doch für jeden modernen Menschen der Wert der Arbeit, welche die Sache hervorbringen musste' (*ERW* 161). When speaking of the production of economic things, Cohen uses the term *Sache*, and thus preserves the Kantian notion of the *Ding an sich* as the thing unknown and uncreated by human consciousness. Although he admired Marx's ethical bent, Cohen considered Marxism to be based on the wrong belief theoretical laws based on reason rule history rather than action and ethics (Schwarzschild, 'The Democratic Socialism of Hermann Cohen' 209).

13 'Am Werte klebt also der Schweiss des Arbeiters, der das flammende Schwert kittet, das die Kultur von dem Paradiese trennt' (*ERW* 161).

14 'Der Wert kann nicht lediglich als Geldwert gedacht werden, wenn nicht zugleich das ganze Wertproblem, in dem der moderne Sozialismus seine wissenschaftliche Grundlage hat, mitgedacht würde' (*ERW* 162).

15 'Angesichts des Volksbegriffes drückt man die Augen zu über die ständischen Unterschiede, die er geschichtlich erfahre, und also auch wohl natürlich zulasse' (*ERW* 253).

16 'Was ist uns Hekuba?' (*ARG* 2:75). See Wiedebach, *Die Bedeutung der Nationalität für Hermann Cohen* 222–5.

17 For a rebuttal of Derrida's comparison of Cohen's pro-German stance to Heidegger's Nazism, see Novak (262–3).

18 'Y a mí me nombraron el caballero de la triste figura, dispuesto a honrarme con esta cortesía. Lamento que no pueda aceptarlo. Para emular a don Quijote hay que cumplir con el rasgo esencial de su persona, hay que quedar sin éxito. Yo he tenido éxito' (Mezquita 378).

19 'Para los que miraban la Reforma desde dentro de la iglesia podía parecerles cóncava y a los reformadores, a los protestantes, la Contra-Reforma, convexa. Y eran lo mismo. Era la necesidad dialéctica' (Mezquita 335).

20 'España … vive en permanente estado de guerra civil, porque el español rehúye la verdadera y santa guerra civil, la que cada uno lleva o debe llevar dentro de sí, con su otro yo' (Mezquita 363).

21 'Una revolución no es nunca un hecho; una revolución es siempre un inacabable quehacer. Porque una revolución se revoluciona a sí misma, se revuelve contra sí misma. Es la serpiente mítica que se devora a sí misma encentándose por la cola' (*PP* 665).

22 'Triste cosa sería que al bárbaro, anti-civil e inhumano régimen bolchevístico se quisiera sustituir con un bárbaro, anti-civil e inhumano régimen de

servidumbre totalitaria. Ni lo uno ni lo otro que en el fondo son lo mismo' (Urrutia 101).

23 'Y yo que creía trabajar por la salud de mi pueblo, llevo también sobre mí la responsabilidad de esta catástrofe. Yo era de los que querían salvar el género humano sin conocer al hombre' ('Carta a un socialista de buena fe' in *La Esfera*, Caracas, 3 January 1937, Mezquita 390).

24 The entire quote reads: 'Un inválido que carezca de la grandeza spiritual de Cervantes, que era un hombre – no un superhombre – viril y completo a pesar de sus mutilaciones, un inválido, como dije, que carezca de esa superioridad del espíritu, suele sentirse aliviado viendo cómo aumenta el número de mutilados alrededor de él' (Carlos Rojas 77). This quote comes from the testimony of Professor Luis Portillo, and is considered authentic by most accounts. Although he doubts that Unamuno would have said the following statements calling the university the temple of intellect and himself its high priest, Azaola considers the comparison of Millán to Cervantes to be 'worthy' of Unamuno (169).

25 According to Lalcona, Ortega's influence on the post-war generation of Spaniards extended beyond his brilliant stylistics and use of new terms to awaken an interest in European history and culture in a generation otherwise completely isolated from the outside world (9–10).

26 'Lejos, sola en la abierta llanada manchega la larga figura de Don Quijote se encorva como un signo de interrogación; y es como un guardián del secreto español, del equívoco de la cultura española' (*MQ* 87).

27 Ortega proposed, but did not write, a section in the *Meditations on Don Quixote* entitled 'The Halcyonic Cervantes.'

28 'Si de un mosaico arrancamos uno de sus trozos, nos queda el perfil de éste en forma de hueco, limitado por los trozos confinantes' (*MQ* 77).

29 We might better understand the metaphor of the book's title as decapitated rather than spineless, since Ortega's diagnosis of Spain's disease hinges on the absence of an intellectual elite that would lead the masses. The missing head, if I may be allowed a gruesome metaphor, is imagined by Ortega throughout his life as that of the philosopher, broadly understood not only as a rigorous logician but also as an intellectual leader of the community. Unamuno referred to the problem of Spain as scoliosis, a disease of the spine (Urrutia Jordana 22).

30 See Guillermo de Torre's letter to *Cuadernos Americanos* from 1942 (Abellán 141–4), and Morán's *El maestro en el erial. Ortega y Gasset y la cultura del franquismo*.

31 For Morán, the possibility that Ortega accepted these funds indicates that the Franco regime bought his silence (485–6). Abellán questions whether

Ortega would have actually received the money registered in the bureaucratic records (166).

32 For transcripts of the documents, see Blanco Alfonso (79–80).

33 As Hirschkop quips, 'For a long time we knew very little about Bakhtin's life. Thanks to the efforts of post-*glasnost* Bakhtin scholarship, we now know even less' (*Mikhail Bakhtin* 111).

34 The volume *Bakhtin and Religion* contains various writings about the influence of Russian Orthodox notions of the Incarnation, spiritual practice, and theology on Bakhtin, including articles by Lock, Pechey, and Mihailovic. Although Lock argues that Bakhtin's understanding of the Incarnation as the coexistence of duality in the person of Christ renders him an opponent of Kantian notions of the unified self (97–119), I tend to see the relation as more dialectical, with the Incarnation providing the young Russian a means to sublate the Kantian transcendental self.

35 'La vida es el texto eterno, la retama ardiente al borde del camino donde Dios da sus voces. La cultura – arte o ciencia o política – es el comentario, es aquel modo de la vida en que, refractándose ésta dentro de sí misma, adquiere pulimento y ordenación' (*MQ* 83).

36 '¿Qué cosa es el hombre? Los clásicos de la filosofía han ido pasándose de mano en mano, siglo tras siglo, esta cuestión, y cuando la pregunta se escurría por descuido o adrede, entre dos manos, cayendo sobre el pueblo, reventaba una revolución' (*OC* 1:92).

37 'La libertad, Sancho, es uno de los más preciosos dones que a los hombres dieron los cielos; con ella no pueden igualarse los tesoros que encierra la tierra ni el mar encubre; por la libertad, así como por la honra, se puede y debe aventurar la vida, y, por el contrario, el cautiverio es el mayor mal que puede venir a los hombres. Digo esto, Sancho, porque bien has visto el regalo, la abundancia que en este castillo que dejamos hemos tenido; pues en mitad de aquellos banquetes sazonados y de aquellas bebidas de nieve, me parecía a mí que estaba metido entre las estrechezas de la hambre, porque no lo gozaba con la libertad que lo gozara si fueran míos; que las obligaciones de las recompensas de los beneficios y mercedes recibidas son ataduras que no dejan campear al ánimo libre. ¡Venturoso aquel a quien el cielo dio un pedazo de pan, sin que le quede obligación de agradecerlo a otro que al mismo cielo!' (*DQM* 2:456).

Bibliography

Abellán, José Luis. *Ortega y Gasset y los orígenes de la transición democrática.* Madrid: Espasa-Calpe, 2000.

Acosta, José de. *Historia natural y moral de las Indias.* Barcelona: Lelio Marini, 1591. Available at Biblioteca Virtual Miguel de Cervantes, http://www.cervantesvirtual.com/FichaObra.html?Ref=22671, accessed on 23 February 2010.

Allemann, Beda. *Ironie und Dichtung.* 2nd ed. Pfullengen: Verlag Günther Neske, 1969.

Allen, Amy. 'Foucault and Enlightenment: A Critical Reappraisal.' *Constellations: An International Journal of Critical and Democratic Theory* 10, no. 2 (June 2003): 180–98.

Alonso, Cecilio. *Intelectuales en crisis. Pío Baroja, militante radical (1905–1911).* Alicante: Instituto de Estudios Juan Gil-Albert, 1985.

Alvar Ezquerra, Alfredo. 'La población española: siglos XVI al XVIII.' In *La sociedad española en la edad moderna.* Edited by Antonio Domínguez Ortiz and Alfredo Alvar Esquerra. Madrid: Ediciones Istmo, 2005. 17–88.

Álvarez Castro, Luis. *La palabra y el ser en la teoría literaria de Unamuno.* Salamanca: Ediciones Universidad de Salamanca, 2005.

Anonymous. *Lazarillo de Tormes.* Edited by Francisco Rico. Madrid: Cátedra, 1999.

Aranguren, José Luis L. *La ética de Ortega.* Madrid: Taurus, 1966.

Arato, Andrew, and Paul Breines. *The Young Lukács and the Origins of Western Marxism.* New York: The Seabury P, 1979.

Arendt, Hannah. *On Revolution.* New York: Penguin, 1987.

Ariel del Val, Fernando. *Historia e ilegitimidad: la quiebra del estado liberal en Ortega: fragmentos de una sociología del poder.* Madrid: Universidad Complutense, 1984.

Aristotle. *Physics. The Complete Works of Aristotle.* Vol. 1. Edited by Jonathan
    Barnes. Princeton, NJ: Princeton UP, 1984.
Arnheim, Rudolf. *The Split and the Structure. Twenty-eight Essays.* Berkeley: U of
    California P, 1996.
Arráez-Aybar, Luis-Alfonso. 'Anatomy in the Pages of *Don Quixote.'*
    Interciencia 31, no. 9 (September 2006): 690–4.
Auerbach, Erich. *Mimesis. The Representation of Reality in Western Literature.*
    Translated by Willard R. Trask. Princeton, NJ: Princeton UP, 1974.
Avalle-Arce, Juan Bautista. *Don Quijote como forma de vida.* Valencia: Fundación
    Juan March and Editorial Castalia, 1976.
Ayala, Francisco. *La novela: Galdós y Unamuno.* Barcelona: Seix Barral, 1974.
Azaola, José Miguel de. *Unamuno y sus guerras civiles.* Bilbao: Ediciones Laga,
    1996.
Bakhtin, Mikhail. *Art and Answerability. Early Philosophical Essays.* Translated
    byVadim Liapunov. Austin: U of Texas P, 1990.
– *The Dialogic Imagination. Four Essays.* Translated by Caryl Emerson and
    Michael Holquist. Austin: U of Texas P, 1988.
– *Problems of Dostoevsky's Poetics.* Translated by Caryl Emerson. Minneapolis:
    U of Minnesota P, 1984.
– *Rabelais and His World.* Translated by Helene Iswolsky. Cambridge, MA:The
    MIT P, 1968.
– *Speech Genres and Other Late Essays.* Translated by Vern W. McGee. Austin:
    U of Texas P, 2007.
– *Toward a Philosophy of the Act.* Translated by Vadim Liapunov. Austin: U of
    Texas P, 1993.
Bakhtin, M.M., and P.N. Medvedev. *The Formal Method in Literary Scholarship.*
    Translated by Albert J. Wehrle. Baltimore: The Johns Hopkins UP, 1978.
Balfour, Sebastian. *The End of the Spanish Empire, 1898–1923.* Oxford:
    Clarendon P, 1997.
Bandera, Cesáreo. *'Monda y desnuda.' La humilde historia de Don Quijote.*
    Reflexiones sobre el origen de la novela moderna. Madrid: Iberoamericana/
    Vervuert, 2005.
Barrera-Osorio, Antonio. *Experiencing Nature. The Spanish American Empire and
    the Early Scientific Revolution.* Austin: U of Texas P, 2006.
Basdekis, Demetrios. *The Evolution of Ortega y Gasset as Literary Critic.* Lanham,
    MD: UP of America, 1986.
Batchelor, R.E. *Unamuno Novelist. A European Perspective.* Oxford: Dolphin, 1972.
Bauman, Zygmunt. *Modernity and the Holocaust.* Ithaca, NY: Cornell UP, 1991.
Behler, Diana. *The Theory of the Novel in Early German Romanticism.* Bern: Peter
    Lang, 1978.

Behler, Ernst. 'Die Auffassung der Revolution in der Frühromantik.' In *Essays on European Literature in Honor of Liselotte Dieckmann*. Edited by Peter Uwe Hohendahl, Herbert Lindenberger, and Egon Schwarz. Saint Louis: Washington UP, 1972. 191–215.

– *Irony and the Discourse of Modernity*. Seattle: U of Washington P, 1990.

– 'Origins of Romantic Aesthetic in Friedrich Schlegel.' *Canadian Review of Comparative Literature* (Winter 1980): 47–66.

Behrens, Klaus. *Friedrich Schlegels Geschichtsphilosophie (1794–1808). Ein Beitrag zur politischen Romantik*. Tübingen: Max Niemeyer Verlag, 1984.

Beiser, Frederick C. *The Romantic Imperative. The Concept of Early German Romanticism*. Cambridge, MA: Harvard UP, 2003.

Beltrán Almería, Luis. 'Bajtín y la nueva historia literaria.' In *Mijail Bajtín en la encrucijada de la hermenéutica y las ciencias humanas*. Edited by Bénédicte Vauthier and Pedro M. Cátedra. Salamanca: Seminario de Estudios Medievales y Renacentistas, 2003. 119–37.

– 'Ortega, Bajtín y *El tema de nuestro tiempo*.' *Berceo* 125 (1993): 137–45.

Benjamin, Walter. 'Der Begriff der Kunstkritik in der deutschen Romantik.' In *Gesammelte Schriften* I-1. Edited by Rolf Tiedemann and Hermann Schweppenhäuser. Frankfurt: Surkamp Verlag, 1974.

Bergel, Lienhard. 'Cervantes in Germany.' In *Cervantes across the Centuries*. Edited by Ángel Flores and M.J. Benardete. New York: Gordian P, 1969. 315–52.

Bergson, Henri. *Creative Evolution*. Translated by Arthur Mitchell. New York: Random House, 1944.

Berkovits, Eliezer. *Major Themes in Modern Philosophies of Judaism*. New York: Ktav Publishing House, 1974.

Bernard-Donals, Michael F. *Mikhail Bakhtin. Between Phenomenology and Marxism*. Cambridge: Cambridge UP, 1994.

Bernstein, J.M. *The Philosophy of the Novel: Lukács, Marxism and the Dialectics of Form*. Minneapolis: U of Minnesota P, 1984.

Berry, Christopher J. 'From Hume to Hegel: The Case of the Social Contract.'*Journal of the History of Ideas* 38, no. 4 (October 1977): 691–703.

Bertrand, Jean-Jacques Achille. *Cervantes en el país de Fausto*. Madrid: Ediciones Cultura Hispánica, 1950.

Bialostosky, Don. 'Architectonics, Rhetoric, and Poetics in the Bakhtin School's Early Phenomenological and Sociological Texts.' *Rhetoric Society Quarterly* 36 (2006): 355–76.

Blackall, Eric A. *Goethe and the Novel*. Ithaca, NY: Cornell UP, 1976.

Blanco, Manuel. *La voluntad de vivir y sobrevivir en Miguel de Unamuno*. Madrid: ABL Editor, 1994.

Blanco Aguinaga, Carlos. 'De Nicodemo a don Quijote.' In *Spanish Thought and Letters in the Twentieth Century*. Edited by Germán Bleiberg and E. Inman Fox. Nashville: Vanderbilt UP, 1966. 75–100.

– *Unamuno, teórico del lenguaje*. Mexico City: Fondo de Cultura Económica, 1954.

Blanco Alfonso, Ignacio. 'Otoño de 1955: conmoción por la muerte de José Ortega y Gasset.' *Revista de Estudios Orteguianos* 10/11 (2005): 79–150.

Blasco, Javier. *Cervantes, raro inventor*. Alcalá de Henares: Ediciones del Centro de Estudios Cervantinos, 2005.

Blumenberg, Hans. *The Legitimacy of the Modern Age*. Translated by Robert M. Wallace. Cambridge, MA: The MIT Press, 1983.

Bodmer, Johann Jakob. *Kritische Betrachtungen über die poetischen Gemälde der Dichter* (Zürich, 1741). Frankfurt am Main: Athenäum Reprints, 1971.

Böer, Joachim. 'José Ortega y Gassets Aufenthalt als Student in Marburg/Lahn.' In *Actas del coloquio celebrado en Marburgo con motivo del centenario del nacimiento de José Ortega y Gasset (1983)*. Edited by Hans-Joachim Lope. Frankfurt am Main: Peter Lang, 1986. 17–27.

Bowie, Andrew. *From Romanticism to Critical Theory: The Philosophy of German Literary Theory*. New York: Routledge, 1997.

Brandist, Craig. 'Bakhtin's Grand Narrative: The Significance of the Renaissance.' *Dialogism* 3 (September 1999): 11–30.

– 'The Hero at the Bar of Eternity: the Bakhtin Circle's Juridical Theory of the Novel.' *Economy and Society* 30, no. 2 (May 2001): 208–28.

Brandist, Craig, and David Shepherd. 'From Saransk to Cyberspace: Towards an Electronic Edition of Bakhtin.' In *Dialogues on Bakhtin: Interdisciplinary Readings*. Edited by Mika Lähteenmäki and Hannele Dufva. Jyväskylä: U of Jyväskylä, 1998. 7–22.

Britt Arredondo, Christopher. *Quixotism. The Imaginative Denial of Spain's Loss of Empire*. Albany: State U of New York P, 2005.

Brito Díaz, Carlos. 'Cervantes al pie de la letra: Don Quijote a lomos del "Libro del Mundo."' *Cervantes: Bulletin of the Cervantes Society of America* 19, no. 2 (Fall 1999): 37–54.

Brown, Marshall. *The Shape of German Romanticism*. Ithaca, NY: Cornell UP, 1979.

Brüggemann, Werner. *Cervantes und die Figur des Don Quijote in Kunstanschauung und Dichtung der deutschen Romantik*. Münster: Aschendorff, 1958.

Bubnova, Tatiana. 'Bajtín en la encrucijada dialógica (datos y comentarios para contribuir a la confusión general).' In *Bajtín y sus apócrifos*. Edited by Iris M. Zavala. Barcelona: Anthropos, 1996. 13–72.

Bullock, Marcus Paul. *Romanticism and Marxism. The Philosophical Development of Literary Theory and Literary History in Walter Benjamin and Friedrich Schlegel*. New York: Peter Lang, 1987.

Cacho Viu, Vicente. 'Prólogo.' In José Ortega y Gasset. *Cartas de un joven español. (1891–1908)*. Edited by Soledad Ortega. Madrid: El Arquero, 1991. 15–38.

– *Repensar el 98*. Madrid: Biblioteca Nueva, 1997.

Calderón de la Barca, Pedro. *La vida es sueño*. In *Diez comedias del siglo de oro*. 2nd ed. Edited by José Martel, Hymen Alpern, and Leonard Mades. Prospect Heights, IL: Waveland P, 1968. 611–97.

Cañizares-Esguerra, Jorge. *Nature, Empire, and Nation. Explorations of the History of Science in the Iberian World*. Stanford, CT: Stanford UP, 2006.

Carpintero, Helio. 'Ortega, Cervantes y las *Meditaciones del Quijote*.' *Revista de filosofía* 30, no. 2 (2005): 7–34.

Cascardi, Anthony J. 'Between Philosophy and Literature: Ortega's *Meditations on Quixote*.' In *Proceedings of the Espectador Universal. International Interdisciplinary Conference Hofstra University*. Ed. Nora de Marval-McNair. Westport, CT: Greenwood P, 1987. 15–50.

– *The Subject of Modernity*. Cambridge: Cambridge UP, 1992.

Cassirer, Ernst. *Platonic Renaissance in England*. New York: Gordian, 1970.

– 'Hermann Cohen and the Renewal of Kantian Philosophy.' Translated by Lydia Patton. *Angelaki. Journal of the Theoretical Humanities* 10, no. 1 (April 2005): 95–108.

Castilla del Pino, Carlos. *Cordura y locura en Cervantes*. Barcelona: Península, 2005.

Castro, Américo. *Cervantes y los casticismos españoles*. Madrid: Alianza, 1974.

– *El pensamiento de Cervantes*. Madrid: Crítica, 1987.

Catalán, Diego. 'Tres Unamunos ante un capítulo del *Quijote*.' In *Spanish Thought and Letters in the Twentieth Century*. Edited by Germán Bleiberg and E. Inman Fox. Nashville: Vanderbilt UP, 1966. 101–41.

Cerezo Galán, Pedro. *El mal del siglo. El conflicto entre Ilustración y Romanticismo en la crisis finisecular del siglo XIX*. Madrid: Biblioteca Nueva, 2003.

– *Las máscaras de lo trágico. Filosofía y tragedia en Miguel de Unamuno*. Madrid: Trotta, 1996.

– *La voluntad de aventura*. Barcelona: Ariel, 1984.

Cervantes, Miguel de. *The Adventures of Don Quixote*. Translated by J.M. Cohen. London: Penguin, 1950.

– *Don Quijote de la Mancha*. Edited by John Jay Allen. Madrid: Cátedra, 2004.

– *Don Quixote*. Translated by Edith Grossman. New York: Harper Collins, 2003.

– *Novelas ejemplares I*. Edited by Juan Bautista Avalle-Arce. Madrid: Clásicos Castalia, 1989.

Chartier, Roger. 'La Europa castellana durante el tiempo del Quijote.' In *España en tiempos del Quijote*. Edited by Antonio Feros and Juan Gelabert. Madrid: Taurus, 2004. 129–58.

Chevalier, Maxime. *Lectura y lectores en la España del siglo XVI y XVII*. Madrid: Ediciones Turner, 1976.

Childers, William. *Transnational Cervantes*. Toronto: U of Toronto P, 2006.

Clark, Katerina, and Michael Holquist. *Mikhail Bakhtin*. Cambridge, MA: Belknap P of Harvard UP, 1984.

Cleveland, Basil. 'The Concept of Reading in Ortega's *Meditations on Quixote*.' *Clio* 34, nos. 1–2 (Fall 2004–Winter 2005): 83–98.

Close, Anthony. *Cervantes and the Comic Mind of his Age*. Oxford: Oxford UP, 2000.

– 'Don Quixote and Unamuno's Philosophy of Art.' In *Studies in Modern Spanish Literature and Art Presented to Helen F. Grant*. Edited by Nigel Glendinning. London: Tamesis, 1972. 25–44.

– *The Romantic Approach to Don Quixote. A Critical History of the Romantic Tradition in Quixote Criticism*. Cambridge: Cambridge UP, 1978.

Coates, Ruth. *Christianity in Bakhtin. God and the Exiled Author*. Cambridge: Cambridge UP, 1998.

Coble, Kelly. 'Should Freedom Be the Ground of Morality? Evaluating Hermann Cohen's Account of the Foundations of Kantian Ethics.' *Idealistic Studies* 34, no. 2 (Summer 2004): 181–97.

Cohen, Hermann. *Ästhetik des reinen Gefühls*. 1, 2. In *Werke*. Vols. 8 and 9. Hildesheim and New York: Georg Olms Verlag, 1982.

– *Ethik des reinen Willens*. In *Werke*. Vol. 7. Hildesheim and New York: Georg Olms Verlag, 1981.

– *Logik der reinen Erkenntnis*. In *Werke*. Vol. 6. Hildesheim and New York: Georg Olms Verlag, 1977.

– *Das Prinzip der Infinitesimal-Methode und seine Geschichte*. In *Werke*. Vol. 5. Edited by Peter Schultheis. Hildesheim: Georg Olms Verlag, 1984.

– '"The Significance of Judaism for the Religious Progress of Humanity" by Hermann Cohen: An Introduction and Translation by Alan Mittleman.' *Modern Judaism* 24, no. 1 (2004): 36–58.

Congdon, Lee. *The Young Lukács*. Chapel Hill: U of North Carolina P, 1983.

Corredor, Eva L. *György Lukács and the Literary Pretext*. New York: Peter Lang, 1987.

Coskun, Deniz. *Law as Symbolic Form. Ernst Cassirer and the Anthropocentric View of Law*. Dordrecht: Springer, 2007.

De la Fuente Ballesteros, Ricardo. 'Mundo fenoménico/mundo nouménico: una clave finisecular (Unamuno/Ganivet/Baroja).' In *La independencia de las últimas colonias españolas y su impacto nacional e internacional.* Edited by José M. Ruano de la Haza. Ottawa: Dovehouse, 1999. 245–60.

Deffis de Calvo, Emilia I. 'El cronotopo de la novela española de peregrinación: Miguel de Cervantes.' *Anales cervantinos* 28 (1990): 99–108.

Derrida, Jacques. *Acts of Religion.* Edited by Gil Anidjar. London: Routledge, 2002.

Derwin, Susan. *The Ambivalence of Form: Lukács, Freud, and the Novel.* Baltimore: The Johns Hopkins UP, 1992.

Díaz, Elías. *Revisión de Unamuno: análisis crítico de su pensamiento político.* Madrid: Tecnos, 1968.

Díaz de Benjumea, Nicolás. *El Quijote de Benjumea.* Edited by Fredo Arias de la Canal. Barcelona: Ediciones Ronda, 1986.

Dobson, Andrew. *An Introduction to the Politics and Philosophy of José Ortega y Gasset.* Cambridge: Cambridge UP, 1989.

Domínguez Ortiz, Antonio and Alfredo Alvar Ezquerra. 'La sociedad Estamental.' In *La sociedad española en la edad moderna.* Edited by Antonio Domínguez Ortiz and Alfredo Alvar Esquerra. Madrid: Ediciones Istmo, 2005. 91–164.

Doody, Margaret Anne. *The True Story of the Novel.* New Brunswick: Rutgers UP, 1997.

Dostoevsky, Fyodor. *A Writer's Diary.* Evanston: Northwestern UP, 1994.

Dudley, Edward J. *The Endless Text: Don Quixote and the Hermeneutics of Romance.* Albany: State U of New York P, 1997.

Dufour, Eric. *Hermann Cohen. Introduction au néokantisme de Marbourg.* Paris: Presses Universitaires de France, 2001.

Earle, Peter G. 'Unamuno and the Theme of History.' *Hispanic Review* 32, no. 4 (October 1964): 319–39.

Egido, Aurora. *Cervantes y las puertas del sueño. Estudios sobre* La Galatea, El Quijote *y* El Persiles. Barcelona: PPU, 1994.

Eichner, Hans. *Friedrich Schlegel.* New York: Twayne, 1970.

– 'Friedrich Schlegel's Theory of Romantic Poetry.' *PMLA* 71, no. 5 (December 1956): 1018–41.

– 'The Genesis of German Romanticism.' *Queen's Quarterly* 72, no. 2 (Summer 1965): 213–31.

Eley, Geoff. *Forging Democracy: The History of the Left in Europe, 1850–2000.* Oxford: Oxford UP, 2000.

Elliott, J.H. *Imperial Spain: 1469–1716.* New York: Meridian, 1977.

Elorza, Antonio. *La razón y la sombra. Una lectura política de Ortega y Gasset.* Barcelona: Anagrama, 1984.

Emerson, Caryl. *The First Hundred Years of Mikhail Bakhtin.* Princeton, NJ: Princeton UP, 1997.

Endress, Heinz-Peter. *Los ideales de Don Quijote en el cambio de valores desde la Edad Media hasta el Barroco.* Pamplona: EUNSA, 2000.

Epistolario completo Ortega-Unamuno. Edited by Laureano Robles Garcedo y Antonio Ramos Gascón. Madrid: Editorial El Arquero, 1987.

Eric Weisstein's World of Mathematics. Available at http://mathworld.wolfram. com/Function.html, accessed 1 May 2007.

Fackenheim, Emil L. *Jewish Philosophers and Jewish Philosophy.* Edited by Michael L. Morgan. Bloomington: Indiana UP, 1996.

Fehér, Ferenc. 'The Last Phase of Anti-Capitalism: Lukács' Response to the War.' *New German Critique* 10 (Winter 1977): 139–54.

– 'Lukács in Weimar.' In *Lukács Reappraised.* Edited by Agnes Heller. New York: Columbia UP, 1983. 75–106.

Fernández, Ana María. *Teoría de la novela en Unamuno, Ortega y Cortázar.* Madrid: Pliegos, 1991.

Fernández, Jaime, S.J. 'La admiración en el *Quijote* y el enigma del paje soldado (*DQ,* II, 24).' *Cervantes : Bulletin of the Cervantes Society of America* 19, no. 1 (Spring 1999): 96–112.

Fernández, Pelayo H. 'La teoría de la novela realista de Ortega y la teoría de lo cómico de Bergson.' *Cuadernos del Sur* 14 (1981): 173–82.

Fernández Cifuentes, Luis. *Teoría y mercado de la novela en España: del 98 a la República.* Madrid: Gredos, 1982.

– 'Unamuno y Ortega: leer una novela, hacer una novela.' In *Essays on Hispanic Literature in Honor of Edmund L. King.* Edited by Sylvia Molloy and Luis Fernández Cifuentes. London: Tamesis, 1983. 45–59.

Fernández de la Mora, Gonzalo. *Ortega y el 98.* Madrid: Ediciones Rialp, 1963.

Fernández Sanz, Amable. 'El problema de España en el pensamiento de Azaña y Ortega hasta 1914.' *Revista de Hispanismo Filosófico* 3 (1998): 59–74.

Fernández-Santamaría, J.A. *The State, War and Peace. Spanish Political Thought in the Renaissance 1516–1559.* Cambridge: Cambridge UP, 1977.

Feros, Antonio. '"Por Dios, por la patria y el rey": el mundo político en tiempos de Cervantes.' In *España en tiempos del Quijote.* Edited by Antonio Feros and Juan Gelabert. Madrid: Taurus, 2004: 61–96.

Ferrari, Massimo. *Retours à Kant. Introduction au néokantisme.* Translated by Thierry Loisel. Paris: Les Éditions du Cerf, 2001.

Ferrater Mora, José. *Unamuno. A Philosophy of Tragedy.* Translated by Philip Silver. Berkeley: U of California P, 1962.

Fisher, Simon. *Revelatory Postivism? Barth's Earliest Theology and the Marburg School.* Oxford: Oxford UP, 1988.

Fitzpatrick, Sheila. *Everyday Stalinism. Ordinary Life in Extraordinary Times: Soviet Russia in the 1930s.* Oxford: Oxford UP, 1999.

Flórez Miguel, Cirilo. 'Política y filosofía en Ortega. Teoría orteguiana de la modernidad.' In *Política y sociedad en José Ortega y Gasset: en torno a 'Vieja y nueva política.'* Edited by María Teresa López de la Vieja de la Torre. Barcelona: Anthropos, 1997. 121–40.

Forcione, Alban K. *Cervantes and the Mystery of Lawlessness: A Study of El casamiento engañoso y El coloquio de los perros.* Princeton, NJ: Princeton UP, 1984.

Fox, E. Inman. *La invención de España. Nacionalismo liberal e identidad nacional.* Madrid: Cátedra, 1997.

– 'Prólogo.' In José Ortega y Gasset. *Meditaciones sobre la literatura y el arte (La manera española de ver las cosas).* Madrid: Castalia, 1987. 7–40.

Franz, Thomas R. *Unamuno's Paratexts: Twisted Guides to Contorted Narratives.* Newark, DE: Juan de la Cuesta Hispanic Monographs, 2006.

Frye, Northrop. *Anatomy of Criticism. Four Essays.* Princeton, NJ: Princeton UP, 1973.

Fuentes, Carlos. *Cervantes o la crítica de la lectura.* Mexico City: Cuadernos de Joaquín Mortiz, 1976.

Funkenstein, Amos. *Perceptions of Jewish History.* Berkeley: U of California P, 1993.

Garagorri, Paulino. *La filosofía española en el siglo XX. Unamuno, Ortega, Zubiri. (Dos precursores, Clarín y Ganivet, y cuatro continuadores).* Madrid: Alianza, 1985.

Garber, Frederick. 'Sterne: Arabesques and Fictionality.' In *Romantic Irony.* Budapest: Akadémiai Kiadó, 1988. 33–40.

García Alonso, Rafael. *El náufrago ilusionado. La estética de José Ortega y Gasset.* Madrid: Siglo XXI de España, 1997.

García Gibert, Javier. *Cervantes y la melancolía. Ensayos sobre el tono y la actitud cervantinos.* Valencia: Novatores, 1997.

García Sánchez, Jesús. *Visiones del Quijote: desde la crisis española de fin del siglo.* Madrid: Visor, 2005.

Garrigues, Emilio. *Ortega y Gasset en su circunstancia alemana.* Bonn: Inter Nationes, 1981.

Gibbs, Robert. 'Jurisprudence Is the Organon of Ethics: Kant and Cohen on Ethics, Law, and Religion.' In *Hermann Cohen's Critical Idealism.* Edited by Reinier Munk. Dordrecht: Springer, 2005. 193–230.

Gigliotti, Gianna. '*Beweis* and *Aufweis*: Transcendental *a priori* and metaphysical *a priori* in Cohen's neo-Kantianism.' In *Hermann Cohen's Critical Idealism.* Edited by Reinier Munk. Dordrecht: Springer, 2005. 97–132.

Gil Villegas M., Francisco. *Los profetas y el mesías. Lukács y Ortega como precursores de Heidegger en el Zeitgeist de la modernidad (1900–1929)*. Mexico City: El Colegio de México y Fondo de Cultura Económica, 1996.

Gilman, Stephen. *The Novel according to Cervantes*. Berkeley: U of California P, 1989.

Gluck, Mary. *Georg Lukács and His Generation 1900–1918*. Cambridge, MA: Harvard UP, 1985.

Goethe, Johann Wolfgang von. *Elective Affinities*. Translated by R.J. Hollingdale. London: Penguin, 1971.

Goldmann, Lucien. *Lukács and Heidegger. Towards a New Philosophy*. London: Routledge and Kegan Paul, 1977.

Gómez, Francisco Vicente. 'El concepto de "dialoguismo" en Bajtín: la otra forma del diálogo renacentista.' *1616: Anuario de la Sociedad Española de Literatura General y Comparada* 5 (1983–4): 47–54.

González, Pedro Blas. *Human Existence as Radical Reality. Ortega y Gasset's Philosophy of Subjectivity*. St Paul, MN: Paragon House, 2005.

González Echevarría, Roberto. *Love and the Law in Cervantes*. New Haven, CT: Yale UP, 2005.

González Landa, María del Carmen, and Eduardo Tejero Robledo. 'La aventura de los molinos de viento: Innovación técnica. Recomposición textual. Valores en educación." *Didáctica. Lengua y literatura* 17 (2005): 147–75.

Goodman, David. *Power and Penury. Government, Technology and Science in Philip II's Spain*. Cambridge: Cambridge UP, 1988.

– 'Science, Medicine, and Technology in Colonial Spanish America: New Interpretations, New Approaches.' In *Science in the Spanish and Portuguese Empires, 1500–1800*. Edited by Daniela Bleichmar, Paula De Vos, Kristin Huffine, and Kevin Sheehan. Stanford, CA: Stanford UP, 2009: 9–34.

Gordon, Peter Eli. 'Science, Finitude, and Infinity: Neo-Kantianism and the Birth of Existentialism.' *Jewish Social Studies* 6, no. 1 (Fall 1999): 30–53.

Gorky, Maxim. 'Soviet Literature.' In *Problems of Soviet Literature. Reports and Speeches at the First Soviet Writer's Congress*. Edited by H.G. Scott. Moscow: Co-operative Publishing Society of Foreign Workers in the U.S.S.R., 1935. 27–69.

Gracia, Jordi. *La resistencia silenciosa. Fascismo y cultura en España*. Barcelona: Anagrama, 2004.

Graham, John T. *A Pragmatist Philosophy of Life in Ortega y Gasset*. Columbia: U of Missouri P, 1994.

– *The Social Thought of Ortega y Gasset. A Systematic Synthesis in Postmodernism and Interdisciplinarity*. Columbia: U of Missouri P, 2001.

– *Theory of History in Ortega y Gasset.'The Dawn of Historical Reason.'* Columbia: U of Missouri P, 1997.

Grauer, Michael. *Die entzauberte Welt. Tragik und Dialektik der Moderne im Frühen Werk von Georg Lukács.* Königstein: Verlag Anton Hain Meisenheim, 1985.

Gray, Rockwell. *The Imperative of Modernity. An Intellectual Biography of José Ortega y Gasset.* Berkeley: U of California P, 1989.

Gullón, Ricardo. *Autobiografías de Unamuno.* Madrid: Gredos, 1964.

– 'Ortega y la teoría de la novela.' *Letras de Deusto* 41 (May–August 1989): 105–21.

Gutiérrez, Carlos M. 'Cervantes, un proyecto de modernidad para el Fin de Siglo (1880–1905).' *Cervantes: Bulletin of the Cervantes Society of America* 19, no. 1 (Spring 1999): 113–24.

Habermas, Jürgen. *The Philosophical Discourse of Modernity. Twelve Lectures.* Translated by Frederick G. Lawrence. Cambridge, MA: The MIT Press, 1995.

Hampton, Warren. 'Ortega in Quest of Don Quixote.' In *Proceedings of the Espectador Universal International Interdisciplinary Conference Hofstra University.* Edited by Nora de Marval-McNair. Westport, CT: Greenwood P, 1987. 47–50.

Hanak, Tibor. *Lukács war anders.* Meisenheim am Glan: Verlag Anton Hain, 1973.

Heimsoeth, Heinz. *The Six Great Themes of Western Metaphysics and the End of the Middle Ages.* Translated by Ramon J. Betanzos. Detroit: Wayne State UP, 1994.

Hegel, Georg Wilhelm Friedrich. *Aesthetics. Lectures on Fine Art.* 2 vols. Translated by T.M. Knox. Oxford: Clarendon P, 1975.

– *Ästhetik.* Frankfurt: Europäische Verlaganstalt, 1966.

– *Hegel's Logic. Part One of the Encyclopedia of the Philosophical Sciences.* Translated by William Wallace. Oxford: Oxford UP, 1975.

– *Hegel's Philosophy of Mind.* Translated by W. Wallace and A.V. Miller. Oxford: Clarendon P, 2007.

– *Phenomenology of Spirit.* Translated by A.V. Miller. Oxford: Clarendon P, 1977.

Heine, Heinrich. 'Einleitung zum Don Quixote.' In *Der sinnreiche Junker Don Quixote de la Mancha* by Miguel de Cervantes. Stuttgart: Brodhagsche Buchhandlung, 1837. Available at http://homepages.compuserve.de/frickew/heine/donquixote.htm, accessed on 4 September 2007.

Heller, Agnes. 'Georg Lukács and Irma Seidler.' In *Lukács Reappraised.* Edited by Agnes Heller. New York: Columbia UP, 1983. 27–72.

- *A Theory of Modernity.* London: Blackwell, 1999.

Hermann Cohen's Philosophy of Religion. International Conference in Jerusalem 1996. Edited by Stéphane Moses and Hartwig Wiedebach. Hildesheim: Georg Olms Verlag, 1997.

Hermann, István. *Die Gedankenwelt von Georg Lukács.* Budapest: Académiai Kiadó, 1978.

Hernández Sánchez, Domingo. *Estética de la limitación. Recepción de Hegel por Ortega y Gasset.* Salamanca: Ediciones Universidad de Salamanca, 2000.

Hirschkop, Ken. 'Bakhtin Myths, or Why We All Need Alibis.' *South Atlantic Quarterly* 97, nos. 3/4 (Summer/Fall 1998): 579–98.

Hirschkop, Ken. *Mikhail Bakhtin. An Aesthetic for Democracy.* Oxford: Oxford UP, 1999.

Hirschkop, Ken and David Shepherd. 'Glossary: Alternative Translations of Key Terms.' In *Bakhtin and Cultural Theory.* Edited by Ken Hirschkop and David Shepherd. Manchester: Manchester UP, 1989. 190–4.

Hitchcock, Peter. 'The Bakhtin Centre and the State of the Archive: An Interview with David Shepherd.' *South Atlantic Quarterly* 97, nos. 3/4 (Summer/Fall 1998): 753–72.

Holmes, Oliver W. *Human Reality and the Social World: Ortega's Philosophy of History.* Amherst: U of Massachusetts P, 1975.

Holquist, Michael. *Dialogism. Bakhtin and His World.* 2nd ed. London: Routledge, 2002.

Holquist, Michael, and Katarina Clark. 'The Influence of Kant in the Early Work of M.M. Bakhtin.' In *Literary Theory and Criticism. Festschrift Presented to René Wellek in Honor of his Eightieth Birthday.* Edited by Joseph Strelka. New York: Peter Lang, 1984. 1:299–313.

Holzhey, Helmut. 'Cohen and the Marburg School in Context.' In *Hermann Cohen's Critical Idealism.* Edited by Reinier Munk. Dordrecht: Springer, 2005. 3–37.

- *Cohen und Natorp. Vol. 1. Ursprung und Einheit.* Basel/Stuttgart: Schwabe and Co. A.G., 1986.

- 'Hermann Cohen: der Philosoph in Auseinandersetzung mit den politischen und gesellschäftlichen Problemen seiner Zeit.' In *Philosophisches Denken-Politisches Wirken. Hermann-Cohen-Kolloquium Marburg 1992.* Edited by Reinhardt Brandt and Franz Orlik. Hildesheim: Georg Olms, 1993. 15–36.

Holzman, Michael. *Lukács's Road to God. The Early Criticism against its Pre-Marxist Background.* Washington, DC: UP of America, 1985.

Huerta Calvo, Javier. 'Lo carnavalesco en la teoría literaria de Mijail Bajtín.' In *Formas carnavalescas en el arte y la literatura.* Edited by Javier Huerta Calvo. Barcelona: Ediciones del Serbal, 1989. 13–31.

Huge, Eberhard. *Poesie und Reflexion in der Aesthetik des frühen Friedrich Schlegel*. Stuttgart: J.B. Metzlersche Verlagsbuchhandlung, 1971.

Huhn, Tom. 'Lukács and the Essay Form.' *New German Critique* 78 (Fall 1999): 183–92.

Hutchinson, Stephen. *Cervantine Journeys*. Madison: The U of Wisconsin P, 1992.

Iffland, James. *De fiestas y aguafiestas: risa, locura e ideología en Cervantes y Avellaneda*. Frankfurt am Main: Vervuert, 1999.

Ilie, Paul. *Unamuno. An Existential View of Self and Society*. Madison: U of Wisconsin P, 1967.

Jameson, Fredric. *Marxism and Form: Twentieth-Century Dialectical Theories of Literature*. Princeton, NJ: Princeton UP, 1971.

– *The Political Unconscious. Narrative as a Socially Symbolic Act*. London: Routledge, 1996.

Jay, Martin. *Marxism and Totality: The Adventures of a Concept from Lukács to Habermas*. Berkeley: University of California Press, 1984.

Jehenson, Miriam Yvonne, and Peter N. Dunn. *The Utopian Nexus in Don Quixote*. Nashville: Vanderbilt UP, 2006.

Johnson, Carroll B. *Cervantes and the Material World*. Urbana: U of Illinois P, 2000.

Johnson, Roberta. *Fuego cruzado: filosofía y novela en España (1900–1934)*. Madrid: Ediciones Libertarias/Prodhuff, 1997.

– *Gender and Nation in the Spanish Modernist Novel*. Vanderbilt: Vanderbilt UP, 2003.

Jospe, Eva. 'Hermann Cohen's Judaism: A Reassessment.' *Judaism* 25, no. 4 (Fall 1976): 461–72.

Kadarkay, Arpad. *Georg Lukács. Life, Thought, and Politics*. Cambridge: Basil Blackwell, 1991.

Kagan, Judif'. 'People Not of Our Time.' In *The Contexts of Bakhtin. Philosophy, Authorship, Aesthetics*. Edited by David Shepherd. Amsterdam: Harwood Academic Publishers, 1998. 3–16.

Kagan, Matvei Isaevich. 'Hermann Cohen (4 July 1842–4 April 1918).' Translated by Craig Brandist and David Shepherd. In *The Bakhtin Circle. In the Master's Absence*. Edited by Craig Brandist, David Shepherd, and Galin Tihanov. Manchester: Manchester UP, 2004. 193–211.

Kamen, Henry. 'Censura y libertad. El impacto de la Inquisición sobre la cultura española.' *Revista de la Inquisición* no. 7 (1998): 109–17.

– *Spain's Road to Empire. The Making of a World Power, 1492–1763*. London: Penguin, 2003.

Kant, Immanuel. *Critique of Judgement*. Translated by J.H. Bernard. New York: Hafner P, 1951.

– *Critique of Pure Reason*. Translated by J.M.D. Meiklejohn. London: Everyman's Library, 1986.

Kaplan, Lawrence. 'Suffering and Joy in the Thought of Hermann Cohen.' *Modern Judaism* 21, no. 1 (2001): 15–22.

Kierkegaard, Søren. *The Concept of Irony with Continual Reference to Socrates.* Translated by Howard V. and Edna H. Hong. Princeton, NJ: Princeton UP, 1989.

Kipperman, Mark. *Beyond Enchantment: German Idealism and English Romantic Poetry.* Philadelphia: U of Pennsylvania P, 1986.

Királyfalvi, Béla. *The Aesthetics of György Lukács.* Princeton, NJ: Princeton UP, 1975.

Klein, Joseph. *Die Grundlegung der Ethik in der Philosophie Hermann Cohens und Paul Natorps – eine Kritik des Neukantianismus.* Göttingen: Vandenhoeck and Ruprecht, 1976.

Kluback, William. *Hermann Cohen: The Challenge of a Religion of Reason.* Chico, California: Scholars P, 1984.

– *The Idea of Humanity. Hermann Cohen's Legacy to Philosophy and Theology.* Lanham, MD: UP of America, 1987.

– 'The Jewish Response to Hegel: Samuel Hirsch and Hermann Cohen.' *The Owl of Minerva* 18, no. 1 (1986): 5–12.

– *The Legacy of Hermann Cohen.* Atlanta: Scholar's P, 1989.

Kristeva, Julia. *Desire in Language. A Semiotic Approach to Literature and Art.* New York: Columbia UP, 1980.

– *Revolution in Poetic Language.* New York: Columbia UP, 1984.

Krois, John Michael. 'Semiotische Transformation der Philosophie: Verkörperung und Pluralismus bei Cassirer und Peirce.' *Dialektik* 1 (1995): 61–72.

Krückeberg, Edzard. *Der Begriff des Erzählens im 20. Jarhhundert. Zu den Theorien Benjamins, Adornos und Lukács.* Bonn: Bouvier Verlag Herbert Grundmann, 1981.

Kruse, Ute. 'Georg Lukács' ungeschriebenes Buch über Friedrich Schlegel.' In *Diskursüberschneidungen Georg Lukács und andere. Akten des Internationalen Georg-Lukács-Symposiums 'Perspektiven der Forschung' Essen 1989.* Edited by Werner Jung. Bern: Peter Lang, 1993. 27–36.

Kruse-Fischer, Ute. *Verzehrte Romantik. Georg Lukács' Kunstphilosophie der esaayistischen Periode (1908–1911).* Stuttgart: M&P, Verlag für Wissenschaft und Forschung, 1991.

Lacoue-Labarthe, Philippe, and Jean-Luc Nancy. *The Literary Absolute. The Theory of Literature in German Romanticism.* Translated by Philip Barnard and Cheryl Lester. Albany: State U of New York P, 1988.

La Rubia Prado, Francisco. *Alegorías de la voluntad. Pensamiento orgánico, retórica y deconstrucción en la obra de Miguel de Unamuno.* Madrid: Libertarias/Prodhufi, 1996.

La Rubia Prado, Francisco. *Unamuno y la vida como ficción.* Madrid: Gredos, 1999.

Laks, André. 'Platon entre Cohen et Natorp. Aspects de l'interprétation néokantienne des idées platoniciennes.' *Cahiers de philosophie politique et juridique* 26 (1994): 15–53.

Lalcona, Javier F. *El idealismo político de Ortega y Gasset. Un análisis sintético de la evolución de su filosofía política.* Madrid: Editorial Cuadernos para el Diálogo, 1974.

Lange, Friedrich Albert. *History of Materialism and Criticism of Its Present Importance.* Vol. 3. Translated by Ernest Chester Thomas. London: Trübner, 1881.

Larraín Acuña, Hernán. *La génesis del pensamiento de Ortega.* Buenos Aires: Compañía General Fabril, 1962.

Leibniz, G.W. *New Essays on Human Understanding.* Translated by Peter Remnant and Jonathan Bennett. Cambridge: Cambridge UP, 1996.

Lenin, V.I. *Materialism and Empirio-Criticism. Critical Comments on a Reactionary Philosophy.* 1908. Available at http://www.marxistsfr.org/archive/lenin/works/1908/mec.html, accessed on 25 June 2009.

Liebeschütz, Hans. *Von Georg Simmel zu Frank Rosenzweig. Studien zum jüdischen Denken im deutschen Kulturbereich.* Tübingen: J.C.B. Mohr (Paul Siebeck), 1970.

Lloréns, Vicente. *Aspectos sociales de la literatura española.* Madrid: Castalia, 1974.

Lock, Charles. 'Bakhtin and the Tropes of Orthodoxy.' In *Bakhtin and Religion. A Feeling for Faith.* Edited by Susan M. Felch and Paul J. Contino. Evanston: Northwestern UP, 2001. 97–119.

López Frías, Francisco. *Etíca y política. En torno al pensamiento de José Ortega y Gasset.* Barcelona: Promociones Publicaciones Universitarias, 1985.

López Piñero, José M. 'The Versalian Movement in Sixteenth-Century Spain.' *Journal of the History of Biology* 12, no. 1 (Spring 1979): 45–81.

Lovejoy, Arthur O. 'Schiller and the Genesis of German Romanticism.' In *Essays in the History of Ideas.* Baltimore: The Johns Hopkins UP, 1948. 207–27.

Löwy, Michael. 'Figures of Weberian Marxism.' *Theory and Society* 25 (1996): 431–46.

– *Georg Lukács: From Romanticism to Bolshevism.* Translated by Patrick Camiller. London: NLB, 1979.

– 'Lukács and Stalinism.' In *Western Marxism: A Critical Reader.* Edited by The New Left Review. London: New Left Review, 1977. 61–82.

Löwy, Michael, and Robert Sayre. *Romanticism against the Tide of Modernity.* Translated by Catherine Porter. Durham: Duke UP, 2001.

Lozano Maneiro, José María. 'Ortega y la teoría de la novela: aproximación a una aproximación.' In *Estética y creatividad en Ortega. Volumen de homenaje a José Ortega y Gasset en el centenario de su nacimiento.* Sociedad Iberoamericana de Filosofía. Madrid: Reus, 1984. 115–19.

Luby, Barry J. *The Uncertainties in Twentieth- and Twenty-first Century Analytic Thought: Miguel de Unamuno the Precursor.* Newark, DE: Juan de la Cuesta Hispanic Monographs, 2008.

Lukács, Georg. 'Aesthetic Culture.' *The Yale Journal of Criticism* 11, no. 2 (Fall 1998): 365–79.

–   'Bolshevism as an Ethical Problem.' In *The Lukács Reader.* Edited by Arpad Kadarkay. London: Blackwell, 1995. 216–21.

–   *Heidelberger Ästhetik (1916–1918).* Edited by György Márkus and Frank Benseler. Darmstadt and Neuwied: Hermann Luchterhand Verlag, 1974.

–   *The Historical Novel.* Translated by Hannah and Stanley Mitchell. Lincoln: U of Nebraska P, 1983.

–   *History and Class Consciousness. Studies in Marxist Dialectics.* Translated by Rodney Livingstone. Cambridge, MA: The MIT P, 1971.

–   *Kurze Skizze einer Geschichte der neueren deutschen Literatur.* Darmstadt and Neuwied: Hermann Luchterhand Verlag, 1975.

–   *The Lukács Reader.* Edited by Arpad Kadarkay. Oxford: Blackwell, 1995.

–   *Political Writings 1919–1929.* Edited by Rodney Livingstone. Translated by Michael McColgan. London: NLB, 1972.

–   *Record of a Life. An Autobiographical Sketch.* Edited by István Eörsi. Translated by Rodney Livingstone. London: Verso Editions, 1983.

–   *Die Seele und die Formen. Essays.* Berlin: Egon Fleischel, 1911.

–   *Selected Correspondence. 1902–1920.* Edited and translated by Judith Marcus and Zoltán Tar. New York: Columbia UP, 1986.

–   *Soul and Form.* Translated by Anna Bostock. London: Merlin P, 1974.

–   *Die Theorie des Romans: ein geschichtsphilosophischer Versuch über die Formen der großen Epik.* Darmstadt: Hermann Luchterhand Verlag, 1971.

–   *The Theory of the Novel: A Historico-philosophical Essay on the Forms of Great Epic Literature.* Translated by Anna Bostock. Cambridge, MA: The MIT Press, 1989.

Lyden, John. 'The Influence of Hermann Cohen on Karl Barth's Dialectical Theology.' *Modern Judaism* 12, no. 2 (May 1992): 167–83.

Maack, Ute. *Ironie und Autorschaft. Zu Friedrich Schlegels Charakteristiken.* Paderborn: Ferdinand Schöningh, 2002.

Madariaga, Salvador de. *Guía del lector del* Quijote: *ensayo psicológico sobre el* Quijote. Buenos Aires: Editorial Sudamericana, 1961.

Malter, Rudolf. 'Grundlinien neukantianischer Kantinterpretation.' In *Neukantianismus: Perspektiven und Problemen*. Edited by Ernst Wolfgang Orth and Helmut Holzhey. Würzburg: Königshausen und Neumann, 1994. 44–58.

Mancing, Howard. '*Don Quixote* and Bakhtin's Two Stylistic Lines of the Novel.' In *Studies in Spanish Literature in Honor of Daniel Eisenberg*. Edited by Tom Lathrop. Newark, DE: Juan de la Cuesta, 2009. 177–98.

Maravall, José Antonio. *El humanismo de las armas en Don Quijote*. Madrid: Instituto de Estudios Políticos, 1948.

Marías, Julián. *Miguel de Unamuno*. Translated by Frances M. López-Morillas. Cambridge, MA: Harvard UP, 1966.

– *Ortega. Circunstancia y vocación*. Madrid: Alianza, 1983.

– *Ortega. Las trayectorias*. Madrid: Alianza, 1983.

Marichal, Juan. *El designio de Unamuno*. Madrid: Taurus, 2002.

Márkus, György. 'Life and the Soul: The Young Lukács and the Problem of Culture.' In *Lukács Reappraised*. Edited by Agnes Heller. New York: Columbia UP, 1983. 1–26.

Márquez Villanueva, Francisco. *Personajes y temas del Quijote*. Madrid: Taurus, 1975.

Martín, Franciso José. 'Hacer concepto. *Meditaciones del Quijote* y filosofía Española.' *Revista de Occidente* 288 (May 2005). Available at www .revistasculturales.com, accessed on 13 Sept. 2007.

– *La tradición velada: Ortega y el pensamiento humanista*. Madrid: Biblioteca Nueva, 1999.

Martín, José F. 'Diálogo y poder en la liberación de los galeotes.' *Cervantes: Bulletin of the Cervantes Society of America* 11, no. 2 (Fall 1991): 27–34.

Martín de la Guardia, Ricardo, and Guillermo Á. Pérez Sánchez. 'En el cincuentenario de la muerte de Ortega y Gasset: el europeísmo de Ortega y el proceso de integración europea.' *Revista de Estudios Europeos* 40 (May–August 2005): 3–10.

Martín Morán, José Manuel. 'Cervantes: el juglar zurdo de la era Gutenberg.' *Cervantes* 17, no. 1 (Spring 1997): 122–44.

Marx, Karl. *Capital: Volume 1*. London: Elecbook, 2001.

– *The German Ideology*. London: Elecbook, 2001.

Massó Lago, Noé. *El joven José Ortega. Anatomía del pensador adolescente*. Castellón: Eliago, 2006.

McClintock, Robert. *Man and His Circumstances. Ortega as Educator*. New York: Teacher's College P, 1971.

McKeon, Michael, ed. *Theory of the Novel. A Historical Approach*. Baltimore: Johns Hopkins UP, 2000.

Medvedev, Pavel N. 'The Immediate Tasks Facing Literary-Historical Science.' Translated by C.R. Pike. In *Bakhtin School Papers*. Edited by Ann Shukman. *Russian Poetics in Translation* 10 (1983): 75–91.

Mennemeier, Franz Norbert. *Friedrich Schlegels Poesiebegriff dargestellt anhand der literaturkritischen Schriften. Die romantische Konzeption einer objektiven Poesie*. Munich: Wilhelm Fink Verlag, 1971.

Mészáros, István. 'Lukács' Concept of Dialectic.' In *Georg Lukács: The Man, His Work and His Ideas*. Edited by G.H.R. Parkinson. London: Weidenfeld and Nicolson, 1970. 34–85.

Meyer, François. *La ontología de Miguel de Unamuno*. Translated by Cesáreo Goicoechea. Madrid: Gredos, 1962.

Mezquita, Eduardo Pascual. *La política del último Unamuno*. Salamanca: Globalia Ediciones Anthema, 2003.

Miles, David H. 'Portrait of the Marxist as a Young Hegelian: Lukács' Theory of the Novel.' *PMLA* 94, no. 1 (January 1979): 22–35.

Millán-Zaibert, Elizabeth. *Friedrich Schlegel and the Emergence of Romantic Philosophy*. Albany: State U of New York P, 2007.

Mittleman, Alan. '"The Significance of Judaism for the Religious Progress of Humanity" by Hermann Cohen. An Introduction and Translation.' *Modern Judaism* 24, no. 1 (February 2004): 36–58.

Molinuevo, José Luis. 'Algunas notas de José Ortega y Gasset.' *Revista de Occidente* 156 (May 1994): 33–52.

– 'Fichte y Ortega (II). Héroes o cuidadanos. El mito de Don Quijote.' *Daimon. Revista de Filosofía* 9 (1994): 341–58.

– 'Fichte y Ortega (III). Superación del idealismo.' In *Trabajos y días salmantinos. Homenaje a D. Miguel Cruz Hernández*. Edited by Pablo García Castillo. Salamanca: Anthema, 1998. 225–42.

– *El idealismo de Ortega*. Madrid: Narcea, 1984.

– 'Literatura y filosofía en Ortega y Gasset.' *Revista de Occidente* 132 (May 1992): 69–94.

– 'Salvar a Fichte en Ortega.' *Azafea. Estudios de historia de la filosofía hispánica* 3 (1990): 103–50.

– 'Sobre Cervantes y *El Quijote* desde el Escorial (Notas de trabajo de José Ortega y Gasset).' *Revista de Occidente* 156 (May 1994): 36–54.

Morán, Gregorio. *El maestro en el erial. Ortega y Gasset y la cultura del franquismo*. Barcelona: Tusquets, 1998.

Morón Arroyo, Ciriaco. 'Álgebra y logaritmo: dos metáforas de Ortega y Gasset.' *Hispania* 49, no. 2 (1966): 232–37.

– *El sistema de Ortega y Gasset*. Madrid: Alcalá, 1968.

– 'Unamuno y Hegel.' In *Miguel de Unamuno*. Edited by A. Sánchez Barbudo. 2nd ed. Madrid: Taurus, 1990. 151–79.

Morris, William. *Politics, Art and Society*. London: The Electric Book Company, 2001.

Morson, Gary Saul. 'Parody, History, and Metaparody.' In *Rethinking Bakhtin: Extensions and Challenges*. Edited by Gary Saul Morson and Caryl Emerson. Evanston, IL: Northwestern UP, 1989. 63–86.

Morson, Gary Saul, and Caryl Emerson. *Mikhail Bakhtin.Creation of a Prosaics*. Stanford, CA: Stanford UP, 1990.

Moynahan, Gregory B. 'Hermann Cohen's *Das Prinzip der Infinitesimelmethode*, Ernst Cassirer, and the Politics of Science in Wilhelmine Germany.' *Perspectives on Science* 11, no. 1 (Spring 2003): 35–75.

Munk, Reinier. 'Alterity in Hermann Cohen's Critical Idealism.' *Journal of Jewish Thought and Philosophy* 9, no. 2 (March 2000): 251–65.

Muñoz, Jerónimo. *Libro del nuevo cometa*. Valencia: Pedro de Huete, 1573.

Muzelle, Alain. 'Friedrich Schlegel et l'arabesque picturale. Le débat néoclassique sur les ornaments.' *Études germaniques* 52, no. 4 (October-December 1997): 649–63.

Myers, David N. *Resisting History. Historicism and Its Discontents in German-Jewish Thought*. Princeton, NJ: Princeton UP, 2003.

Natorp, Paul. 'Hermann Cohens philosophische Leistung unter dem Gesichtspunkte des Systems.' In *Auslegungen Hermann Cohen*. Edited by Helmut Holzhey. Frankfurt am Main: Peter Lang, 1994.

Natorp, Paul. 'Philosophische Propadeutik. (Allgemeine Einleitung in die Philosophie und Anfansgründe der Logik, Ethik und Psychologie).' In *Leitsätzen zu akademischen Vorlesungen*. 3rd revised ed. Marburg: N.G. Elwert'sche Verlagsbuchhandlung, 1909.

Navajas, Gonzalo. *Miguel de Unamuno: bipolaridad y síntesis ficcional. Una lectura posmoderna*. Barcelona: PPU, 1988.

Navarro, Alberto. 'Introducción.' In Miguel de Unamuno, *Vida de Don Quijote y Sancho*. Madrid: Cátedra, 1988. 42–75.

Navarro Brotóns, Victor. 'The Cultivation of Astronomy in Spanish Universities in the Latter Half of the Sixteenth Century.' In *Universities and Science in the Early Modern Period*. Edited by Mordechai Feingold. Dordrecht: Springer, 2006. 83–98.

Nerlich, Michael. *Ideology of Adventure. Studies in Modern Consciousness, 1100–1750*. Translated by Ruth Crowley. Minneapolis: U of Minnesota P, 1987.

Nietzsche, Friedrich. *Beyond Good and Evil*. Edited by Rolf-Peter Horstmann and Judith Norman. Cambridge: Cambridge UP, 2002.

Nikolaev, Nikolai I. 'Introduction to M.M. Bakhtin's Lectures and Comments of 1924–1925.' Translated by Vadim Liapunov. In *Bakhtin and Religion. A Feeling for Faith.* Edited by Susan M. Felch and Paul J. Contino. Evanston, IL: Northwestern UP, 2001. 193–205.

Nonnenmann, K. Rainer. *'Variationen über kein Tema.* Die romantische *Arabeske* als ästhetische Kategorie in Robert Schumanns op. 18.' *Die Musikforschung* 54, no. 3 (July–September 2001): 243–54.

Norman, Judith. 'Squaring the Romantic Circle. Hegel's Critique of Schlegel's Theories of Art.' In *Hegel and Aesthetics.* Edited by William Maker. Albany: State U of New York P, 2000. 131–44.

Novak, David. 'Hermann Cohen on State and Nation: A Contemporary Review.' In *Hermann Cohen's Critical Idealism.* Edited by Reinier Munk. Dordrecht: Springer, 2005. 259–79.

Nozick, Martin. *Miguel de Unamuno. The Agony of Belief.* Princeton, NJ: Princeton UP, 1971.

Ollig, Hans-Ludwig. *Der Neukantianismus.* Stuttgart: Metzler, 1979.

Olson, Paul R. *The Great Chiasmus. Word and Flesh in the Novels of Unamuno.* West Lafayette, IN: Purdue UP, 2003.

O'Malley. C. Donald. 'Andreas Vesalius' Pilgrimage.' *Isis* 45, no. 2 (July 1954): 138–44.

Orringer, Nelson R. *Hermann Cohen (1842–1918). Filosofar como fundamentar.* Madrid: Ediciones del Orto, 2000.

– 'Kant, Ortega y la "posesión"de una filosofía.' *Anales del seminario de metafísica. Num. extra. Homenaje a S. Rábade* (1992): 109–25.

– 'Ortega, psicólogo y la superación de sus maestros.' *Azafea. Estudios históricos de la filosofía hispánica* 1 (1985): 185–236.

– *Ortega y sus fuentes germánicas.* Madrid: Gredos, 1979.

– 'Ortega's Dialogue with Heidegger in *What Is Philosophy?.*' In *Ortega y Gasset Centennial/Centenario Ortega y Gasset.* Madrid: José Porrúa Turanzas, 1985. 45–56.

– 'Ser y no-ser en Platón, Hartmann y Ortega.' *Nueva revista de filología hispánica* 29 (1986): 60–86.

– 'El Unamuno casticista en "Meditaciones del Quijote".' *Cuadernos salmantinos de filosofía* 10 (1983): 37–54.

– *Unamuno y los protestantes liberales (1912). Sobre las fuentes de 'Del sentimiento trágico de la vida.'* Madrid: Gredos, 1985.

Ortega y Gasset, José. *Cartas de un joven español. (1891–1908).* Edited by Soledad Ortega. Madrid: Fundación José Ortega y Gasset and El Arquero, 1991.

– *La deshumanización del arte.* Madrid: Espasa-Calpe, 1987.

- 'El estilo de una vida (Notas de trabajo de José Ortega y Gasset).' *Revista de Occidente* 132 (May 1992): 51–68.
- *Kant, Hegel, Scheler.* Madrid: Revista de Occidente/Alianza, 1983.
- 'El manifiesto de Marcela.' In *Para la cultura del amor.* Madrid: Arquero, 1988. 25–33.
- *Meditaciones del Quijote/Ideas sobre la novela.* 9th ed. Madrid: Revista de Occidente, 1975.
- *Obras completas.* Madrid: Revista de Occidente, 1962–65.
- *El tema de nuestro tiempo.* Santiago de Chile: Editorial Cultura, 1937.
Ortega y Gasset and the Question of Modernity. Edited by Patrick H. Durst. Minneapolis: The Prisma Institute, 1989.
Ouimette, Victor. *Los intelectuales españoles y el naufragio del liberalismo (1923–1936).* 2 vols. Valencia: Pre-Textos, 1998.
- *José Ortega y Gasset.* Boston: Twayne, 1982.
- *Reason Aflame. Unamuno and the Heroic Will.* New Haven, CT: Yale UP, 1974.
Øveraas, Anne Marie. *Nivola contra novela.* Salamanca: Ediciones Universidad Salamanca, 1993.
Pan'kov, Nikolai. '"Everything else depends on how this business turns out …": Mikhail Bakhtin's Dissertation Defense as Real Event, as High Drama and as Academic Comedy.' In *Bakhtin and Cultural Theory.* 2nd ed. Edited by Ken Hirschkop and David Shepherd. Manchester: Manchester UP, 2001. 26–61.
Pardo Tomás, José. *Ciencia y censura. La Inquisición española y los libros científicos en los siglos XVI y XVII.* Madrid: CSIC, 1991.
París, Carlos. *Unamuno. Estructura de su mundo intelectual.* Barcelona: Anthropos, 1989.
Parkinson, G.H.R. *Georg Lukács.* London: Routledge and Kegan Paul, 1977.
Parlej, Piotr. *The Romantic Theory of the Novel. Genre and Reflection in Cervantes, Melville, Flaubert, Joyce, and Kafka.* Baton Rouge and London: Louisiana State UP, 1997.
Parr, James A. *Don Quixote. A Touchstone for Literary Criticism.* Kassel: Edition Reichenberger, 2005.
Pascal, Blaise. *Pensées.* Accessible at http://www.ub.unifreiburg.de/referate/04/pascal/pensees.pdf, accessed on 28 May 2009.
Pasternak, Boris. *Safe Conduct. An Early Autobiography and Other Works.* Translated by Alec Brown. London: Elek Books, 1959.
Patton, Lydia. 'The Critical Philosophy Renewed. The Bridge between Hermann Cohen's Early Work on Kant and Later Philosophy of Science.' *Angelaki: Journal of the Theoretical Humanities* 10, no. 1 (April 2005): 109–18.

Pavel, Thomas. 'Literary Genres as Norms and Good Habits.' *New Literary History: A Journal of Theory and Interpretation* 34, no. 2 (Spring 2003): 201–10.

Pechey, Graham. *Mikhail Bakhtin: The Word in the World.* New York: Routledge, 2007.

Pérez, Joseph. *La Inquisición española. Crónica negra del Santo Oficio.* Madrid: Ediciones Martínez Roca, 2003.

Peter, Klaus. *Stadien der Aufklärung. Moral und Politik bei Lessing, Novalis und Friedrich Schlegel.* Wiesbaden: Akademische Verlagsgesellschaft Athenaion, 1980.

Philonenko, Alexis. *L'école de Marbourg. Cohen-Natorp-Cassirer.* Paris: Librairie Philosophique J. Vrin, 1989.

– *Métaphysique et politique chez Kant et Fichte.* Paris: Librairie Philosophique J. Vrin, 1997.

Piché, Claude. 'Heidegger et Cohen, lecteurs de Kant.' *Archives de Philosophie* 61, no. 4 (1998): 603–28.

Piskunova, Svetlana. 'Motivos e imágenes de las fiestas vernales en el *Quijote*.' In *Volver a Cervantes. Actas del IV Congreso Internacional de la Asociación de Cervantistas. Lepanto 1/8 de octubre de 2000.* Edited by Antonio Bernat Vistarini. Palma de Mallorca: Universitat de les Illes Balears, 2001. 623–9.

Plato. *Five Dialogues. Euthyphro, Apology, Crito, Meno, Phaedo.* Translated by G.M.A. Grube. Indianapolis: Hackett Publishing, 1981.

– *The Republic. The Portable Plato.* Translated by Benjamin Jewett. New York: Penguin, 1977. 281–696.

Polheim, Karl Konrad. *Die Arabeske. Ansichten und Ideen aus Friedrich Schlegels Poetik.* Paderborn: Verlag Ferdinand Schöningh, 1966.

Poma, Andrea. *The Critical Philosophy of Hermann Cohen.* Translated by John Denton. Albany: State U of New York P, 1997.

– *The Yearning for Form and Other Essays on Hermann Cohen's Thought.* Dordrecht: Springer, 2006.

Poole, Brian. 'Bakhtin and Cassirer: The Philosophical Origins of Bahktin's Carnival Messianism.' *The South Atlantic Quarterly* 97, nos. 3/4 (Summer/Fall 1998): 537–78.

– 'From Phenomenology to Dialogue: Max Scheler's Phenomenological Tradition and Mikhail Bakhtin's Development from "Toward a Philosophy of the Act" to his Study of Dostoevsky.' In *Bakhtin and Cultural Theory.* 2nd ed. Edited by Ken Hirschkop and David Shepherd. Manchester: Manchester UP, 2001. 109–35.

Portuondo, María M. *Secret Science. Spanish Cosmography and the New World.* Chicago: U of Chicago P, 2009.

Pumpiansky, L.V. 'Appendix: M.M. Bakhtin's Lectures and Comments of 1924–1925. From the Notebooks of L.V. Pumpiansky.' Translated by Vadima Liapunov. In *Bakhtin and Religion. A Feeling for Faith.* Edited by Susan M. Felch amd Paul J. Contino. Evanston: Northwestern UP, 2001. 193–237.

Quint, David. *Cervantes's Novel of Modern Times. A New Reading of* Don Quijote. Princeton, NJ: Princeton UP, 2003.

Rabaté, Jean-Claude. *Guerra de ideas en el joven Unamuno (1880–1900).* Madrid: Biblioteca Nueva, 2001.

Radnóti, Sándor. 'Lukács and Bloch.' In *Lukács Reappraised.* Edited by Agnes Heller. New York: Columbia UP, 1983. 63–74.

Redondo, Augustin. 'La tradición carnavalesca en el "Quijote".' In *Formas carnavalescas en el arte y la literatura.* Edited by Javier Huerta Calvo. Barcelona: Ediciones del Serbal, 1989. 153–81.

Reed, Cory. *The Novelist as Playwright: Cervantes and the Entremes Nuevo.* Bern: Peter Lang, 1993.

Reed, Walter L. 'The Problem of Cervantes in Bakhtin's Poetics.' *Cervantes* 7, no. 2 (1987): 29–37.

Regalado García, Antonio. *El laberinto de la razón: Ortega y Heidegger.* Madrid: Alianza, 1990.

– *El siervo y el señor. La dialéctica agónica de Miguel de Unamuno.* Madrid: Gredos, 1968.

Renfrew, Alastair. *Toward a New Material Aesthetics. Bakhtin, Genre and the Fates of Literary Theory.* Oxford: Legenda, 2006.

Renner, Rolf Günter. *Ästhetische Theorie bei Georg Lukács. Zu ihrer Genese und Struktur.* Bern and Munich: Francke Verlag, 1976.

Reyero, Carlos. *Cervantes y el mundo cervantino en la imaginación romántica.* Alcalá de Henares: Casa de la Entrevista and Capilla del Oidor, 1997.

Ribbans, Geoffrey. *Niebla y Soledad. Aspectos de Unamuno y Machado.* Madrid: Gredos, 1971.

Riegl, Alois. *Problems of Style. Foundations for a History of Ornament.* Translated by Evelyn Kain. Princeton, NJ: Princeton UP, 1992.

Riley, E.C. *Cervantes's Theory of the Novel.* Oxford: Clarendon P, 1962.

Ringer, Fritz K. *The Decline of the German Mandarins. The German Academic Community, 1890–1938.* Cambridge, MA: Harvard UP, 1969.

Robert, Marthe. 'From *Origins of the Novel.*' In *Theory of the Novel: A Historical Approach.* Edited by Michael McKeon. Baltimore: Johns Hopkins UP, 2000. 160–77.

– *Roman des origines et origines des romans.* Paris: Gallimard, 1972.

Roberts, Stephen G.H. *Miguel de Unamuno o la creación del intelectual español moderno*. Translated by María José Martínez Jurico. Salamanca: Ediciones Universidad de Salamanca, 2007.

Rockmore, Tom. *Irrationalism. Lukács and the Marxist View of Reason*. Philadelphia: Temple UP, 1992.

Rodríguez Huéscar, Antonio. *José Ortega y Gasset's Metaphysical Innovation. A Critique and Overcoming of Idealism*. Translated by Jorge García-Gómez. Albany: State U of New York P, 1995.

– *Perspectiva y verdad: el problema de la verdad en Ortega*. Madrid: Revista de Occidente, 1966.

Rodríguez Mansilla, Fernando. 'A vueltas con los autores del *Lazarillo de Tormes* (a propósito del libro de Mercedes Agulló).' *Boletín de la Academia Peruana de la Lengua*. Forthcoming.

Rojas, Carlos. *Unamuno y Ortega: intelectuales frente al drama*. Barcelona: Editorial Dirosa, 1977.

Rojas, Fernando de. *La Celestina*. Barcelona: Círculo de Lectores, 1966.

Romero Salvadó, Francisco J. *Spain: Between War and Revolution*. London: Routledge, 1999.

Rosales, Luis. *Cervantes y la libertad*. Madrid: Sociedad de Estudios y Publicaciones, 1960.

Rudd, Margaret Thomas. *The Lone Heretic. A Biography of Miguel de Unamuno y Jugo*. Austin: U of Texas P, 1963.

Rukser, Udo. *Discurso académico pronunicado en la sesión de la Facultad de Filosofía y Educación celebrada para recibir al miembro académico Dr. Udo Rukser*. Santiago de Chile: Ed. Universitaria, 1967.

Rzhevsky, Nicholas. 'Kozhinov on Bakhtin.' *New Literary History* 25, no. 2 (Spring 1994): 429–44.

Salas Fernández, Tomás J. *Ortega y Gasset: teórico de la novela*. Málaga: Universidad de Málaga, 2001.

Salazar Rincón, Javier. *El mundo social del Quijote*. Madrid: Gredos, 1986.

Salmerón, Fernando. *Las mocedades de Ortega y Gasset*. Mexico City: Universidad Nacional Autónoma de México, 1971.

Salomon, Noël. *La vida rural en tiempos de Felipe II*. Barcelona: Planeta, 1973.

Samuelson, Norbert. *An Introduction to Modern Jewish Philosophy*. Albany: State U of New York P, 1989.

San Martín, Javier. *Ensayos sobre Ortega*. Madrid: UNED, 1994.

– *Fenomenología y cultura en Ortega. Ensayos de interpretación*. Madrid: Tecnos, 1998.

San Miguel, Ángel. 'Ortega y Gasset cervantista. Pre-historia de las *Meditaciones del Quijote*.' In *Actas del coloquio cervantino Würzburg 1983*.

Edited by Theodor Berchem and Hugo Laitenberger. Münster/Westfalen: Aschendorffsche Verlagsbuchhandlung, 1987. 109–17.

Sánchez Barbudo, A. *Estudios sobre Galdós, Unamuno y Machado.* Madrid: Ediciones Guadarrama, 1968.

Schanze, Helmut. 'Friedrich Schlegels Theorie des Romans.' In *Deutsche Romantheorien. Beiträge zu einer historischen Poetik des Romans in Deutschland.* Edited by Reinhold Grimm. Frankfurt am Main and Bonn: Athenäum Verlag, 1968. 61–80.

Schaub, Jean-Frédéric. 'La monarquía hispana en el sistema europeo de estados.' In *España en tiempos del Quijote.* Edited by Antonio Feros and Juan Gelabert. Madrid: Taurus, 2004. 97–128.

Scheunemann, Dietrich. 'The Problem of the Book: *Don Quixote* in the Age of Mechanical Reproduction.' In *Cervantes and the Modernists. The Question of Influence.* Edited by Edwin Williamson. London: Tamesis, 1994. 135–48.

Schlegel, Friedrich. *Charakteristiken und Kritiken I (1796–1801).* In *Kritische Friedrich-Schlegel Ausgabe.* Vol. 2. Edited by Hans Eichner. Paderborn: Thomas-Verlag, 1967.

– *Dialogue on Poetry and Literary Aphorisms.* Translated by Ernst Behler and Roman Struc. University Park: Pennsylvania State UP, 1968.

– *Fragmente zur Poesie und Literatur.* In *Kritische Friedrich-Schlegel Ausgabe.* Vol. 16–17. Edited by Ernst Behler. Paderborn: Ferdinand Schöningh, 1958–1983.

– *Geschichte der alten und neuen Literatur.* In *Kritische Friedrich-Schlegel Ausgabe.* Vol. 6. Edited by Hans Eichner. Paderborn: Ferdinand Schöningh, 1961.

– *Kritische Friedrich-Schlegel Ausgabe.* Edited by Ernst Behler, Hans Eichner, and Jean-Jacques Anstett. Paderborn: Ferdinand Schöningh, 1981.

– *Literarische Notizen 1797–1801.* Frankfurt am Main: Ullstein Materialen, 1980.

– *Literary Notebooks 1797–1801.* Edited by Hans Eichner. Toronto: U of Toronto P, 1957.

– *Philosophical Fragments.* Translated by Peter Firchow. Minneapolis: U of Minnesota P, 1991.

Schmid, Peter A. *Ethik als Hermeneutik. Systematische Untersuchungen zu Hermann Cohens Rechts- und Tugendlehre.* Würzburg: Königshausen und Neumann, 1995.

– 'Hermann Cohen's Theory of Virtue.' In *Hermann Cohen's Critical Idealism.* Edited by Reinier Munk. Dordrecht: Springer, 2005. 231–57.

Schmidt, Rachel. 'Beyond Words: Cervantes Iconography in the 1905 Centenary and the Following Decade.' In *Don Quixote Illustrated: Textual Images and Visual Readings. Iconografía del Quijote.* Edited by Eduardo Urbina and Jesús G. Maestro. Pontevedra, Spain: Editorial Mirabel, 2005. 39–75.

– 'Cervantes's *Galatea* and Friedrich Schlegel's *Lucinde*, or Unmasking the Pastoral and the Allegorical as Modes of the Modern Novel.' *Anuario de estudios cervantinos* III (2007): 23–35.

– 'Women in the 1905 and 1916 Cervantes Centenary Activities.' *Romance Quarterly* 52, no. 4 (Fall 2005): 294–311.

Scholz, Bernhard F. 'Bakhtin's Concept of 'Chronotope': The Kantian Connection.' In *The Contexts of Bakhtin. Philosophy, Authorship, Aesthetics.* Edited by David Shepherd. Amsterdam: Harwood Academic Publishers, 1998. 141–72.

Schreiber, Jens. *Das Symptom des Schreibens. Roman und absolutes Buch in der Fruhromantik (Novalis/Schlegel).* Frankfurt am Main: Peter Lang, 1983.

Schultheis, Peter. 'Einleitung.' In Hermann Cohen, *Das Prinzip der Infinitesimal-Methode und seine Geschichte.* In *Werke*, vol. 5. Hildesheim: Georg Olms Verlag, 1984. 7*–46*.

– 'Platon: Geburstätte des Cohenschen Apriori?' In *Philosophisches Denken-Politisches Wirken. Hermann-Cohen-Kolloquium Marburg 1992.* Edited by Reinhardt Brandt and Franz Orlik. Hildesheim: Georg Olms, 1993. 55–75.

Schwarzschild, Steven S. 'The Democratic Socialism of Hermann Cohen.' In *Hermann Cohen. Auslegungen.* Edited by Helmut Holzhey. Frankfurt am Main: Peter Lang, 1994. 205–27.

– 'Introduction.' In Hermann Cohen. *Ethik des reinen Willens.* In *Werke*, vol. 7. Hildesheim and New York: Georg Olms Verlag, 1981. vii*–xxxv*.

– 'The Tenability of Hermann Cohen's Construction of the Self.' *Journal of the History of Philosophy* 13, no. 3 (July 1975): 361–84.

Senabre, Ricardo. *Lengua y estilo de Ortega y Gasset.* Salamanca: Universidad de Salamanca, 1964.

Shaitanov, Igor'. 'The Concept of the Generic Word: Bakhtin and the Russian Formalists.' In *Face to Face. Bakhtin in Russia and the West.* Edited by Carol Adlam, Rachel Falconer, Vitalii Makhlin, and Alastair Renfrew. Sheffield, UK: Sheffield Academic P, 1997. 233–53.

Shklovsky, Viktor. *Theory of Prose.* Translated by Benjamin Sher. Elmwood Park, IL: Dalkey Archive P, 1990.

Silver, Philip W. *Ortega as Phenomenologist. The Genesis of* Meditations on Quixote. New York: Columbia UP, 1978.

Silverblatt, Irene. 'The Black Legend and Global Conspiracies. Spain, the Inquisition, and the Emerging Modern World.' In *Rereading the Black Legend: The Discourses of Religious and Racial Difference in the Renaissance Empires.* Edited by Margaret R. Greer, Walter D. Mignolo, and Maureen Quilligan. Chicago: U of Chicago P, 2007. 99–116.

Sim, Stuart. *Georg Lukács.* Hemel Hempstead, UK: Harvester Wheatsheaf, 1994.

Sinclair, Alison. *Uncovering the Mind. Unamuno, the Unknown and the Vicissitudes of Self.* Manchester: Manchester UP, 2001.

Spitzer, Leo. *Linguistics and Literary History: Essays in Stylistics*. New York: Russell and Russell, 1962.

Stanley, Patricia. 'Hoffmann's 'Phantasiestücke im Callots Manier' in Light of Friedrich Schlegel's Theory of the Arabesque.' *German Studies Review* 8, no. 3 (October 1985): 399–417.

Stedman Jones, Garth. 'The Marxism of the Early Lukács.'In *Western Marxism: A Critical Reader*. Edited by New Left Review. London: New Left Review, 1977. 11–60.

Storm, Eric. 'El tercer centenario del *Don Quijote* en 1905 y el nacionalismo español.' *Hispania* 57, no. 58, (May–August 1998): 625–54.

– *Het perspectif van de vooruitgang. Denken over politiek in het spaanse fin de siècle.* Baarn: Agora, 1999.

Strathman, Christopher A. *Romantic Poetry and the Fragmentary Imperative. Schlegel, Byron, Joyce, Blanchot*. Albany: State U of New York P, 2006.

Stuart Mill, John. 'An Examination of Sir William Hampton's Philosophy.' In *Collected Works*. Vol. 9. Edited by J.M. Robson. Toronto: U of Toronto P and Routledge and Kegan Paul, 1979.

Szondi, Peter. *On Textual Understanding and Other Essays*. Translated by Harvey Mendelsohn. Minneapolis: U of Minnesota P, 1986.

Tarr, Zoltan. 'A Note on Weber and Lukács.' *International Journal of Politics, Culture, and Society*. 3, no. 1 (Fall 1989): 131–9.

Ter Horst, Robert. *The Fortunes of the Novel. A Study in the Transposition of a Genre*. New York: Peter Lang, 2003.

Thayer, Harvey W. 'Hudibras in Germany.' *PMLA* 24, no. 3 (1909): 547–84.

Thomson, Clive, and Anthony Wall. 'Cleaning Up Bakhtin's Carnival Act.' *Diacritics* 23, no. 2 (Summer 1993): 47–70.

Thompson, G.R. 'Romantic Arabesque, Contemporary Theory, and Postmodernism: The Example of Poe's *Narrative*.' *ESQ* 35, nos. 3–4 (1989): 163–271.

Thompson, I.A.A. 'La guerra y el soldado.' In *España en tiempos del Quijote*. Edited by Antonio Feros and Juan Gelabert. Madrid: Taurus, 2004. 159–96.

Tierno Galván, Enrique. 'El tacitismo en las doctrinas políticas del siglo de oro español.' In *Escritos*. Madrid: Tecnos, 1971. 11–93.

– 'Ortega y la metafísica. La influencia alemana a través de la Universidad de Marburgo.' In *Actas del coloquio celebrado en Marburgo con motivo del centenario del nacimiento de José Ortega y Gasset (1983)*. Edited by H.-J. Lope. Frankfurt am Main: Peter Lang, 1986. 53–66.

Tihanov, Galin. 'Bakhtin, Joyce and Carnival: Towards the Synthesis of Epic and Novel in Rabelais.' *Paragraph* 24, no. 1 (2001): 66–83.

– 'Bakhtin's Essays on the Novel (1935–41): A Study of their Intellectual Background and Innovativeness.' *Dialogism* 1 (1998): 30–56.

– 'Ethics and Revolution: Lukács's Responses to Dostoevsky.' *Modern Language Review* 94, no. 3 (July 1999): 609–25.
– *The Master and the Slave. Lukács, Bakhtin, and the Ideas of Their Time*. Oxford: Clarendon P, 2000.
Todorov, Tzvetan. *Mikhail Bakhtin. The Dialogical Principle*. Translated by Wlad Godzich. Minneapolis: U of Minnesota P, 1984.
Toulmin, Stephen. *Cosmopolis. The Hidden Agenda of Modernity*. New York: The Free P, 1990.
Trapiello, Andrés. *Las armas y las letras. Literatura y guerra civil (1936–1939)*. Barcelona: Planeta, 1994.
Trilling, James. *Ornament. A Modern Perspective*. Seattle: U of Washington P, 2003.
Turgenev, Ivan. *Hamlet and Don Quixote*. London: Hendersons, 1972.
Turkevich, Ludmilla Buketoff. *Cervantes in Russia*. Princeton, NJ: Princeton UP, 1950.
Turner, David G. *Unamuno's Webs of Fatality*. London: Tamesis, 1974.
Tuttle, Howard N. *The Dawn of Historical Reason. The Historicality of Human Existence in The Thought of Dilthey, Heidegger and Ortega y Gasset*. New York: Peter Lang, 1994.
– *Human Life Is Radical Reality. An Idea Developed from the Conceptions of Dilthey, Heidegger, and Ortega y Gasset*. New York: Peter Lang, 2005.
Uhlig, Claus. 'Shakespeare between Antiquity and Modernity. A Theme of Aesthetics in Hegel and Cohen.' *Anglia* 122, no. 1 (2004): 24–43.
Unamuno, Miguel de. *Del sentimiento trágico de la vida*. In *Obras completas*. Vol. 7. Madrid: Escelicer, 1966. 109–302.
– *En torno al casticismo*. In *Obras completas*. Vol. 1. Madrid: Escelicer, 1966. 775–869.
– *Manual de Quijotismo. Cómo se hace una novela. Epistolario Miguel de Unamuno/Jean Cassou*. Edited by Bénédicte Vauthier. Salamanca: Ediciones Universidad Salamanca, 2005.
– *Niebla*. Edited by Mario J. Valdés. Madrid: Cátedra, 1993.
– *Obras completas*. Madrid: Escelicer, 1966.
– *Pensamiento político*. Edited by Elías Díaz. Madrid: Tecnos, 1965.
– *El resentimiento trágico de la vida. Notas sobre la revolución y guerra civil españolas*. Madrid: Alianza, 1991.
– *Vida de Don Quijote y Sancho*. 5th ed. Buenos Aires: Espasa-Calpe, 1943.
Urrutia, Manuel María. 'Un documento excepcional: el *manifiesto* de Unamuno a finales de octubre-principios de noviembre de 1936.' *Revista de hispanismo filosófico* 3 (1998): 95–102.

Urrutia Jordana, Ana. *La poetización de la política en el Unamuno exiliado. De Fuerteventura a París y Romancero del Destierro.* Salamanca: Ediciones Universidad de Salamanca, 2003.

Valdés, Mario J. *Death in the Literature of Unamuno.* Urbana: U of Illinois P, 1964.

– 'Salamanca 1898: Unamuno en la hoguera.' In *La independencia de las últimas colonias españolas y su impacto nacional e internacional.* Edited by José M. Ruano de la Haza. Ottawa: Dovehouse, 1999. 261–78.

Valera, Juan. 'Sobre la *Estafeta de Urganda, o Aviso de Cide Asam Ozoud Benengeli, sobre el desencanto del <<Quijote>>, escrito por Nicolás Díaz de Benjumea.'* Available at http://www.cervantesvirtual.com/servlet/SirveObras/vlr/01371296877811677440035/index.htm, accessed on 30 July 2009.

Van der Linden, Harry. *Kantian Ethics and Socialism.* Indianapolis: Hackett, 1988.

Varela, Javier. *La novela de España. Los intelectuales y el problema español.* Madrid: Taurus, 1999.

Varela Olea, María Ángeles. *Don Quijote, mitologema nacional. (Literatura y Política entre la Septembrina y la II República).* Alcalá de Henares: Centro de Estudios Cervantinos, 2003.

Vauthier, Bénédicte. 'Bajtín en la encrucijada de las ciencias humanas europeas "en crisis". Revisión de un debate.' In *Mijail Bajtín en la encrucijada de la hermenéutica y las ciencias humanas.* Edited by Bénédicte Vauthier and Pedro M. Cátedra. Salamanca: Seminario de Estudios Medievales y Renacentistas, 2003. 45–74.

– 'Estudio preliminar.' In Miguel de Unamuno, *Manual de Quijotismo. Cómo se hace una novela. Epistolario Miguel de Unamuno/Jean Cassou.* Edited by Bénédicte Vauthier. Salamanca: Ediciones Universidad Salamanca, 2005. 13–61.

Villacañas Berlanga, José Luis. 'Kant desde dentro.' *Isegoria* 30 (2004): 67–90.

Vuillemin, Jules. *L'héritage kantien et la révolution copernicienne. Fichte-Cohen-Heidegger.* Paris: Presses Universitaires de France, 1954.

Wagner, Peter. *Theorizing Modernity: Inescapability and Attainability in Social Theory.* London: Sage Publications, 2001.

Wall, Anthony. 'A Broken Thinker.' *The South Atlantic Quarterly* 97, nos. 3/4 (Summer/Fall 1998): 669–98.

Watt, Ian. *The Rise of the Novel. Studies in Defoe, Richardson and Fielding.* Berkeley: U of California P, 1957.

Weiland, Werner. *Der junge Friedrich Schlegel oder Die Revolution in der Frühromantik.* Stuttgart: W. Kohlhammer Verlag, 1968.

Wiedebach, Hartwig. 'Aesthetics in Religion: Remarks on Hermann Cohen's Theory of Jewish Existence.' *The Journal of Jewish Thought and Philosophy* 11, no. 1 (May 2002): 63–73.

– *Die Bedeutung der Nationalität für Hermann Cohen.* Hildesheim: Georg Olms Verlag, 1997.

Willey, Thomas E. *Back to Kant. The Revival of Kantianism in German Social and Historical Thought, 1860–1914.* Detroit: Wayne State UP, 1978.

Winter, Eggert. 'Ethik als Lehre vom Menschen.' In *Hermann Cohen. Auslegungen.* Edited by Helmut Holzhey. Frankfurt am Main: Peter Lang, 1994. 311–38.

Wogenstein, Sebastian. 'Concepts of Alterity and Liminality in Hermann Cohen's Writings.' *Naharaim. Journal of German Jewish Literature and Culture History* 2, no. 2 (2008): 159–73.

Woland, Gerd. 'Introduction.' In Hermann Cohen, *Ästhetik des reinen Gefühls.* Hildesheim and New York: Georg Olms Verlag, 1982.

Wyers, Frances. *Miguel de Unamuno: The Contrary Self.* London: Tamesis, 1976.

Zambrano, María. *Unamuno.* Barcelona: Debate, 2003.

Zamora Bonilla, Javier. *Ortega y Gasset.* Barcelona: Plaza & Janés, 2002.

Zavala, Iris M. *La posmodernidad y Mijail Bajtín. Una poética dialógica.* Madrid: Espasa-Calpe, 1991.

– *Unamuno y el pensamiento dialógico.* Barcelona: Anthropos, 1991.

Zbinden, Karine. *Bakhtin between East and West. Cross-Cultural Transmission.* London: Legenda, 2006.

– 'Traducing Bakhtin and Missing Heteroglossia.' *Dialogism* (April 1999): 41–60.

Zeuch, Ulrike. *Das Unendliche – höchste Fülle oder Nichts? Zur Problematik von Friedrich Schlegels Geist-Begriff und dessen geistesgeschichtlichen Voraussetzungen.* Würzburg: Königshausen und Neumann, 1991.

Ziolkowski, Eric. *The Sanctification of Don Quixote: from Hidalgo to Priest.* University Park: Pennsylvania State UP, 1991.

Ziolkowski, Theodore. *German Romanticism and Its Institutions.* Princeton, NJ: Princeton UP, 1990.

Zubizarreta, Armando F. *Unamuno en su nivola.* Madrid: Taurus, 1960.

Index

Abellán, José Luis, 199, 297–8, 345n30, 345–6n31
absence, 32, 55, 89, 103, 223, 256, 293, 304–5, 330n9, 345n29; and meaning, 100, 110, 113–15, 117, 223. *See also* meaning
absolute, the, 38–40, 42, 44–5, 48–9, 53, 61, 63, 66–71, 76, 86, 101, 119, 126–7, 146, 179, 194–5, 209, 276, 278, 316n5, 317n12, 318nn17–18, 20, 22, 321n9, 334n57
abstract idealist, 91, 97, 101–3, 265, 305
abstraction, ix, 32, 68–9, 98, 106, 163, 169, 219
Academy of the Lynx, 12
Acosta, José de, 12
action, xii, xiv, 9, 12, 14, 22, 25–6, 28, 37, 39, 42, 46, 85, 87, 94, 97, 101–2, 107, 109, 111–12, 114, 118, 130–1, 134–8, 142–5, 149–52, 155–6, 159, 179, 187, 190, 198–9, 201, 203–4, 206, 209–10, 216, 228–30, 243–7, 268–9, 276, 280, 283–5, 292, 296–8, 300, 304, 326n42, 328n73, 344n12; as *Handlung*, 136–7, 144, 152, 201–2, 284, 324nn26–7, 326nn46–7, 336nn11–12

actuality (also *Wirklichkeit*), xv, 4, 15, 34, 40, 44, 61, 82, 91, 96, 104, 108, 113, 133, 146, 149, 156–7, 163, 169, 230, 245, 269, 283, 285, 305, 309, 325n39, 328–9n74, 330n9, 334n53, 335nn6–7; as opposed to the virtual, xv, 146, 149, 217–21, 305, 334n53, 339n46
Adorno, Theodor, x, 45, 49
adventure, 8, 11, 28, 43, 72, 81, 90–1, 160, 166, 218, 222, 225, 228, 280, 309, 336n11; literature of, 217–19, 220, 222; misadventures, 105, 166; will to, 221, 225, 293
Aeschylus, 79
aesthetics, xiii, 38–42, 45, 47, 51, 56, 58–9, 75, 77, 100, 121, 123–6, 143–4, 146, 148–51, 189, 193, 195, 198, 200, 202, 204, 219, 223, 241, 243, 245–6, 250, 265, 285, 301, 321n15, 322n5, 323n10, 326n50, 327n52, 328n73, 339n53
Agathon, 226
agency, xi, 8, 20, 106, 111, 113, 116–17, 140, 204–5, 240, 282, 305–6
Agincourt, 20
Agulló, Mercedes, 312n7